GAAP

Practical Implementation
Guide and Workbook

GAAP

Practical Implementation Guide and Workbook

Barry J. Epstein   **Nadira M. Saafir**

WILEY

JOHN WILEY & SONS, INC.

ISBN: 978-0-470-59906-8

Printed in the United States of America

10 9 8 7 6 5 4 3 2 1

Contents

About the Authors

Barry J. Epstein, PhD, CPA, is a partner with Chicago-based Russell Novak & Company, LLP, where he specializes in technical consultation on accounting and auditing matters and corporate governance, and maintains a national practice as a consulting and testifying expert for commercial and other litigation matters, including accountants' malpractice, contractual dispute resolution, damages modeling, and white-collar criminal defense. He has previously served in senior technical and litigation consulting positions with several regional and national CPA firms and as a corporate finance executive and college professor. Dr. Epstein has authored or coauthored six books (including *Wiley IFRS Interpretation and Application*), hundreds of professional education courses, several articles in business or professional journals, and a weekly business column for an international newspaper. He has served on several state and national technical committees, including the AICPA's Board of Examiners, served as chair of the Illinois CPA Society's senior accounting technical committee, and held teaching positions at several universities. Dr. Epstein received his doctorate from the University of Pittsburgh and also holds degrees from DePaul University and the University of Chicago. He is a member of the Illinois CPA Society, the AICPA, and the American Accounting Association.

Nadira M. Saafir, CPA, is a senior litigation consultant with Chicago-based Russell Novak & Company LLP. Prior to joining Russell Novak & Company in 2009, she served as a senior auditor at Deloitte, where she gained an extensive knowledge base regarding the theory and practical application of generally accepted accounting principles. She received her master's degree in accounting from the University of Illinois at Chicago and holds a bachelor's of business administration degree from Grand Valley State University. She is a member of the AICPA.

Chapter 1

RESEARCHING GAAP

BACKGROUND AND INTRODUCTION

Overview of GAAP

This chapter provides an overview of generally accepted accounting principles (GAAP), including the processes involved in its development.

GAAP Defined

The phrase "generally accepted accounting principles" is a technical accounting term that encompasses the conventions, rules, and procedures necessary to define accepted accounting practice at a particular time. It includes not only broad guidelines of general application but also detailed practices and procedures. Those conventions, rules, and procedures provide a standard by which to measure financial presentations.

—U.S. Auditing Standards Board, AU §411

OBJECTIVE OF GAAP REPORTING

Generally accepted accounting principles (GAAP) are concerned with the measurement of economic activity, the timing when such measurements are to be made and recorded, the disclosures surrounding this activity, and the preparation and presentation of summarized economic information in the form of financial statements.

There are two broad categories of accounting principles: those dealing with *recognition and measurement*, and those dealing with *presentation and disclosure*.

Recognition and measurement principles determine when and how transactions and events items enter the accounting cycle and impact the financial statements. These quantitative standards require economic information to be reflected numerically.

Presentation and disclosure principles involve qualitative considerations regarding information that is deemed an essential ingredient of a full set of financial statements, the absence or inappropriate presentation of which would make the financial statements materially misleading.

Disclosure principles complement recognition principles by explaining assumptions underlying the numerical information and by providing additional information about accounting policies, contingencies, uncertainties, and other matters that are essential to fully understand the performance and financial condition of the reporting entity.

WHO CREATED GAAP?

Over time, different professional and statutory bodies have been given responsibility for the promulgation of GAAP, with multiple organizations often sharing this responsibility. All GAAP established by earlier standard-setting bodies, to the extent not withdrawn or superseded, continues in effect. GAAP in effect as of July 1, 2009, have been incorporated in the Accounting Standards Codification (ASC) of the Financial Accounting Standards Board (FASB), and that promulgated hereinafter will be set forth as changes to ASC and not as freestanding pronouncements, such as FASB statements.

Committee on Accounting Procedure

The 1929 market crash led to the first serious attempt to create formalized generally accepted accounting principles in 1930, in the hope that a set of uniform and stringent financial reporting requirements would prevent a recurrence. The American Institute of Accountants (which in 1957 was renamed the American Institute of Certified Public Accountants [AICPA]) created a special committee to work with the New York Stock Exchange toward the goal of establishing standards for accounting procedures. The special committee recommended five rules to the Exchange, published in 1938 as Accounting Research Bulletin (ARB) 1 of the Committee on Accounting Procedure. The Committee subsequently published 51 such Bulletins, including ARB 43, which consolidated and superseded all prior bulletins and also attempted to achieve uniformity in accounting terminology. However, its limited resources and lack of serious research efforts in support of its pronouncements were questioned in the late 1950s as a number of very complex controversial topics loomed on the horizon.

Accounting Principles Board

In response, the Accounting Principles Board (APB) was created to facilitate the development of principles that were to be based primarily on the research of a separate Accounting Research Division of the AICPA. The Division was to undertake extensive research, publish its findings, and then permit the APB to take the lead in the discussions that would ensue concerning accounting principles and practices. The Board's authority was enforced primarily through its prestige and Rule 203 of the AICPA Code of Professional Conduct. Furthermore, formal approval of Board issuances by the Securities and Exchange Commission (SEC) gave additional support to its activities.

During the Board's 14 years of existence, it issued 31 authoritative Opinions plus 4 nonauthoritative Statements. The Board made only scant use of the efforts of the Accounting Research Division, which published 15 research studies during its lifetime, and the respective agendas of the two bodies were independently arrived at. The general opinion was that the APB did not, ultimately, operate differently or more effectively than had the Committee on Accounting Procedure, resulting in calls for its replacement.

Financial Accounting Standards Board

Based on findings by the Wheat Study Group, the independent Financial Accounting Standards Board (FASB) was created in 1972. The Board currently consists of five members (until 2008, there were seven full-time members) having diverse backgrounds in public accounting, private industry, and academia. The Board is assisted by a staff of professionals that conducts research and works directly with the Board. FASB is recognized as authoritative through Financial Reporting Release (FRR) 1 of the SEC and through Rule 203 of the AICPA Code of Professional Conduct.

FASB is an independent body, relying on the Financial Accounting Foundation for selection of its members and approval of its budgets. FASB is supported by the sale of its publications and by fees assessed on all public companies (imposed under the Sarbanes-Oxley Act of 2002) based on their market capitalizations. The Board of Trustees of the Foundation is composed of members of the

- American Accounting Association
- American Institute of Certified Public Accountants
- CFA Institute

- Financial Executives International
- Government Finance Officers Association
- Institute of Management Accountants
- National Association of State Auditors, Comptrollers, and Treasurers
- Securities Industry Association

From its inception through the mid-2009 implementation of the Accounting Standards Codification (discussed below), the Board issued several types of pronouncements.[1] The most important of these were Statements of Financial Accounting Standards and the FASB Interpretations, the latter of which were used to clarify or elaborate on existing Statements or pronouncements of predecessor bodies. Under the GAAP hierarchy that existed prior to mid-2009, FASB Standards and Interpretations constituted category A GAAP, which also included FASB Staff Positions—a more recent form of official guidance—and the Board's FAS 133 implementation issues. Technical Bulletins, which were formerly category B GAAP, usually addressed issues not covered directly by existing standards and were primarily used to provide guidance where it was not expected to be costly or require a major change in practice. Bulletins were discussed at Board meetings and subject to Board veto. Both Technical Bulletins and Interpretations were designed to be responsive to implementation and practice problems on relatively narrow subjects.

The FASB staff was empowered to issue Implementation Guides and Staff Positions, which were included in category D of the former GAAP hierarchy. In a question-and-answer format, these implementation guides addressed specific questions that arose when a Standard was initially issued. FASB Staff Positions (FSP), of which many were produced over several years through mid-2009, were responses to questions on appropriate application of FASB literature that were expected to have widespread relevance. Implementation guides and Staff Positions were drafted by the staff and then issued, provided that a majority of the FASB Board members did not object.

Effective July 1, 2009, all codified GAAP was placed in a single level of the hierarchy (a second, lower level contains what formerly was defined as category E, consisting of scholarly writings, texts and guides by private-sector authors, guidance by other relevant bodies, etc.). The formerly important distinctions among categories A to D have completely evaporated.

American Institute of Certified Public Accountants (AICPA)

The Accounting Standards Executive Committee (AcSEC) has been the senior technical committee at the AICPA. It was authorized to set accounting standards and to speak for the AICPA on accounting matters. These were prepared largely through the work of various AICPA committees and task forces. AcSEC issued Statements of Position (SOPs) and industry audit and accounting guides (AAG), which were reviewed and cleared by the FASB and thus constituted category B GAAP under the former hierarchy. SOPs provided guidance on financial accounting and reporting issues. AAGs were intended to provide guidance to auditors in examining and reporting on financial statements of entities in specific industries and provided standards on accounting problems unique to a particular industry. AcSEC Practice Bulletins (formerly category C GAAP) usually provided guidance on very narrowly defined accounting issues. Effective November 2002, however, FASB reclaimed the sole authority to promulgate general-purpose GAAP, relegating AcSEC to the issuance of industry-specific accounting and auditing standards. Its role in the future has not yet been made clear.

Emerging Issues Task Force (EITF)

The Emerging Issues Task Force (EITF), formed by FASB in 1984 to assist in identifying current or emerging issues and implementation problems before divergent practices become entrenched, has most often restricted its attention to narrow issues. Task Force members have been drawn primarily from public accounting firms but also included individuals who would be aware of

---

[1] *Through July 1, 2009, the FASB issued 168 Statements on Financial Accounting Standards, 48 Interpretations, 51 Technical Bulletins as well as over 88 Staff Positions and over 30 implementation compilations. Most, but not all, of this literature remained in effect as of mid-2009. The preponderance of currently effective GAAP is the product of the FASB, and not of its predecessors, although a small number of such older standards remain in effect.*

issues and practices that should be considered by the group. Nonvoting representatives of the SEC and the FASB attend EITF for discussion purposes.

In terms of operations, an issues paper is prepared for each EITF agenda item; after discussion, if a consensus is reached, the consensus is referred to the FASB for ratification. Absent a consensus, the matter may end up on FASB's agenda or be resolved by the SEC, or may simply remain unresolved, with no standard-setting body currently considering it.

FASB has historically published a volume of EITF Abstracts, which are summaries of each Issue Paper and the results of Task Force discussion. Under the Accounting Standards Codification process, there will be no freestanding EITF consensuses (nor FASB Statements, etc.) but rather only amendments to or replacements of specific provisions in the Codification, issued as Accounting Standards Updates (ASU).

Effective status of consensuses. Although EITF pronouncements were technically category C GAAP, they were so specialized that generally there had been no salient category A or B GAAP on the respective topics, making the consensuses the highest-ranking guidance. The SEC was of the view that Task Force consensuses constituted GAAP for public companies, and it would question any accounting that differed from them. The SEC believed that the EITF supplied a public forum to discuss accounting concerns and assist in providing advice, and it had always been supportive of the Task Force's work.

Discussion topics. The EITF also previously published Discussion Issues, which were FASB and SEC staff announcements regarding technical matters that were deemed important but that did not relate specifically to a numbered EITF issue. These announcements were designed to help provide guidance on the application of relevant accounting pronouncements. These were increasingly infrequent over recent years, and it is anticipated that further discussion issues will not be produced.

Other Sources

Not all GAAP resulted from a deliberative process and the issuance of pronouncements by authoritative bodies. Historically, certain principles and practices evolved into acceptability without formal adoption of standards. Examples include straight-line and declining balance depreciation methods and last-in, first-out (LIFO) and first-in, first-out (FIFO) inventory costing methods. There are also many disclosure principles that evolved into general accounting practice after first being required by the SEC in submissions made to it—for example, reconciliations of the effective and statutory tax rates. Even much of the content of statements of financial position and income statements has evolved over the years in the absence of adopted standards. These other sources of GAAP remain relevant and will be found in the second (i.e., nonauthoritative) level of the new hierarchy.

ACCOUNTING STANDARDS CODIFICATION

Following a costly five-year effort, FASB in 2008 largely completed its project to codify GAAP. After a one-year test period, FASB determined that the codification would become effective July 1, 2009, superseding all existing GAAP literature.

The accounting standards Codification eliminated the multilevel hierarchy that previously existed in favor of a simple bifurcation between authoritative and nonauthoritative guidance. The Codification does not change GAAP, per se, but instead introduces a new, more readily accessible, user-friendly online research system. It reorganizes the multitude of GAAP pronouncements into about 90 accounting topics and displays all topics using a consistent structure. The Codification also includes relevant SEC guidance, which follows the same topical structure used in the Codification. This structure permits real-time updating as new standards are released and offers many other advantages, although users first will have to incur the substantial fixed cost of learning the new system.

HOW IS GAAP CREATED?

For many decades, GAAP has been created by the promulgation of standards and interpretations by the bodies granted statutory and professional authority to make such rules. Prior to the ASC, the FASB and AICPA both long adhered to rigorous "due process" when creating new guidance in category A and category B GAAP. The goal was to involve constituents who would be affected by the newly issued guidance, so that any new standards would result in information that would more meaningfully report economic activity without attempting to influence behavior in any particular direction. The FASB's due process procedures are described next. (The AICPA followed similar procedures but in the future it will have a reduced role.) Due process will remain as a guiding principle in the overall development of GAAP under the ASC structure.

Due Process prior to ASC. The FASB received requests for new standards from its diverse constituency, which includes reporting entities, auditors, industry groups, users, the EITF, and the SEC. Requests for action may have included suggestions for new topics as well as for reconsideration of existing pronouncements. For each major project added to its technical agenda, the FASB appointed an advisory task force of approximately 15 outside experts, taking care that various points of view were represented. The Task Force would meet with and advise the Board and staff on the definition and scope of the project and the nature and extent of any additional research that appeared to be needed. The FASB and its staff then debated the significant issues in the project and arrived at tentative conclusions, after studying existing literature and conducting or commissioning additional research, as needed. Task Force and Board meetings were open to public observation, and a public record was maintained. Many of these proceedings were also available by live or archived audio Webcast as well as via telephone.

If the accounting problem being considered by the Board was especially complex, the FASB began by publishing a discussion memorandum or another discussion document, generally setting forth the definition of the problem, the scope of the project, and the financial accounting and reporting issues; discussing research findings and relevant literature; and presenting alternative solutions to the issues under consideration and the arguments and implications relative to each. This was distributed to interested parties by request and was available on the FASB Web site, with a deadline for written comments specified and often with an invitation to present viewpoints at a public hearing.

Any individual or organization could request to speak at the public hearing, which was conducted by the FASB and the staff assigned to the project, with public observers welcome. After individual presentations, the FASB and staff asked questions that were based on written material submitted by the speakers prior to the hearing as well as on the speaker's oral comments. In addition, all written comments submitted were analyzed. The FASB members studied this analysis and read the comment letters to help them reach conclusions. The hearing transcript and written comments became part of the public record.

After the comment letters and oral presentations responding to the discussion document had been considered, formal deliberations began. (For less complex accounting issues, if no discussion document was prepared, the due process began at this point.) The FASB deliberated at meetings that are open to public observation, although observers could not participate in the discussions. Prior to each Board meeting, the staff presented a written analysis and recommendations of the issues to be discussed. During the meeting, the staff would present a summary of the written materials and the Board would discuss each issue. The Board would meet as many times as necessary to resolve the issues.

When the Board reached tentative conclusions on all the issues in the project, the staff prepared an Exposure Draft, which would set forth the Board's conclusions about the proposed standard (or interpretation) of financial accounting and reporting, the proposed effective date and method of transition, background information, and an explanation of the basis for the Board's conclusions. The Board would review and, if necessary, revise, the Exposure Draft. Then a vote would be taken about whether the Exposure Draft could be published for public comment. A majority of the Board members had to vote to approve an Exposure Draft for issuance for comment. If three votes were not obtained (after the Board was reduced to five members; when the Board consisted of seven members, four votes were required), the FASB would hold additional meetings and redraft the Exposure Draft until the necessary support could be obtained.

Any individual or organization could provide comments about the conclusions in the Exposure Draft during the exposure period, which was generally sixty days or more. The Board sometimes would decide to have a public hearing to hear constituents' views. At the conclusion of the comment period, all comment letters and oral presentations were analyzed by the staff, and the Board members read the letters and the staff analysis. At that point, the Board was ready to redeliberate the issues, with the goal of issuing final accounting standards.

If substantial modifications had been made, the Board would issue a revised Exposure Draft for additional public comment. If so, the Board also might have decided that another public hearing was warranted. When the Board was finally satisfied that all reasonable alternatives had been adequately considered, the staff would draft a final pronouncement for the Board's vote. Three votes were required for adoption of a pronouncement (now that the Board has been reduced to five members). Once issued, the standards become GAAP after the effective date stated in the pronouncement.

Due Process under ASC

The process to be followed under the new ASC structure largely follows that that previously existed. Public involvement and due process continue to be key elements in the standard-setting process; the major difference is that revisions, deletions, or additions to the ASC, rather than full-fledged freestanding pronouncements, will normally be the end product of the process.

For major projects, FASB has established the next procedures for developing accounting standards, some of which may be omitted for those projects that are focused on narrower application and implementation issues. Additional steps may be inserted during the course of any given project, even if not specifically required by FASB's Rules of Procedures.

First, FASB will receive from various sources requests or recommendations for possible projects and reconsideration of existing standards. The FASB chair will then decide whether to add a project to the technical agenda. This decision will be subject to oversight by the Financial Accounting Foundation's Board of Trustees, after appropriate consultation with FASB members and others.

Next, the Board will deliberate at one or more public meetings the various issues identified and analyzed by its staff. FASB will then issue an Exposure Draft. (Optionally, as may be deemed needed, a discussion paper may be issued to obtain input that is used to develop an Exposure Draft.)

Subsequently, FASB may hold a public roundtable meeting on the Exposure Draft, if that is seen as being useful or necessary. The staff will analyze comment letters, any public roundtable discussion, and any other information. FASB then will redeliberate the proposed provisions at public meetings.

Finally, the Board will issue an Accounting Standards Update (ASU) describing amendments to the Accounting Standards Codification (ASC). The ASU will delete, add, or revise specific paragraphs in the ASC, and a given ASU may alter a variety of existing topics and subtopics on an as-needed basis. Thus, a given ASU is not necessarily a coherent whole setting forth the entirety of a new standard, as was past practice, when FASB standards, interpretations, technical bulletins, or staff positions were promulgated.

HIERARCHY OF GAAP UNDER THE CODIFICATION

Hierarchy

On July 1, 2009, the FASB Accounting Standards Codification™ became the single official source of authoritative, nongovernmental U.S. generally accepted accounting principles (GAAP). It thus supersedes all extant FASB, AICPA, EITF, and related literature. After that date, only one level of authoritative GAAP exists, excluding the guidance issued by the Securities and Exchange Commission. All other literature will be nonauthoritative. In effect, therefore, the former five-level U.S. GAAP hierarchy has been compressed to two levels.

Only "As Amended" Guidance Included in ASC

The Codification includes all the former category A to D GAAP issued by accounting standard-setters, including pronouncements issued by the FASB, EITF, the Accounting Standards Executive Committee (AcSEC), the Accounting Principles Board, and so on, to the extent still binding on financial reporting practice. The materials used to create the Codification are the "as-amended" versions of those original accounting standards. Therefore, the Codification does **not** identify as sources any documents that solely amend other standards.

For example, FAS 149 was an amendment of FAS 133, so the content of FAS 149 is included through the as-amended version of FAS 133. Similarly, a great deal of literature (FASB Statements, Technical Bulletins, and Interpretations, as well as scores of EITF Issues, etc.) amended the venerable lease accounting standard, FAS 13, and those amending materials also are no longer referenced.

As with former practice, when certain standards and other guidance were issued with delayed effective dates, the Codification will include materials that may not yet be mandatorily effective. The content from new standards that are not yet fully effective for all reporting entities appears in the Codification as boxed text and is labeled as *pending content*. The pending content text box includes the earliest transition date and a link to the related transition guidance, also found in the Codification.

For reference purposes, the Codification permits backward tracing to the actual literature from which the Codification was derived. Of course, in the future, new pronouncements will add to or amend the Codification only, and no stand-alone FASB Statements or other guidance will be promulgated; thus, there will be no original source to be referenced as a stand-alone pronouncement.

For this reason, researching GAAP in official sources will now demand familiarity with, and access to, the Accounting Standards Codification™ issued by FASB. Understanding the structure of the Codification will thus be of great importance to all who have a need to understand GAAP and to research and apply GAAP to specific facts and circumstances.

SEC Guidance Included in ASC

Included in the Codification is relevant SEC guidance, which follows the same topical structure used throughout the Codification. This represents a departure from past practice, since SEC materials were not previously included in official GAAP guidance (although it obviously still had been binding on publicly held reporting entities and also was to be given some consideration as "category E" hierarchy literature, even by nonissuers, since it represented the best thinking on a given topic). To increase the utility of the Codification for public companies, relevant portions of authoritative content issued by the SEC and selected SEC staff interpretations and administrative guidance have been included for reference in the Codification. The sources include Regulation S-X, Financial Reporting Releases (FRR)/Accounting Series Releases (ASR), Interpretive Releases (IR), and SEC staff guidance in Staff Accounting Bulletins (SAB), EITF Topic D, and SEC Staff Observer comments. The Codification does not, however, incorporate the entire population of SEC rules, regulations, interpretive releases, and staff guidance, such as content related to matters outside of the basic financial statements, including Management's Discussion and Analysis (MD&A), or to auditing or independence matters.

Using the ASC

The Codification content is arranged within *Topics, Subtopics, Sections,* and *Subsections.* All accountants should quickly develop a facility to navigate through this material. Use of obsolete references (e.g., in audit file memoranda) will imply a lack of technical competence and may pose litigation or other risks for both preparers and auditors.

Topics represent a collection of related guidance. The topics correlate closely to standards issued by the International Accounting Standards Board (IASB), consistent with the agreed-upon plan to converge U.S. GAAP and IFRS. (The widely discussed potential supersession of U.S. GAAP by IFRS would likely render the ASC useless.) Topics reside in four main areas as follows:

1. *Presentation.* Topics relating only to presentation matters; they do not address recognition, measurement, and derecognition matters. Examples of these topics are income statement, balance sheet, and earnings per share.
2. *Financial statement accounts.* The Codification organizes topics into a financial statement order, including assets, liabilities, equity, revenue, and expenses. Topics include, for example, receivables, revenue recognition, and inventory.
3. *Broad transactions.* These topics relate to multiple financial statement accounts and are generally transaction oriented. Topics include, for example, business combinations, derivatives, and nonmonetary transactions.
4. *Industries.* These topics relate to accounting that is unique to an industry or type of activity. Topics include, for example, airlines, software, and real estate.

Subtopics represent subsets of a topic and typically are identified by type or by scope. For example, operating leases and capital leases are two separate subtopics of the leases topic, distinguished by type of lease. Each topic contains an *overall subtopic* that generally represents the pervasive guidance for the topic, which includes guidance that applies to all other subtopics. Each additional subtopic represents incremental or unique guidance not contained in the overall subtopic.

Sections represent the nature of the content in a subtopic—for example, recognition, measurement, and disclosure. The sectional organization for all subtopics is the same. In a manner similar to that used for topics, sections correlate closely with sections of individual International Accounting Standards.

Sections are further broken down into *subsections, paragraphs,* and *subparagraphs*, depending on the specific content of each section.

Hybrid Classification Scheme Used in ASC

FASB has developed a hybrid classification system specifically for the Codification. The structure of the classifications system is: XXX-YY-ZZ-PP, where XXX = Topic, YY = Subtopic, ZZ = Section, PP = Paragraph. An "S" preceding the section number denotes SEC guidance.

New standards will be composed of two items: the standard (similar to existing standards with a *Basis for Conclusions*) and an appendix of *Codification Update* instructions. The title of the combined set of standard and instructions will be *Codification Update YYXX,* where YY is the last two digits of the year and XX is the sequential number for each update. For example, the combined numbers would be 09-01, 09-02, and so on. All authoritative GAAP issued by the FASB will be issued in this format, regardless of the form in which such guidance may have been issued previously (e.g., EITF Abstracts, FASB Staff Positions, FASB Statements, and FASB Interpretations).

The FASB will organize the content of new standards using the same Section headings as those used in the Codification. The Codification Update Instructions are similar to the Amendments sections of current FASB standards. They will display marked changes to the pertinent sections of the Codification. New standards will not be deemed authoritative in their own right; instead, the new standards will serve only to update the Codification and provide the historical basis for conclusions of a new standard.

IMPORTANT CONCEPT OF MATERIALITY IN APPLYING GAAP

Materiality as a concept has great significance in researching, understanding, and implementing GAAP. Each standard or other document that has been issued by the FASB concludes by stating that its provisions need not be applied to immaterial items. Disputes over financial statement presentations often turn on the materiality of items that were, or were not, recognized, measured, and presented in certain ways.

Materiality Defined

Materiality is defined by the FASB as the magnitude of an omission or misstatement in the financial statements that makes it probable that a reasonable person relying on those financial statements would have been influenced by the omitted information or made a different judgment if the correct information had been known. However, due to its inherent subjectivity, the definition does not provide definitive guidance in distinguishing material information from immaterial information. The individual accountant must exercise professional judgment in evaluating information and concluding on its materiality. Materiality as a criterion has both quantitative and qualitative aspects, and items should not be deemed *immaterial* unless all potentially applicable quantitative and qualitative aspects are given full consideration and found not relevant.

Quantitative Component to Materiality

Quantitatively, materiality has been defined in relatively few pronouncements, which is a testament to the great difficulty of setting precise measures for materiality. For example, in ASC 280-10, addressing segment disclosures, a material segment or customer is defined as representing 10% or more of the reporting entity's revenues (although, even given this rule, qualitative considerations may cause smaller segments to be deemed reportable). The SEC has in various of its pronouncements defined materiality as 1% of total assets for receivables from officers and stockholders, 5% of total assets for separate balance sheet disclosure of items, and 10% of total revenue for disclosure of oil and gas producing activities.

Although materiality judgments traditionally have been primarily based on quantitative assessments, the nature of a transaction or event can affect a determination of whether that transaction or event is material. For example, a transaction that, if recorded, changes a profit to a loss or changes compliance with ratios in a debt covenant to noncompliance would be material even if it involved an otherwise immaterial amount. Also, a transaction that might be judged immaterial if it occurred as part of routine operations may be material if its occurrence helps meet certain objectives. For example, a transaction that allows management to achieve a target or obtain a bonus that otherwise would not become due would be considered material, regardless of the actual amount involved.

Another factor in judging materiality is the degree of precision that may be attained when making an estimate. For example, accounts payable usually can be estimated more accurately than a possible loss from the incurrence of an asset retirement obligation. An error that would be material in estimating accounts payable might be acceptable in estimating the retirement obligation.

Certain events or transactions may be deemed material because of their nature, regardless of the dollar amounts involved, and thus require disclosure under any circumstances. Offers to buy or sell assets for more or less than book value, litigation proceedings against the company pursuant to price-fixing or antitrust allegations, and active negotiations regarding their settlement can have a material impact on the enterprise's future profitability and, thus, are all examples of items that would not be capable of being evaluated for materiality based solely on numerical calculations.

It is clear that materiality, as traditionally defined by the accounting and auditing establishment, may no longer align with the definition implicitly applied by financial statement users, including the SEC and other regulatory authorities. It has become clear that a more nuanced and complex definition of materiality may now be required. In general, a decision regarding the application of GAAP (e.g., the choice of a nonstandard costing or revenue recognition method for a particular transaction) should be viewed as being immaterial only if all conceivable effects, such as the impact on common financial statement ratios or trends, are expected to be truly immaterial. A strict application of a quantitative threshold—say, 5% of net income—should be avoided, and once a materiality level is established, it should be strictly maintained in the face of identified errors or warranted adjustments in amounts greater than what had been defined.

The SEC, in its Staff Accounting Bulletin 99 (SAB 99), provides a useful discussion of this issue. Although not strictly applicable to nonpublic preparers of financial statements, this guidance is worthy of consideration by all accountants and auditors. Among other things, SAB 99 notes that deliberate application of nonacceptable accounting methods cannot be justified merely because the impact on the financial statements is deemed to be immaterial. SAB 99 also usefully reminds preparers and others that materiality has both quantitative and qualitative dimensions, which must both be given full consideration. Staff Accounting Bulletin 108 (SAB 108) later added to the literature of materiality with its discussion of considerations applicable to prior period restatements.

Qualitative Component to Materiality

In addition to the more obvious quantitative aspect to materiality, there is an equally important, but more elusive, qualitative aspect to be considered. Examples of qualitative factors that could possibly cause a quantitatively immaterial misstatement or omission to be deemed material, as cited by SAB 99, are

- Whether the misstatement arises from an item capable of precise measurement or whether it arises from an estimate and, if so, the degree of imprecision inherent in the estimate
- Whether the misstatement masks a change in earnings or other trends
- Whether the misstatement hides a failure to meet analysts' consensus expectations for the enterprise
- Whether the misstatement changes a loss into income or vice versa
- Whether the misstatement concerns a segment or other portion of the registrant's business that has been identified as playing a significant role in the registrant's operations or profitability
- Whether the misstatement affects the registrant's compliance with regulatory requirements
- Whether the misstatement affects the registrant's compliance with loan covenants or other contractual requirements
- Whether the misstatement has the effect of increasing management's compensation—for example, by satisfying requirements for the award of bonuses or other forms of incentive compensation
- Whether the misstatement involves concealment of an unlawful transaction

THE SARBANES-OXLEY ACT OF 2002

One result of a spate of business failures and accounting scandals occurring in the late 1990s/early 2000s was the enactment of the Sarbanes-Oxley Act, which included among its provisions these five sweeping changes:

1. Establishment of the Public Company Accounting Oversight Board (PCAOB), to oversee the audits of public companies that are subject to the securities laws of the United States (referred to as "issuers") and to establish auditing, quality control, ethics, independence, and other standards relating to the auditing of the financial statements of issuers. Three of the five PCAOB members cannot be and must not have been certified public accountants.
2. Placing of severe limits on an audit firm's ability to provide nonaudit services to its issuer audit clients.
3. Establishment of a requirement that the chief executive officer (CEO) and the chief financial officer (CFO) of each issuer certify in each periodic report to the SEC

   a. The appropriateness of the financial statements and disclosures.
   b. That those financial statements and disclosures fairly present, in all material respects, the operational and financial condition of the issuer.

4. Requirement for the SEC to conduct a study of off-balance-sheet transactions and the use of special-purpose entities, and to report its recommendations to Congress.
5. Requirement for the U.S. Government Accountability Office (GAO) to conduct a study regarding the consolidation of public accounting firms since 1989, including the present and future impact of the consolidation, and the solutions to any problems it discovers.

Internal Control Assessments

Another important provision of the Sarbanes-Oxley Act, set forth in Section 404, increases corporate management's responsibility for assessing the effectiveness of internal control over financial reporting. Operational management, as well as financial management, must now be more cognizant of their joint responsibility for quality financial reporting. Management's methods for assessing internal control will, and should, vary from company to company.

Corporate management must assess the risk of material financial statement misstatement along two dimensions: (1) inherent risk—the susceptibility of one or more financial statement assertions to a material misstatement, and (2) fraud risk—the risk of material misstatement due to fraudulent financial reporting or theft of assets.

Sarbanes-Oxley and the Development of GAAP

The principal regulatory focus of the Sarbanes-Oxley Act is on auditors and corporate management, which is appropriate because major financial reporting debacles such as Enron and WorldCom were primarily the result of management fraud and audit failures rather than of inherently faulty accounting standards. However, several requirements of the Act have the possibility of affecting future GAAP and its standards setters.

The Act defined the required characteristics of an accounting standards-setting body. For the time being, standards will continue to be set by FASB. The SEC reaffirmed in 2003 that it will continue to acknowledge FASB's pronouncements as being generally accepted. However, FASB is expected to announce some changes to demonstrate that it "has adopted procedures to ensure prompt consideration, by majority vote of its members, of changes to accounting principles necessary to reflect emerging accounting issues and changing business practices" and "considers, in adopting accounting principles . . . the extent to which international convergence on high quality accounting standards is necessary or appropriate."

Debate over Principles- and Rules-Based Standards

Sarbanes-Oxley required that the SEC conduct a study on the adoption by the United States financial reporting system of a principles-based accounting system. The study was to

include an examination of—(i) the extent to which principles-based accounting and financial reporting exists in the United States; (ii) the length of time required for change from a rules-based to a principles-based financial reporting system; (iii) the feasibility of and proposed methods by which a principles-based system may be implemented; and (iv) a thorough economic analysis of the implementation of a principles-based system.

That study was conducted as mandated, and the report thereon was released in 2003. (It can be found on the Special Studies section of the SEC's Web site, at www.sec.gov/news/studies/ principlesbasedstand.htm.) Briefly, it found that the oft-cited distinction between rules-based and principles-based standards was largely illusory, inasmuch as high-quality financial reporting standards must be (and have generally been) based on sound principles, but that a pure, principles-only set of standards, without practical guidance, would not serve the public interest.

Principles-based standards. Some have suggested that rules-based accounting standards contributed to the Enron, WorldCom, and other collapses. It is true that certain detailed rules found under U.S. GAAP (e.g., capital lease requirements such as the "90% test") have encouraged carefully constructed evasions (e.g., so-called 89% leases), which often provoke even more detailed rules, followed by yet more "engineered" transactions and reporting stratagems. Some observers suggested that the answer to the problems of "gaming the rules" and the ever-increasing complexity of resulting standards might have been found in embracing a principles-based, as opposed to a rules-based, approach to standards setting. To some (limited) extent, the standards published by the International Accounting Standards Board exhibited that characteristic, and some therefore argued that a movement toward principles-based standards might be facilitated by the convergence of U.S. GAAP and international standards.

The idea of a principles-based approach to U.S. standard setting is not new. FASB's conceptual framework, summarized later in this chapter, contains the body of principles that underlies U.S. accounting and reporting. The FASB has used the conceptual framework in developing its accounting standards for almost 30 years. However, FASB sometimes has bowed to pressure to provide exceptions to its principles in order to achieve other "desired" accounting results (e.g., to limit the volatility of reported earnings, as with current pension accounting requirements under FAS 87). Indeed, it is probably the existence of multiple exceptions to the promulgated standards, more than any failure to ground these in general principles, that opened the door to various reporting practices that, in certain circumstances, permitted the conduct of financial reporting frauds.

If a principles-based approach were implemented by FASB, accounting standards would continue to be developed from the conceptual framework (which is, as of early 2010, currently under revision), but the principles would apply more broadly than under existing standards. That is, there would be fewer exceptions to the principles in the standards. In addition, standard-setters would provide less interpretive and implementation guidance for applying the standards because the overall principle would ostensibly provide the necessary foundation for the answer with such guidance being considered superfluous. Exceptions would be extremely limited, or nonexistent, under a principles-based approach.

In addition, a principles-based approach requires accountants to more diligently exercise good professional judgment and to resist the urge to seek specific answers and rulings on every implementation issue. It also would require that the SEC and users of financial information accept the consequences of applying professional judgment, which means there would undoubtedly be some divergence in practice, possibly resulting in some loss of comparability of the financial statements of reporting enterprises.

As of early 2010, it appears that the debate over rules- or principles-based standards may be implicitly resolved by either the full convergence of U.S. GAAP with International Financial Reporting Standards (IFRS) or, in what was formerly thought to be unlikely but which is now deemed to be a very real possibility, having IFRS supersede U.S. GAAP. The fact that well over 100 other nations have opted to endorse IFRS (at least for publicly held companies' financial reporting), with as many as another 50 now taking steps to have IFRS supersede their respective national GAAP regimes, coupled with the possible granting of permission for IFRS-based reporting by U.S. companies registered with the SEC, makes this further development increasingly probable, in the authors' view.

Standards Overload

The recent criticisms of rules-based standards join earlier criticisms about the complexity of accounting standards. Some accountants complain about "standards overload," saying that there are too many accounting standards, which are individually too complex to be understood and implemented, and that too many organizations (SEC, FASB, EITF, AICPA, etc.) have historically been empowered to issue these pronouncements. Complaints regarding standards overload are not new, and with about 168 FASB Statements (some no longer effective) and myriad other standards (including hundreds of EITF Issues), these complaints must be given credence. (The process of Codification has eliminated the original standards and other authoritative literature but has not reduced the amount of guidance contained therein.) However, the solution, if there is one, is not obvious. Nor is it clear that financial reporting frauds, audit failures, or other such phenomena have been the result of this overload. Overwhelmingly, frauds result from the deliberate misapplication of GAAP and not from an inability on the part of preparers and auditors to comprehend the requirements of the standards.

Some have said that a solution would be to reduce and simplify GAAP, especially for entities having characteristics suggesting that the risk of misleading the users of the financial statements might be low. For example, some recommend a size test, with smaller entities following a subset of the standards that are mandated for larger entities (a system now used in the United Kingdom and soon being proposed by IASB as well). Even this simple suggestion has complications, however; size could arguably be determined by the amount of assets, revenues, or net worth, or the number of owners. Others recommend that public entities, regardless of size, follow a more comprehensive set of standards than privately owned businesses. The recently promulgated IFRS for Small and Medium-Sized Entities (IFRS for SMEs), which currently can be utilized by U.S.-based reporting entities that do not have public ownership or accountability, is the most prominent example of such a solution to this perceived problem.

Those who disagree say that differing standards would reduce the quality of financial reporting. For example, if decisions about which entities should follow which standards were made using a single criterion for all standards (such as size or ownership), some entities that engage heavily in a certain type of transaction (e.g., derivative financial instruments) might not be subject to the standards for that transaction—even though the recognition, measurement, and disclosure of those transactions were critical to understanding the financial condition and results of operations of the entity. To solve that problem, criteria would need to be based in some way on the underlying subject matter of the standard, which would result in an accountant having to examine each standard to determine if it would apply to a particular entity. That could compound the standards overload problem rather than solve it.

To respond to the demand for simpler standards for smaller or nonpublic reporting entities, FASB has endeavored over recent decades to offer somewhat differentiated standards for disclosures. ASC 825-10-50 exempts nonpublic companies from certain financial instrument disclosures if the entity's total assets are less than $100 million and the entity has not held or issued any derivative financial instruments. Nonpublic companies also are not required to disclose earnings per share (ASC 260-10), segment information (ASC 220-10), or certain pension and postretirement information (ASC 715-20). These exemptions have not, however, been widely hailed as representing significant progress against the perceived problem of standards overload.

To obtain better insight into these issues, in early 2004, the AICPA formed a Private Company Financial Reporting Task Force and charged it with conducting empirical research on the needs of preparers and users of private company financial statements and how well GAAP was meeting those needs, and developing recommendations based upon the results of the study. The findings were mixed, at best, showing a lack of clear consensus on this issue. Further efforts will doubtless be made in the near term to research and perhaps resolve what has been a many-decades-long debate.

Other FASB Initiatives to Reduce Complexity

In addition to the codification project, FASB has attempted to reduce the complexity of accounting standards by reducing the number of standard-setting bodies that issue authoritative accounting pronouncements. FASB changed the process of the EITF to give FASB more direct involvement with its agenda, deliberations, and conclusions. Two FASB board members were added to the EITF Agenda Committee, and FASB was required to ratify each EITF consensus at a public board meeting before the consensus officially becomes GAAP. Also, FASB and the AICPA agreed that AcSEC would cease issuing Statements of Position that create broadly applicable GAAP, instead limiting its work to specialized industry accounting standards. FASB announced its intention to collaborate with representatives from the EITF, AICPA, and SEC to develop a model for deciding if additional authoritative standards are necessary on a given topic and then how to most effectively segregate duties among those bodies with respect to issuing those standards.

FASB also expressed its intent to more thoroughly assess the cost-benefit relationships of proposed standards. Presumably, complex standards are more costly to implement, and thus the costs are more likely to outweigh the expected benefits to users. If so, enactment would be less probable. To understand the costs of a proposed standard, FASB intends to actively engage its constituents in a discussion of the costs as a formal step in the Board's due process. To understand more fully the benefits of a proposed standard, FASB has created a User Advisory Council, a group of 40 professionals representing a variety of investment and analytical disciplines, which will be consulted on specific projects as well as helping the Board formulate its overall agenda. FASB also established a Small Business Advisory Committee (SBAC) in order to obtain additional needed input from its small business constituents.

In 2005, the FASB and AICPA separately issued Exposure Drafts proposing to move the nongovernmental GAAP Hierarchy, discussed earlier in this chapter, from the auditing literature to the accounting literature. In connection with this change, the Exposure Drafts also designated FASB Staff Positions (FSP) and Derivatives Implementation Group Issues (DIG) as "category A" GAAP. This resulted in FAS 162, issued in May 2008. FAS 162 was only transitional in nature and is not included in the Codification, which streamlined the hierarchy to only two categories or levels: guidance within the Codification and all other guidance.

Although these FASB initiatives are viewed by many as a step in the right direction, it remains to be seen whether they successfully answer criticisms of standards overload. The financial environment is increasingly complex and litigious, which makes a lessening of the burden of GAAP unlikely in the near term.

AICPA and Its Diminished Influence

In the aftermath of the various financial reporting scandals previously discussed, many in the business and accounting communities criticized the AICPA for not proactively and forthrightly acknowledging systematic shortcomings in both the financial reporting and auditing realms and for not taking a visible leadership role in developing proposed solutions regarding their remediation. This perception that the AICPA was sitting on the sidelines as these scandals unfolded undoubtedly contributed to the creation, by the Sarbanes-Oxley Act, of the Public Company Accounting Oversight Board and its charge to oversee the auditing profession with respect to the audits of issuers (i.e., public companies). The PCAOB assumed the AICPA's previous responsibilities for ethics, independence, quality control, continuing professional education, peer review, and auditing standards as they relate to auditors of public company issuers.

Under these circumstances, the AICPA was (and still is) in danger of being rendered irrelevant as a standard setter and, no less, as a standard bearer for the profession. Its Auditing Standards Board (ASB) has continued to issue pronouncements that are binding on auditors of nonissuers (i.e., nonpublic companies) while the PCAOB has diverged from the AICPA's auditing standards by issuing its own standards. This action has fueled the debate regarding the advisability of "big GAAS, little GAAS." To the detriment of the auditing profession, the ultimate resolution of this conflict might be left to the judiciary if, as is quite conceivable, a nonissuer audit failure is alleged to have occurred that the plaintiff alleges might have been prevented had the auditor followed the PCAOB Standards instead of the Auditing Standards Board Standards.

Alleged Harmful Effects Caused by Financial Reporting Standards

In general, reporting entities have not welcomed proposals for new standards, since these inevitably involve change, costs of implementation, and, perhaps, a period of confusion while the marketplace assimilates the new information. In addition, the business community often claims that FASB does not understand the economic impact of new standards on their businesses. It complains that the implementation of certain accounting standards will harm businesses' ability to compete in the global marketplace and will impede their ability to raise debt or equity capital on favorable terms.

Two early examples of such resistance accompanied the issuance of FAS 43 (compensated absences) and FAS 106 (postretirement benefits). In both cases, the business community said that the new standard would cause it to reduce benefits to employees—and in some cases it did just that. The counterargument was perhaps more impressive, however: As a consequence of formerly failing to fully account for the actual economics of promises made or benefits granted, companies were misled regarding their true financial condition, which, once exposed, resulted in changes in behavior that were arguably long overdue. Managers were harmed by their former ignorance and by the delay; they were not hurt by the truth. (Proposed changes to accounting for pensions and other postemployment benefits, discussed in Chapter 16, will inevitably also trigger much anguish and again, quite possibly, reductions in promised benefits).

In two recent cases, dissatisfaction with proposed standards escalated to the point where the business community asked the federal government to intervene. When, in the mid-1990s, FASB proposed that the value of stock options granted to employees be reflected as an expense in the financial statements, the business community, and particularly technology firms, loudly claimed that the proposed recognition would have a dramatic and negative economic effect. First, the argument went, it would force them to discontinue issuing stock options, which would prevent the companies from compensating valuable employees, leading to increased turnover, loss of key talent, and dire macrolevel economic consequences. Second, to the extent options were granted and reflected in expense, it would cause the firms' costs of capital to increase significantly because of lower levels of reported profitability. Finally, it arguably would put U.S. firms at a competitive disadvantage to foreign companies that did not have to expense the value of stock options (or were not offering this benefit to employees), although IFRS does demand accounting for the economic cost of stock-based compensation in a manner quite similar to that under current U.S. GAAP (based on FAS 123[R]).

Before that battle ended, "sense of the House" and "sense of the Senate" resolutions had been introduced, objecting to FASB's tentative conclusions, and a bill had been introduced that would have, if enacted, precluded the recognition of the value of stock options as an expense as a matter of law. This debate threatened not only the stock-based compensation standard but also the future of accounting standard setting in the private sector itself. That concern contributed to FASB's decision to issue FAS 123 with only a requirement for disclosure of the value of stock options, with recognition and measurement optionally continuing under prior (APB 25) rules. Not surprisingly, virtually all publicly held companies continued to utilize the "implicit value" approach of APB 25, even though FAS 123 clearly stated that the "fair value" approach was preferable GAAP.

Another such situation arose later, when FASB was pursuing its derivative financial instruments project, when the business community again approached the Congress with a request for it to intercede in the debate. Although the federal government was not as quick to intervene in this instance, FASB was again criticized by several members of Congress and by their staff. To have been thus criticized and, in part, thwarted by influential government officials twice in a span of five years might have proved to be detrimental as the Congress considered legislation in response to the collapse of Enron Corp. However, standard setting in the private sector, and the supremacy of FASB in the standard-setting role, appear to have survived those challenges, at least for the immediate future. It remains to be seen how, if at all, convergence with—or possible supersession by—IFRS might be responded to by those who wish to see a more prominent role by government in the financial reporting standard-setting sphere.

The most recent example of claims being made that financial reporting requirements were causing harm to specific reporting entities, entire industry segments, or the domestic and international economies as a whole arose during the recent (and continuing) financial crisis affecting many nations. Arguably, this has been a natural bubble-bursting process that has its roots in the vast expansion of credit granting, particularly for domestic residences, and the rapidly escalating asset prices that resulted therefrom. The diminished valuations of financial instruments precipitated by the subprime mortgage crisis, followed by declining home prices, followed by economic contraction overall, coupled with the widespread required use of fair value ("mark to market") for such instruments, led to a demand that the *accounting rules* be relaxed or permanently changed, in order to ameliorate the *economic* and *financial* effects that were seen as being a consequence of financial reporting requirements. (For example, financial firms reported about $175 billion of value writedowns in 2008, in the aggregate, with further losses taken in 2009.)

In this instance (as with the reaction against fair value accounting for stock-based compensation proposals in the mid-1990s), powerful business and political interest lined up to pressure the accounting standardsetters, arguing that perceived or potential bad consequences should serve to derail rational financial reporting objectives. The large declines in fair (i.e., market) values of financial instruments held by banks, dutifully reported in accordance with GAAP, were said to somehow *not* be representative of actual fair values (due to reportedly unprecedented illiquidity and other market anomalies) and thus in need of modification, thereby understating actual losses and overstating bank and thrift capital.

FASB responded, under duress, by issuing some clarification (which should have been unnecessary, since GAAP—found at ASC 820-10—already provides guidance for valuing instruments when nominal market quotes are unreliable) and addresses circumstances when markets may be inactive and/or when market prices reflect only distressed sales. The effects on reported earnings and capital of banks and thrifts have been significant, according to reports that were circulated beginning in early 2009. Concerns about the impact of, and the virtue of using, fair values have continued to be raised, although, in the authors' opinion, the trend toward the incorporation of fair values into GAAP-basis financial reporting is unstoppable, and warranted.

RESEARCHING GAAP PROBLEMS

The research procedures presented here are intended to serve as a general model for approaching research on accounting issues or questions you may have. These procedures are only intended as an illustration of the process, not as a "cookbook" approach. These procedures should be refined and adapted to each individual fact situation.

Research Procedures

Step 1: Identify the problem. It has been observed that the mere act of defining a problem contributes mightily to solving the problem. This certainly applies to the domain of researching financial reporting issues. Most often it is found that incorrect answers (e.g., regarding the proper way to report revenue-producing activities) flow from improper definition of the actual question to be resolved. Provisional definitions of problems should be vigorously challenged *before* attempting to search for solutions. The process to be employed is to

- Gain an understanding of the problem or question.
- Challenge the tentative definition of the problem and revise, as necessary.
- Problems and research questions can arise from new authoritative pronouncements, changes in a firm's economic operating environment, or new transactions, as well as from the realization that the problem had not been properly defined in the past.
- It is important to remember that research can be performed before or after the critical event has occurred. However, if proposed transactions and potential economic circumstances are anticipated, more deliberate attention can be directed at finding the correct solution, and certain proposed transactions having deleterious reporting consequences might be avoided altogether or structured more favorably.
- If little is known about the subject area, it may be useful to consult general reference sources (e.g., *Journal of Accountancy, CPA Journal, BusinessWeek*) to become more familiar with the topic and build up some economic horse sense in the area (i.e., the basic what, why, how, when, who, where). Web-based research vastly expands the ability to gather useful information.
- If you are a preparer/auditor, ensure that you have sufficiently determined whether the issue you are researching is a GAAP issue or an auditing issue so that your search is directed to the appropriate literature.
- With the ongoing process of convergence with IFRS (and possible IFRS adoption) a reality, it will be wise to consider not merely short-term implications under U.S. GAAP but longer-term potential ramifications if changes are made to existing GAAP.

Step 2: Analyze the problem

- Identify critical factors, issues, and questions that relate to the research problem.
- What are the options? Brainstorm possible alternative accounting treatments. Note that alternatives continue to narrow both under U.S. GAAP and also due to ongoing efforts to converge to IFRS.
- What are the goals of the transaction? Are these goals compatible with full and transparent disclosure and recognition? Evolving GAAP and IFRS will both place greater emphasis on "transparency" in financial reporting.
- What is the economic substance of the transaction, irrespective of the manner in which it appears to be structured?
- What limitations or factors can impact the accounting treatment?

Step 3: Refine the problem statement

- Clearly articulate the critical issues in a way that will facilitate research and analysis.

Step 4: Identify plausible alternatives

- Plausible alternative solutions are based upon prior knowledge or theory.
- Additional alternatives may be identified as steps 5 to 7 are completed.
- The purpose of identifying and discussing different alternatives is to be able to respond to key accounting issues that arise out of a specific situation.
- The alternatives are the potential methods of accounting for the situation from which only one will ultimately be chosen.
- Exploring alternatives is important because many times there is no single cut-and-dried financial reporting solution to the situation.

- Ambiguity often surrounds many transactions and related accounting issues. Accordingly, the accountant and business advisor must explore the alternatives and use professional judgment in deciding on the proper course of action.
- Remember that other accountants may reasonably disagree with the judgment used or conclusions made, but this does not necessarily mean they are right.

Step 5: Develop a research strategy

- Determine which authorities or literature needs to be searched. Often it will be necessary to search all authoritative literature, which is now combined in the Accounting Standards Codification™ promulgated by FASB. The topic-based organization of this material should facilitate conducting such research, allowing the user to zero in on a detailed-level issue by beginning with a broad topic definition.
- Generate keywords or phrases that will form the basis of an electronic search.
- Consider trying a broad search to

  - Assist in developing an understanding of the area.
  - Identify appropriate search terms.
  - Identify related issues and terminology.

- Consider trying very precise searches to identify if there is authoritative literature directly on point.

Step 6: Search authoritative literature. This step involves implementation of the research strategy through searching, identifying, and locating applicable information.

- Research published GAAP, now codified in the ASC.
- Research using *Wiley GAAP*.
- Research other literature.
- Research practice.
- Use theory.
- Find analogous events and/or concepts that are reasonably similar.

Step 7: Evaluation

- Analyze and evaluate all of the information obtained.
- This evaluation should lead to the development of a solution or recommendation. Again it is important to remember that steps 3 to 7 describe activities that will interact with each other and lead to a more refined process in total, and a more complete solution. These steps may involve several iterations.

Researching Nonpromulgated GAAP

Researching nonpromulgated GAAP consists of reviewing pronouncements in areas similar to those being researched, reading accounting literature mentioned in the GAAP hierarchy as "other sources," and careful reading of the relevant portions of the FASB Conceptual Framework summarized later in this chapter. Understanding concepts and intentions espoused by accounting experts can give the essential clues to a logical formulation of alternatives and conclusions regarding problems that have not yet been addressed by the standard-setting bodies.

Both the AICPA and FASB publish a myriad of nonauthoritative literature. FASB publishes the documents it uses in its due process: Discussion Memorandums, Invitations to Comment, Exposure Drafts, and Preliminary Views as well as minutes from its meetings. It also publishes research reports, newsletters, and implementation guidance. The AICPA publishes its Exposure Drafts, as well as Technical Practice Aids, Issues Papers, comment letters on proposals of other standard-setting bodies, and the monthly periodical, *Journal of Accountancy*. Technical Practice Aids are answers published by the AICPA Technical Information Service to questions about accounting and auditing standards. AICPA Issues Papers are research documents about accounting and reporting problems that the AICPA believes should be resolved by FASB. They provide information about alternative accounting treatments used in practice. These two AICPA publications, which are not approved by FASB, have no authoritative status, but those who depart from their guidance should be prepared to justify that departure based on the facts and circumstances of the particular situation. Listings of FASB and AICPA publications are available at their Web sites. (A list of Web site addresses is located at the end of this chapter.)

The Securities and Exchange Commission issues Staff Accounting Bulletins and makes rulings on individual cases that come before it, which create and impose accounting standards on those whose financial statements are to be submitted to the Commission. The SEC, through acts passed by Congress, has been given broad powers to prescribe accounting practices and methods for all statements filed with it.

The International Accounting Standards Board publishes its standards, interpretations, the *Framework for the Preparation and Presentation of Financial Statements*, and project archives. Summaries of the standards and interpretations and the project archives are available at the Board's Web site, along with instructions for purchasing the complete standards, interpretations, and other materials.

The American Accounting Association (AAA) is an organization consisting primarily of accounting educators. It is devoted to encouraging research into accounting theory and practice. The issuances of the AAA tend to be normative, that is, prescribing what GAAP ought to be like, rather than explaining current standards. However, the monographs, committee reports, and *The Accounting Review* published by the AAA may be useful sources for research into applicable accounting standards.

Governmental agencies, such as the Government Accountability Office, the Federal Accounting Standards Advisory Board, and the Cost Accounting Standards Board, have certain publications that may assist in researching written standards. Also, industry organizations and associations may be other helpful sources.

Certain publications are helpful in identifying practices used by entities that may not be promulgated as standards. The AICPA publishes an annual survey of the accounting and disclosure policies of many public companies in *Accounting Trends and Techniques* and maintains a library of financial statements that can be accessed through a computerized search process (NAARS). EDGAR (Electronic Data Gathering, Analysis, and Retrieval) publishes the SEC filings of public companies, which includes the companies' financial statements. Through selection of keywords and/or topics, these services can provide information on how other entities resolved similar problems.

Internet-Based Research Sources

There has been and continues to be an information revolution affecting the exponential growth in the volume of materials, authoritative and nonauthoritative, that are available on the Internet. A listing of just a small cross-section of these sources is presented next.

Accounting Web Sites

AICPA Online	www.aicpa.org	Includes accounting news section; CPE information; section on professional ethics; information on relevant congressional/ executive actions; online publications, such as the *Journal of Accountancy*; Accounting Standards Executive Committee; also has links to other organizations; includes links to authoritative standards for nonissuers including auditing standards, attestation standards, and quality control standards.
American Accounting Association	www.aaahq.org	Accounting news; publications; faculty information; searchable; links to other sites.
FASB	www.fasb.org	Information on FASB; includes list of new Pronouncements/Statements; summaries of selected projects; summaries/status of all FASB Statements. Due to funding provided by PCAOB, FASB now posts its Statements, Interpretations, Staff Positions, and newly issued EITF Issues on its Web site.

FASB Codification	asc.fasb.org/home	Searchable database using the new accounting codification; includes cross-referencing and tutorials
GASB	www.gasb.org	Information on GASB; new GASB documents; summaries/status of all GASB statements; proposed Statements; Technical Bulletins; Interpretations
IASB	www.iasb.org.uk	Information on the IASB; lists of Pronouncements, Exposure Drafts, project summaries, and conceptual framework
NASBA	www.nasba.org	National State Boards of Accountancy (NASBA); includes listings of registered CPE sponsors and links to state boards of accountancy, as well as standards governing continuing professional education that it jointly issues with the AICPA
PCAOB	www.pcaobus.org	Sections on rulemaking, standards (including the interim auditing, attestation, quality control, ethics, and independence standards), enforcement, inspections and oversight activities
Rutgers Accounting Web	www.accounting.rutgers.edu	Includes links to journals and publications, software, publishers, educational institutions, government agencies, and information regarding continuous auditing initiatives
SEC	www.sec.gov	SEC digest and statements; EDGAR searchable database; information on current SEC rulemaking; links to other sites
WebCPA	www.webcpa.com	Breaking news regarding the profession, links to regulators, taxing agencies, associations, and agencies

Example of How to Solve a GAAP Problem

As an example of how to solve a GAAP problem, let us examine how the FASB and its staff approached a question raised by the Edison Electric Institute (EEI) in the project that eventually led to FAS 143, *Asset Retirement Obligations* (now ASC 410-20).

The EEI requested that the FASB add a project to its agenda to determine the appropriate accounting for removal costs, such as the costs of nuclear decommissioning and similar costs affecting other industries. At the time this was raised, the existing accounting practices for removal costs were inconsistent as to the criteria used for recognition, measurement, and the presentation of the obligation in the financial statements. Some entities did not recognize any obligations for removal costs until actually incurred. Other entities estimated the cost of retiring the asset and accrued a portion of that amount each period as an expense, with an offsetting liability, so that when the asset was retired, a liability for the full amount of the removal costs would already be on the ledger. Still others recognized the expense but displayed the credit side of the entry as a contra asset rather than a liability.

FASB looked for an analogous situation and found one in FAS 19, *Financial Accounting and Reporting by Oil and Gas Producing Companies* (ASC 932-235-10). Paragraph 37 of that standard states that "estimated dismantlement, restoration, and abandonment cost shall be taken into account in determining amortization and depreciation rates." The effect of that paragraph was that the credit side of the entry was to accumulated depreciation, which could result in an accumulated depreciation amount that exceeded the cost of the asset. There was no recognition of an obligation to dismantle and restore the property (a liability). Instead the focus was on achieving a particular pattern of expense recognition. Because the amount of the obligation that the entity had incurred was not a central concern under ASC 932, the FASB (which embraced a balance sheet orientation in its conceptual framework, which was issued after ASC 932 was promulgated) rejected it and sought another solution.

FASB next considered the definition of a liability in paragraphs 36-40 of Statement of Financial Accounting Concepts (CON) 6 to determine whether nuclear decommissioning and similar asset retirements could be considered liabilities of the entities owning the assets. Since the first characteristic of a liability—that an entity has "a present duty or responsibility to one or more other entities that entails settlement by probable future transfer or use of assets at a specified or determinable date, on occurrence of a specified event, or on demand"—would be met when an entity is required by current laws, regulations, or contracts to settle an asset retirement obligation upon retirement of the asset, FASB concluded that accounting for this liability would be the central goal of the new standard.

In some situations, the duty or responsibility to remove the asset is created by an entity's own promise. In other situations, the duty or responsibility is created by circumstances in which an entity finds itself bound to perform, and others are justified in relying on the entity to perform. Thus, in its initial deliberations, the FASB decided that entities should report both legal and constructive obligations in their financial statements. Paragraph 36 of CON 6, which defines the essential characteristics of a liability, recognizes both types of obligations. It states:

> *[A]lthough most liabilities rest generally on a foundation of legal rights and duties, existence of a legally enforceable claim is not a prerequisite for an obligation to qualify as a liability if for other reasons the entity has the duty or responsibility to pay cash, to transfer other assets, or to provide services to another entity.*

Paragraph 40 of CON 6 provides further insight. It states:

> *Liabilities stemming from equitable or constructive obligations are commonly paid in the same way as legally binding contracts, but they lack the legal sanction that characterizes most liabilities and may be binding primarily because of social or moral sanctions or custom. An equitable obligation stems from ethical or moral constraints rather than from rules of common or statute law.*

During its due process, FASB heard from constituents that without improved guidance for determining whether a constructive obligation exists, inconsistent application of the final standard would result. After further consideration of the qualitative characteristics of reliability and comparability found in CON 2, and the recognition characteristic of reliability in CON 5, the FASB decided to confine recognition only to legal obligations, including legal obligations created under the doctrine of promissory estoppel.

FASB also considered the second characteristic of a liability, that "the duty or responsibility obligates a particular entity, leaving it little or no discretion to avoid the future sacrifice." It concluded that an asset retirement obligation had that characteristic.

FASB considered the third and final characteristic of a liability, namely that "the transaction or other event obligating the entity has already happened." It concluded that an entity must look to the nature of the duty or responsibility to assess whether the obligating event has occurred. FASB provides the example of a nuclear power facility: Although the operator assumes responsibility for decontamination upon receipt of a license, it is not until the facility is operated and contamination occurs that there is an obligating event.

When contemplating the manner in which the asset retirement obligation could be measured, FASB was guided by CON 7. In that concepts statement, FASB concluded that "the only objective of present value, when used in accounting measurements at initial recognition and fresh-start measurements, is to estimate fair value." Based on this, FASB determined that an asset retirement obligation should be measured at fair value, but in the (typical) absence of quoted market prices or prices for similar liabilities, entities should use present value techniques to measure the liability.

In deciding on the appropriate designation of the debit offsetting the entry recording the obligation, FASB first made reference to the definition of an asset under CON 6. FASB concluded that capitalized asset retirement costs would not qualify for presentation as a separate asset because no separate future economic benefit flows from these costs. Thus, asset retirement costs do not meet the definition of an asset in paragraph 25 of CON 6. However, FASB observed that current accounting practice includes in the historical cost basis of an asset all the costs that are necessary to prepare the asset for its intended use. FASB concluded that the requirement for capitalization of the asset retirement cost as part of the historical cost of the asset and then depreciating that asset both (1) obtains a measure of cost that more closely reflects the entity's total investment in the asset, and (2) permits the allocation of that cost to expense in the periods over which the related asset would be expected to provide benefits.

Thus, in this actual situation, by reasoning from analogous situations and applying established accounting concepts, FASB was able to develop an important new standard. In a like manner, solutions to GAAP practice problems can be reached. Those solutions will serve the reporting entity in achieving GAAP-compliant financial reporting until a standards-setting body resolves the problem by issuing authoritative guidance.

FASB CONCEPTUAL FRAMEWORK

FASB has issued seven pronouncements (six of which remain extant) called Statements of Financial Accounting Concepts (CON) in a series designed to constitute a foundation of financial accounting standards. This conceptual framework is designed to prescribe the nature, function, and limits of financial accounting and to be used as a guideline that will lead to consistent standards. These conceptual statements do not establish accounting standards or disclosure practices for particular items. They are not enforceable under the AICPA Code of Professional Conduct.

FASB's conceptual framework is intended to serve as the foundation upon which the Board can construct standards that are both sound and internally consistent. The fact that the framework was intended to guide FASB in establishing standards is embodied in the preface to each of the Concepts Statements. The preface to CON 6 states:

> *The Board itself is likely to be the most direct beneficiary of the guidance provided by the Statements in this series. They will guide the Board in developing accounting and reporting standards by providing the Board with a common foundation and basic reasoning on which to consider merits of alternatives.*

The conceptual framework is also intended for use by the business community to help understand and apply standards and to assist in their development. This goal is also mentioned in the preface to each of the Concepts Statements, as this excerpt from CON 6 shows:

> *However, knowledge of the objectives and concepts the Board will use in developing standards also should enable those who are affected by or interested in financial accounting standards to understand better the purposes, content, and characteristics of information provided by financial accounting and reporting. That knowledge is expected to enhance the usefulness of, and confidence in, financial accounting and reporting. The concepts also may provide some guidance in analyzing new or emerging problems of financial accounting and reporting in the absence of applicable authoritative pronouncements.*

The FASB Special Report, *The Framework of Financial Accounting Concepts and Standards* (1998), states that the conceptual framework should help solve complex financial accounting or reporting problems by

- *Providing a set of common premises as a basis for discussion;*
- *Providing precise terminology;*
- *Helping to ask the right questions;*
- *Limiting areas of judgment and discretion and excluding from consideration potential solutions that are in conflict with it; and*
- *Imposing intellectual discipline on what traditionally has been a subjective and ad hoc reasoning process.*

Of the seven Concepts Statements, the fourth, *Objectives of Financial Reporting by Nonbusiness Organizations*, is not covered here due to its specialized nature.

Components of the conceptual framework. The components of the conceptual framework for financial accounting and reporting include objectives, qualitative characteristics, elements, recognition, measurement, financial statements, earnings, funds flow, and liquidity. The relationship between these components is illustrated in the following diagram reproduced from a FASB Invitation to Comment, *Financial Statements and Other Means of Financial Reporting*.

In the diagram, components to the left are more basic and those to the right depend on components to their left. Components are closely related to those above or below them.

The most basic component of the conceptual framework is the objectives. The objectives underlie the other phases and are derived from the needs of those for whom financial information is intended. The qualitative characteristics are the criteria to be used in choosing and evaluating accounting and reporting policies.

Elements of financial statements are the components from which financial statements are created. They include assets, liabilities, equity, investments by owners, distributions to owners, comprehensive income, revenues, expenses, gains, and losses. In order to be included in financial statements, an element must meet criteria for recognition and possess a characteristic that can be reliably measured.

Conceptual Framework for Financial Accounting and Reporting

Reporting or display considerations is concerned with what information should be provided, who should provide it, and where it should be displayed. How the financial statements (financial position, earnings, and cash flow) are presented is the focal point of this part of the conceptual framework project.

A CON does not establish GAAP. Since GAAP may be inconsistent with the principles set forth in the conceptual framework, the FASB expects to reexamine existing accounting standards. Until that time, a CON does not require a change in existing GAAP. CON do not amend, modify, or interpret existing GAAP, nor do they justify departing from GAAP based upon interpretations derived from them.

Complete coverage of the FASB Concepts Statements is offered in *Wiley GAAP 2010*.

CONDUCTING RESEARCH THROUGH THE FASB CODIFICATION WEB SITE

As noted previously in this chapter, the FASB has completed its project to codify GAAP, thereby eliminating the multilevel hierarchy in favor of a single, centralized database of authorized documentation. The FASB has compiled this Codification into a Web site, which is located at http://asc.fasb.org/home. The site is intended to be easily searchable for research purposes. This section provides an overview of the site's contents and search functionality.

On all pages of the site, all categories of the Codification are listed down the vertical menu bar on the left side of the page, revealing these primary topics, and the numbering series for each one:

- *Presentation (200)*. Covers the reporting aspects of GAAP, such as the balance sheet, income statement, and segment reporting.
- *Assets (300)*. Contains GAAP for all types of assets, such as receivables, investments, and intangibles.
- *Liabilities (400)*. Contains GAAP for all types of liabilities, such as commitments, contingencies, and guarantees.
- *Equity (500)*. Covers GAAP for such topics as stock, stock dividends, and treasury stock.

- *Revenue (600).* Includes all revenue topics, including product revenue, services revenue, and a great deal of industry-specific topics.
- *Expenses (700).* Clusters all types of expense-related GAAP into five broad categories, which are cost of goods sold, research and development, compensation, income taxes, and other expenses.
- *Broad Transactions (800).* Contains the major transactional topics, such as business combinations, derivatives, and foreign currency matters.
- *Industry (900).* Itemizes GAAP for specific industries, such as entertainment, real estate, and software.
- *Master Glossary.* Includes a compilation of terminology assembled from the multitude of original GAAP source documents.

The numbering series indicated next to each bullet point shows the three-digit number assigned to each topic. For example, the Presentation topic contains a number of subtopics, all indexed with numbers in the 200 range; the Balance Sheet subtopic is numbered 210, while the Interim Reporting subtopic is numbered 270. These index numbers become more apparent while perusing the submenus attached to each primary topic. For example, the submenu for the Presentation topic reveals 14 subcategories, numbered from 205 (for Presentation of Financial Statements) to 280 (for Segment Reporting).

At the most granular level of detail, the Codification has a two-digit numerical code for a standard set of categories, which follow:

- *Overview and Background (05).* Provides overview and background material.
- *Scope and Scope Exceptions (15).* Outlines the transactions, events, and other occurrences to which the subtopic guidance does or does not apply.
- *Glossary (20).* Contains definitions for terms found within the subtopic guidance.
- *Recognition (25).* Defines the criteria and timing for recording an item in the financial statements.
- *Initial Measurement (30).* Provides guidance on the criteria and amounts used to measure a transaction at the initial date of recognition.
- *Subsequent Measurement (35).* Provides guidance on the subsequent measurement and recognition of an item.
- *Other Presentation Matters (45).* A catchall category providing guidance not included in the preceding sections.
- *Disclosure (50).* Provides guidance regarding disclosure in the notes to or on the face of the financial statements.
- *Implementation Guidance and Illustrations (55).* Contains illustrations of the guidance provided in the preceding sections.
- *Relationships (60).* Contains links to guidance that may be helpful to the reader of the subtopic.
- *SEC Materials (S99).* Contains selected SEC content for use by public companies.

By drilling down through the various topics and subtopics in the sidebar, a researcher can eventually locate the relevant GAAP information. However, there are three other ways to access GAAP information through the Codification site that may prove to be easier.

- *Cross-referencing.* If the researcher knows the reference number of an original GAAP source document, such as an EITF consensus or a FASB Staff Position, then s/he can enter this information through the Cross-Reference tab, which is located at the top center of the Codification home page. A By Standard search box will appear, where the researcher can select from a drop-down menu containing three-digit abbreviations for all of the various GAAP source documents. For example, FTP represents the FASB Staff Positions, while APB represents the Accounting Principles Board Opinions. After making a selection from this menu, the available list of all corresponding documents will appear next to it, in the Standard Number drop-down menu. Selecting a document from this list will bring up the corresponding topic, subtopic, section, and paragraph number in the Codification, as well as a hyperlink to the underlying text.

- *Codification search.* If the researcher is searching for specific words or phrases, then the best search tool is the Codification search bar, which is located in the upper right corner of any page on the site. To use it for a precision search, enter quotes around the search text; for a less precise search that returns individual words within the search text, do not use quotes. If the resulting set of links is too voluminous, then use the Narrow by Topic option on the right side of the page. This option allows the researcher to reduce the number of selections to only certain topic areas. For example, to determine the appropriate presentation of cash on the balance sheet, search on the word Cash, and then narrow the selection to just the Presentation topic, and then narrow further to just the Balance Sheet subtopic.
- *Advanced search.* The most detailed researching method is the Advanced Search option, which is located below the search bar in the upper right corner of any site page. The resulting search page reveals a combination of options; the researcher can use text, Codification numbers, document titles, and topics to prepare a more refined search.

The simplified structure of the Codification makes it a much simpler database than the old GAAP hierarchy for researching purposes, which is also enhanced by the Codification Web site's excellent search tools.

Chapter 2

STATEMENT OF FINANCIAL POSITION
(ASC 210)

INTRODUCTION

Statements of financial position present information about assets, liabilities, and owners' equity. They reflect an entity's resources (assets) and its financing structure (liabilities and equity) in conformity with generally accepted accounting principles (GAAP). The statement of financial position reports the aggregate, cumulative effect of economic transactions at a point in time.

SCOPE

The requirements of ASC 210 apply to all entities that prepare "general-purpose financial statements" that are stated to be presented in accordance with GAAP. "General-purpose financial statements" are those intended to meet the needs of users who are not in a position to demand reports that are tailored according to their information needs.

DEFINITIONS OF KEY TERMS

Assets. Probable future economic benefits obtained or controlled by a particular entity as a result of past transactions or events.

Contributed capital. Contributed or paid-in capital is the amount of equity invested in a corporation by its owners. It consists of capital stock and additional paid-in capital.

Equity. The residual interest in assets of the reporting entity that remains after deducting its liabilities.

Liabilities. Probable future sacrifices of economic benefits arising from present obligations of past transactions or events.

STRUCTURE AND CONTENT

The format of the statement of financial position is not specified by any authoritative pronouncement. Instead, formats and titles have developed as a matter of tradition and, in some cases, through industry practice. Two basic formats are used:

1. The balanced format, in which the sum of the amounts for liabilities and equity are added together on the face of the statement to illustrate that assets equal liabilities plus equity. This is the reason for the formerly commonly used title, "balance sheet."
2. The less frequently presented equity format, which shows totals for assets, liabilities, and equity but no sums illustrating that assets less liabilities equals equity. An infrequently seen variation on this is to show assets minus liabilities as being equal to equity.

Those two formats can take one of two forms.

1. The account form, presenting assets on the left-hand side of the page and liabilities and equity on the right-hand side.
2. The report form, which is the top-to-bottom or running presentation.

The use of the title "balance sheet," "statement of financial position," or "statement of financial condition" implies that the statement is presented using GAAP. If, instead, some other comprehensive basis of accounting, such as income tax basis or cash basis, is used, the financial statement title must be revised to reflect this fact. The use of a title such as "Statements of Assets and Liabilities—Income Tax Basis" is necessary to differentiate the financial statement being presented from a GAAP statement of financial position.

In order to increase the usefulness of financial statements, many entities include financial statements for one or more prior years in their annual reports, although comparative information is not actually required under current U.S. GAAP (but will be under proposed revisions to GAAP).

Assets

Current assets are cash and other assets that are reasonably expected to be realized in cash or sold or consumed during the normal operating cycle of the business. When the normal operating cycle is less than one year, a one-year period is used to distinguish current assets from noncurrent assets. When the operating cycle is very long, the usefulness of the concept of current assets diminishes. The next items are classified as current assets:

- Cash and cash equivalents
- Short-term investments
- Receivables
- Inventories
- Prepaid expenses

Excluded from the classification of current assets are assets that will not be realized in cash during the next year (or operating cycle, if longer). These assets are classified as noncurrent assets:

- Long-term investments (including debt and equity securities, tangible assets, and investments held in special funds)
- Property, plant, and equipment
- Intangible assets
- Other assets (assets that do not fit neatly into any of the other asset categories)

Liabilities

Liabilities are displayed on the statement of financial position in the order of expected payment. The distinction between current and noncurrent assets and liabilities generally rests on both the ability and intent of the enterprise to liquidate or not to liquidate within the traditional one-year time frame or the operating cycle, if longer.

Obligations are classified as current if their liquidation is reasonably expected to require the use of existing resources properly classifiable as current assets or to create other current obligations. Obligations that are due on demand or that are callable at any time by the lender are classified as current regardless of the intent of the reporting entity or lender. These liabilities are classified as current liabilities:

- Accounts payable
- Trade notes payable

- Dividends payable
- Advances and deposits
- Agency collections and withholdings
- Current portion of long-term debt
- Accrued expenses

Obligations that are not expected to be liquidated within one year (or the current operating cycle, if longer) are classified as noncurrent. These obligations are classified as noncurrent:

- Notes and bonds payable
- Capital lease obligations
- Written put options on the option writer's (issuer's) equity shares and forward contracts to purchase an issuer's equity shares that require physical or net cash settlement
- Contingent obligations
- Mandatorily redeemable shares
- Other noncurrent liabilities (including defined benefit pension obligations, postemployment obligations, and postretirement obligations)

Offsetting

In general, assets and liabilities are not permitted to be offset against each other unless certain specified criteria are met. ASC 210-20-45 permits offsetting only when all of these conditions, which constitute a right of offset, are met:

- Each of the two parties owes the other determinable amounts (although they may be in different currencies and bear different rates of interest).
- The enterprise has the right to offset the amount it owes against the amount owed to it by the other party.
- The enterprise intends to offset the two amounts.
- The right of offset is legally enforceable.

Stockholders' Equity

Stockholders' equity represents the residual interest in the assets of the reporting entity after liabilities are subtracted from assets. In a corporation, shareholders' equity arises from three sources: contributed (paid-in) capital, retained earnings, and accumulated other comprehensive income.

Contributed, or paid-in, capital is the amount of equity invested in a corporation by its owners. It consists of capital stock and additional paid-in capital. Contributed capital arises from the issuance of common and preferred stock to investors, from transaction by the corporation in its own stock (e.g., treasury stock, stock dividends, conversion of convertible bonds), and from the donation of assets or services.

Capital stock is the par or stated value of preferred and common shares. The face of the statement of financial position often provides information about the type of issues, the par or stated value per share, and the number of shares authorized, issued, and outstanding.

Retained earnings are the cumulative net income of the corporation from the date of its inception (or reorganization) to the date of the financial statements, less the cumulative distribution to shareholders either directly (dividends) or indirectly (treasury stock).

Accumulated other comprehensive income is the change in equity of a business entity during a period that arises from sources other than net income and transactions with its owners. Under current accounting standards, its accumulated components include net unrealized holding gains and losses on investments classified as available-for-sale securities, the effective portion of the gain or loss on derivative instruments designated and qualified as either cash flow hedges or hedges of forecasted foreign currency–denominated transactions, the excess of minimum pension liability over unrecognized prior service cost, and unrealized gains on foreign currency translation. The components of accumulated other comprehensive income are shown either in the statement of changes in shareholders' equity or in the shareholders' equity section of the statement of financial position.

EXTRACTS FROM PUBLISHED FINANCIAL STATEMENTS

Champions Biotechnology, Inc.
CONSOLIDATED BALANCE SHEETS

	April 30	
	2009	*2008*
Assets		
Current assets		
Cash and cash equivalents	$1,728,000	$3,709,000
Short-term investments	1,017,000	—
Prepaid expenses, deposits, and other receivables	1,125,000	53,000
Total current assets	3,870,000	3,762,000
Property and equipment, net	81,000	—
Intangible assets	—	227,000
Goodwill	669,000	662,000
Total assets	$4,620,000	$4,651,000
Liabilities and Stockholders' Equity		
Current liabilities		
Accounts payable	$1,414,000	$ 113,000
Accrued liabilities	67,000	35,000
Deferred revenue	1,223,000	505,000
Accrued salary due to officer	—	361,000
Total current liabilities	2,704,000	1,014,000
Commitments and Contingencies		
Stockholders' equity		
Preferred stock, $10 par value; 56,075 shares authorized; no shares issued or outstanding	—	—
Common stock, $.001 par value; 50,000,000 shares authorized; 33,579,000 and 33,338,000 issued at April 30, 2009 and 2008, respectively, and 32,989,000 and 33,248,000 shares outstanding, respectively	34,000	33,000
Treasury stock, at cost, 590,000 and 90,000 shares, respectively	(1,000)	—
Additional paid-in capital	11,640,000	11,119,000
Accumulated deficit	(9,757,000)	(7,515,000)
Total stockholders' equity	1,916,000	3,637,000
Total liabilities and stockholders' equity	$4,620,000	$4,651,000

The accompanying notes are an integral part of these consolidated financial statements.

Disclosures

In addition to the measurement accounting principles that guide the value placed on the elements included in the statement of financial position, there are accounting principles specifying the informative disclosures that are necessary because, without the information they provide, the financial statements would be misleading. Some examples of disclosure techniques are discussed next.

Parenthetical Explanations

Information sometimes is disclosed by means of parenthetical explanations appended to the appropriate balance sheet caption. Parenthetical explanations place the disclosure prominently in the body of the statement instead of in a note or schedule where they are more likely to be overlooked. For example,

- Common stock ($10 par value, 200,000 shares authorized, 150,000 issued) $1,500,000

Notes to Financial Statements

If information cannot be disclosed in a relatively short and concise parenthetical explanation, a note disclosure is used.

Cross-References

Cross-referencing is used when there is a direct relationship between two accounts on the statement of financial position. For example, among the current assets, the next bulleted item might be shown if $1,500,000 of accounts receivable were pledged as collateral for a $1,200,000 bank loan:

- Accounts receivable pledged as collateral on bank loan payable $1,500,000

Included in the current liabilities would be

- Bank loan payable—collateralized by accounts receivable $1,200,000

Valuation Allowances

Valuation allowances are used to reduce or increase the carrying amounts of certain assets and liabilities. Accumulated depreciation reduces the carrying value of property, plant, and equipment, and a bond premium (discount) increases (decreases) the face value of a bond payable.

Supporting Schedules

A supporting schedule might be used to provide additional detail about an item in the financial statements. For example, consolidating schedules might be included in addition to the basic consolidated financial statements, or a five-year summary of selected financial data might be included. In general, supporting schedules are not used to provide information required by GAAP because those schedules are not part of the basic financial statements and typically are subjected to only limited procedures by auditors.

Accounting Policies

There are many different methods of valuing assets, recognizing revenues, and assigning costs. Financial statement users must be aware of the accounting policies used by entities so that sound economic decisions can be made. The disclosures are to identify and describe the accounting principles followed by the reporting entity and methods of applying those principles that materially affect the determination of financial position, changes in cash flows, or results of operations. The disclosure is to encompass those accounting principles and methods that involve selection from acceptable GAAP alternatives, principles and methods peculiar to the industry, and unique applications of GAAP.

Related Parties

Financial statements are required to disclose material related-party transactions other than compensation arrangements, expense allowances, or other similar items that occur in the ordinary course of business. A related party is essentially any party that controls or can significantly influence the management or operating policies of the company to the extent that the company may be prevented from fully pursuing its own interests.

Transactions with related parties are to be disclosed even if there is no account recognition made for such transactions. Disclosures are not permitted to assert that the terms of related-party transactions were essentially equivalent to arm's-length dealings unless those claims can be substantiated.

Subsequent Events

The statement of financial position is dated as of the last day of the fiscal period, but a period of time usually elapses before the financial statements are issued or available to be issued. During this period, significant events or transactions may occur that materially affect the company's financial position. The failure to disclose significant events occurring between the date of the statement of financial position and the date the financial statement is issued or available to be issued could mislead a reader who is otherwise unaware of those events.

Contingencies

A contingency is an existing condition, situation, or set of circumstances involving uncertainty as to possible gain or loss. The uncertainty ultimately will be resolved when one or more future events occur or fail to occur. If it is probable that an asset has been impaired or that a liability has been incurred at the date of the statement of financial position and the amount of that loss can be reasonably estimated, the loss is accrued by a charge to earnings and the recognition of a liability. However, if it is only reasonably possible that a future event will confirm that an asset was impaired or a liability was incurred at the date of the statement of financial position, the reporting entity must disclose the contingency if the amount involved could have a material effect on the financial statements.

Commitments

All significant contractual commitments are to be disclosed in the notes to the financial statements.

MULTIPLE-CHOICE QUESTIONS

1. Which of the following is **not** a current asset?
    (a) Inventory.
    (b) Receivables.
    (c) Intangible assets.
    (d) Prepaid expenses.

2. Which of the following conditions is **not** a criterion for offsetting under ASC 210-20-45?
    (a) The right of offset is legally enforceable.
    (b) The enterprise intends to offset the two amounts.
    (c) The enterprise has the right to offset the amount it owes against the amount owed to it by the other party.
    (d) Only one of the parties owes the other a determinable amount.

3. Which of the following statements is true?
    (a) Accumulated other comprehensive income is the change in equity of a business enterprise that arises from sources other than net income and transactions with its owners.
    (b) Paid-in capital is the par or stated value of preferred and common shares.
    (c) Stockholders' equity is the cumulative net income of the corporation from the date of its inception to the date of the financial statements, less the cumulative distributions to shareholders.

4. Which of the following statements is **not** true?
    (a) Obligations that are callable at any time by the lender may be classified as either current or noncurrent liabilities.
    (b) A note payable is an example of a noncurrent liability.
    (c) Liabilities are displayed on the statement of financial position in the order of expected payment.
    (d) Obligations that are not expected to be liquidated within one year are classified as noncurrent.

5. Which of the following is not specifically required to be disclosed under GAAP?
    (a) Related-party transactions.
    (b) Names of major/significant shareholders of the entity.
    (c) Significant contractual commitments.
    (d) Significant subsequent events.

Chapter 3

INCOME STATEMENT (ASC 225)

INTRODUCTION

A primary focus of financial reporting is to provide information about an entity's performance that is useful to present and potential investors, creditors, and others when they are making financial decisions. Performance is measured primarily by net income and its components, which are provided in the income statement. An income statement reflects information about transactions and events occurring over a period of time.

SCOPE

The requirements of ASC 225 apply to general-purpose financial statements that purport to present the results of operations in conformity with generally accepted accounting principles (GAAP).

DEFINITIONS OF KEY TERMS

Comprehensive income. The change in equity of a business entity during a reporting period from transactions and other events and circumstances from nonowner sources. It includes all changes in equity during a period, except those resulting from investments by and distributions to owners.

Expenses. Decreases in assets or increases in liabilities during a period resulting from delivery of goods, rendering of services, or other activities constituting the reporting entity's central operations.

Extraordinary item. Events and transactions that are distinguished by their unusual nature and by the infrequency of their occurrence.

Revenues. Increases in assets or decreases in liabilities during a period from delivering goods, rendering services, or other activities constituting the entity's central operations.

CONTENT

Revenues

Revenues represent actual or expected cash inflows that result from an entity's central operations. Revenues generally are recognized at the culmination of the earnings process—when the entity has substantially completed all it must do to be entitled to future cash inflows (or to retain cash already transferred).

Revenues are commonly distinguished from gains in these ways:

- Revenues result from an entity's central operations; gains result from incidental or peripheral activities of the entity.
- Revenues usually are earned; gains result from nonreciprocal transactions (such as winning a lawsuit or from the forgiveness of a debt) or other economic events for which there is no earnings process.
- Revenues are reported gross; gains are reported net.

Expenses

Expenses generally are recognized when an asset either is consumed in an entity's central operations or is no longer expected to provide the level of future benefits expected when that asset was recognized.

Expenses commonly are distinguished from losses in these three ways:

1. Expenses result from an entity's central operations; losses result from incidental or peripheral activities of the entity.
2. Expenses often are incurred during the earnings process; losses often result from nonreciprocal transactions (such as thefts or fines, or from an adverse litigation result) or other economic events unrelated to an earnings process.
3. Expenses are reported gross; losses are reported net.

The general approach for recognizing expenses is first to attempt to match cost with the related revenues. Next, a method of systematic and rational allocation should be attempted. If both of those measurement principles are inappropriate, the cost should be immediately expensed.

Other Comprehensive Income

Comprehensive income is the change in equity that results from revenue, expenses, gains, and losses during a period as well as any other recognized changes in equity that occur for reasons other than investments by owners and distributions to owners.

Other comprehensive income (comprehensive income less net income) is defined to include the effects of foreign currency translation, minimum pension liability adjustments, the effective portion of the gain or loss on derivative instruments designated and qualified as either a cash-flow hedging item or a hedge of a forecasted foreign currency–denominated transaction, and unrealized gains and losses on certain investments in debt and equity securities.

Extraordinary Items

An event or transaction should be presumed to be an ordinary and usual activity (and thus not be described as extraordinary) unless the event or transaction is both of an unusual nature and is infrequent in its occurrence.

In determining whether an event or transaction is of an unusual nature, these special characteristics of the reporting entity are considered:

- Type and scope of operations
- Lines of business
- Operating policies
- Industry (or industries) in which the reporting entity operates
- Geographic locations of its operations
- Nature and extent of government regulation

These items are by definition *not* extraordinary:

- Write-downs or write-offs of receivables, inventories, equipment leased to others or intangible assets
- Foreign currency gains and losses
- Gains and losses on the disposal of a segment of a business
- Gains and losses from sale or abandonment of property, plant, or equipment used in operations
- Effects of a strike
- Adjustment of accruals on long-term contracts

FORMAT

The basic order of presentation of information in an income statement is shown next.

- Income from continuing operations
- Results from discontinued operations
- Extraordinary items
- Net income
- Other comprehensive income
- Earnings per share (basic and diluted)

Entities are not required to present information about comprehensive income in a combined statement of income and comprehensive income. Instead, they need only present the components of other comprehensive income along with totals for net income, other comprehensive income, and comprehensive income in a statement of the same prominence as other financial statements. Thus, two other alternatives are available:

1. An expanded statement of changes in stockholders' equity
2. A stand-alone statement of comprehensive income

An acceptable practice is to combine the income statement and the statement of retained earnings into a single statement called the statement of income and retained earnings. The income statement is prepared in the normal manner. The beginning balance in retained earnings is added to the net income (loss) figure. Declared dividends are deducted to obtain the retained earnings ending balance.

If a component of an entity either is classified as held for sale or has been disposed of during the period, the results of its operations are reported in discontinued operations if both of these two conditions are met:

1. The operations and cash flows of the component have been or will be removed from the ongoing operations of the entity as a result of the disposal transactions.
2. The equity will have no significant continuing involvement in the operations of the component after the disposal transaction.

Extraordinary items should be segregated from the results of ordinary operations and be shown net of taxes in a separate section of the income statement, following "discontinued operations." If more than one extraordinary item occurs during a period, they should be reported separately or details should be included in the notes to the financial statements.

Earnings per share is a measure often used in evaluating a firm's stock price and in assessing the firm's future earnings and ability to pay dividends. Because of the importance of earnings per share, the profession has concluded that it should be disclosed on the face of the income statement.

EXTRACTS FROM PUBLISHED FINANCIAL STATEMENTS

Harris Corporation
CONSOLIDATED STATEMENT OF INCOME

| | Fiscal years ended | | |
	2009	2008	2007
(In millions, except per share amounts)			
Revenue from product sales and services			
Revenue from product sales	$3,915.3	$3,544.2	$2,937.6
Revenue from services	1,089.7	1,051.9	800.3
	5,005.0	4,596.1	3,737.9
Cost of product sales and services			
Cost of product sales	(2,498.0)	(2,289.7)	(1,826.3)
Cost of services	(922.2)	(855.9)	(693.5)
	(3,420.2)	(3,145.6)	(2,519.8)
Engineering, selling, and administrative expenses	(791.3)	(746.5)	(656.7)
Impairment of goodwill and other long-lived assets	(255.5)	—	—
Nonoperating income (loss)	(3.1)	11.4	(16.2)
Interest income	3.2	5.2	11.8
Interest expense	(52.8)	(53.1)	(38.9)
Income from continuing operations before income taxes	485.3	667.5	518.1
Income taxes	(172.9)	(214.0)	(170.9)
Income from continuing operations	312.4	453.5	347.2
Discontinued operations (including a $62.6 million loss on disposition), net of income taxes	(274.5)	(9.3)	133.2
Net income	$37.9	$444.2	$480.4
Net income per common share			
Basic	$2.36	$3.39	$2.62
Continuing operations	(2.07)	(0.07)	1.01
Discontinued operations	$0.29	$3.32	$3.63
Diluted	$2.35	$3.33	$2.49
Continuing operations	(2.07)	(0.07)	0.94
Discontinued operations	$0.28	$3.26	$3.43

See accompanying Notes to Consolidated Financial Statements.

Harris Corporation
CONSOLIDATED STATEMENT OF COMPREHENSIVE INCOME
AND SHAREHOLDERS' EQUITY

(In millions, except share and per share amounts)	Common stock	Other capital	Retained earnings	Accumulated other comprehensive income (loss)	Total
Balance at June 29, 2007	**129.6**	**283.1**	**1,472.5**	**18.6**	**1,903.8**
Net income	—	—	444.2	—	444.2
Foreign currency translation	—	—	—	22.2	22.2
Net unrealized loss on hedging derivatives, net of income taxes of $0.7	—	—	—	(1.1)	(1.1)
Net unrealized loss on securities available-for-sale, net of income taxes of $7.3	—	—	—	(11.9)	(11.9)
Loss on treasury stock, net of income taxes of $3.2	—	—	—	(5.2)	(5.2)
Net unrecognized pension obligation, net of income taxes of $(1.6)	—	—	—	3.4	3.4
Comprehensive income					451.6
Shares issued under stock incentive plans	1.4	37.9	—	—	39.3
Share-based compensation expense	—	31.8	—	—	31.8
Debt converted to shares of common stock	6.6	156.9	—	—	163.5
Repurchases and retirement of common stock	(4.0)	(56.1)	(174.5)	—	(234.6)
Adjustment for initial implementation of FIN 48	—	—	0.1	—	0.1
Cash dividends ($0.60 per share)	—	—	(81.5)	—	(81.5)
Balance at June 27, 2008	**133.6**	**453.6**	**1,660.8**	**26.0**	**2,274.0**
Net income	—	—	37.9	—	37.9
Foreign currency translation	—	—	—	(64.0)	(64.0)
Net unrealized gain on hedging derivatives, net of income taxes of $(1.4)	—	—	—	2.3	2.3
Net unrealized loss on securities available-for-sale, net of income taxes of $3.1	—	—	—	(5.0)	(5.0)
Amortization of loss on treasury stock, net of income taxes of $(0.4)	—	—	—	0.6	0.6
Net unrecognized pension obligation, net of income taxes of $6.9	—	—	—	(11.3)	(11.3)
Comprehensive loss					(39.5)
Shares issued under stock incentive plans	0.5	7.2			7.7
Share-based compensation expense	—	39.2	—	—	39.2
Repurchases and retirement of common stock	(2.7)	(33.7)	(95.9)	—	(132.3)
Spin-off of Harris Stratex Networks, Inc.	—	—	(173.1)	—	(173.1)
Cash dividends ($.80 per share)	—	—	(106.6)	—	(106.6)
Statement 158 transition adjustment	—	—	(0.3)	—	(0.3)
Balance at July 3, 2009	**$131.4**	**$466.3**	**$1,322.8**	**$(51.4)**	**$1,869.1**

See accompanying Notes to Consolidated Financial Statements.

MULTIPLE-CHOICE QUESTIONS

1. When preparing an income statement, which of the following is **not** true?

(a) Basic and diluted earnings per share should be presented.

(b) The income statement may be combined with the statement of retained earnings.

(c) Extraordinary items may be included with the results of ordinary operations.

(d) Entities may present information about comprehensive income in a separate statement.

2. Which of the following best describes comprehensive income?

(a) It includes the effects of foreign currency translation, minimum pension liability adjustments, the effective portion of the gain or loss on derivative instruments designated as a cash flow hedge, and unrealized gains and losses on certain investments in debt and equity securities.

(b) The change in equity of a business enterprise during a period from transactions with nonowner sources.

(c) Increases in assets or decreases in liabilities during a period from delivering goods and rendering services.

(d) Events and transactions that are distinguished by their unusual nature and by the infrequency of their occurrence.

3. Which of the following is **not** considered an extraordinary item?

(a) The investor's share of an investee's extraordinary item when the investor uses the equity method of accounting for the investee.

(b) The remaining excess of the fair value of acquired net assets over their cost.

(c) Gain or losses on the disposal of a segment of a business.

Chapter 4

STATEMENT OF CASH FLOWS
(ASC 230)

INTRODUCTION

The statement of cash flows presents information about cash receipts by and payments to an entity during a period, as well as information about the entity's investing and financing activities. Since the ultimate objective of investment and credit decisions is the maximization of net cash inflows, information for assessing the amounts, timing, and uncertainty of prospective cash flows is needed by potential investors, creditors, and others making investment and credit decisions.

SCOPE

The requirements of ASC 230 apply to all entities, including both businesses and not-for-profits that prepare "general-purpose financial statements" that have to be presented in accordance with generally accepted accounting principles (GAAP).

DEFINITIONS OF KEY TERMS

Direct method. A method that derives the net cash provided by operating activities from the components of operating cash receipts and payments as opposed to adjusting net income for items not affecting cash.

Financing activities. The transactions an entity engages in to acquire and repay capital (e.g., borrowings, sale of capital stock, repayments, etc.).

Indirect method. A method that derives the net cash provided by operating activities by adjusting net income for revenue and expense items not resulting from cash transactions.

Investing activities. The transactions the entity engages in that affect its investments in noncurrent assets (e.g., purchase or sale of plant, property, and equipment).

Operating activities. The transactions not classified as financing or investing activities, generally involving producing and delivering goods or providing services.

OVERALL CONSIDERATIONS

A statement of cash flows is a required part of a complete set of financial statements for business entities and not-for-profit organizations. Only defined benefit plans, certain other employee benefit plans, and highly liquid investment companies that meet specified conditions are not required to present this statement.

Investment enterprises or a common trust fund held for the collective investment and reinvestment of money are not required to provide a cash flow statement if these conditions are met:

- Substantially all of the entity's investments are highly liquid.
- The entity's investments are carried at market value.
- The entity has little or no debt.
- The entity provides a statement of changes in net assets.

The primary purpose of the statement of cash flows is to provide information about cash receipts and cash payments of an entity during a period. A secondary purpose is to provide information about the entity's investing and financing activities during the period. Specifically, the statement of cash flows helps investors and creditors assess the

- Ability to generate future positive cash flows.
- Ability to meet obligations and pay dividends.
- Reasons for differences between net income and net cash receipts and payments.
- Cash and noncash aspects of investing and financing transactions on an entity's financial position.

CLASSIFICATION

Investing Activities

Investing activities include the acquisition and disposition of long-term productive assets or securities held in available-for-sale or held-to-maturity portfolios that are not considered cash equivalents. Investing activities also include the lending of money and the collection on loans. Examples of cash flows from investing activities include

- Receipts from collections or sales of loans made by the entity and of other entities' debt instruments that were purchased by the entity.
- Receipts and disbursements from sales of equity instruments of other entities and from returns of investment in those instruments.
- Receipts or payments from sales and purchases of property, plant, and equipment and other productive assets.
- Receipts from sales of loans that were not specifically acquired for resale. For example, if loans were acquired initially as investments, cash receipts from the sale of those loans must be classified as investing activities regardless of the change in purpose for holding the loan.
- Disbursements for loans made by the entity and payments to acquire debt instruments of other entities.

Financing Activities

Financing activities result from transactions with owners and lenders that provide financial resources to the reporting entity or return or repay those resources to those owners and lenders. The financing activities of not-for-profit organizations also include receiving contributions from donors that require the resources to be used for long-term purposes, such as an endowment restricted for the purchase of long-lived assets. Examples of cash flows from financing activities include

- Proceeds from issuing equity instruments, bonds, mortgages, notes and from other short- or long-term borrowings.
- Receipts from contributions and investment income that by donor stipulation is restricted for the purposes of acquiring, constructing, or improving property, plant, equipment, or

other long-lived assets or establishing or increasing a permanent endowment or term endowment.

- Proceeds received from or distributions paid to derivative instruments that include financing elements at inception, whether the proceeds were received at inception or over the term of the derivative instrument, other than a financing element inherently included in an at-the-market derivative instrument with no repayments.
- Cash retained as a result of the tax deductibility of increases in the value of equity instruments issued under share-based payment arrangements that are not included in the cost of goods sold or services that is recognizable for financial reporting purposes.
- Payments of dividends or other distributions to owners, including outlays to reacquire the entity's equity instruments.
- Repayments of amounts borrowed.
- Other principal payments to creditors who have extended long-term credit.
- Payments for debt issue costs.

Operating Activities

Operating activities include all transactions that are not classified as investing or financing activities. Operating activities include delivering or producing goods for sale and providing services. Examples of operating activities include

- Cash receipts from the sale of goods or services.
- Cash receipts from returns on loans, other debt instruments of other entities, and equity securities (interest and dividends).
- Cash payments to acquire material for manufacture of goods for resale.
- Cash payments to other suppliers and employees for other goods or services.
- Cash payments to the government for taxes, duties, fines, and other fees or penalties.
- Cash payments to lenders and other creditors for interest.
- Cash payments made to settle an asset retirement obligation.
- All other payments and receipts that do not stem from transactions defined as investing or financing activities.

Noncash Disclosures

Disclosure of these noncash investing and financing activities may be appended to the statement or reported in the accompanying notes:

- Acquiring an asset through a capital lease or by incurring long-term debt.
- Conversion of debt to equity.
- Exchange of noncash assets or liabilities for other noncash assets or liabilities.
- Issuance of ownership shares to acquire assets.
- Obtaining an investment asset or a building by receiving a contribution.

PRESENTATION

Direct Method versus Indirect Method

The operating activities section of the statement of cash flows can be presented under the direct or indirect method. The Financial Accounting Standards Board (FASB), however, has expressed a preference for the direct method of presenting net cash flows from operating activities. Despite the user community's frequently voiced preferences for the direct method of presentation, the indirect method always has been vastly preferred by preparers.

The direct method shows the items that affected cash flow during the period. Cash received and cash paid are presented, as opposed to converting accrual-basis income to cash flow information. At a minimum, entities using the direct method are required to report these classes of operating cash receipts and payments:

- Cash collected from customers
- Interest and dividends received

- Other operating cash receipts
- Cash paid to employees and other suppliers
- Income taxes paid, including separate identification of the cash that would have been paid if the reporting entity had not received an income tax benefit resulting from increases in the fair value of its shares associated with share-based compensation arrangements
- Interest paid
- Other operating cash payments

The direct method allows the user to clarify the relationship between the company's net income and its cash flows. For example, payments of expenses are shown as cash disbursements and are deducted from cash receipts. In this way, the user is able to recognize the cash receipts and cash payments for the period.

When the direct method is used, a separate schedule reconciling net income to net cash flows from operating activities also must be provided. That schedule reports the same information as the operating activities section prepared using the indirect method. Therefore, both the direct and indirect methods must be prepared when using the direct method for reporting cash flows from operating activities.

The indirect method focuses on the differences between net income and cash flows. This format begins with net income, which is obtained directly from the income statement. Revenue and expense items not affecting cash are added or deducted to arrive at net cash provided by operating activities. For example, depreciation and amortization would be added back because they reduce net income without affecting cash.

The indirect method emphasizes change in the components of most current asset and current liability accounts. Changes in inventory, accounts receivable, and other current accounts are used to determine the cash flow from operating activities. Note that the change in accounts receivable should be calculated using the balance net of allowance account in order to ensure that write-offs of uncollectible accounts are treated properly.

GROSS VERSUS NET BASIS

The emphasis in the statement of cash flows is on gross cash receipts and payments. For instance, reporting the net change in bonds payable would obscure the financing activities of the entity by not disclosing separately cash inflows from issuing bonds and cash outflows from retiring bonds.

In a few circumstances, netting of cash flows is allowed. Items having quick turnovers, large amounts, and short maturities may be presented as net cash flows if the cash receipts and payments pertain to

- Investments (other than cash equivalents)
- Loans receivable
- Debts (original maturity of three months or less)

CASH FLOW PER SHARE

Cash flow per share may not be displayed in the financial statements of a reporting entity because the FASB does not want the cash flow statement to have equal status with the income statement. If a single cash-flow-per-share amount were reported, it would conflate operating cash flows with those from investing and financing activities and thus would not represent a meaningful construct in any event.

EXTRACTS FROM PUBLISHED FINANCIAL STATEMENTS (INDIRECT METHOD)

Shengkai Innovations, Inc.
(F/K/A Southern Sauce Company, Inc.)
CONSOLIDATED STATEMENTS OF CASH FLOWS
For the Years Ended June 30, 2009, and 2008
(Stated in U.S. Dollars)

	2009	2008
Cash flows from operating activities		
Net income	$13,577,694	$10,087,039
Depreciation	172,185	154,557
Amortization	778,115	719,171
Gain on disposal of property, plant, and equipment	—	(31,712)
Adjustments to reconcile net income to net cash provided by operating activities:		
Trade receivables	(450,979)	(1,604,622)
Notes receivable	(283,286)	(8,230)
Other receivables	(3,108)	35,246
Prepaid VAT	(194,439)	—
Deposits and prepaid expenses	639,067	37,106
Amounts due from directors and shareholders	—	36,630
Advances to suppliers	(316,230)	179,708
Inventories	(179,522)	842,385
Notes payable	984,074	(34,602)
Accounts payable	178,912	86,038
Advances from customers	212,911	(26,341)
Other payables	242,840	(566,625)
Accruals	14,440	(36,116)
Income tax payable	516,342	31,153
Net cash provided by operating activities	$15,889,016	$ 9,900,785
Cash flows from investing activities		
Sales proceeds of property, plant, and equipment	$ —	$68,581
Purchase of property, plant, and equipment	(564,609)	(295,841)
Payment of intangible assets	(1,895,099)	—
Payment of deposits on computer system	—	(4,114,871)
Increase in pledged deposits	(440,232)	(475,434)
Net cash used in investing activities	$(2,899,940)	$ (4,817,565)
Cash flows from financing activities		
Proceeds from stock issued, net of transaction costs of $1,275,000	$ —	$13,725,000
Proceeds from stock issued, net of transaction costs of $386,210	4,613,790	—
Net cash provided by financing activities	$ 4,613,790	$13,725,000

MULTIPLE-CHOICE QUESTIONS

1. Which of the following is **not** an investing activity?

    (a) Receipts from sales of loans made by the entity.

    (b) Repayments of amounts borrowed.

    (c) Disbursements for loans made by the entity.

    (d) Receipts from sales of property, plant, and equipment.

2. Which of the following describes financing activities?

    (a) Transactions a firm engages in to acquire and repay capital.

    (b) Transactions a firm engages in that affect its investments in noncurrent assets.

    (c) Transactions involving producing and delivering goods or providing services.

3. Which of the following is **not** a criterion for exemption from presenting a statement of cash flows?

    (a) Substantially all of the entity's investments are highly liquid.

    (b) The entity has little or no debt.

    (c) The entity provides a statement of changes in net assets.

    (d) The entity has a small cash balance at the end of the year.

4. If a company makes payments of cash dividends, it should be classified as a(n)

    (a) Investing activity.

    (b) Financing activity.

    (c) Operating activity.

    (d) Noncash transaction in the notes to the financial statements.

5. Which of the following is **not** a criterion for presenting cash flows on a net basis?

    (a) Items have quick turnovers, large amounts, and short maturities related to investments.

    (b) Items have quick turnovers, large amounts, and short maturities related to loans receivable.

    (c) Items have quick turnover, small amounts, and short maturities related to investments.

    (d) Items have quick turnover, large amounts, and short maturities related to debts.

Chapter 5

ACCOUNTING POLICIES, CHANGES IN ACCOUNTING ESTIMATES, AND ERRORS (ASC 250)

BACKGROUND AND INTRODUCTION

When contemplating a change in accounting principle, a primary focus of management should be to consider its effect on financial statement comparability. For users of financial statements, it is important to be able to compare not only the financial statements of an entity from one period to another but also the financial statements of different entities. Such information is needed in order to make relative comparisons of financial performance and financial position and changes in financial position.

ASC 250 prescribes criteria for selecting and changing accounting policies and the disclosures thereof and also sets out the requirements and disclosures for changes in accounting estimates and corrections of errors. In doing so, it purports to

- Enhance the relevance and reliability of an entity's financial statements
- Ensure the comparability of the financial statements of an entity over time as well as with financial statements of other entities

---

DEFINITIONS OF KEY TERMS (in accordance with ASC 250)

Accounting policies. The accounting principles of a reporting entity and the methods of applying them.

Change in accounting estimate. A revision of an accounting measurement based on the occurrence of new events, additional experience, subsequent developments, better insight, and improved judgement.

Errors. Mathematical mistakes, mistakes in applying accounting principles, oversight or misuse of available facts, and use of unacceptable generally accepted accounting principles (GAAP).

Restatement. The revision of previously issued financial statements in order to correct an error made in preparing them. Under ASC 250, this term is only to be used in the context of error corrections, and not to describe any other types of financial statement changes.

ACCOUNTING POLICIES

Accounting policies are essential for a proper understanding of the information contained in the financial statements prepared by the management of an entity. An entity should clearly outline all significant accounting policies it has used in preparing the financial statements. Because under generally accepted accounting principles (GAAP) alternative treatments are possible, it becomes all the more important for an entity to clearly state which accounting policy it has used in the preparation of the financial statements. For instance, under ASC 330-10-30, an entity has the choice of the weighted-average method; last-in, first-out (LIFO); or the first-in, first-out (FIFO) method in valuing its inventory. Unless the entity discloses which method of inventory valuation it has used in the preparation of its financial statements, users would not be able to use the financial statements properly to make relative comparisons with other entities.

CONSISTENCY OF ACCOUNTING POLICIES

Once selected, accounting policies must be applied consistently for similar transactions, other events, and conditions.

FACTORS GOVERNING CHANGES IN ACCOUNTING POLICIES

Once selected, an accounting policy may be changed only if the change

- Is required by a newly issued accounting pronouncement; or
- Results in financial statements providing reliable and more relevant information.

PRACTICAL INSIGHT

In the year in which an entity changes its accounting system from manual to computerized, it may be required to switch from the first-in, first-out (FIFO) method (which it used while valuing inventory manually) to the weighted-average method. This change is essential because the computerized system, which is tailor-made for the industry to which the entity belongs, is capable of valuing inventories only under the weighted-average method and is not equipped to value inventories under the FIFO method. Under these circumstances, this change in method of valuing inventories from the FIFO to the weighted-average method is justified because it results in financial statements providing reliable and more relevant information (and is comparable to other entities within the industry to which the entity belongs).

These items are **not** considered changes in accounting policies:

- The application of an accounting policy for transactions, other events, or conditions that differs in substance from those previously occurring
- The application of a new accounting policy for transactions, other events, or conditions that did not occur previously or were immaterial

APPLYING CHANGES IN ACCOUNTING POLICIES

A change in accounting policy required by a new accounting pronouncement shall be applied *retrospectively* to all prior periods presented, unless it is impracticable to do so. That is to say, the new policy is applied to transactions, other events, and conditions as if the policy had always been applied.

The practical impact of this is that corresponding amounts (or "comparatives") presented in financial statements must be restated as if the new policy had always been applied. The impact of the new policy on the retained earnings prior to the earliest period presented should be adjusted against the opening balance of retained earnings.

Case Study 1

Facts

(a) Newburger Co. changed its accounting policy in 200Y with respect to the valuation of inventories. Up to 200X, inventories were valued using a weighted-average cost (WAC) method. In 200Y the method was changed to first-in, first-out (FIFO), as it was considered to more accurately reflect the usage and flow of inventories in the economic cycle. The impact on inventory valuation was determined to be

At December 31, 200W:	an increase of $20,000
At December 31, 200X:	an increase of $30,000
At December 31, 200Y:	an increase of $40,000

(b) The income statements prior to adjustment are

	200Y	200X
Revenue	$500,000	$400,000
Cost of sales	200,000	160,000
Gross profit	300,000	240,000
Administration costs	120,000	100,000
Selling and distribution costs	50,000	30,000
Net profit	$130,000	$110,000

Required

Present the change in accounting policy in the Income Statement and the Statement of Changes in Equity in accordance with requirements of ASC 250.

Solution

The income statements after adjustment would be

Newburger Co.
INCOME STATEMENT
For the Year Ended December 31, 200Y

	200Y	200X (restated)
Revenue	$500,000	$400,000
Cost of sales	190,000	150,000
Gross profit	310,000	250,000
Administration costs	120,000	100,000
Selling and distribution costs	50,000	30,000
Net profit	$140,000	$120,000

Explanation

In each year, cost of sales will be reduced by $10,000, the net impact on the opening and closing inventories of change in accounting policy.

The impact on the "retained earnings" included in the "Statement of Changes in Equity" would be as follows. (The shaded figures represent the situation if there had been no change in accounting policy.)

Newburger Co.
STATEMENT OF CHANGES IN EQUITY
(Retained earnings columns only)
For the Year Ended December 31, 200Y

	Retained earnings	Retained earnings
At January 1, 200X, as originally stated (say)	$600,000	$600,000
Change in accounting policy for valuation of inventory	20,000	
At January 1, 200X, as restated	620,000	
Net profit for the year as restated	120,000	110,000
At December 31, 200X	740,000	710,000
Net profit for the year	140,000	130,000
At December 31, 200Y	$880,000	$840,000

Explanation

The cumulative impact at December 31, 200X, is an increase in retained earnings of $30,000 and at December 31, 200Y, of $40,000.

LIMITATIONS OF RETROSPECTIVE APPLICATION

Retrospective application of a change in accounting policy need not be made if it is *impracticable* to determine either the period-specific effects or the cumulative effect of the change. "Impracticable" is very strictly defined in the Standard in order to preclude simplistic statements used to avoid restating earlier periods.

Applying a requirement of a pronouncement is "impracticable" when the entity cannot apply it after making every effort to do so. For a particular prior period, it is "impracticable" to apply a change in an accounting policy if

- The effects of the retrospective application are not determinable;
- Retrospective application requires assumptions about management's intent in a prior period that cannot be independently substantiated; or
- The retrospective application requires significant estimates of amounts, and it is impossible to distinguish objectively, from other information, information about those estimates that

  - Provides objective information of circumstances that existed at the time the prior period financial statements were issued; and
  - Would have been available when the prior period financial statements were issued.

When it is "impracticable" to apply a change in policy retrospectively, the entity applies the change to the earliest period to which it is possible to apply the change.

DISCLOSURES WITH RESPECT TO CHANGES IN ACCOUNTING POLICIES

When initial application of an accounting pronouncement has an effect on current or prior periods, or would have an effect but it is impracticable to determine, an entity shall disclose

- The nature and reason for the change, including an explanation of why the newly adopted accounting principle is preferable;
- A description of the prior period information that has been retrospectively adjusted;
- The effect of the change on income from continuing operations, net income, and any other affected financial statement line item;
- The cumulative effect of the change on retained earnings or other components of equity or net assets in the statement of financial position as of the earliest period presented; and
- If retrospective application is impracticable, the circumstances making it impracticable and a description of the alternative method used to report the change.

In addition to the foregoing, disclosures *are required* regarding new accounting pronouncements that *have been issued but are not yet effective.* Such disclosures comprise the fact that certain accounting pronouncements have been issued (at the date of authorization of the financial statements) but were not effective **and** known or reasonably estimable information relevant to assessing the possible impact of the new accounting pronouncement.

CHANGES IN ACCOUNTING ESTIMATES

Many items in the financial statements cannot be measured with accuracy and are thus estimated. This is due to uncertainties inherent in business activities. These uncertainties must be translated into figures that are then reported in the financial statements. Thus accounting estimates are a very important part of the process of financial reporting. Common examples of accounting estimates include

- Pension costs
- Asset impairments
- Useful lives of property, plant, and equipment
- Salvage values
- Provision for warranty obligations

Future conditions and events cannot be estimated with certainty. Therefore, changes in estimates will be inevitable as new information and more experience is obtained. Thus, a change in estimate does not warrant restating the financial statements of a prior period because it is not a correction of an error.

Case Study 2

Facts

On January 1, 2010, a machine purchased for $10,000 was originally estimated to have a 10-year useful life and a salvage value of $1,000. On January 1, 2015 (five years later), the asset is expected to last another 10 years and have a salvage value of $800. As a result, both the current period (the year ending December 31, 2010) and subsequent periods are affected by the change.

Required

Compute the annual depreciation expense over the estimated remaining useful life.

Solution

Original cost	$10,000
Less estimated salvage (residual) value	(1,000)
Depreciable amount	9,000
Accumulated depreciation based on original assumptions (10-yr life)	
2010	900
2011	900
2012	900
2013	900
2014	4,500
Carrying value at 1/1/2015	5,500
Revised estimate of salvage value	(8,000)
Depreciable amount	4,700
Remaining useful life at 1/1/2015	10 years
	470 depreciation per year
Effect on 2014 net income	$470 – $900 = $430 increase

Occasionally it may be difficult to distinguish between changes in measurement bases (i.e., accounting policies) and changes in estimate. In such cases, the change is treated as a change in estimate.

Changes in accounting estimates are to be adjusted prospectively in the period in which the estimate is amended and, if relevant, to *future periods* if they are also affected.

Disclosures with Respect to Changes in Accounting Estimates

An entity should disclose amounts and nature of changes in accounting estimates. In addition, it should also disclose changes relating to future periods, unless impracticable. The definition of "impracticable," which has been explained for the purposes of "change in accounting policy," applies in case of "changes in accounting estimates" as well.

CHANGE IN REPORTING ENTITY

An accounting change resulting in financial statements that are, in effect, of a different reporting entity than previously reported on is retrospectively applied to the financial statements of all prior periods presented in order to show financial information for the new reporting entity for all periods. The change is also retrospectively applied to previously issued interim financial information. These items qualify as changes in reporting entity:

- Consolidated or combined financial statements in place of individual entities' statements
- A change in the members of the group of subsidiaries that comprise the consolidated financial statements
- A change in the companies included in combined financial statements

Specifically excluded from qualifying as a change in reporting entity are

- A business combination accounted for by the purchase method
- Consolidation of a variable interest entity under FIN 46(R)

CORRECTION OF PRIOR PERIOD ERRORS

Errors can arise in recognition, measurement, presentation, or disclosure of items in financial statements. Errors result from mathematical mistakes, mistakes in the application of GAAP, or the oversight or misuse of facts known or available to the accountant at the time the financial statements were prepared.

ASC 250 specifies that, when correcting an error in prior period financial statements, the term *restatement* is to be used. That term is exclusively reserved for this purpose so as to effectively communicate to users of financial statements the reason for a particular change in previously issued financial statements.

Disclosures in Respect of Correction of Prior Period Errors

When restating previously issued financial statements, management is to disclose

- The fact that the financial statements have been restated.
- The nature of the error.
- The effect of the restatement on each line item in the financial statements.
- The cumulative effect of the restatement on retained earnings (or other applicable components of equity or net assets).
- The effect on net income, both gross and net of income taxes.
- For public companies (or others electing to report earnings on per share data), the effect of the restatement on affect per share amounts for each prior period presented.

*Once disclosed, these disclosures are **not** to be repeated in financial statements of subsequent periods.*

Case Study 3

Facts

Assume that Truesdell Company had overstated its depreciation expense by $50,000 in 2008 and $40,000 in 2009, both due to mathematical mistakes. The errors affected both the financial statements and the income tax returns in 2008 and 2009 and are discovered in 2010.

Truesdell's balance sheets and statements of income and retained earnings as of and for the year ended prior to restatement were as follows:

Truesdell Company
STATEMENT OF INCOME AND RETAINED EARNINGS
Prior to Restatement
Year Ended December 31, 2009

	2009
Sales	$ 2,000,000
Cost of sales	
Depreciation	750,000
Other	390,000
	1,140,000
Gross profit	860,000
Selling, general and administrative expenses	450,000
Income from operations	410,000
Other income (expense)	10,000
Income before income taxes	420,000
Income taxes	168,000
Net income	252,000
Retained earnings, beginning of year	6,463,000
Dividends	(1,200,000)
Retained earnings, end of year	$ 5,515,000

Truesdell Company
STATEMENT OF POSITION
Prior to Restatement
Year Ended December 31, 2009

	2009
Current assets	$2,540,000
Property and equipment	
Cost	3,500,000
Accumulated depreciation and amortization	(430,000)
	3,070,000
Total assets	$5,610,000
Liabilities and stockholders' equity	
Income taxes payable	$ —
Other current liabilities	12,000
Total current liabilities	12,000
Noncurrent liabilities	70,000
Total liabilities	82,000
Stockholders' equity	
Common stock	13,000
Retained earnings	5,515,000
Total stockholders' equity	5,528,000
Total liabilities and stockholders' equity	$5,610,000

Required

What steps are necessary to restate Truesdell's prior period financial statements?

Solution

Step 1. Adjust the carrying amounts of assets and liabilities at the beginning of the first period presented in the financial statements for the cumulative effect of correcting the error on periods prior to those presented in the financial statements.

The first period presented in the financial statements is 2009. At the beginning of that year, $50,000 of the mistakes had been made and reflected on both the income tax return and financial statements. Assuming a flat 40% income tax rate and ignoring the effects of penalties and interest that would be assessed on the amended income tax returns, the following adjustment would be made to assets and liabilities at January 1, 2009:

Decrease in accumulated depreciation	$50,000
Increase in income taxes payable	(20,000)
	$30,000

Step 2. Offset the effect of the adjustment in Step 1 by adjusting the opening balance of retained earnings (or other components of equity or net assets, as applicable to the reporting entity) for that period.

Retained earnings at the beginning of 2009 will increase by $30,000 as the offsetting entry resulting from Step 1.

Step 3.   Adjust the financial statements of each individual prior period presented for the effects of correcting the error on that specific period (referred to as the period specific effects of the error).

The 2009 prior period financial statements will be corrected for the period-specific effects of the restatement as follows:

Decrease in depreciation expense and accumulated depreciation	$40,000
Increase in income tax expense and income taxes payable	(16,000)
Increase 2009 net income	$24,000

The restated financial statements are presented next.

Truesdell Company
STATEMENT OF INCOME AND RETAINED EARNINGS
As Restated
Year Ended December 31, 2010

	2010	2009 restated
Sales	$2,100,000	$2,000,000
Cost of sales		
Depreciation	740,000	710,000
Other	410,000	390,000
	1,150,000	1,100,000
Gross profit	950,000	900,000
Selling, general and administrative expenses	460,000	450,000
Income from operations	490,000	450,000
Other income (expense)	(5,000)	10,000
Income before income taxes	485,000	460,000
Income taxes	200,000	184,000
Net income	285,000	276,000
Retained earnings, beginning of year, as originally reported	5,569,000	6,463,000
Retained earnings, beginning of year, as restated	—	30,000
Dividend	(800,000)	(1,200,000)
Retained earnings, end of year	$5,054,000	$5,569,000

Truesdell Company
STATEMENT OF POSITION
As Restated
Year Ended December 31, 2010

	2010	2009 restated
Current assets	$2,840,000	$2,540,000
Property and equipment		
Cost	3,750,000	3,500,000
Accumulated depreciation and amortization	(1,050,000)	(340,000)
	2,700,000	3,160,000
Total assets	$5,540,000	$5,700,000
Liabilities and stockholders' equity		
Income taxes payable	$ 50,000	$36,000
Other current liabilities	110,000	12,000
Total current liabilities	160,000	48,000
Noncurrent liabilities	313,000	70,000
Total liabilities	473,000	118,000
Stockholders' equity		
Common stock	13,000	13,000
Retained earnings	5,054,000	5,569,000
Total stockholders' equity	5,067,000	5,582,000
Total liabilities and stockholders' equity	$5,540,000	$5,700,000

EXTRACTS FROM PUBLISHED FINANCIAL STATEMENTS

USG Corporation, December 31, 2008

Notes to the Consolidated Financial Statements

Change in accounting principle

Prior to the fourth quarter of 2008, we valued our inventories in the United States under the last-in, first-out (LIFO) cost method. As of October 1, 2008, we changed our method of accounting for these inventories from the LIFO method to the average cost method. As of September 30, 2008, the inventories in the United States for which the LIFO method of accounting was applied represented approximately 79% of total gross inventories. We believe that this change is to a preferable method which better reflects the current cost of inventory on our consolidated balance sheets. Additionally, this change conforms virtually all of our worldwide inventories to a consistent inventory costing method and provides better comparability to our peers. We applied this change in accounting principle retrospectively to all prior periods presented herein in accordance with Statement of Financial Accounting Standards, or SFAS, 154, *Accounting Changes and Error Corrections*. As a result of this accounting change, our retained earnings (deficit) as of January 1, 2006 decreased to $(572) million using the average cost method from $(595) million as originally reported using the LIFO method for inventories in the United States.

MULTIPLE-CHOICE QUESTIONS

1. ABC Inc. changes its method of valuation of inventories from first-in, first-out (FIFO) to last-in, first-out (LIFO) method. ABC Inc. should account for this change as
- (a) A change in estimate and account for it prospectively.
- (b) A change in accounting policy and account for it prospectively.
- (c) A change in accounting policy and account for it retrospectively.
- (d) Account for it as a correction of an error and account for it retrospectively.

2. Which of the following is **not** considered a change in accounting policy?
- (a) Change in useful life from 5 years to 7 years.
- (b) Change of method of valuation of inventory from FIFO to weighted-average.
- (c) Change of method of valuation of inventory from LIFO to FIFO.
- (d) A change in the companies included in combined financial statements.

3. If an entity has a change in the members of the group of subsidiaries that comprise the consolidated financial statements, it should
- (a) Restate prior year's financial statements to incorporate the correct subsidiaries.
- (b) Present the change as a disclosure in the notes to the financial statements only.
- (c) Retrospectively apply the accounting change to the financial statements of all prior periods presented.
- (d) Account for the change in the current and future periods.

4. When an entity determines that the collectability of its accounts receivables has changed by a material amount as a result of the downturn in the economy, the entity should
- (a) Retrospectively change the bad debt allowance.
- (b) Change the bad debt allowance and treat it as a correction of an error.
- (c) Change its bad debt allowance for the current year and future years.
- (d) Ignore the effect of the change on bad debts, because the economy is expected to recover and accounts receivable may be collectible in the future.

Chapter 6

FAIR VALUE (ASC 820)

SCOPE

ASC 820 was issued to establish a single, consistent, generally accepted accounting principles (GAAP) definition of fair value; provide uniform, consistent guidance on how to measure fair value, including the establishment of a hierarchical fair value measurement framework that classifies measurement inputs based on their level of market observability; and expand the information required to be provided to financial statement users about fair value measurements.

DEFINITION OF KEY TERMS

(in accordance with ASC 820)

Active market. A market in which transactions occur with sufficient frequency and volume to provide pricing information on an ongoing basis.

Bond. A debt instrument evidencing a transaction whereby a borrower (referred to as the bond's issuer) agrees to pay a sum of money at a designated future date plus periodic interest payments at the stated rate. The contract between the issuer and the bondholder (also known as the holder or investor) is referred to as an indenture. Bonds are used by commercial enterprises; municipalities; federal, state, and foreign governments; colleges and universities; hospitals; and other entities to finance a wide variety of activities or special projects.

Exit price. For valuing assets, the price that a reporting entity that holds the asset would hypothetically receive by selling it on the measurement date. For valuing liabilities, the price that a hypothetical marketplace participant would pay to transfer the liability on the measurement date, which hypothetically is also the amount that the holder of a reporting entity's debt (i.e., holding it as an asset) would receive to transfer its interest in the reporting entity's liability to another market participant on the measurement date.

Fair value. The price that would be received to sell an asset or paid to transfer a liability in an orderly transaction between market participants at the measurement date. Although GAAP literature has focused primarily on fair value in the context of assets and liabilities, the definition also applies to instruments classified in equity.

Financial asset. Cash, evidence of an ownership interest in an entity, or a contract that conveys to one entity a right (1) to receive cash or another financial instrument from a second entity or (2) to exchange other financial instruments on potentially favorable terms with the second entity.

Financial instrument with off-balance-sheet risk. A financial instrument has off-balance-sheet risk of accounting loss if the risk of accounting loss to the entity can exceed the amount recognized as an asset, if any, or if the ultimate obligation can exceed the amount that is recognized as a liability in the statement of financial position.

Financial liability. A contract that imposes on one entity an obligation (1) to deliver cash or another financial instrument to a second entity or (2) to exchange other financial instruments on potentially unfavorable terms with the second entity.

Firm commitment. A binding, legally enforceable agreement between unrelated parties that includes

1. All significant terms including the quantity of goods or services to be exchanged, a fixed price, and the transaction's timing. The fixed price may be denominated in the reporting entity's functional currency or in a foreign currency. It might also be stated as a specified interest rate or effective yield.
2. A disincentive for nonperformance sufficient to make performance probable.

Highest and best use. The use of an asset by market participants that would maximize its value or the value of the group of assets in which those market participants would use it. An asset is valued using one of the following approaches:

1. In-use. This approach is used if the maximum value would be provided to market participants by using the asset in combination with other assets as a group. The asset could be used as it is installed and configured at the measurement date or in a different configuration. An in-use fair value measurement is based on the price that would be received by the reporting entity on the measurement date in a current transaction to sell the asset along with the other assets in the group using consistent assumptions regarding the highest and best use of all of the assets in the group.
2. In-exchange. This approach is used if the maximum value would be provided to market participants from the asset on a stand-alone basis. An in-exchange fair value measurement is based on the price that would be received on the measurement date in a current transaction to sell the asset individually and not as part of a group of assets.

Indicative price. A bid or offer price that represents a preliminary estimate of the price for a prospective transaction. These prices are quoted to customers for planning and informational purposes, but are not firm or binding offers for an actual transaction.

Market participants. Buyers and sellers in the principal or most advantageous market for an asset or liability who are

1. Independent of the reporting entity (i.e., other than related parties).
2. Knowledgeable to the extent that they have a reasonable understanding about the asset or liability and the transaction based on all available information, including information that is obtainable through the performance of usual and customary due diligence efforts.
3. Able to buy or sell the asset or liability.
4. Willing to enter into a transaction for the asset or liability (i.e., they are not under duress that would force or compel them to enter into the transaction).

Market risk premium. The adjustment to a fair value measurement necessary to reflect the premium that would be demanded by a market participant for bearing the uncertainties and unforeseeable circumstances associated with the item being measured (Source: ASC 410-20-55-13, in the context of asset retirement obligations).

Most advantageous market. From the standpoint of a reporting entity that does not have access to the principal market (see definition below) for an asset or liability, the market in which the reporting entity would sell the asset for the maximum amount or transfer the liability for the minimum amount, taking into consideration the costs of executing the transaction in the respective markets. Although transaction costs are considered in making a determination of the market that is most advantageous, such costs are not to be factored into the fair value valuation determined by reference to that market.

Net realizable value. The amount of cash anticipated to be produced in the normal course of business from an asset, net of any direct costs of the conversion into cash.

Orderly transaction. A sale or transfer by the reporting entity that holds an asset or owes a liability that

- Is not a forced liquidation or distress sale.
- Assumes exposure of the asset or liability to the market for a period prior to the measurement date to facilitate marketing activities that are usual and customary for transactions involving such assets or liabilities.

Principal market. From the standpoint of the reporting entity, the market that it would use to sell the asset or transfer the liability that has the highest volume of transactions and level or activity for the asset or liability. If there is a principal market for an asset or liability, fair value is required to be determined by reference to that market, even if the reporting entity could receive a more favorable price in a different market. This is the case even if the price is not directly observable and, instead, is determined using a valuation technique with assumptions (inputs) derived from market data.

SCOPE EXCEPTIONS

- Share-Based Payments (ASC 718 and ASC 505-50)
- Measurement models that are based on vendor-specific objective evidence (VSOE), such as

  - Multiple-deliverable arrangements.
  - Software revenue recognition.
  - Software stored on another entity's hardware.

- Market value of inventory for the purposes of applying the lower of cost or market model to measure inventory realizability.

ASC 820-10-15 includes a scope exception excluding from its provisions the fair value measurements for purposes of lease classification or measurement.

MEASUREMENT PRINCIPLES

These procedures and decisions need to be applied and made in order to value an asset or liability at fair value under ASC 820:

1. Identify the item to be valued and the unit of account.
2. Determine the principal or most advantageous market and the relevant market participants.
3. Select the valuation premise to be used for asset measurements.
4. Consider the risk assumptions applicable to liability measurements.
5. Identify available inputs.
6. Select the appropriate valuation technique(s).
7. Make the measurement.
8. Determine amounts to be recognized and information to be disclosed.

The issuer is not to include the effect of the credit enhancement in its fair value measurement of the liability.

Inputs are the assumptions that market participants would use in pricing an asset or liability, including assumptions regarding risk. Inputs can be either observable or unobservable. ASC 820 requires the evaluator to maximize the use of relevant observable inputs and minimize the use of unobservable inputs.

An observable input is based on market data obtainable from sources independent of the reporting entity. Observable inputs are either directly observable or indirectly observable.

ASC 820 provides a fair value input hierarchy that serves as a framework for classifying inputs.

- Level 1. *Directly observable inputs.* Includes quoted prices in active markets for identical assets or liabilities that the reporting entity has the ability to access at the measurement date.
- Level 2. *Indirectly observable inputs.* Includes directly or indirectly observable prices in active markets for similar assets or liabilities, quoted prices for identical or similar items in markets that are not active, and inputs other than quoted prices (i.e., interest rates, yield curves, etc.), and market corroborated inputs.
- Level 3. *Unobservable inputs.* Includes inputs that are unobservable and that reflect management's own assumptions about the assumptions market participants would make.

Classification of inputs as to the level of the hierarchy in which they fall serves two purposes:

1. It provides the evaluator with a means of prioritizing assumptions used as to their level of objectivity and verifiability in the marketplace.
2. As discussed later in this chapter, the hierarchy provides a framework to provide informative disclosures that enable readers to assess the reliability and market observability of the fair value estimates embedded in the financial statements.

Level 1 inputs are considered to be the most reliable and therefore should be used whenever they are available. The use of a Level 2 or 3 input is generally prohibited if a Level 1 input is available.

It is important to assess available inputs and their relative classification in the hierarchy prior to selecting the valuation technique or techniques to be applied to measure fair value for a particular asset or liability.

Quoted bid prices represent the maximum price at which market participants are willing to buy an asset; quoted ask prices represent the minimum price at which market participants are willing to sell an asset. If available market prices are expressed in terms of bid and ask prices, management is to use the price within the bid-ask spread (the range of values between bid and ask prices) that is most representative of fair value, irrespective of where in the fair value hierarchy the input would be classified.

ASC 820 permits the use of pricing conventions, such as midmarket pricing, as a practical alternative for determining fair value measurements within a bid-ask spread.

VALUATION TECHNIQUES

Management is required to consistently apply the valuation techniques it elects to use to measure fair value. Three valuation approaches may be used:

1. *Market approach.* This valuation approach uses information generated by actual market transactions for identical or comparable assets or liabilities (including a business in its entirety).
2. *Income approach.* Techniques classified as income approaches measure fair value based on current market expectations about future amounts (such as cash flows or net income) and discount them to an amount in measurement date dollars.
3. *Cost approach.* This approach is based on quantifying the amount required to replace an asset's remaining service capacity (i.e., the asset's current replacement cost).

MEASUREMENT CONSIDERATIONS

When the reporting entity first acquires an asset or incurs (or assumes) a liability in an exchange transaction, the transaction price represents an entry price, the price paid to acquire the asset and the price received to assume the liability.

Fair value measurements are not based on entry prices but rather on exit prices: the price that would be received to sell the asset or paid to transfer the liability.

Entry and exit prices differ conceptually, but in many cases they may be identical and can be considered to represent fair value of the asset or liability at initial recognition.

However, there are situations in which the transaction price is not representative of fair value at initial recognition. Four examples include

1. Related-party transactions.
2. Transactions occurring under duress, such as a forced or liquidation transaction. Such transactions do not meet the criterion in the definition of fair value that they be representative of an "orderly transaction."
3. The exchange transaction occurs in a market different from the principal or most advantageous market in which the reporting entity would sell the asset or transfer the liability (i.e. when the reporting entity is a securities dealer that enters into transactions in different markets depending on whether the counterparty is a retail customer or another securities dealer).
4. Different units of account that apply to the transaction price and the assets/liabilities being measured (i.e., where the transaction price includes other elements besides the assets/liabilities that are being measured, such as unstated rights and privileges that are subject to separate measurement, or when the transaction price includes transaction costs).

FAIR VALUE DISCLOSURES

ASC 820 encourages, but does not require, management to combine its fair value disclosures with other required disclosures, such as the financial instrument disclosures required by ASC 825.

ASC 820 uses a hybrid principles-based approach and rules-based approach to detailing the fair value disclosures.

The two requirements are

1. For assets and liabilities measured at fair value on a recurring basis subsequent to their initial recognition, management is to provide information that will enable financial statement users to assess the inputs used to develop those measurements and, further, for measurements using significant unobservable (Level 3) inputs, the effect of those measurements on earnings for the period.
2. For assets and liabilities measured at fair value on a nonrecurring basis subsequent to their initial recognition (such as impaired assets), management is to provide information that will enable financial statement users to assess the inputs used to develop those measurements.

ASC 820 requires substantial and detailed disclosures.

Quantitative disclosures are required to be presented in a tabular format and are to be presented separately for each major category of assets and liabilities. For debt and equity securities, "major category" is synonymous with "major security type."

Management should consider these five characteristics of a particular security type to determine whether disclosure is necessary and whether it is necessary to further separate a security type into greater detail to provide sufficiently informative disclosure:

1. Shared activity or business sector
2. Vintage[1]
3. Geographic concentration
4. Credit quality
5. Economic characteristic

Additional disclosures are required to be made with respect to assets and liabilities measured at fair value on a recurring basis in periods subsequent to initial recognition.

Additional disclosures are required to be made with respect to assets and liabilities measured at fair value on a nonrecurring basis in periods subsequent to initial recognition (i.e., impaired assets).

The FASB has decided to increase the frequency of disclosures that previously had been required to be made only on an annual basis.

The FASB established a disclosure framework to respond to concerns about a lack of transparency regarding derivative and hedging activities. This framework is intended to enhance the understanding of financial statement users about

---

[1] *The term* vintage *is used in the context of mortgage-backed securities (MBS) to refer to when a particular issue originated. The vintage of an MBS can be an indicator of the underlying risks of prepayment and default (credit loss) of the mortgages that comprise the security.*

- How and why the reporting entity uses derivative instruments.
- How derivative instruments and related hedged items are accounted for.
- How derivative instruments and related hedged items affect the reporting entity's financial position, financial performance, and cash flows.

FAIR VALUE OPTION

ASC 825-10-25, *The Fair Value Option*, encourages reporting entities to elect to use fair value to measure eligible assets and liabilities in their financial statements.

Electing entities would obtain relief from the onerous and complex documentation requirements that apply to certain hedging transactions under ASC 815 while reducing the financial statement effects of volatility caused by differing measurement methods for qualifying assets and related liabilities.

Five items are eligible for the election:

1. Most recognized financial assets and financial liabilities.
2. Firm commitments that would otherwise not be recognized at inception and that involve only financial instruments (i.e., a forward purchase contract for a loan that is not readily convertible to cash). The commitment involves only financial instruments (the loan and cash) and would not be recognized at inception since it does not qualify as a derivative.
3. A written loan commitment.
4. Rights and obligations under insurance contracts or warranties that are not financial instruments but whose terms permit the insurer (warrantor) to settle claims by paying a third party to provide goods and services to the counterparty (insured party or warranty claimant).
5. A host financial instrument resulting from bifurcating an embedded nonfinancial derivative instrument from a nonfinancial hybrid instrument under ASC 815-15-25 (i.e., an instrument in which the value of the bifurcated embedded derivative is payable in cash, services, or merchandise but the host debt contract is payable only in cash).

ASC 825-10-25 provides management with flexibility in electing the fair value option (FVO). However, once it is elected, the election is irrevocable.

Management may elect the FVO for an eligible item in one of two ways:

1. Based on an established policy for specified types of eligible items that it follows consistently
2. On the date of occurrence of events as specified in the standard

PRESENTATION AND DISCLOSURE

ASC 825-10-25 requires the reporting entity to report assets and liabilities for which the FVO was elected in a manner that separates those amounts from carrying amounts of similar assets and liabilities measured using another measurement method.

PRACTICAL INSIGHT

To avoid misleading disclosures, an entity should disclose all components of an account balance—those related to the fair value option, as well as any other measurement attribute applied.

Private equity investments

($75 measured at fair value; $50 measured using the equity method) $125

Separate sections of assets and liabilities could contain separate line items enumerating the eligible items within each for which the FVO was elected by management. For example:

Young Aviation Chopper and Helicopter Works, Inc.
CONSOLIDATED STATEMENT OF FINANCIAL POSITION
(Unclassified for illustrative purposes)
December 31, 2010

	Amounts measured under the company's customary accounting policies at *other than fair value*	Amounts required to be measured at fair value or whose carrying values *approximate fair value*	Eligible amounts measured at fair value at management's election	*Total*
Assets				
Cash and cash equivalents		$ 38		$ 38
Accounts receivable	$ 97			97
Notes receivable	400		$150	550
Inventory	134			134
Investments				
Trading securities		115		115
Securities available-for-sale		75		75
Securities held-to-maturity	32			32
Derivatives		60		60
Private equity	50		75	125
Property and equipment, net	10			10
Other assets	20		—	20
Total assets	$ 743	$288	$225	$1,256
Liabilities				
Borrowings under short-term line of credit	$ 128			$ 128
Long-term debt	140		$ 60	200
Accounts payable		$110		110
Accrued liabilities	130			130
Other liabilities	555	—	—	555
Total liabilities	953	110	60	1,123
Stockholders' equity				
Common stock	4			4
Additional paid-in capital	88			88
Retained earnings	42			42
Accumulated other comprehensive income	(1)	—	—	(1)
Total stockholders' equity	133	—	—	133
Total liabilities and stockholders' equity	$1,086	$110	$ 60	$1,256

The disclosures required by ASC 825-10-25 do not apply to the next three items. However, any existing disclosures required by the cited pronouncements continue to be required under GAAP.

1. Investments in securities classified as trading securities under ASC 320, *Investments—Debt and Equity Securities.*
2. Life settlement contracts measured at fair value pursuant to ASC 325-30-30, *Investments in Insurance Contracts.*
3. Servicing rights measured at fair value under ASC 860-50-35, *Servicing Assets and Liabilities.*

Additional disclosures are required as of the date of each interim and annual statement of financial position.

Also, disclosures are required about items for which the fair value option has been elected for each interim and annual period for which an income statement is presented.

EXTRACTS FROM PUBLISHED FINANCIAL STATEMENTS

Nike, Inc. Form 10-K dated May 31, 2009

Note 6. Fair Value Measurements

Effective June 1, 2008, the Company adopted FAS 157, *Fair Value Measurements*, for financial assets and liabilities. FAS 157 establishes a hierarchy that prioritizes fair value measurements based on the types of inputs used for the various valuation techniques (market approach, income approach, and cost approach). FAS 157 is applied under existing accounting pronouncements that require or permit fair value measurements and, accordingly, does not require any new fair value measurements.

The levels of hierarchy are described below:

- Level 1: Observable inputs such as quoted prices in active markets for identical assets or liabilities.
- Level 2: Inputs other than quoted prices that are observable for the asset or liability, either directly or indirectly; these include quoted prices for similar assets or liabilities in active markets and quoted prices for identical or similar assets or liabilities in markets that are not active.
- Level 3: Unobservable inputs in which there is little or no market data available, which require the reporting entity to develop its own assumptions.

The Company's assessment of the significance of a particular input to the fair value measurement in its entirety requires judgment and considers factors specific to the asset or liability. Financial assets and liabilities are classified in their entirety based on the most stringent level of input that is significant to the fair value measurement.

The following table presents information about the Company's financial assets and liabilities measured at fair value on a recurring basis as of May 31, 2009, and indicates the fair value hierarchy of the valuation techniques utilized by the Company to determine such fair value.

| | Fair value measurements using | | | Assets/liabilities | |
	Level 1	*Level 2*	*Level 3*	*at fair value*	*Balance sheet classification*
Assets			*(In millions)*		
Derivatives	$ —	$ 378.7	$ —	$ 378.7	Other current assets and other long-term assets
Available-for-sale securities	240.0	1,314.8	—	1,554.8	Cash equivalents
Available-for-sale securities	467.9	696.1	—	1,164.0	Short-term investments
Total assets	$707.9	$2,389.6	$ —	$3,097.5	
Liabilities					
Derivatives	$ —	$ 68.9	$ —	$ 68.9	Accrued liabilities and other long-term liabilities
Total liabilities	$ —	$ 68.9	$ —	$ 68.9	

Derivative financial instruments include foreign currency forwards, option contracts, and interest rate swaps. The fair value of these derivatives contracts is determined using observable market inputs such as the forward pricing curve, currency volatilities, currency correlations, and interest rates, and considers nonperformance risk of the Company and that of its counterparties. Adjustments relating to these risks were not material for the year ended May 31, 2009.

Available-for-sale securities are primarily comprised of investments in U.S. Treasury and agency securities, corporate commercial paper, and bonds. These securities are valued using market prices on both active markets (Level 1) and less active markets (Level 2). Level 1 instrument valuations are obtained from real-time quotes for transactions in active exchange markets involving identical assets. Level 2 instrument valuations are obtained from readily available pricing sources for comparable instruments.

The Company had no material Level 3 measurements as of May 31, 2009.

In accordance with the requirements of SFAS 107, *Disclosures about Fair Value of Financial Instruments*, the Company annually discloses the fair value of its debt, which is recorded on the consolidated balance sheets at adjusted cost. Refer to Note 8, Long-Term Debt, for additional detail.

Harley-Davidson, Inc. Form 10-K dated December 31, 2008

Note 17. Fair Value of Financial Instruments

The Company's financial instruments consist primarily of cash and cash equivalents, marketable securities, trade receivables, finance receivables held for investment, net, finance receivables held for sale, trade payables, debt, foreign currency contracts, and interest rate swaps. Under U.S. GAAP certain of these items are required to be recorded in the financial statements at fair value, while other are required to be recorded at historical cost.

Cash and Cash Equivalents, Trade Receivables, and Trade Payables. With the exception of certain money-market investments, these items are recorded in the financial statements at historical cost. The historical cost basis for these amounts is estimated to approximate their respective fair values due to the short maturity of these instruments.

Marketable Securities. Marketable securities are recorded in the financial statements at fair value. The fair value of marketable securities is based primarily on quoted market prices. Changes in fair value are recorded, net of tax, as other comprehensive income and included as a component of shareholders' equity.

Finance Receivables Held for Investment, Net. Finance receivables held for investment are recorded in the financial statements at historical cost. The historical cost basis of wholesale finance receivables approximates fair value because they are either short-term or have interest rates that adjust with changes in market interest rates.

The fair value of investment in retained securitization interests is recorded in the financial statements at fair value and is estimated based on the present value of future expected cash flows using management's best estimates of the key assumptions. Changes in fair value are recorded, net of tax, as other comprehensive income and included as a component of shareholders' equity.

Finance Receivables Held for Sale. Finance receivables held for sale in the aggregate are recorded at the lower of cost or estimated fair value. HDFS uses discounted cash flow methodologies to estimate the fair value of finance receivables held for sale that incorporate appropriate assumptions for discount rate, funding costs, and credit enhancement, as well as estimates concerning credit losses and prepayments that, in management's judgment, reflect assumptions marketplace participants would use at December 31, 2008 and 2007. Any amount by which cost exceeds fair value is accounted for as a valuation adjustment with an offset to other income. The fair value of the finance receivables held for sale at December 31, 2008 was $2.44 billion, which is net of a $31.7 million valuation adjustment. The carrying value of finance receivables held for sale at December 31, 2007, approximated the fair value.

Debt. Debt is generally recorded in the financial statements at historical cost. The carrying value of debt provided under the Global Credit Facilities approximates fair value since the interest rates charged under this facility are tied directly to market rates and fluctuate as market rates change. The carrying value of commercial paper approximates fair value due to their short maturity. The carrying value of the asset-backed commercial paper conduit facility approximates the fair value due to its short maturity.

At December 31, 2008 and 2007, the fair value of the Medium-Term Notes was $1.03 billion and $1.00 billion, respectively. The fair value of the Medium-Term Notes issued during 2008 and 2007 is estimated based upon rates currently available for debt with similar terms and remaining maturities. The remaining Medium-Term Notes are carried at fair value and include a fair value adjustment due to the interest rate swap agreement, designated as a fair value hedge, which effectively converts a portion of the note from a fixed to a floating rate.

Derivative Financial Instruments. The Company uses a variety of derivative financial instruments to manage foreign currency exchange rate, commodity price and interest rate risk. All derivative instruments are recognized on the balance sheet at fair value. A specific description of each of the Company's derivative instruments follows.

Foreign Currency Contracts. During 2008 and 2007, the Company utilized foreign currency contracts to hedge its sales transactions denominated in Euros and Australian dollars. The foreign currency contracts were designated as cash flow hedges and generally had lives of less than one year. The Company bases the fair value of its foreign currency contracts on quoted market prices. Information related to the Company's foreign currency contracts as of December 31 is as follows (in millions):

	2008	*2007*
Euro value	€ 275.0	€170.0
Australian dollar value	AUD 25.0	AUD —
Notional U.S. dollar value	$ 419.3	$227.8
Fair value of contracts recorded as current assets (liabilities)	$ 19.1	$(20.2)
Unrealized gain (loss) recorded in accumulated other comprehensive loss, net of tax	$ 8.3	$(11.4)

The effectiveness of these hedges is measured based on changes in fair value of the contract attributable to changes in the forward exchange rate. During 2008 and 2007, the hedges were highly effective and, as a result, the amount of hedge ineffectiveness recognized during the year was not material. During 2008, net losses on foreign currency contracts reclassified from other comprehensive income and recognized in earnings totaled $5.6 million, or $3.5 million net of tax. The Company expects that the unrealized gains, net of taxes, as of December 31, 2008, of $8.3 million will be reclassified to earnings within one year. Realized gains and losses on foreign currency contracts are recorded in cost of goods sold and the related cash flows are included in cash flows from operations.

Natural Gas Contracts. During 2008, the Company utilized natural gas contracts to hedge the cost of natural gas consumption. The natural gas contracts were designated as cash flow hedges and had lives of less than one year. The Company bases the fair value of its natural gas contracts on quoted market prices. Information related to the Company's natural gas hedges as of December 31 is as follows (in millions):

	2008
Therms	$ 5.8
Notional value	$ 4.8
Fair value of contracts recorded as current liabilities	$ (1.3)
Unrealized loss recorded in accumulated other comprehensive loss, net of tax	$ (0.8)

During 2008, the hedges were highly effective and, as a result, the amount of hedge ineffectiveness recognized during the year was not material. The Company expects that the unrealized losses, net of taxes, as of December 31, 2008, of $0.8 million will be reclassified to earnings within one year.

Interest Rate Swaps, Securitization Transactions. During 2008 and 2007, HDFS utilized interest rate swaps to reduce the impact of fluctuations in interest rates on its securitization transactions. These interest rate derivatives are designated as cash flow hedges and generally have a life of less than six months. Information related to these swap agreements as of December 31 is as follows (in millions):

	2008	*2007*
Notional value	$ —	$535.9
Fair value of swaps recorded as current assets (liabilities)	$ —	$ (6.7)
Unrealized loss recorded in accumulated other comprehensive loss, net of tax	$ —	$ (3.9)

During 2008 and 2007, the hedges were highly effective and, as a result, the amount of hedge ineffectiveness recognized during the year was not material. During 2008, net losses on securitization related interest rate swaps reclassified from other comprehensive income and recognized in earnings totaled $16.1 million, or $10.4 million net of tax.

HDFS entered into derivative contracts to facilitate its first-quarter 2008 and third-quarter 2007 securitization transactions. These derivatives do not qualify for hedge accounting treatment and have a life of one to five years. Changes in the fair value of these derivatives are recognized in current-period earnings within other operating expenses. Information related to these derivative contracts as of December 31 is as follows (in millions):

	2008	*2007*
Notional value	$881.9	$700.0
Fair value of swaps recorded as current assets (liabilities)	$ 1.1	$ (0.1)
Unrealized gain (loss) recorded in earnings, net of tax	$ 1.3	$ (0.1)

Interest Rate Swaps, Unsecured Commercial Paper. In April 2008, HDFS entered into an amortizing $137.0 million interest rate swap agreement that effectively converts a portion of its floating-rate debt to a fixed-rate basis for a period of five years. This replaced a $50.0 million swap agreement, which expired in March 2008. Additionally, HDFS has a $175.0 million amortizing interest rate swap agreement that expires in 2012. This interest rate swap agreement also effectively converts a portion of its floating-rate debt to a fixed-rate basis. The differential paid or received on these swaps is recognized on an accrual basis as an adjustment to interest expense. As of December 31, 2008, and 2007, the agreements were designated as cash flow hedges. Information related to the swap agreements as of December 31 is as follows (in millions):

	2008	*2007*
Notional value	$ 233.1	$ 204.2
Fair value of swaps recorded as current assets (liabilities)	$ (17.0)	$ (6.2)
Unrealized gain (loss) recorded in accumulated other comprehensive loss, net of tax	$ (10.9)	$ (4.0)

During 2008 and 2007, the hedges were highly effective, and, as a result, the amount of hedge ineffectiveness recognized during the year was not material. During 2008, net losses on commercial paper related interest rate swaps reclassified from other comprehensive income and recognized in earnings totaled $5.9 million, or $3.8 million net of tax. HDFS expects to reclassify $5.2 million of the unrealized loss, net of taxes, as of December 31, 2008, to earnings within one year. The unrealized loss will be in addition to the payment of variable interest associated with the floating-rate debt.

Interest Rate Swaps, Asset-Backed Commercial Paper Conduit Facility. In December 2008, HDFS entered into $300.0 million and $200.0 million amortizing interest rate swaps that effectively convert its floating-rate debt to a fixed-rate basis for a period of twenty-two months. The differential paid or received is recognized on an accrual basis as an adjustment to interest expense. As of December 31, 2008, these agreements were designated as cash flow hedges. Information related to the swap agreements as of December 31 is as follows (in millions):

	2008
Notional value	$500.0
Fair value of swaps recorded as current liabilities	$ (5.2)
Unrealized loss recorded in accumulated other comprehensive loss, net of tax	$ (3.2)

During 2008, the hedges were highly effective and, as a result, the amount of hedge ineffectiveness recognized during the year was not material. Net losses on asset-backed commercial conduit facility related interest rate swaps were reclassified from other comprehensive income and recognized in earnings totaled $0.2 million, or $0.1 million net of tax.

In December 2008, HDFS entered into derivative contracts to facilitate its participation in the asset-backed commercial paper conduit facility. These derivatives do not qualify for hedge accounting and have a life of three years. Changes in the fair value of these derivatives are recognized in current-period earnings within other operating expenses. Information related to these derivative contracts as of December 31 is as follows (in millions):

	2008
Notional value	$22.8
Fair value of swaps recorded as current assets	$ 0.5
Unrealized gain recorded in earnings, net of tax	$ 0.5

Interest Rate Swaps, Medium-Term Notes. During 2005 and 2003, HDFS entered into interest rate swap agreements that effectively convert a portion of its fixed-rate debt to a floating-rate basis for a period of five years. The differential paid or received on these swaps is recognized on an accrual basis as an adjustment to interest expense. As of December 31, 2008, and 2007, the agreements were designated as fair value hedges. During 2008 and 2007, the hedges were highly effective and, as a result, there was no ineffectiveness recognized on these hedges during the year. Information related to these swap agreements as of December 31 is as follows (in millions):

	2008	*2007*
Notional value	$150.0	$550.0
Fair value of swaps recorded as current assets	$ 9.7	$ 1.3

No ready market exists for swaps utilized by HDFS. Fair value is determined by an independent third party using established valuation methods.

Note 18. Fair Value Measurements

The carrying value of those financial assets and liabilities recorded at fair value is measured on a recurring or nonrecurring basis. Financial assets and liabilities measured on a recurring basis are those that are adjusted to fair value each time a financial statement is prepared. Financial assets and liabilities measured on a nonrecurring basis are those that are adjusted to fair value when a significant event occurs. In determining fair value of financial assets and liabilities, the Company uses various valuation techniques. The availability of inputs observable in the market varies from instrument to instrument and depends on a variety of factors including the type of instrument, whether the instrument is actively traded, and other characteristics particular to the transaction. For many financial instruments, pricing inputs are readily observable in the market, the valuation methodology used is widely accepted by market participants, and the valuation does not require significant management discretion. For other financial instruments, pricing inputs are less observable in the market and may require management judgment.

The Company assesses the inputs used to measure fair value using a three-tier hierarchy. The hierarchy indicates the extent to which inputs used in measuring fair value are observable in the market. Level 1 inputs include quoted prices for identical instruments and are the most observable. Level 2 inputs include quoted prices for similar assets and observable inputs such as interest rates, foreign currency exchange rates, commodity rates, and yield curves. Level 3 inputs are not observable in the market and include management's own judgments about the assumptions market participants would use in pricing the asset or liability. The use of observable and unobservable inputs is reflected in the hierarchy assessment disclosed in the table below.

The following table presents information about the Company's assets and liabilities measured at fair value on a recurring basis as of December 31, 2008, and indicates the fair value hierarchy of the valuation techniques utilized by the Company to determine such fair value (in thousands):

	Balance as of December 31, 2008	*Quoted prices in active markets for identical assets (Level 1)*	*Significant other observable inputs (Level 2)*	*Significant unobservable inputs (Level 3)*
Assets				
Cash equivalents	$380,082	$380,082	—	—
Derivatives	31,508	—	$31,508	—
Investment in retained securitization interests	330,674	—	—	$330,674
	$742,264	$380,082	$31,508	$330,674
Liabilities				
Derivatives	$ 23,503	—	$23,503	—

The investment in retained securitization interests is valued using discounted cash flow methodologies incorporating assumptions that, in management's judgment, reflect the assumptions marketplace participants would use at December 31, 2008. The following table presents additional information about the investment in retained securitization interests which is measured at fair value on a recurring basis using significant unobservable inputs (Level 3) at December 31, 2008 (in thousands):

	2008
Balance, beginning of period	$407,742
Total gains or losses (realized/unrealized):	
Included in financial services income[a]	18,808
Included in other comprehensive income	(29,090)
Sales, repurchases and settlements, net	(66,786)
Balance, end of period	$330,674

[a] *Total gains or losses included in financial services income includes an impairment charge of $41.4 million as discussed in Note 8.*

Finance receivables held for sale in the aggregate are carried at the lower of cost or estimated fair value and are measured at fair value on a nonrecurring basis using significant unobservable inputs (Level 3).

During 2008, the Company recorded noncash charges of $37.8 million due to a decline in the fair value below cost on finance receivables held for sale. The fair value of the finance receivables held for sale at December 31, 2008, was $2.44 billion, which is net of a $31.7 million valuation adjustment.

MULTIPLE-CHOICE QUESTIONS

1. Which of the following procedures and decisions does **not** need to be applied and made in order to value an asset or liability at fair value under ASC 820?
  (a) Identify the item to be valued and the unit of account.
  (b) Determine the principal or most advantageous market and the relevant market participants.
  (c) Include the effect of the credit enhancement in the fair value measurement of the liability.
  (d) Identify available inputs.

2. Which valuation technique is **not** permitted to be used to measure fair value?
  (a) Market approach.
  (b) Valuation approach.
  (c) Income approach.
  (d) Cost approach.

3. In which of the following situations would the transaction price **not** be representative of fair value at initial recognition?
  (a) Related-party transactions.
  (b) Transactions occurring under duress such as a forced or liquidation transaction.
  (c) The exchange transaction occurs in a market different from the principal or most advantageous market in which the reporting entity would sell the asset or transfer the liability.
  (d) Different units of account that apply to the transaction price and the assets/liabilities being measured.
  (e) All of the above.

4. Which of the following is **not** a disclosure *requirement* under ASC 820?
  (a) Management must combine its fair value disclosures with other required disclosures.
  (b) For assets and liabilities measured at fair value on a recurring basis subsequent to their initial recognition, management is to provide information that will enable financial statement users to assess the inputs used to develop those measurements.
  (c) For assets and liabilities measured at fair value on a nonrecurring basis subsequent to their initial recognition, management is to provide information that will enable financial statement users to assess the inputs used to develop those measurements.
  (d) Quantitative disclosures are required to be presented in a tabular format and are to be presented separately for each major category of assets and liabilities.

5. Which of the following would **not** be eligible to elect to use fair value to measure eligible assets and liabilities in their financial statements?
  (a) Most recognized financial assets and financial liabilities.
  (b) Firm commitments that would otherwise not be recognized at inception and that involve only financial instruments.
  (c) An oral loan commitment.
  (d) Rights and obligations under insurance contracts or warranties that are not financial instruments but whose terms permit the insurer (warrantor) to settle claims by paying a third party to provide goods and services to the counterparty (insured party or warranty claimant).

Chapter 7

CASH, RECEIVABLES, AND PREPAID EXPENSES (ASC 305, 310, 860)

BACKGROUND AND INTRODUCTION

Assets displayed on the statement of financial position are the resources available to the reporting entity to support its current and future operations.

To provide information about liquidity, the assets often are divided into current and noncurrent assets.

- When the normal operating cycle is less than one year, a one-year period is used to distinguish current assets from noncurrent assets.
- If the operating cycle exceeds one year, the operating cycle is the proper period to use for current asset identification.

Current assets consist of cash and other assets (e.g., short-term investments, receivables, inventory, and prepaid expenses) that are reasonably expected to be realized in cash or sold or consumed during the normal operating cycle of the business.

DEFINITIONS OF KEY TERMS
(in accordance with ASC 305, 310, and 860)

Accounts receivable. Amounts due from customers for goods or services provided in the normal course of business operations.

Aging the accounts. Computation of the adjustment for uncollectibility of accounts receivable outstanding at the end of the period based upon the length of time the accounts have been unpaid.

Cash. Coins and currency on hand and balances in checking accounts available for immediate withdrawal.

Cash equivalents. Short-term, highly liquid investments that are readily convertible to known amounts of cash and are so near their maturity that they present negligible risk of changes in value due to changes in interest rates. Examples include Treasury bills, commercial paper, and money market funds.

Current assets. Those assets that are reasonably expected to be realized in cash or sold or consumed within a year or within the normal operating cycle of the reporting entity, if longer than a year.

Factoring. The outright sale of accounts receivable to a third-party financing entity. The sale may be with or without recourse.

Recourse. The right of a transferee (factor) to receive payment from the transferor of receivables for uncollectible accounts, prepayments by the debtors, merchandise returns, or other defects in the eligibility of the receivables.

Transfer. Conveyance of a noncash financial asset by or to someone other than the issuer of the financial asset.

CASH

To be included as cash in the statement of financial position, funds must be represented by coins, currency, undeposited checks, money orders, drafts, and demand deposits that are immediately available without restriction. Cash that is restricted as to use would not be included with cash unless the restrictions on it expire within the year (or the operating cycle, if longer). Thus, cash contractually required to be held in a sinking fund is classified as a current asset if it will be used to retire the current portion of long-term debt. However, if material, it would be reported on a separate line rather than included with cash.

Cash in a demand deposit account that is being held for the retirement of long-term debts that do not mature currently is excluded from current assets and shown as a noncurrent investment. Cash in transit to the reporting entity (e.g., checks already mailed by the customer) cannot be included in cash because it is not under the control of the reporting entity.

It has long been common to see the caption "Cash and Cash Equivalents" in the statement of financial position. That caption includes other forms of near cash as well as demand deposits and liquid, short-term securities. Cash equivalents must be available upon demand in order to justify inclusion. However, a current joint FASB-IASB project, addressing financial statement presentation, might restore the prominence of "cash," excluding equivalents, by dispensing with the concept of cash and equivalents. Such a change would affect both the statement of financial position and the statement of cash flows, as these two financial statements must articulate.

Compensating Balances

An entity often will be required to maintain a minimum amount of cash on deposit, generally in connection with having a borrowing arrangement with a financial institution (compensating balance). The purpose of this balance may be to substitute for service fees forgone by the bank (or fees at a rate less than market) or simply to increase the yield on a loan to the lender. Since most organizations must maintain a certain working balance in their cash accounts simply to handle routine transactions and to cushion against unforeseen variations in the demand for cash, borrowers often will not find compensating balance arrangements objectionable.

The compensating balance is not available for unrestricted use and penalties will result if it is used. If material, the portion of the reporting entity's cash account that is a compensating balance must be segregated and shown as a separate caption on the statement of financial position, and this should be included in noncurrent assets if related borrowings are noncurrent liabilities. If the borrowings are current liabilities or if the compensating balance reduces fees that would have been incurred in the next year, it is acceptable to show the compensating balance as a separately captioned current asset.

Example of Compensating Balance Disclosure

The Arkansas Billboard Company (ABC) has obtained a short-term, $10 million line of credit with Premier Bank. The loan agreement with Premier includes a requirement that ABC maintain a compensating balance of 5% of the maximum amount of the line of credit (5% × $10 million = $500,000). ABC also has a loan with First National Bank involving a single balloon payment of $200,000 due in two years, and requiring a compensating balance of 10% (10% × $200,000 = $20,000). At year-end, ABC has cash balances of $782,000 at Premier and $28,000 at First National. ABC's reporting of cash on its statement of financial position is

Current assets:	
Cash	290,000
Restricted cash compensating balances	500,000
Noncurrent assets:	
Restricted cash compensating balances	20,000

Cash Not Immediately Available

Cash in savings accounts subject to a statutory notification requirement and cash in certificates of deposit maturing during the current operating cycle or within one year may be included as current assets but, if material, is to be separately captioned in the statement of financial position to avoid the misleading implication that these funds are available immediately upon demand. Typically, such items will be included in the short-term investments caption, but these could be labeled as time deposits or restricted cash deposits.

Overdrafts

A reporting entity may issue checks with a dollar value exceeding the balance in its checking account. If the excess amount of these checks over the checking account balance has not yet cleared the bank, the overage is called a book overdraft, since the overdraft exists only in the reporting entity's accounting records. For reporting purposes, although the bank is yet unaware of this situation, the overdraft is reported as a liability, since the checks already have been released and thus are no longer under the control of the reporting entity. If the checks have cleared the bank, and the bank has advanced the reporting entity the funds (sometimes marketed as "automatic overdraft protection"), then this borrowing is also reported as a liability.

Petty Cash

Petty cash and other imprest cash accounts usually are combined in financial statements with other cash accounts.

RECEIVABLES

There are several types of receivables: accounts receivable, open accounts, trade accounts receivable, trade acceptances, third-party instruments, and amounts due from officers, shareholders, employees, or affiliated companies.

Accounts receivable, open accounts, and trade accounts are agreements by customers to pay for services received or merchandise obtained.

Notes receivable are formalized obligations evidenced by written promissory notes.

Receivables due within one year (or one operating cycle, if longer) generally should be presented at outstanding face value (principal amount), adjusted for any write-offs already taken and valuation allowances.

Example

Snowy Winters & Sons is a purveyor of fine books about the Alaska heartland. Its total ending receivable balance is $420,000. The receivable balance is affected by the following items:

- The allowance for uncollectible accounts receivable is $17,000, reflecting a historical rate of bad debts equal to 4% of receivables.
- It ships books on a subscription basis, resulting in a 15% return rate. Winters has recorded an allowance for returns of $63,000.
- It offers an early payment discount of 1%, which is generally taken. Winters maintains a 1% early payment allowance of $4,200 to reflect this arrangement.
- One large customer, Anchorage Book Company (ABC), is delinquent in its payments, so the collections department has converted ABC's outstanding balance of $58,000 into a short-term note receivable, payable over 10 months at a 12% interest rate.

- The Winters legal staff has won a lawsuit from which the company can expect to receive a total of $12,000, payable over two years.
- Early Winters, the family patriarch, borrowed $15,000 from the company to purchase an antique dogsled.

Snowy Winters' controller reports this information on the Winters statement of financial position in the following manner:

Accounts receivable, trade	335,000	
Less: Allowance for doubtful accounts	(17,000)	
Returns allowance	(63,000)	
Early payment for discount allowance	(4,200)	250,800
Receivables due from officers		15,000
Notes receivable due in current year		58,000
Noncurrent receivables		
Claims receivable (litigation settlement to		
be collected over two years)		12,000

Valuation Allowance for Uncollectible Amounts

The recording of a valuation allowance for anticipated uncollectible amounts is almost always necessary. The direct write-off method, in which a receivable is charged off only when it is clear that it cannot be collected, even if mandated for tax purposes, is unsatisfactory from a GAAP perspective since it overstates assets and also results in a mismatching of revenues and expenses.

Proper matching can be achieved only if bad debts are recorded in the same fiscal period as the revenues to which they are related. Since the amount of uncollectible accounts is not known with certainty at the time, an estimate must generally be made.

There are two methods of estimation: the percentage-of-sales method and the aging-the-accounts method.

1. The percentage-of-sales method is geared more to matching of revenues and expenses.
2. The aging-the-accounts method is more inclined toward the presentation of the correct net realizable value of the trade receivables in the statement of financial position.

For the percentage-of-sales method, historical data are analyzed to ascertain the relationship between bad debts and credit sales. The derived percentage is then applied to the current period's sales revenues in order to arrive at the appropriate debit to bad debts expense for the year. The offsetting credit is made to allowance for uncollectible accounts (often still referred to as the reserve for bad debts). When specific customer accounts subsequently are identified as uncollectible, they are written off against this allowance.

Care must be taken to ensure that the bad debt ratio computed will be representative of uncollectibility of the current period's credit sales. A ratio based on historical experience may require an adjustment to reflect the current economic climate. For example, if a large percentage of customers is concentrated in a geographic area that is experiencing an economic downturn, the rate of default may increase over that previously suffered. Changes in credit terms and in customer mix also may affect the relationship between sales and bad debts, and should be given consideration in determining the bad debt percentage to be applied to current period credit sales. In practice, these relationships evolve slowly over time and may not always be observed over the short term.

When aging the accounts, an analysis is prepared of the customer receivables at the date of the statement of financial position. Each customer's balance is categorized by the number of days or months the underlying invoices have remained outstanding. Based on the reporting entity's past experience or on other available statistics, such as industry trends, historical bad debts percentages are applied to each of these aggregate amounts, with larger percentages being applied to the older accounts. The end result of this process is a computed total dollar amount that implies the proper ending balance in the allowance for uncollectible receivables at the date of the statement of financial position. The computed amount is compared to the balance in the valuation account, and an adjustment is made for the differences. Thus, the adjustment needed will be an amount other than the amount computed by the aging.

Case Study 1

Percentage-of-sales method

Facts

Assume the following.

Total credit sales for year	$ 7,500,000
Bad debt ratio from prior years or other data source	1.75% of credit sales
Computed year-end adjustment for bad debts expense	$ 131,250 ($7,500,000 × .0175)

Required

What is the entry required to record the estimate for uncollectible accounts?

Solution

The entry required is

Bad debts expense	131,250	
Allowance for uncollectible receivables		131,250

Case Study 2

Aging Method

Facts

Assume the following.

	Age of accounts			
	Under 30 days	*30–90 days*	*Over 90 days*	*Total*
Gross receivables	$1,100,000	$425,000	$360,000	
Bad debt percentage	0.5%	2.5%	15%	
Provision required	$ 5,500	$ 10,625	$ 54,000	$70,125

Assume that a debit balance of $58,250 already exists in the allowance account (from charge-offs during the year that exceeded the credit balance in the allowance account at the previous year-end).

Required

What is the entry required to record the estimate for uncollectible accounts?

Solution

The credit balance required in the allowance account is $70,125. Assuming that a debit balance of $58,250 already exists in the allowance account (from charge-offs during the year that exceeded the credit balance in the allowance account at the previous year-end), the necessary entry is

Bad debts expense	128,375	
Allowance for uncollectible receivables		128,375

Both of the estimation techniques should produce approximately the same result over the course of a number of years. Nonetheless, these adjustments are based on estimates and will never predict ultimate results precisely. When facts subsequently become available to indicate that the amount provided as an allowance for uncollectible accounts was incorrect, an adjustment classified as a change in estimate is made, unless this was the consequence of a failure to consider facts available at the time the estimate was made, in which case a correction of an accounting error will have to be recognized.

Imputed Interest

If a receivable is due on terms exceeding one year, the proper valuation is the present value of future payments to be received, determined by using an interest rate commensurate with the risks involved at the date of the receivable's creation. In many situations, the interest rate commensurate with the risks involved is the rate stated in the agreement between the payee and the debtor. However, if the receivable is noninterest-bearing or if the rate stated in the agreement is not indicative of the market rate for a debtor of similar creditworthiness under similar terms, interest is imputed at the market rate.

A valuation allowance is used to adjust the face amount of the receivable to the present value at the market rate. The balance in the valuation allowance is amortized as additional interest income so that interest income is recognized using a constant rate of interest over the life of the agreement. Initial recording of such a valuation allowance also results in the recognition of an expense, typically (for customer receivables) reported as selling expense or as a contra revenue item (sales discounts).

When a note is issued solely for cash, its present value is necessarily assumed to be equal to the cash proceeds. The interest rate is that rate which equates the cash proceeds received by the borrower to the amounts to be paid in the future.

When a note receivable that bears an unrealistic rate of interest is issued in exchange for cash, an additional right or privilege usually is granted, unless the transaction was not conducted at arm's length. If there was an added right or privilege involved, the difference between the present value of the receivable and the cash advanced is the value assigned to the right or privilege. It will be accounted for as an addition to the cost of the products purchased for the purchaser/lender and as additional revenue to the debtor.

Example of Accounting for a Note Issued for Both Cash and a Contractual Right

1. Schwartz borrows $10,000 from Weiss via an unsecured five-year note. Simple interest at 2% is due at maturity.
2. Schwartz agrees to sell Weiss a car for $15,000, which is less than its market price.
3. The market rate of interest on a note with similar terms and a borrower of similar creditworthiness is 10%.

The present value factor for an amount due in five years at 10% is .62092. Therefore, the present value of the note is $6,830 [= ($10,000 principal + $1,000 interest at the stated rate) × .62092]. According to ASC 835, the $3,170 (= $10,000 – $6,830) difference between the present value of the note and the face value of the note is regarded as part of the cost/purchase price of the car. Weiss would make the next entry to record the transaction:

Note receivable	10,000	
Car	18,170	
Cash		25,000
Discount on note receivable		3,170

The discount on note receivable is amortized using the effective interest method, as follows:

	Effective interest (10%)	*Stated interest (2%)*	*Amortization*	*Note and interest receivable*
01/01/10				6,830
01/01/11	683	200	(483)	7,513
01/01/12	751	200	(551)	8,264
01/01/13	826	200	(626)	9,091
01/01/14	909	200	(709)	10,000
01/01/15	1,000	200	(800)	11,000

The entry for the first year would be

Discount on note receivable	483	
Interest receivable	200	
Interest revenue		683

When a note is issued in exchange for property, goods, or services and the transaction is entered into at arm's length, the stated interest rate is presumed to be fair unless

1. No interest rate is stated.
2. The stated rate is unreasonable.
3. The face value of the note receivable is materially different from fair value of the property, goods, or services received.

4. The face value of the note receivable is materially different from the current market value of the note at the date of the transaction.

According to ASC 835, when the rate on the note is not fair, the note is to be recorded at the fair market value of the property, goods, or services sold or the market value of the note, whichever is the more clearly determinable. The difference is recorded as a discount or premium and amortized to interest income.

Example of Accounting for a Note Exchanged for Goods

1. Green sells Brown inventory that has a fair market value of $8,573.
2. Green receives a two-year noninterest-bearing note having a face value of $10,000.

In this situation, the fair market value of the consideration is readily determinable and, thus, represents the amount at which the note is to be recorded. Green would make this entry:

Notes receivable	10,000	
Discount on notes receivable		1,427
Sales revenue		8,573

The discount will be amortized to interest expense over the two-year period using the interest rate implied in the transaction, which is 8%. The present value factor is .8573 ($8,573/$10,000). Using a present value table for amount due in two years, .8573 is located under the 8% rate.

If neither the fair value of the property, goods, or services sold nor the fair value of the note receivable is determinable, then the present value of the note must be determined using an imputed market interest rate. This rate then will be used to establish the present value of the note by discounting all future payments on the note at that rate.

Pledging, Assigning, and Factoring Receivables

An organization can alter the timing of cash flows resulting from sales to its customers by using its accounts receivable as collateral for borrowings or by selling the receivables outright. A wide variety of arrangements can be structured by the borrower and lender, but the most common are pledging, assignment, and factoring.

Pledging is an agreement in which accounts receivable are used as collateral for loans. The customers whose accounts have been pledged are not aware of this event, and their payments still are remitted to the original entity to which the debt was owed. The pledged accounts merely serve as security to the lender, giving comfort that sufficient assets exist to generate cash flows adequate in amount and timing to repay the debt. However, the debt is paid by the borrower, whether the pledged receivables are collected or not and whether the pattern of their collection matches the payments due on the debt or not.

The only accounting issue relating to pledging is that of adequate disclosure. The accounts receivable, which remain assets of the borrowing entity, continue to be shown as current assets in its financial statements but must be identified as having been pledged. This identification can be accomplished either parenthetically or by note disclosures. Similarly, the related debt should be identified as having been collateralized by the receivables.

Example of Disclosure for Pledged Receivables

Current assets:	
Accounts receivable ($3,500,000 of which has been pledged as collateral for bank loans), net of allowance for doubtful accounts of $600,000	8,450,000
Current liabilities:	
Bank loans payable (collateralized by pledged accounts receivable)	2,700,000

A more common practice is to include the disclosure in the notes to the financial statements. Since the borrower has not surrendered control of the pledged receivables, it continues to carry the pledged receivables as its assets (ASC 860).

The assignment of accounts receivable is a more formalized transfer of the receivables to the lending institution. The lender investigates the specific receivables that are being proposed for assignment and approves those that it deems worthy as collateral. Usually customers are not aware that their accounts have been assigned, and they continue to forward their payments to the original obligee (the borrowing entity). In some cases, the assignment agreement requires that collection proceeds be delivered to the lender immediately. The borrower is, however, the primary obligor of the debt and is required to make timely payment on the debt, whether the receivables are collected as anticipated or not. The borrowing is with recourse, and the general credit of the borrower is pledged to the payment of the debt.

Since the lender knows that not all the receivables will be collected on a timely basis by the borrower, only a fraction of the face value of the receivables will be advanced as a loan to the borrower. Typically, this fraction ranges from 70% to 90%, depending on the credit history and collection experience of the borrower.

Assigned accounts receivable remain the assets of the borrower and continue to be presented in its financial statements, with appropriate disclosure of the assignment similar to that illustrated for pledging. Prepaid finance charges would be recorded as a prepaid expense and amortized to expense over the period to which the charges apply.

In the typical case involving the assignment of receivables, the borrower retains control of the receivables, and it is clear that the transaction is a secured borrowing rather than a sale. If it is unclear whether the borrower has retained control of the receivables, a determination must be made as to whether to account for the transfer as a sale or as a secured borrowing.

Factoring traditionally involves the outright sale of receivables to a finance company, known as a factor. These arrangements involve (1) notification to the customer to remit future payments to the factor and (2) the transfer of receivables to the factor without recourse to the transferor. The factor assumes the risk of an inability to collect. Thus, once a factoring arrangement is completed, the transferor has no further involvement with the accounts, except for a return of merchandise.

In its simplest form, the receivables are sold and the difference between the cash received and the carrying value is recognized as a gain or loss.

Case Study 3

Factoring of Receivables without Recourse

Facts

Thirsty Corp. enters into an agreement with Rich Company to sell a group of its receivables without recourse for $180,055. A total face value of $200,000 accounts receivable (against which a 5% allowance had been recorded) are involved.

Required

What is the entry required to record the transaction?

Solution

Cash	180,055	
Allowance for bad debts (200,000 × .05)	10,000	
Loss on sale of receivables	19,945	
Bad debts expense		10,000
Accounts receivable		200,000

The classic variety of factoring provides two financial services to the business: It permits the reporting entity to obtain cash earlier than waiting for customers to pay, and it transfers the risk of bad debts to the factor. The factor is compensated for each of these services. Interest is charged based on the anticipated length of time between the date the factoring arrangement is consummated and the expected collection date of the receivables sold. A fee is charged based on the factor's anticipated bad debt losses.

Case Study 4

Factoring of Receivables without Recourse

Facts

Thirsty Corp. enters into an agreement with Rich Company to sell a group of its receivables without recourse. The receivables have a total face value of $200,000 (against which a 5% allowance had been recorded). The factor will charge 20% interest computed on the weighted-average time to maturity of the receivables of 36 days plus a 3% fee.

Required

What is the entry required to record the transaction?

Solution

Cash	180,055	
Allowance for bad debts (200,000 × .05)	10,000	
Interest expense (or prepaid) (200,000 × .20 × 36/365)	3,945	
Factoring fee (200,000 × .03)	6,000	
Loss on sale of receivables	10,000	
Bad debts expense		10,000
Accounts receivable		200,000

Some companies factor receivables as a means of transferring bad debt risk but leave the cash on deposit with the factor until the weighted-average due date of the receivables, thereby avoiding interest charges. This arrangement is still referred to as factoring, since the customer receivables have been sold. However, the borrowing entity does not receive cash but instead records a new receivable, usually captioned "Due from Factor." This receivable, in contrast to the original customer receivables, is essentially without risk and is presented in the statement of financial position without a deduction for estimated uncollectible receivables.

Merchandise returns are normally the responsibility of the transferor, who must then make the appropriate settlement with the factor. To protect against the possibility that merchandise returns will diminish the total of receivables to be collected, a factor frequently advances only a portion of the face amount of the factored receivables (less any interest and factoring fee deductions). The factor will retain a certain fraction of the total proceeds relating to the portion of sales that are anticipated to be returned by customers. This sum is known as the factor's holdback. When merchandise is returned to the transferor, an entry is made offsetting the receivable from the factor. At the end of the return privilege period, any remaining holdback will become due and payable to the transferor.

Case Study 5

Factoring of Receivables without Recourse

Facts

1. Thirsty Corp. enters into an agreement with Rich Company to sell a group of its receivables without recourse. The receivables have a total face value of $200,000 (against which a 5% allowance had been recorded). The factor will charge 20% interest computed on the weighted-average time to maturity of the receivables of 36 days plus a 3% fee. A 5% holdback will also be retained.
2. Thirsty's customers return for credit $4,800 of merchandise.
3. The customer return privilege period expires and the remaining holdback is paid to the transferor.

Required

What is the entry required to record the transaction?

Solution

1. Cash   180,055
       Allowance for bad debts (200,000 × .05)   10,000
       Interest expense (or prepaid) (200,000 × .20 × 36/365) 3,945
       Factoring fee (200,000 × .03)   6,000
       Factor's holdback receivable
         [$10,000/($10,000 + $190,000) × $190,000]   9,500
       Loss on sale of receivables   500
         Bad debts expense   10,000
         Accounts receivable   200,000

The interest expense, factor's fee, and loss can be combined into a $10,445 charge to loss on the sale of receivables.

2. Sales returns and allowances   4,800
         Factor's holdback receivable   4,800

3. Cash   5,200
         Factor's holdback receivable   4,700
         Loss on sale of receivables   500

The factor's holdback receivable recorded by the seller is required by ASC 860 to be an allocation of the carrying value of the receivables ($190,000) between the assets sold (the receivables) and the assets retained (the holdback) based on their relative fair values at the date of the factoring agreement. The factor holds back 5% of the face value ($200,000) for a total of $10,000. Upon settlement the loss or gain recorded at the origination of the factoring arrangement needs to be adjusted because the factor pays the remaining holdback of $5,200 ($10,000 holdback – $4,800 returns) in settlement of an asset with a carrying value of $4,700 ($9,500 – $4,800).

Factoring results in a transfer of title to the factored receivables. Where there is a no-recourse provision or other continuing involvement with the receivables, the removal of the receivables from the borrower's statement of financial position is clearly warranted.

Another variation is known as factoring with recourse. Accounting for factoring with recourse requires a determination of whether the transfer is a sale or a secured borrowing. That determination is made by applying ASC 860.

PREPAID EXPENSES

Prepaid expenses are amounts paid to secure the use of assets or the receipt of services at a future date or continuously over one or more future periods. Prepaid expenses will not be converted to cash, but they are classified as current assets because, if not prepaid, they would have required the use of current assets during the coming year (or operating cycle, if longer). Examples of items that are often prepaid include dues, subscriptions, maintenance agreements, memberships, licenses, rents, and insurance.

The examples of prepaid expenses cited in the previous paragraph are unambiguous. This is, however, not always the case. In negotiating union labor contracts, the parties may agree that the union employees will be entitled to receive a lump-sum cash payment or series of payments in exchange for agreeing to little or no increase in the employees' base wage rate.

These lump-sum arrangements ordinarily do not require the employee to refund any portion of the lump sum to the employer in the event that the employee terminates employment during the term of the labor agreement. Further, it is assumed by the parties that, upon termination of a union member, the employer will replace that individual with another union member at the same base wage rate to whom no lump sum would be due. Management believes that the lump-sum payment arrangement will reduce or eliminate raises during the contract term and that these lump-sum payments will benefit future periods.

In order to record these lump sums as prepaid expenses, ASC 710-10-25 specifies that, based on a careful review of the facts and circumstances around the contract and negotiations, the payments must clearly benefit a future period in the form of a lower base wage rate than would otherwise have been in effect.

Further, the amortization period is not permitted to extend beyond the term of the union contract. The presumption of replacing terminating union members with other union members at the same wage rate is essential to this conclusion and, thus, this accounting treatment is applicable only to union contracts and is not permitted to be applied by analogy to account for individual employment contracts or other compensation arrangements.

The Securities and Exchange Commission Observer noted that accounting for this transaction as a prepaid expense is appropriate only when there is no evidence of any kind that the lump-sum payment or payments are related to services rendered in the past.

Amortization

Prepaid expenses are amortized to expense on a ratable basis over the period during which the benefits or services are received. For example, if rent is prepaid for the quarter at the beginning of the quarter, two months of the rent will be included in the prepaid rent account. At the beginning of the second month, the equivalent of one month's rent (half the account balance) would be charged to rent expense. At the beginning of the third month, the remaining prepayment would be charged to rent expense.

Example of Prepaid Expenses

The PipeTrak Company starts using geographical information systems (GIS) software to track the locations of the country's pipeline infrastructure under a contract for the Department of Homeland Security. It pays maintenance fees on three types of GIS software, for which the following maintenance periods are covered:

Software name	Maintenance start date	Maintenance duration	Maintenance fee
Culture Data (CD)	February	Annual	$4,800
Map Layering (ML)	April	Semiannual	18,000
Land Grid (LG)	June	Quarterly	6,000

It initially records these fee payments as prepaid expenses. PipeTrak's controller then uses this amortization table to determine the amount of prepaid expenses to charge to expense each month:

Software	Feb	Mar	Apr	May	Jun	Jul	Aug	Sep	Oct	Nov	Dec
CD	400	400	400	400	400	400	400	400	400	400	400
ML			3,000	3,000	3,000	3,000	3,000	3,000			
LG					2,000	2,000	2,000				
Totals	400	400	3,400	3,400	5,400	5,400	5,400	3,400	400	400	400

In June, PipeTrak records the next entry to charge a portion of its prepaid software maintenance to expense:

| Software maintenance expense | 5,400 | |
| Prepaid expenses | | 5,400 |

DISCLOSURES

ASC 942 includes disclosure requirements for all entities involved in financing activities, including trade receivables.

1. The following amounts must be reported separately on the face of the statement of financial position:

    a. The amount of receivables held for sale.
    b. The amount of foreclosed or repossessed assets, which can be included in the other assets category if the notes to the financial statements disclose the amount.

2. The statement of financial position or notes are to report

    a. Separately, each major category of loans and trade receivables.
    b. The allowance for doubtful accounts or loan losses.
    c. Any unearned income, unamortized premiums or discounts, and any net unamortized deferred fees and costs related to loans or trade receivables.

d. The recorded investment in loans (and trade receivables, if applicable) on nonaccrual status, as of each statement of financial position presented.

e. The recorded investment in loans (and trade receivables, if applicable) on accrual status that are past due 90 days or more, as of each statement of financial position presented.

f. The carrying amount of financial instruments that serve as collateral for borrowings.

3. The "summary of significant accounting principles" note is to include

a. The basis for accounting for trade receivables, loans receivable, and lease financings, including those held for sale.

b. Whether aggregate or individual asset basis is used in determining the lower of cost or fair value of nonmortgage loans held for sale.

c. The classification and method of accounting for receivables that can be contractually prepaid or otherwise settled in a way that the reporting entity would not recover substantially all of its recorded investment.

d. The method for recognizing interest income on loan and trade receivables, including related fees and costs, and the method of amortizing net deferred fees or costs.

EXTRACTS FROM PUBLISHED FINANCIAL STATEMENTS

IMAX Corporation December 31, 2008

Critical Accounting Policies

Allowances for Accounts Receivable and Financing Receivables

Allowances for doubtful accounts receivable are based on the Company's assessment of the collectability of specific customer balances, which is based upon a review of the customer's creditworthiness, past collection history and the underlying asset value of the equipment, where applicable. Interest on overdue accounts receivable is recognized as income as the amounts are collected.

The Company monitors the performance of the theaters to which it has leased or sold theater systems which are subject to ongoing payments. When facts and circumstances indicate that there is a potential impairment in the accounts receivable, net investment in lease or a financing receivable, the Company will evaluate the potential outcome of either renegotiations involving changes in the terms of the receivable or defaults on the existing lease or financed sale agreements. The Company will record a provision if it is considered probable that the Company will be unable to collect all amounts due under the contractual terms of the arrangement or a renegotiated lease amount will cause a reclassification of the sales-type lease to an operating lease.

When the net investment in lease or the financing receivable is impaired, the Company will recognize a provision for the difference between the carrying value in the investment and the present value of expected future cash flows discounted using the effective interest rate for the net investment in the lease or the financing receivable. If the Company expects to recover the theater system, the provision is equal to the excess of the carrying value of the investment over the fair value of the equipment.

When the minimum lease payments are renegotiated and the lease continues to be classified as a sales-type lease, the reduction in payments is applied to reduce unearned finance income.

These provisions are adjusted when there is a significant change in the amount or timing of the expected future cash flows or when actual cash flows differ from cash flow previously expected.

Once a net investment in lease or financing receivable is considered impaired, the Company does not recognize interest income until the collectability issues are resolved. When finance income is not recognized, any payments received are applied against outstanding gross minimum lease amounts receivable or gross receivables from financed sales.

MULTIPLE-CHOICE QUESTIONS

1. Which of the following would **not** be an acceptable method of recording a valuation allowance related to accounts receivables?

    (a) Percentage-of-sales method.

    (b) Direct write-off.

    (c) Aging method.

2. Which of the following items would **not** be included in cash?

    (a) Money orders.

    (b) Immediately available demand deposits.

    (c) Undeposited checks.

    (d) Cash in transit to the reporting entity.

3. An agreement in which receivables are used as collateral for loans is

    (a) Factoring.

    (b) Pledging.

    (c) Assigning.

    (d) Both (a) and (c).

    (e) Both (b) and (c).

    (f) All of the above.

4. Which of the following is **not** true of factoring receivables?

    (a) The lender investigates the specific receivables that are being proposed for factoring and approves those items that it deems worthy as collateral.

    (b) It involves the outright sale of receivables to a finance company.

    (c) The customer is notified to remit future payments to the factor.

    (d) The difference between the cash received and the carrying value is recognized as a gain or loss.

Chapter 8

INVENTORY (ASC 330)

BACKGROUND AND INTRODUCTION

The Standard prescribes the accounting treatment for inventories. The main issue with respect to accounting for inventory is the amount of cost to be recognized as an asset. The Standard provides guidance on the determination of the cost and subsequent recognition of expense (including write-down of inventory to its market value). The Standard also provides guidance on the cost flow assumptions ("cost formulas") that are to be used in assigning costs to inventories.

SCOPE

This Standard applies to all inventories other than

- Not-for-profit entities.
- Regulated entities.

DEFINITIONS OF KEY TERMS

Dollar-value LIFO. A variation of conventional LIFO in which layers of inventory are priced in dollars adjusted by price indices instead of being priced at unit prices.

Gross profit method. A method used in interim periods to estimate the amount of ending inventory based on the cost of goods available for sale, sales, and the expected gross profit percentage.

Inventory. Those items of tangible personal property that are (1) held for sale in the normal course of business (finished goods), (2) in the process of being produced for that purpose (work-in-process), or (3) to be used in the production of such items (raw materials).

LIFO liquidation. The permanent elimination of all or part of the LIFO base or old inventory layers when inventory quantities decrease. This inventory decrement can distort gross profit, operating income, and net income since old costs are being reflected in cost of goods sold and matched against current revenues.

Lower of cost or market. Inventories are required to be valued at the lower of cost or market. Market is generally considered to be replacement cost; however, for the purpose of this computation, market is not permitted to exceed the ceiling (net realizable value) or to be less than the floor (net realizable value less a normal markup).

Net realizable value. The selling price of an item, less selling costs and costs to complete.

OWNERSHIP OF GOODS

In order to obtain an accurate measurement of inventory quantity, it is necessary to determine when title legally passes between the buyer and seller. The exception to this general rule arises from situations when the buyer assumes the significant risks of ownership of the goods prior to taking title and/or physical possession of the goods.

Goods in Transit

At year-end, any goods in transit from seller to buyer must be included in one of those parties' inventories based on the conditions of the sale. Such goods are included in the inventory of the firm financially responsible for transportation costs. The responsibility may be indicated by the shipping terms.

FOB

The term *FOB* is an abbreviation of "free on board." If goods are shipped FOB destination, transportation costs are paid by the seller and title does not pass until the carrier delivers the goods to the buyer. These goods are part of the seller's inventory while in transit. If goods are shipped FOB shipping point, transportation costs are paid by the buyer and title passes when the carrier takes possession of the goods. These goods are part of the buyer's inventory while in transit.

FAS

A seller who ships FAS (free alongside) must bear all expense and risk involved in delivering the goods to the dock next to (alongside) the vessel on which they are to be shipped. The buyer bears the cost of loading and shipment. Title passes when the carrier, as agent for the buyer, takes possession of the goods.

Consignment

In consignment arrangements, the consignor ships goods to the consignee, who acts as the agent of the consignor in trying to sell the goods. In some consignments, the consignee receives a commission and is, in effect, acting as an agent of the consignor. In other arrangements, the consignee "purchases" the goods simultaneously with the sale of the goods to the customer. Goods on consignment are included in the inventory of the consignor and excluded from the inventory of the consignee.

Product Financing Arrangement

A product financing arrangement is a transaction in which an entity (referred to as the "sponsor") simultaneously sells and agrees to repurchase inventory to and from a financing entity. The repurchase price is contractually fixed at an amount equal to the original sales price plus the financing entity's carrying and financing costs. The purpose of the transaction is to enable the sponsor enterprise to arrange financing of its original purchase of the inventory.

The substance of this transaction is that of a borrowing transaction, not a sale. That is, the transaction is, in substance, no different from the sponsor directly obtaining third-party financing to purchase inventory.

The proper accounting by the sponsor is to record the liability in the amount of the selling price when the funds are received from the financing entity in exchange for the initial transfer of inventory. The sponsor accrues carrying and financing costs in accordance with its normal accounting policies. These accruals are eliminated and the liability is satisfied when the sponsor repurchases the inventory. The inventory is not removed from the statement of financial position of the sponsor and a sale is not recorded. Thus, although legal title has passed to the financing entity, for purposes of measuring and valuing inventory, the inventory is considered to be owned by the sponsor.

Right of Return

Another issue requiring special consideration exists when a buyer is granted a right of return. The seller must consider the propriety of recognizing revenue at the point of sale under such a situation. As per ASC 605-15-25-1, the sale is recorded when these six specified conditions are met:

1. The seller's price to the buyer is substantially fixed or determinable at the date of sale.
2. The buyer has paid the seller, or the buyer is obligated to pay the seller and the obligation is not contingent on resale of the product. If the buyer does not pay at time of sale and the buyer's obligation to pay is contractually or implicitly excused until the buyer resells the product, then this condition is not met.
3. The buyer's obligation to the seller would not be changed in the event of theft or physical destruction or damage of the product.
4. The buyer acquiring the product for resale has economic substance apart from that provided by the seller. This condition relates primarily to buyers that exist on paper, that is, buyers that have little or no physical facilities or employees. It prevents entities from recognizing sales revenue on transactions with parties that the sellers have established primarily for the purpose of recognizing such sales revenue.
5. The seller does not have significant obligations for future performance to directly bring about resale of the product by the buyer.
6. The amount of future returns can be reasonably estimated.

If these criteria are not met, then the sale is not recorded until the earlier of the expiration date of the return privilege or the date when all six conditions are met. This situation results in the seller continuing to include the goods in its measurement and valuation of inventory even though legal title has passed to the buyer.

ACCOUNTING FOR INVENTORIES

A major objective of accounting for inventories is the matching of appropriate costs to the period in which the related revenues are earned in order to properly compute gross profit. Inventories are recorded in the accounting records using either a periodic or perpetual system.

In a periodic inventory system, inventory quantities are determined by physical count. The quantity of each item counted is then priced using the cost flow assumption that the entity had adopted as its accounting policy for that type of inventory. Cost of goods sold is computed by adding beginning inventory and net purchases (or cost of goods manufactured) and subtracting ending inventory.

Using a periodic inventory system necessitates the taking of physical inventory counts to determine the quantity of inventory on hand at the end of a reporting period. In order to facilitate accurate annual financial statements, in practice, physical counts are performed at least annually on the last day of the fiscal year.

A perpetual inventory system keeps a running total of the quantity (and possibly cost) of inventory on hand by maintaining subsidiary inventory records that reflect all sales and purchases as they occur. When inventory is purchased, inventory (rather than purchases) is debited. When inventory is sold, cost of goods sold and corresponding reduction of inventory are recorded.

If the entity maintains a perpetual inventory system, it must regularly and systematically verify the accuracy of its perpetual records by physically counting inventories and comparing the quantities on hand with the perpetual records.

MEASUREMENT OF INVENTORIES

In general, inventories are valued at the "lower of cost or market." One notable exception to recording inventories at cost is provided by the hedge accounting requirements of ASC 815-25. If inventory has been designated as the hedged item in a fair value hedge, changes in the fair value of the hedged inventory are recognized on the statement of financial position as they occur, with the offsetting charge or credit recognized currently in earnings.

COST OF INVENTORIES

Cost is defined as the sum of applicable expenditures and charges directly or indirectly incurred in bringing an article to its existing condition and location.

Raw Material and Merchandise Inventory

The cost of these purchased inventories will include all expenditures incurred in bringing the goods to the point of sale and converting them to a salable condition. These costs include the purchase price, transportation costs, insurance while in transit, and handling costs charged by the supplier.

Purchases can be recorded at their gross amount or net of any allowable discount. If recorded gross, the discounts taken represent a reduction in the purchase cost for purposes of determining cost of goods sold. If they are recorded net, however, any lost discounts are treated as a financial expense, not as cost of goods sold. The net method theoretically is considered to be preferable, but the gross method is simpler and, thus, more commonly used. Either method is acceptable under generally accepted accounting principles (GAAP), provided that it is consistently applied.

Manufacturing Inventories

Inventory cost in a manufacturing entity is to include both acquisition and production costs. This concept is commonly referred to as full absorption or full costing. As a result, the work-in-process and finished goods inventories include direct materials, direct labor, and an appropriately allocated portion of indirect production costs referred to as indirect overhead.

Under full absorption costing, indirect overhead costs—costs that are incidental to and necessary for production—are allocated to goods produced and, to the extent those goods are uncompleted or unsold at the end of a period, are included in ending work-in-process or finished goods inventory, respectively. Indirect overheard costs include such costs as

- Depreciation and cost depletion
- Maintenance and repairs
- Factory rent and utilities
- Indirect labor
- Normal rework labor, scrap, and spoilage
- Production supervisory wages
- Indirect materials and supplies
- Quality control and inspection
- Small tools not capitalized

Indirect overhead is comprised of two elements, variable and fixed overhead. Variable overhead is to be allocated to work-in-process and finished goods based on the actual usage of the production facilities. Fixed overhead, however, is to be allocated to work-in-process and finished goods based on the normal expected capacity of the entity's production facilities with the overhead rate recomputed in instances when actual production exceeds the normal capacity.

For the purpose of determining normal productive capacity, it is expected that capacity will vary from period to period based on entity-specific or industry-specific experience. Management is to formulate a judgment regarding a reasonable range of normal production levels expected to be achieved under normal operating conditions. Should the entity incur unusually large expenses resulting from idle facilities, excessive waste, spoilage, freight, or handing costs, the abnormal portion of these expenses is to be treated as a cost of the period incurred and not to be allocated to inventory.

Case Study 1

Facts

The InCase Manufacturing Company (IMC) uses injection molding to create two types of plastic CD cases—regular size and mini—on a seven-day, three-shift production schedule. During the current month, it records the following overhead expenses:

Depreciation of machinery	$232,000
Indirect labor	208,000
Indirect materials	58,000
Maintenance	117,000

Production supervisory wages	229,000
Quality control	82,000
Rent	30,000
Repairs	12,000
Small tools	28,000
Scrap and spoilage	49,000
Utilities	37,000

IMC's controller analyzed scrap and spoilage and determined that abnormal losses of $32,000 were incurred due to a bad batch of plastic resin pellets.

For allocation purposes, IMC's controller elects to group the adjusted overhead expenses into two cost pools. Pool #1 contains all expenses related to machinery operation, which includes depreciation, indirect labor, indirect materials, maintenance, rent, repairs, small tools, and utilities. Pool #2 contains all expenses related to production runs, which includes production of supervisory wages, quality control, scrap, and spoilage.

Required

1. How should the abnormal scrap and spoilage expense be treated and what is the required journal entry?
2. What is the journal entry to record the allocation of costs to the machinery cost pool?
3. What is the journal entry to record the allocation of costs to the production runs cost pool?

Solution

1. Scrap and spoilage should be adjusted by charging the cost of the bad batch of pellets to cost of goods sold during the current period. The journal entry to record the expense is

| Cost of goods sold | 32,000 | |
| Scrap and spoilage expense | | 32,000 |

2. The entry to allocate costs to the machinery cost pool is

Machinery operation	722,000	
Depreciation		232,000
Indirect labor		208,000
Indirect materials		58,000
Maintenance		117,000
Rent		30,000
Repairs		12,000
Small tools		28,000
Utilities		37,000

3. The entry to allocate costs to the production runs cost pool is

Production runs	328,000	
Production supervisory wages		229,000
Quality control		82,000
Scrap and spoilage		17,000

Note that scrap and spoilage has been reduced by the abnormal spoilage expense, which was charged to cost of goods sold (= $49,000 − $32,000 = $17,000).

COST FLOW ASSUMPTIONS

In selecting which cost flow assumption to adopt as its accounting policy for a particular type of industry, management should consider a variety of factors. First, the industry norm should be examined, as this will facilitate intercompany comparison by financial statement users. The appropriateness of using a particular cost flow assumption will vary depending on the nature of the industry and the expected economic climate. The appropriate method in a period of rising prices differs from the method that is appropriate for a period of declining prices. Each of the foregoing assumptions and their relative advantages is discussed in the next subsections.

First-In, First-Out (FIFO)

The FIFO method of inventory valuation assumes that the first goods purchased are the first goods used or sold, regardless of the actual physical flow. This method is thought to most closely parallel the physical flow of the units in most industries.

The strength of this cost flow assumption lies in the inventory amount reported on the statement of financial position. Because the earliest goods purchased are the first ones removed from the inventory account, the remaining balance is composed of items priced at more recent cost. This yields results similar to those obtained under current cost accounting on the statement of financial position. However, the FIFO method does not necessarily reflect the most accurate income figures as older, historical costs are being charged to cost of goods sold and matched against current revenues.

In periods of rising prices, the FIFO method will result in higher income taxes than the other alternatives, while in a deflationary period, FIFO provides for a lesser income tax burden. However, a major advantage of the FIFO method is that it is not subject to all of the complex regulations and requirements of the income tax code that govern the use of LIFO.

The FIFO method provides the same results under either the periodic or perpetual inventory tracking system.

Case Study 2

First-in, First-out (FIFO) Method

Facts

Aaron Inc. is a newly established international trading company. It commenced its operation in 2010. Aaron imports goods from Belgium and sells in the local market. It uses the FIFO method to value its inventory. Listed next are the purchases and sales made by the entity during the year 2010:

Purchases

January 2010	20,000 units @ $ 25 each
March 2010	30,000 units @ $ 30 each
September 2010	40,000 units @ $ 35 each

Sales

May 2010	30,000 units
November 2010	40,000 units

Required

Based on the FIFO cost flow assumption, compute the value of inventory at May 31, 2010; September 30, 2010; and December 31, 2010.

Solution

(a)	January 2010	Purchase	+ 20,000 units @ $25	=	$ 500,000
	March 2010	Purchase	+ 30,000 units @ $30	=	900,000
			Total		$ 1,400,000
(b)	May 2010	Sales (30,000 units)	− 20,000 units @ $25	=	$ (500,000)
			− 10,000 units @ $30	=	(300,000)
					$ (800,000)

(c) **Inventory valued on FIFO basis at May 31, 2010:**

	20,000 units @ $30	=	$ 600,000

(d)	September 2010	Purchase	+ 40,000 units @ $35	=	$ 1,400,000

(e) **Inventory valued on FIFO basis at September 30, 2010:**

20,000 units @ $30	=	$ 600,000
40,000 units @ $35	=	1,400,000
		$ 2,000,000

(f)	November 2010	Sales (40,000 units)	– 20,000 units @ $30	= $ (600,000)
			– 20,000 units @ $35	= (700,000)
				$(1,300,000)

(g) **Inventory valued on FIFO basis at December 31, 2010:**

	20,000 units @ $35	= $ 700,000

Last-In, First-Out (LIFO)

The LIFO method of inventory valuation assumes that the last goods purchased are the first goods used or sold. This allows the matching of current costs with current revenues and provides the best measure of gross profit. However, unless costs remain relatively unchanged over time, the LIFO method usually will misstate the ending inventory balance sheet amount because LIFO inventory usually includes costs of acquiring or manufacturing inventory that were incurred in earlier periods. LIFO usually does not follow the physical flow of merchandise or materials. However, the matching of the physical flow with the cost flow is not an objective of accounting for inventories.

In periods of rising prices, the LIFO method is generally thought to best fulfill the objective of providing the clearest measure of periodic net income. It does not, however, provide an accurate estimate of inventory cost in an inflationary environment. However, this shortcoming usually can be overcome by providing additional disclosures in the notes to the financial statements. In periods of rising prices, a prudent business should use the LIFO method because it will result in a decrease in the current income tax liability when compared to other alternatives. In a deflationary period, the opposite is true.

LIFO accounting is actually an income tax concept. Thus, the rules regarding the application of the LIFO method are not set forth in U.S. GAAP but rather are found in the U.S. Internal Revenue Code (IRC) §472. U.S. Treasury regulations provide that any taxpayer who maintains inventories may select LIFO application for any or all inventoriable items. This election is made with the taxpayer's income tax return on Form 970 after the close of the first tax year that the taxpayer intends to use (or expand the use of) the LIFO method. Partial adoption of LIFO is allowed for both accounting and income tax purposes.

The quantity of ending inventory on hand at the beginning of the year of election is termed the "base layer." This inventory is valued at actual (full absorption) cost, and unit cost for each inventory item is determined by dividing the total cost by the quantity on hand. At the end of the initial and subsequent years, increases in the quantity of inventory on hand are referred to as increments, or LIFO layers. These increments are valued individually by applying one of these costing methods to the quantity of inventory representing a layer:

- The actual cost of the goods most recently purchased or produced
- The actual cost of the goods purchased or produced in order of acquisition
- An average unit cost of all goods purchased or produced during the current year
- A hybrid method that more clearly reflects income (For income tax purposes, this method must meet with the approval of the IRS Commissioner.)

Thus, after using the LIFO method for five years, it is possible that an entity could have ending inventory consisting of the base layer and five additional layers (or increments), provided that the quantity of ending inventory increased every year.

LIFO LIQUIDATION

When ending inventory decreases from the level established at the close of the preceding year, the entity experiences a decrement, or LIFO liquidation. Decrements reduce or eliminate previously established LIFO layers. Once any part of a LIFO layer has been eliminated, it cannot be reinstated after year-end. For example, if in its first year after the election of LIFO an entity establishes a LIFO layer (increment) of 10 units, then, in the next-year inventory, decreases by 4 units leaving the first layer at 6 units, the entity is not permitted in any succeeding year to increase the number of units in the first-year layer back up to the original 10 units. The quantity in the first layer remains at a maximum of 6 units subject to further reduction if decrements occur in future years. Any unit increases in future years will create one or more new layers.

The effect of LIFO liquidations in periods of rising prices is to transfer, from ending inventory into cost of goods sold, costs that are below the current cost being paid. Thus, the resultant effect of a LIFO liquidation is to increase income for both accounting and income tax purposes. Because of this, LIFO is most commonly used by companies in industries in which levels of inventories are consistently maintained or increased over time.

To determine the effect of the liquidation, management must compute the difference between actual cost of sales and what cost of sales would have been had the inventory been reinstated. The Internal Revenue Service has ruled that this hypothetical reinstatement must be computed under the company's normal pricing procedures for valuing its LIFO increments. The next disclosure is considered acceptable GAAP disclosure in the event of a LIFO liquidation:

> During 2010, inventory quantities were reduced below their levels at December 31, 2009. As a result of this reduction, LIFO inventory costs computed based on lower prior years' acquisition costs were charged to cost of goods sold. If this LIFO liquidation had not occurred and cost of sales had been computed based on the cost of 2010 purchases, cost of goods sold would have increased by approximately $xxx and net income decreased by approximately $xx or $x per share.

Case Study 3

Last-in, First-out (FIFO) Method

Facts

Thomas Co. is in its first year of operation and elects to use the periodic LIFO method of inventory valuation. The company sells only one product. Thomas applies the LIFO method using the order of current year acquisition cost. The following data are given for years 1 through 3:

		Units			Purchase cost	
Year 1	*Beginning inventory*	*Purchased*	*Sold*	*Ending inventory*	*Unit cost*	*Total cost*
Purchase		200	—		$2.00	$400
Sale		—	100		—	—
Purchase		200	—		3.00	$600
Sale		—	150		—	—
	—	400	250	150		
Year 2						
Purchase		300	—		$3.20	$960
Sale		—	200		—	—
Purchase		100	—		3.30	330
	150	400	200	350		
Year 3						
Purchase		100	—		$3.50	$350
Sale		—	200		—	—
Sale		—	100		—	—
	350	100	300	150		

Required

Compute the ending inventory value at the end of (1) year 1, (2) year 2, and (3) year 3.

Solution

Year 1

Cost of goods sold	*Units*	*Unit cost*	*Total cost*
	200	$3.00	$600
	50	2.00	100
	250		700
Ending inventory	150	2.00	$300

NOTE: The base-year cost is $2.00 and the base-year level is 150 units. Therefore, if ending inventory in subsequent periods exceeds 150 units, a new layer will be created.

Year 2

		Units	Unit cost	Total cost	
Cost of goods sold		100	$3.30	$330	
		100	3.20	320	
		200		650	
Ending inventory		150	2.00	$300	Base-year layer
		200	3.20	640	Year 2 increment
		350		$940	

Year 3

		Units	Unit cost	Total cost	
Cost of goods sold		100	$3.50	$350	
		200	3.20	640	
		300		$990	
Ending inventory		150	2.00	$300	Base-year layer

NOTE: The decrease of 200 units in year 3 eliminated the entire year 2 increment. Thus, any year 4 increase in the quantity of inventory would result in a new increment, which would be valued at year 4 prices.

Pooling Approach

Applying the unit LIFO method requires a substantial amount of recordkeeping. The recordkeeping becomes more burdensome as the number of products increases. For this reason, a "pooling" approach often is used to compute LIFO inventories.

Pooling is the process of grouping items that are naturally related and then treating this group as a single unit in determining LIFO cost. Because the ending inventory normally includes many items, decreases in one item can be offset by increases in others, whereas under the unit LIFO approach, a decrease in any one item results in a liquidation of all or a portion of a LIFO layer.

Complexity in applying the pooling method arises from the income tax regulations. These regulations require that the opening and closing inventories of each type of good be similar as to character, quality, and price. This qualification generally has been interpreted to mean identical. The effect of this interpretation is to require a separate pool for each item under the unit LIFO method. To provide a simpler, more practical approach to applying LIFO and allow for increased use of LIFO pools, election of the dollar-value LIFO method is permitted.

Dollar-Value LIFO

Under the dollar-value LIFO method of inventory valuation, the cost of inventories is computed by expressing base-year cost in terms of total dollars rather than specific prices of specific units. The dollar-value method also provides an expanded interpretation of the use of LIFO pools. Increments and decrements are treated in the same manner as under the unit LIFO approach but are reflected only in terms of a net increment or liquidation for the entire pool.

Three alternatives exist for determining pools under dollar-value LIFO:

1. The natural business unit method
2. The multiple-pooling method
3. Pools for wholesalers, retailers, jobbers, etc.

The natural business unit is defined by the existence of separate and distinct processing facilities and operations and the maintenance of separate income (loss) records. The concept of the natural business unit generally is dependent on the type of product being produced, not the various stages of production for that product. Thus, the pool of a manufacturer can (and will) contain raw materials, work-in-progress, and finished goods.

The treasury regulations require that a pool consist of all items entering into the entire inventory investments of a natural business unit, unless the taxpayer elects to use the multiple-pooling method.

The multiple-pooling method is the grouping of "substantially similar" items. In determining substantially similar items, consideration is given to the processing applied, the interchangeability, the similarity of use, and the customary practice of the industry. Although the election of multiple pools will necessitate additional recordkeeping, it may result in a better estimation of gross profit and periodic net income.

According to Reg. § 1.472-8(c), inventory items of wholesalers, retailers, jobbers, and distributors are to be assigned to pools by major lines, types, or classes of goods. The natural business unit method may be used with the permission of the Commissioner.

Computing Dollar-Value LIFO

The purpose of the dollar-value LIFO method of valuing inventory is to convert inventory priced at end-of-year prices to that same quantity of inventory priced at base-year (or applicable LIFO layer) prices. The dollar-value method achieves this result through the use of a conversion price index. The inventory computed at current year cost is divided by the appropriate index to arrive at its base-year cost. The main computational focus is on the determination of the conversion price index. Three methods that can be used in the computation of the ending inventory amount of a dollar-value LIFO pool:

1. Double-extension
2. Link-chain
3. Indexing

Double-extension method. The double-extension method was originally developed to compute the conversion price index. It involves extending the entire quantity of ending inventory for the current year at both base-year prices and end-of-year prices to arrive at a total dollar value for each. The dollar total computed at end-of-year prices is referred to as the conversion price index. This index indicates the relationship between base-year and current prices in terms of a percentage. Each layer (or increment) is valued at its own percentage. Although a representative sample is allowed (meaning that not all of the items need to be double-extended), the recordkeeping under this method is very burdensome. The base-year price must be maintained for each inventory item. Depending on the number of different items included in the inventory of the entity, the necessary records may be too detailed to keep past the first year or two.

Link-chain method. The link-chain method of applying dollar-value LIFO was developed to mitigate the effects of the complexity associated with the double-extension method. This method was originally developed for (and limited to) those companies that wanted to use LIFO but, because of a substantial change in product lines over time, were unable to reconstruct or maintain the historical records necessary to make accurate use of the double-extension method.

The link-chain method is the process of developing a single cumulative index that is applied to the ending inventory amount priced using the beginning-of-the-year costs. Thus, the index computed at the end of each year is "linked" to the index from all previous years. A separate cumulative index is used for each pool regardless of the variations in the components of these pools over the years. The index is calculated by double-extending a representative sample of items in the pool at both beginning-of-year prices and end-of-year prices. This annual index is then applied to (multiplied by) the previous period's cumulative index to arrive at the new current year cumulative index.

It is important to note that the double-extension and link-chain methods are not elective alternatives for the same situation. For income tax purposes, the link-chain election requires that substantial changes in product lines be evident over the years; the method may not be elected solely because of its ease of application. The double-extension and index methods must be demonstrably impractical in order to elect the link-chain method. However, an entity may use different computational techniques for financial reporting and income tax purposes. Therefore, the link-chain method could be used for financial reporting purposes even if a different application is used for income tax purposes. The recordkeeping burdens imposed by using different LIFO methods (including the deferred income tax accounting that would be required for the temporary difference between the GAAP and income tax bases of the LIFO inventories) would, however, make this a highly unlikely scenario.

Indexing methods. Indexing methods basically can be broken down into two types:

1. Internal index
2. External index

Internal index. The internal index is merely a variation of the double-extension method. The regulations allow for the use of a statistically valid representative sample of inventory to be double-extended. The index computed from the sample is then used to restate the inventory to base-year cost and to value the new layer.

External index. The external index method, referred to in Treasury regulations as the Inventory Price Index Computation (IPIC) method, involves using indices published by the U.S. Department of Labor's Bureau of Labor Statistics (BLS) and applying them to specified categories of inventory included in the taxpayer's LIFO pools.

Case Study 4

Link-Chain Method

Facts

Assume the following inventory data for years 1 to 4 for Dempster Distributors, Inc. Year 1 is assumed to be the initial year of operation for the company. Assume that A and B constitute a single pool.

Product	Ending inventory quantity	Cost per unit Beg. of year	End of year	Extension Beginning	End
Year 1					
A	5,000	N/A	$ 6.00	N/A	$ 30,000
B	7,000	N/A	10.00	N/A	70,000
					$100,000
Year 2					
A	6,000	$ 6.00	6.30	$ 36,000	$ 37,800
B	7,500	10.00	11.00	75,000	82,500
				$111,000	$120,300
Year 3					
A	5,800	6.30	6.40	$ 36,540	$ 37,120
B	7,400	11.00	11.50	81,400	85,100
				$117,940	$122,220
Year 4					
A	6,200	6.40	6.50	$ 39,680	$ 40,300
B	7,800	11.50	12.00	89,700	93,600
				$129,380	$133,900

Required

Calculate the base index for each year and the LIFO cost at the end of year four.

Solution

1. The initial year (base year) does not require the computation of an index under any LIFO method. The base year indeed will always be 1.00.
2. In year 2, the Index and LIFO cost are

	Base-year cost	Index	LIFO cost
Base-year Layer	$100,000	1.000	$100,000
Year 2 Layer	11,000	1.084	11,924
	$111,000		$111,924

The year 2 index is calculated as 120,300/111,000 = 1.084

3. The index for year 3 is computed as 122,220/117,940 = 1.036

The next step is to determine the cumulative index, which is the product of the preceding year's cumulative index and the current year index, or 1.084 × 1.036 = 1.123. The new cumulative index is used to restate the inventory at end-of-year dollars to base-year cost. This is accomplished by dividing the end-of-year inventory by the new cumulative index, or 122,220/1.123 = 108,833. In this instance we have experienced a decrement (a decrease from the prior year's $111,000). Ending inventory at the end of year 3 is

	Base-year cost	Index	LIFO cost
Base-year Layer	$100,000	1.000	$100,000
Year 2 Layer	8,833	1.084	9,575
Year 3 Layer	—	1.123	—
	$108,833		$109,575

4. The same steps are performed for the year 4 computation. The current-year index is 133,900/129,380 = 1.035. The new cumulative index is 1.035 × 1.123 = 1.162. The base-year cost of the current inventory is 133,390/1.162 = $115,232. Thus, LIFO inventory at the end of year 4 is

	Base–year cost	Index	LIFO cost
Base-year Layer	$100,000	1.000	$100,000
Year 2 Layer	8,833	1.084	9,575
Year 3 Layer	—	1.123	—
Year 4 Layer	6,399	1.162	7,435
	$115,232		$117,010

LIFO CONFORMITY RULE

A unique rule regarding LIFO inventories is referred to as the LIFO conformity rule. A taxpayer may not use a different inventory method in reporting profit or loss of the entity for external financial reports. Thus, if LIFO is elected for income tax purposes, it must also be used for accounting purposes.

Another important consideration in applying the LIFO conformity rule is the law concerning related corporations. In accordance with the Tax Reform Act of 1984, all members of the same group of financially related corporations are treated as a single taxpayer when applying the conformity rule. Previously, taxpayers were able to circumvent the conformity rule by having a subsidiary on LIFO while the non-LIFO parent presented combined non-LIFO financial statements. This is a violation of the conformity requirement.

Weighted-Average and Moving-Average

Another method of inventory valuation involves averaging and is commonly referred to as the weighted-average method. This method is permitted for financial reporting purposes but is not permitted for income tax purposes.

Under this method, the cost of goods available for sale (beginning inventory plus net purchases) is divided by the number of units available for sale to obtain a weighted-average cost per unit. Ending inventory and cost of goods sold are then priced at this average cost.

Case Study 5

Weighted-Average Method

Facts

Blue Corp. uses a software package to cost and value its inventory. The software uses the weighted-average cost method to value inventory. The following are the purchases and sales made by Blue Corp. LLC during 2009.

	Units available	Units sold	Actual unit cost	Actual total cost
Beginning inventory	100	—	$2.10	$210
Sale	—	75	—	—
Purchase	150	—	2.80	420
Sale	—	100	—	—
Purchase	50	—	3.00	150
Total	300	175		$780

Required

Calculate Blue Corp.'s (1) weighted-average cost per unit, (2) ending inventory value, and (3) cost of goods sold.

Solution

1. The weighted-average cost per unit is $780/300, or $2.60.
2. Ending inventory is 125 units (300 – 175) at $2.60, or $325.
3. Cost of goods sold is 175 units at $2.60, or $455.

When the weighted-average assumption is applied using a perpetual inventory system, the average cost is recomputed after each purchase. This process is referred to as moving average. Cost of goods sold is recorded using the most recent average. This combination is called the moving-average method. As an example

	Units on hand	Purchases in dollars	Cost of sales in dollars	Inventory total cost	Inventory moving-average unit cost
Beginning inventory	100	$ —	$ —	$210.00	$2.10
Sale					
(75 units @ $2.10)	25	—	157.50	52.50	2.10
Purchase					
(150 units, $420)	175	420.00	—	472.50	2.70
Sale 100 units					
@ $2.70)	75	—	270.00	202.50	2.70
Purchase					
(50 units, $150)	125	150.00	—	352.50	2.82

Cost of goods sold is 75 units at $2.10 and 100 units at $2.70, or $427.50.

The average methods do not provide an estimate of current cost information on either the statement of financial position or income statement. The average methods are not permitted to be used from income tax purposes. Therefore, their use for financial reporting purposes would necessitate the use of FIFO for income tax reporting purposes, since LIFO requires financial statement conformity.

Of the three cost flow assumptions, FIFO and LIFO produce the most extreme results; results from using the weighted-average method generally fall somewhere in between. The selection of one of these methods involves a detailed analysis of the organization's objectives, industry practices, current and expected future economic conditions, and, most important, needs of the intended users of the financial statements.

PRACTICAL INSIGHT

There is some question about the future of LIFO for inventory costing purposes. Few have ever defended LIFO as a realistic cost flow assumption, and without the LIFO conformity rule imposed under U.S. tax law, most accountants would have supported another method of costing, probably FIFO, as being more representationally faithful for financial reporting purposes. Under International Financial Reporting Standards, LIFO is not permitted. Now that FASB and IASB are formally committed to converge their respective financial reporting standards, there will be more pressure on FASB to derecognize LIFO as appropriate for financial reporting purposes. The logical strategy would be to seek repeal of the LIFO conformity rule, thereby permitting LIFO for tax purposes without forcing the financial statements to report under a costing method that does not describe real economic events. To date, there has been little discussion of this issue, which would appear to be an impediment to full convergence of the standards.

LOWER OF COST OR MARKET

As per ASC 330-10-35-1, a departure from the cost basis of pricing the inventory is required when the utility of goods, in their disposal in the ordinary course of business, will be less than cost. Whether due to physical deterioration, obsolescence, changes in price levels, or other causes, the difference shall be recognized as a loss in the current period. The application of lower of cost or market (LCM) is a means of attempting to measure loss of utility and recognize the effects in the period in which this occurs.

The term *market* means current replacement cost not to exceed a ceiling of net realizable value or to be less than a floor of net realizable value adjusted for a normal profit margin.

LCM is not applied in conjunction with the LIFO method of inventory valuation for income tax purposes. However, it is important to note that LCM/LIFO is applied for financial reporting purposes. Such application gives rise to a temporary difference in the carrying value of inventory between financial statements and income tax returns.

LCM may be applied either to the entire inventory or to each individual inventory item. The primary objective for selecting between the alternative methods of applying the LCM rule is to select the one that most clearly reflects periodic income. The rule is most commonly applied to the inventory on an item-by-item basis. There are two reasons for this application:

1. It is required by income tax purposes unless it involves practical difficulties.
2. It provides the most conservative valuation of inventories, because decreases in the value of one item are not offset by increases in the value of another.

Replacement cost is a valid measure of the future utility of the inventory item since increases or decreases in the entity's purchase price generally foreshadow related increases or decreases in the price at which it is able to sell the item. The ceiling and the floor provide safeguards against the recognition of either excessive profits or excessive losses in future periods in those instances where the selling price and replacement cost do not move in the same direction in a proportional manner. The ceiling avoids the recognition of additional losses in the future when the selling price is falling faster than the replacement cost. Without the ceiling constraint, inventories would be carried at an amount in excess of their net realizable value. The floor avoids the recognition of abnormal profits in the future when replacement cost is falling faster than the selling price. Without the floor, inventories would be carried at a value less than their net realizable value minus a normal profit.

The loss from writing inventories down to LCM generally is reflected on the income statement in cost of goods sold. If material, the loss must be captioned separately in the income statement. The write-down is recorded as a debit to a loss account and a credit to either an inventory or a valuation allowance account.

Case Study 6

Lower of cost or market

Facts

Assume the following information for products A, B, C, D, and E:

Item	Cost	Replacement cost	Est. selling price	Cost to complete	Quantity on hand	Normal profit %	Normal profit amount
A	$2.00	$1.80	$2.50	$0.50	100	24%	$0.60
B	4.00	1.60	4.00	0.80	200	24%	0.96
C	6.00	6.60	10.00	1.00	300	18%	1.80
D	5.00	4.75	6.00	2.00	400	20%	1.20
E	1.00	1.05	1.20	0.25	500	12.5%	0.15

Required

Compute the valuation of each item using the LCM principle

Solution

Item	Cost	Replacement cost	NRV (ceiling)	NRV less profit (floor)	Market	LCM
A	$2.00	$1.80	$2.00	$1.40	$1.80	$1.80
B	4.00	1.60	3.20	2.24	2.24	2.24
C	6.00	6.60	9.00	7.20	7.20	6.00
D	5.00	4.75	4.00	2.80	4.00	4.00
E	1.00	1.05	0.95	0.80	0.95	0.84

OTHER INVENTORY TOPICS

Purchase Commitments

Purchase commitments generally are not recognized in the financial statements because they are executory in nature. However, disclosure in the notes to the financial statements is required for firm purchase commitments that are material in amount. If at the date of the statement of financial position the contract price of these commitments exceeds the market value, the estimated loss is accrued and reported as a loss in the income statement. This results in recognition of the loss before the inventory actually is purchased.

Inventories Valued at Selling Price

In exceptional cases, inventories may be reported at sales price less estimated disposal costs. Such treatment is justified when cost is difficult to determine, quoted market prices are available, marketability is assured, and units are interchangeable. Precious metals, certain agricultural products, and meat are examples of inventories valued in this manner. When inventory is valued above cost, revenue is recognized before the time of sale.

Stripping Costs Incurred during Production in the Mining Industry

Stripping costs incurred during a mine's production phase are to be accounted for as variable production costs and, therefore, allocated to inventory. This is limited to stripping costs incurred during the period when inventory is being produced (i.e., extracted), not during the preproduction phase of the mine.

INTERIM REPORTING

The principles used to determine ending inventory and cost of goods sold in annual reports are also used in interim reports, although four exceptions are allowed:

1. The gross profit method may be used to estimate cost of goods sold and ending inventory.
2. When LIFO layers are liquidated during the interim period but are expected to be replaced by year-end, cost of goods sold is adjusted to reflect current costs rather than older LIFO costs.
3. Temporary market declines need not be recognized if substantial evidence exists that market prices will recover. If LCM losses are recorded in one or more interim periods and are recovered by year-end, the recovery is recognized as a fourth-quarter gain.
4. Planned standard cost variances expected to reverse by year-end are not recognized.

DISCLOSURE

The financial statements should disclose

- Accounting policies adopted for measuring inventories and the cost flow assumption (i.e., cost formula) used.
- Where inventories are stated at sale prices.
- Where goods are stated above cost.
- When substantial and unusual losses result from the application of LCM, the loss may be stated in the income statement separately from cost of goods sold.

EXTRACTS FROM PUBLISHED FINANCIAL STATEMENTS

Trudy Corporation, Annual Report March 31, 2009

Notes to Financial Statements

Accounting Policies

Inventories

Inventories, which consist principally of finished goods, are stated at the lower of cost or market. Cost is determined using the first-in, first-out method. The Company reviews its inventory for obsolescence and provides for obsolescence when the inventory is deemed to be unsalable over a reasonable time.

Alanco Technologies Inc. and Subsidiaries, Annual Report June 30, 2009

Notes to the Financial Statements

6. Inventories

	2009	*2008*
Raw materials and purchased parts	$2,935,600	$4,304,100
Finished goods	172,600	359,800
	3,108,200	4,663,900
Less reserve for obsolescence	(773,400)	(676,300)
	2,334,800	3,987,600

Inventory for the Data Storage segment is included in Assets Held for Sale in the consolidated balance sheets at both June 30, 2009 and 2008. If the Data Storage segment's inventory balance is included in the consolidated inventory, inventory balances would increase by $527,200, net of a $59,300 reserve, and $803,300, net of a $56,000 reserve, at June 30, 2009 and 2008, respectively.

MULTIPLE-CHOICE QUESTIONS

1. Inventory should be stated at
    (a) Lower of cost and net realizable value.
    (b) Lower of cost or market.
    (c) Lower of cost and nominal value.
    (d) Lower of cost and net selling price.
    (e) Choices (b) and (d).
    (f) Choices (a) and (c).
    (g) Choices (a), (b), and (d).

2. Which of the following is **not** considered an indirect overhead cost?
    (a) Depreciation.
    (b) Factory rent and utilities.
    (c) Labor used in the production of goods.
    (d) Production supervisory wages.

3. Net realizable value is
    (a) The sum of all applicable expenditures and charges incurred in bringing an article to its existing condition and location.
    (b) The replacement cost of the item.
    (c) The selling price of an item, less selling costs and costs to complete.
    (d) The sum of all indirect and direct overhead costs.

4. In a period of rising prices, which valuation method provides the clearest measure of periodic net income?
    (a) LIFO.
    (b) Weighted-average.
    (c) Gross profit method.
    (d) FIFO.

Chapter 9

REVENUE RECOGNITION (ASC 605)

BACKGROUND AND INTRODUCTION

According to CON 5, *Recognition and Measurement in Financial Statements of Business Enterprises,* "an entity's revenue-earning activities involve delivering or producing goods, rendering services, or other activities that constitute its ongoing major or central operations, and revenues are considered to have been earned when the entity has substantially accomplished what it must do to be entitled to the benefits represented by the revenues."

In order to be recognized, revenue must be realized or realizable, and it must have been earned. CON 5 notes that "the two conditions (being realized or realizable, and being earned) are usually met by the time product or merchandise is delivered or services are rendered to customers, and revenues from manufacturing and selling activities and gains and losses from sales of other assets are commonly recognized at the time of sale (usually meaning delivery)."

"Revenue" should be distinguished from "gains." Revenue arises from an entity's ordinary activities. Gains, however, include such nonroutine items as the profit on disposal of noncurrent assets, or on retranslating balances in foreign currencies, or fair value adjustments to financial and nonfinancial assets.

The SEC, reflecting on the conceptual foundation for revenue recognition, observed first in Staff Accounting Bulletin 101, and then in its replacement, SAB 104, that "revenue generally is realized or realizable and earned when all of the following criteria are met":

1. There is persuasive evidence that an arrangement exists.
2. Delivery has occurred or services have been rendered.
3. The seller's price to the buyer is fixed or determinable.
4. Collectibility is reasonably assured.

This Standard prescribes the requirements for the recognition of revenue in an entity's financial statements. Revenue can take various forms, such as sales of goods, provision of services, royalty fees, franchise fees, management fees, dividends, interest, subscriptions, and so on.

The principal issue in the recognition of revenue is its timing—at what point is it probable that future economic benefit will flow to the entity and the benefit can be measured reliably?

Some of the recent highly publicized financial scandals that caused turmoil in the financial world globally were allegedly the result of financial manipulations resulting from recognizing revenue based on inappropriate accounting policies. Such financial missteps resulting from the use of aggressive revenue recognition policies have drawn the attention of the accounting world to the importance of accounting for revenue.

It is absolutely critical that the point of recognition of revenue is properly determined. For instance, in case of sale of goods, is revenue to be recognized on receipt of the customer order, on completion of production, on the date of shipment, or on delivery of goods to the customer? The decision as to when and how revenue should be recognized has a significant impact on the determination of "net income" for the year (i.e., the "bottom line"), and thus it is a very critical element in the entire process of the preparation of the financial statements.

SCOPE

The guidance in ASC 605 applies to all entities and applies to these types of transactions and revenue recognition considerations:

- Revenue and gains
- Installment and cost recovery methods of revenue recognition

---

DEFINITIONS OF KEY TERMS
(in accordance with ASC 605)

Fair value. The amount in cash or cash equivalent value of other consideration that a real estate parcel would yield in a current sale between a willing buyer and a willing seller (other than in a forced or liquidation sale). The fair value of a parcel is affected by its physical characteristics, ultimate use, and the time required to make such use of the property considering access, development plans, zoning restrictions, and market absorption factors.
Revenue. The gross inflow of resources that a company receives from its normal business activities, usually from the sale of goods and the provision of services to customers.

PRACTICAL INSIGHT

"Revenue" refers only to those amounts received or receivable by an entity on its own account. Amounts received or receivable for the accounts of others are not classified as income as there is no increase in equity; such items are liabilities. Examples include sales taxes (amounts owed to the government), insurance premiums collected by an agent (revenue in this case would be the commission), and the like.

MEASUREMENT OF REVENUE

Revenue is to be measured at the fair value of the consideration received or receivable. In most cases, the value is easily determined by the sales contract after taking into account trade discounts or rebates.

Case Study 1

Facts

Big Bulk has arrangements with its customers that, in any 12-month period ending March 31, if they purchase goods for a value of at least $1 million, they will receive a retrospective discount of 2%. Big Bulk's year-end is December 31, and it has made sales to a customer during the period April 1 to December 31 of $900,000.

Required

How much revenue should Big Bulk recognize?

Solution

Based on a prorated calculation, Big Bulk will make sales to its customer of $1.2 million ($900,000 × 12/9). Therefore, Big Bulk should accrue a retrospective rebate of 2% on $900,000 and recognize revenue of $882,000.

However, transactions can be more complex, for example, if longer-than-normal credit is offered at below-market rates of interest or if assets are exchanged. In both cases, the transaction needs to be carefully analyzed.

Case Study 2

Facts

Nice Guy Inc. sells goods with a cost of $100,000 to Start-up Co. for $140,000 and a credit period of six months. Nice Guy Inc.'s normal cash price would have been $125,000 with a credit period of one month or with a $5,000 discount for cash on delivery.

Required

How should Nice Guy Inc. measure the income from the transaction?

Solution

Effectively, Nice Guy Inc. is financing Start-up Co. for a period of six months. The normal price would have been $120,000 ($125,000 – the cash discount of $5,000). Therefore, revenue should be accounted at an amount that discounts the actual sale amount of $140,000 back to $120,000.

The difference between the nominal amount of $140,000 and the discounted value would be recognized as interest income over the period of finance of six months.

Barter transactions (nonmonetary exchanges, as described in ASC 845-10) are not a problem, assuming that they represent the culmination of an earnings process. However, in recent years there have been many reports of transactions that appear to have been concocted merely to create the illusion of revenue-generating activities (i.e., including advertising swaps engaged in by some entities, most commonly dot-com enterprises, and the excess capacity swaps of fiber-optic communications concerns under "indefeasible right to use" agreements.)

Both of these and many other situations involved immediate recognition of revenues coupled with deferred recognition of costs and typically, in aggregate, were equal exchanges that did not provide profits to either party. Furthermore, these examples do not represent culminations of the normal earnings process (e.g., fiber-optic networks were built in order to sell communications services to end users, not for the purpose of swapping capacity with other similar operations).

IDENTIFICATION OF A TRANSACTION

Usually when applying the recognition criteria of the Standard, one applies it to each transaction. However, occasions arise with more complex transactions when the criteria need to be applied to *components* of a transaction.

Case Study 3

Facts

Full Service Co. sells some equipment, the cash price of which is $100,000, for $140,000 with a commitment to service the equipment for a period of two years, with no further charge.

Solution

Full Service Co. would recognize revenue on the sale of goods of $100,000. The balance of $40,000 would be recognized over two years as service revenue.

SALE OF GOODS

The Standard prescribes that in order to be recognized, revenue must be realized or realizable, and it must have been earned. Revenue generally is realized or realizable and earned when all of these criteria are met:

- There is persuasive evidence that an arrangement exists.
- Delivery has occurred or services have been rendered.
- The seller's price to the buyer is fixed or determinable.
- Collectibility is reasonably assured.

It is also essential for there to be a transfer of "significant" risks. For example, if goods are sold but the receivable will be collected only if the buyer is able to sell, then "significant" risks of ownership are retained by the original seller and no sale is recognized.

The point of time at which significant risks and rewards of ownership transfer to the buyer requires careful consideration of the circumstances surrounding the transaction. Generally, the transfer of significant risks and rewards of ownership takes place when title passes to the buyer or the buyer receives possession of the goods. However, in some circumstances, the transfer of risks and rewards of ownership does not coincide with the transfer of legal title or the passing of possession, as when a building that is still under construction is sold.

PRACTICAL INSIGHT

In the case of retail sales, wherein customers have a right to return the goods or right to seek a refund, the retention of risks and rewards is not considered that "significant" that revenue from the sale of goods is *not* recognized at the point when goods are sold to the customers. The risk not transferred is the risk of goods sold being returned by customers or the risk of customers seeking refunds. Revenue in such a situation is recognized at the time of sale, provided the seller can reliably estimate future returns (based on some rational basis, such as past experience and other pertinent factors) and recognize a provision under ASC 605.

Furthermore, the *costs* incurred in respect of the transaction must be reliably measured.

Case Study 4

Facts

Bespoke Inc. has manufactured a machine specifically to the design of its customer. The machine could not be used by any other party. Bespoke Inc. has never manufactured this type of machine before and expects a number of faults to materialize in its operation during its first year of use, which Bespoke Inc. is contractually bound to rectify at no further cost to the customer. The nature of these faults could well be significant. As of Bespoke Inc.'s year-end, the machine had been delivered and installed, the customer invoiced for $100,000 (the contract price), and the costs incurred by Bespoke Inc. up to that date amounted to $65,000.

Required

How should Bespoke Inc. recognize this transaction?

Solution

As Bespoke Inc. has not manufactured this type of machine earlier, it is not in a position to reliably measure the cost of rectification of any faults that may materialize. Consequently, the cost to Bespoke Inc. of the transaction cannot be reliably measured and no sale should be recognized.

Very often, contracts for sale of goods can be *subject to conditions*, such as

- Subject to inspection and/or installation. If installation is a quick and simple process (i.e., it forms an insignificant part of the sales contract), revenue can be recognized on delivery.
- On approval with a right of return. The contract is recognized when goods are accepted or the period of right of return has lapsed.
- On consignment. The contract is recognized only when the consignee has sold the goods.
- Cash on delivery. The contract is recognized when cash is received.
- "Layaway" when goods are delivered on receipt of the final installment payment. If history shows that full payment is normally received, revenue could be recognized when a significant deposit is received and the goods are on hand and ready for delivery. Otherwise, revenue would be recognized only on delivery.

In other words, if the seller retains significant risks of ownership, the transaction is not regarded as a sale for the purposes of recognizing revenue. A seller may retain significant risks of ownership, which may be manifested in numerous ways. The next case study shows circumstances wherein the seller retains significant risks of ownership.

Case Study 5

Which of the following situations signify that "risks and rewards" have **not** been transferred to the buyer?

(a) XYZ Inc. sells goods to ABC Inc. In the sales contract, there is a clause that the seller has an obligation for unsatisfactory performance, which is not governed by normal warranty provisions.

(b) Zeta Inc. shipped machinery to a destination specified by the buyer. A significant part of the transaction involves installation that has not yet been fulfilled by Zeta Inc.

(c) The buyer has the right to cancel the purchase for a reason not specified in the contract of sale (duly signed by both parties), and the seller is uncertain about the outcome.

Solution

(a) According to the clause in the sales contract, XYZ Inc. has an obligation beyond the normal warranty provision. Thus, "risks and rewards of ownership" have not been transferred to the buyer on the date of the sale.

(b) "Risks and rewards of ownership" have not been transferred to the buyer on the date of the delivery of the machinery because a significant part of the transaction (i.e., installation) is yet to be done.

(c) "Risks and rewards of ownership" will not be transferred to the buyer due to the "unspecified uncertainty" arising from the terms of the contract of sale (duly signed by both parties), which allow the buyer to retain the right of cancellation of the sale due to which the seller is uncertain of the outcome.

A transaction is not deemed a sale until it is probable that the future economic benefits will flow to the entity. In some of the cases, the receipt of consideration may be doubtful. Until the uncertainty is removed, the sale should not be recognized.

PRACTICAL INSIGHT

When uncertainty arises about collectibility of revenue booked in an earlier period, then a valuation allowance should be established, as opposed to adjusting the revenue originally recognized in an earlier period.

Revenues recognized and the costs (expenses) associated with them should be matched and recognized simultaneously. This is essential because if costs cannot be measured reliably, then the related revenue should not be recognized. In such a situation, any consideration received from such transactions is booked as a liability.

RENDERING OF SERVICES

Revenue from the rendering of services can be recognized by reference to the stage of completion if the final outcome can be reliably estimated. This would be the case if

- The amount of revenue can be measured reliably.
- It is probable that economic benefits associated with the transaction will flow to the seller.
- The stage of completion can be measured reliably.
- The costs incurred and the cost to complete can be measured reliably.

Examples

- Installation fees are recognized over the period of installation by reference to the stage of completion.
- Subscriptions usually are recognized on a straight-line basis over the subscription period.
- Insurance agency commissions would be recognized on commencement of the insurance *unless* the agent is likely to have to provide further services, in which case a portion of the revenue would be deferred to cover the cost of providing that service.
- Fees from development of customized software are recognized by reference to stage of completion, including postdelivery support.
- Event admission fees are recognized when the event occurs. If subscription to a number of events is sold, the fee is allocated to each event.
- Tuition fees would be recognized over the period in which tuition is provided.
- Financial service fees depend on the services that are being rendered. Very often they are treated as an adjustment to the effective interest rate on the financial instrument that is being created. This would be the case for origination and commitment fees. Investment management fees would be recognized over the period of management.

DISCLOSURES

ASC 235 requires disclosures of "important judgments as to appropriateness of principles relating to the recognition of revenue." SAB 101 expressed the opinion of the SEC staff that because revenue recognition generally involves the exercise of judgment, companies always are required to disclose their revenue recognition policies. SAB 101 also provided that, when applicable, the notes to the financial statements are to include disclosure of

- The revenue recognition policy for each material type of transaction.
- If the company enters into multiple-element sales arrangements (e.g., bundling of related products and/or services), the method of accounting for each element and the method used to determine each element and value it.
- Material changes in estimates of returns in accordance with ASC 605-15 (e.g., changing the percentage of sales used to establish the allowance).

EXTRACTS FROM PUBLISHED FINANCIAL STATEMENTS

Nike, Inc., Annual Report, 2009 (May 31, 2009)

Recognition of Revenues

Wholesale revenues are recognized when the risks and rewards of ownership have passed to the customer, based on the terms of sale. This occurs upon shipment or upon receipt by the customer depending on the country of the sale and the agreement with the customer. Retail store revenues are recorded at the time of sale. Provisions for sales discounts, returns, and miscellaneous claims from customers are made at the time of sale.

Smurfit-Stone Container Enterprises, Inc., Annual Report 2008

Revenue Recognition

The Company recognizes revenue at the time persuasive evidence of an agreement exists, price is fixed and determinable, title passes to external customers, and collectibility is reasonably assured. Shipping and handling costs are included in cost of goods sold.

The Company records certain inventory buy/sell transactions between counterparties within the same line of business as a single exchange transaction on a net basis in the consolidated statement of operations.

MULTIPLE-CHOICE QUESTIONS

1. "Bill and hold" sales, in which delivery is delayed at the buyer's request but the buyer assumes title and accepts invoicing, should be recognized when
  (a) The buyer makes an order.
  (b) The seller starts manufacturing the goods.
  (c) The title has been transferred but the goods are kept on the seller's premises.
  (d) It is probable that the delivery will be made, payment terms have been established, and the buyer has acknowledged the delivery instructions.

2. ABC Inc. is a large manufacturer of machines. XYZ Ltd., a major customer of ABC Inc., has placed an order for a special machine for which it has given a deposit of $112,500 to ABC Inc. The parties have agreed on a price for the machine of $150,000. As per the terms of the sales agreement, it is an FOB (free on board) contract, and the title passes to the buyer when goods are loaded onto the ship at the port. When should the revenue be recognized by ABC Inc.?
  (a) When the customer orders the machine.
  (b) When the deposit is received.
  (c) When the machine is loaded on the port.
  (d) When the machine has been received by the customer.

3. Revenue from an artistic performance is recognized once
  (a) The audience register for the event online.
  (b) The tickets for the concert are sold.
  (c) Cash has been received from the ticket sales.
  (d) The event takes place.

4. X Ltd., a large manufacturer of cosmetics, sells merchandise to Y Ltd., a retailer, which in turn sells the goods to the public at large through its chain of retail outlets. Y Ltd. purchases merchandise from X Ltd. under a consignment contract. When should revenue from the sale of merchandise to Y Ltd. be recognized by X Ltd.?
  (a) When goods are delivered to Y Ltd.
  (b) When goods are sold by Y Ltd.
  (c) It will depend on the terms of delivery of the merchandise by X Ltd. to Y Ltd. (i.e., CIF [cost, insurance, and freight] or FOB).
  (d) It will depend on the terms of payment between Y Ltd. and X Ltd. (i.e., cash or credit).

5. M Ltd., a new company manufacturing and selling consumable products, has come out with an offer to refund the cost of purchase within one month of sale if the customer is not satisfied with the product. When should M Ltd. recognize the revenue?

  (a) When goods are sold to the customers.
  (b) After one month of sale.
  (c) Only if goods are not returned by the customers after the period of one month.
  (d) At the time of sale along with an offset to revenue of the liability of the same amount for the possibility of the return.

6. Micrium, a computer chip manufacturing company, sells its products to its distributors for onward sales to the ultimate customers. Due to frequent fluctuations in the market prices for these goods, Micrium has a "price protection" clause in the distributor agreement that entitles it to raise additional billings in case of upward price movement. Another clause in the distributor's agreement is that Micrium can at any time reduce its inventory by buying back goods at the cost at which it sold the goods to the distributor. Distributors pay for the goods within 60 days from the sale of goods to them. When should Micrium recognize revenue on sale of goods to the distributors?
  (a) When the goods are sold to the distributors.
  (b) When the distributors pay to Micrium the cost of the goods (i.e., after 60 days of the sale of goods to the distributors).
  (c) When goods are sold to the distributor, provided estimated additional revenue is also booked under the "protection clause" based on past experience.
  (d) When the distributor sells goods to the ultimate customers and there is no uncertainty with respect to the "price protection" clause or the buyback of goods.

7. Company XYZ Inc. manufacturers and sells standard machinery. One of the conditions in the sales contract is that installation of machinery will be undertaken by XYZ Inc. During December 2009, XYZ received a special onetime contract from ABC Ltd. to manufacture, install, and maintain customized machinery. It is the first time XYZ Inc. will be producing this kind of machinery, and it is expecting that numerous changes would need to be made to the machine after the installation is completed, which one period is described in the contract of sale as the "maintenance period." The total cost of making the changes during the maintenance period cannot be reasonably estimated at the time of the installation. When should the revenue from sale of this special machine be recognized?
  (a) When the machinery is produced.
  (b) When the machinery is produced and delivered.
  (c) When the installation is complete.
  (d) When the maintenance period as per the contract of sale expires.

Chapter 10

PROPERTY, PLANT, AND EQUIPMENT
(ASC 360)

BACKGROUND AND INTRODUCTION

This Standard prescribes rules regarding the recognition, measurement, and disclosures relating to property, plant, and equipment (often referred to as fixed assets) that would enable users of financial statements to understand the extent of an entity's investment in such assets and the movements therein.

The principal issues involved relate to the recognition of items of property, plant, and equipment; determining their costs; and assessing the depreciation and impairment losses that need to be recognized.

DEFINITIONS OF KEY TERMS

Cost. The amount paid or fair value of other consideration given to acquire or construct an asset.

Depreciable amount. The cost of an asset less its residual value.

Depreciation. The systematic allocation of the depreciable amount of an asset over its expected useful life.

Fair value. The amount for which an asset could be exchanged between knowledgeable willing parties in an arm's-length transaction.

Property, plant, and equipment. Tangible assets that are held for use in production or supply of goods and services, for rental to others, or for administrative purposes *and* are expected to be used during more than one period.

Residual value (of an asset). The estimated amount, less estimated disposal costs, that could currently be realized from the asset's disposal if the asset were already of an age and condition expected at the end of its useful life.

Useful life. The period over which an asset is expected to be utilized or the number of production units expected to be obtained from the use of the asset.

RECOGNITION OF AN ASSET

Criteria for Recognition

An item of property, plant, and equipment should be recognized as an asset *if and only if* it is probable that future economic benefits associated with the asset will flow to the entity *and* the cost of the item can be measured reliably.

Upon acquisition, the reporting entity capitalizes all the costs necessary to deliver the asset to its intended location and prepare it for its productive use, including interest.

Replacement costs that add to the utility of an existing asset in effect create a new asset that has been acquired and are subject to the same capitalization considerations applied in recognizing the original asset. As a practical expedient, most reporting entities establish a dollar threshold under which such costs are charged to expense, irrespective of their purpose. This is done under the assumption that the costs of capitalizing and depreciating the item far exceed the benefits to users of the financial statements. In practice, then, these items are generally considered to be immaterial to the financial statements, both individually and in the aggregate.

If the cost increases the future service potential of the asset, it is accounted for in one of these two manners, depending on the individual facts and circumstances:

1. *Costs that do not extend the overall useful life of the asset.* If a portion of the original asset is being replaced, theoretically, the carrying value, if any, of the corresponding portion of the asset that is being replaced (cost less accumulated depreciation and less any impairment charges recognized in prior periods) should be removed from the accounting records and recorded as a loss in the period of the replacement. This accounting is seldom used in practice because, in general, accounting records for fixed assets are not maintained in the painstaking detail necessary to determine the carrying value of the individual components that comprise each asset. Instead, most companies will capitalize the replacement components under the rationale that the portion of the asset being replaced would have been depreciated sufficiently based on the useful life of the host asset so that, at the time of replacement, little or no carrying value would remain to be removed.

2. *Costs that extend the overall useful life of the asset.* If, as a result of incurring a cost, the useful life of the host asset is extended without increasing its productivity or capacity, it has been suggested that the costs be recorded as a charge to accumulated depreciation rather than capitalizing them as additions to fixed assets. Recording the transaction in this manner effectively recovers previously recognized depreciation and has the same effect on the net carrying value as capitalizing the addition. This treatment is seldom used in practice and has little theoretical appeal unless it is accompanied by a prospective change in the remaining estimated useful life of the host asset.

If a cost, such as repairs and maintenance, does not extend an asset's useful life, increase its productivity, improve its operating efficiency, or add additional production capacity, the cost is to be recognized as an expense as incurred.

The costs of moving a fixed asset to a new location at which it will operate in the same manner and with the same functionality as it did at its former location does not result in any future benefits, and therefore the costs of dismantlement, packaging/crating, shipping, and reinstallation are to be recognized as an expense as incurred.

Measurement at Recognition

An item of property, plant, and equipment that satisfies the recognition criteria should be recognized initially at its cost. Cost comprises items such as

- Purchase price, including import duties, nonrefundable purchase taxes, less trade discounts and rebates.
- Costs directly attributable to bringing the asset to the location and condition necessary for it to be used in a manner intended by the entity.
- Installation and setup costs.
- Testing and breaking-in costs.

- Foundations and other costs related to providing proper support for the asset.
- Costs of reconditioning assets that are purchased used in order to prepare them for use.
- Freight costs and related shipping insurance.

Case Study 1

Facts

Extravagant Inc. is installing a new plant at its production facility. It has incurred these costs:

1.	Cost of the plant (cost per supplier's invoice plus taxes)	$2,500,000
2.	Initial delivery and handling costs	200,000
3.	Cost of site preparation	600,000
4.	Consultants used for advice on the acquisition of the plant	700,000
5.	Interest charges paid to supplier of plant for deferred credit	200,000
6.	Operating losses before commercial production	400,000

Required

Please advise Extravagant Inc. on the costs that can be capitalized in accordance with ASC 360.

Solution

These costs can be capitalized:

1.	Cost of the plant	$2,500,000
2.	Initial delivery and handling costs	200,000
3.	Cost of site preparation	600,000
4.	Consultants' fees	700,000
		$4,000,000

Interest charges paid on "deferred credit terms" to the supplier of the plant (*not* a qualifying asset) of $200,000 and operating losses before commercial production amounting to $400,000 are not costs necessary to deliver the asset to its intended location and prepare it for its productive use and thus cannot be capitalized. They should be written off to the income statement in the period they are incurred.

Measurement of Cost

The cost of an asset is measured at the cash price equivalent at the date of acquisition. If payment is "deferred" beyond normal credit terms, then the difference between the cash price and the total price is recognized as a finance cost and treated accordingly.

If an asset is acquired in exchange for another asset, then the acquired asset is measured at its fair value unless the exchange lacks commercial substance or the fair value cannot be measured reliably, in which case the acquired asset should be measured at the carrying amount of the asset given up, where carrying amount is equal to cost less accumulated depreciation and any impairment losses already recognized.

Measurement after Recognition

After initial recognition of an item of property, plant, and equipment, the asset should be measured using the cost model.

The cost model requires an asset, after initial recognition, to be carried at cost less accumulated depreciation and impairment losses.

DEPRECIATION

Each part of an item of property, plant, and equipment with a cost that is significant in relation to the whole shall be depreciated separately, and such depreciation charge shall be charged to the income statement unless it is included in the cost of producing another asset.

Depreciation is to be applied to the depreciable amount of an asset on a systematic and rational basis over its expected useful life. Expected *useful* life is the period used, *not* the asset's *economic* life, which could be appreciably longer.

The depreciable amount takes account of the expected residual or salvage value of the assets.

Depreciation still needs to be charged even if the fair value of an asset exceeds its residual value. The rationale for this is the definition of residual value, detailed earlier. Residual value is the estimated amount, less estimated disposal costs, that could be currently realized from the asset's disposal if the asset were *already of an age and condition expected at the end of its useful life*. This definition precludes the effect of inflation and, in all likelihood, will be less than fair value.

Depreciation commences when an asset is in the location and condition that enables it to be used in the manner intended by management. Depreciation shall cease at the earlier of its derecognition (sale or scrapping) or its reclassification as "held for sale." Temporary idle activity does not preclude depreciating the asset, as future economic benefits are consumed not only through usage but also through wear and tear and obsolescence. Useful life, therefore, needs to be determined carefully based on use, maintenance programs, expected capacity, expected output, expected wear and tear, technical or commercial innovations, and legal limits.

Straight-Line Method

Depreciation expense is recognized evenly over the estimated useful life of the asset.

Accelerated Methods

Depreciation expense is higher in the early years of the asset's useful life and lower in the later years. These methods are more appropriate than the straight-line method if the asset depreciates more quickly or has greater production capacity in the earlier years than it does as it ages. They are also sometimes used on the theory that maintenance and repair costs typically increase as assets age; therefore, in conjunction with accelerated depreciation, total ownership costs (depreciation, maintenance and repairs) will approximate straight-line methods.

Declining Balance

Annual depreciation is computed by multiplying the book value at the beginning of the fiscal year by a multiple of the straight-line rate of depreciation.

When an asset is either acquired or disposed of during the year, the full-year depreciation calculation is prorated between the accounting periods involved.

Case Study 2

Methods of Depreciation

Facts

Michele Corporation purchased a production machine and placed it in service on January 1, 2010. The machine cost $100,000, has an estimated salvage value of $10,000, and an estimated useful life of five years.

Required

    1. Calculate depreciation using straight-line depreciation.
    2. Calculate depreciation using double-declining balance.
    3. Calculate depreciation using sum-of-the-years' digits.

Solution

    1. Formula

        a. Compute the straight-line depreciation rate as

$$\frac{1}{\text{Estimated useful life}}$$

        b. Multiply the depreciation rate by the cost less estimated salvage value.

        c. Straight-line depreciation = $\frac{1}{5}$ = 20% per year

        d. 20% × ($100,000 – $10,000) = $18,000 annual depreciation

2. Double-declining balance (ceases when the book value = the estimated salvage value)

$$2 \times \text{Straight-line depreciation rate} \times \text{Book value at the beginning of the year}$$

Year	Net book value, beginning of year	Double-declining balance depreciation computed as 2 × SL rate × beginning NBV	Net book value, end of year
1	$100,000	$40,000	$60,000
2	60,000	24,000	36,000
3	36,000	14,400	21,600
4	21,600	8,640	12,960
5	12,960	2,960	10,000 limited by salvage value
Total		$90,000	

3. Sum-of-the-years' digits (SYD) depreciation

Formula

$$(\text{Cost} - \text{Estimated salvage value}) \times \text{Applicable percentage}$$

$$\text{Applicable percentage} = \frac{\text{Number of years of estimated life remaining at the beginning of the year}}{\text{SYD}}$$

$$\text{SYD} = \frac{n(n + 1)}{2} \quad \text{where } n = \text{estimated useful life}$$

$$\text{SYD} = \frac{5(5 + 1)}{2} = 15$$

This formula yields the sum of each year of the estimated useful life:

$$1 + 2 + 3 + 4 + 5 = 15$$

Year	Remaining estimated useful life at beginning of year	SYD	Applicable percentage	Annual depreciation
1	5	5/15	33.33%	$30,000
2	4	4/15	26.67	24,000
3	3	3/15	20.00	18,000
4	2	2/15	13.33	12,000
5	1	1/15	6.67	6,000
Totals	15		100.00%	$90,000

DERECOGNITION

The carrying amount of an item of property, plant, and equipment shall be derecognized on disposal or when no future economic benefit is expected from its use or disposal. Any gain on disposal is the difference between the net disposal proceeds and the carrying amount of the asset. Gains on disposal are *not* to be classified in the income statement as revenue.

DISCLOSURE

Disclosures with respect to each class of property, plant, and equipment are extensive and comprise

- Classes of assets, including separate identification of assets held and used, assets held for sale, assets under construction and not in service, and idle assets.
- The bases of valuation.
- The methods of computing depreciation.
- The amount of accumulated depreciation either by classes of assets or in total.
- A description of and the amount of any assets pledged as collateral.
- Capitalized interest cost.

- Estimated costs to complete for major construction.
- Capitalized preproduction costs related to long-term supply agreements. Aggregate amounts of assets recognized.
- Asset retirement obligations.
- Impairment of assets classified as held and used.

EXTRACTS FROM PUBLISHED FINANCIAL STATEMENTS

Beacon Roofing Supply, Annual Report 2009

Notes to Financial Statements

6. Property and Equipment, net

Property and equipment, net, consisted of the following:

	September 30, 2009	September 30, 2008
Land	$ 3,190	$ 2,159
Buildings and leasehold improvements	18,725	16,651
Equipment	100,731	95,774
Furniture and fixtures	10,478	10,092
	133,124	124,676
Less: accumulated depreciation and amortization	80,159	67,964
	$ 52,965	$ 56,712

Depreciation and amortization of property and equipment totaled $17,394, $18,381, and $17,792 in 2009, 2008, and 2007, respectively.

Evolution Resources, Inc. Annual Report 2009

Note 6. Property, Plant, and Equipment

The Company had no property, plant, and equipment as of April 9, 2009. As of October 31, 2009, property, plant, and equipment consisted principally of the assets related to the Liquafaction business acquired on July 14, 2009, as follows:

Description:	
Production facilities	$10,631,970
Fixtures and equipment	–
Total cost	10,631,970
Accumulated depreciation	(93,000)
Net property, plant, and equipment	$10,538,970

In conjunction with the Liquafaction purchase on July 14, 2009, the Company engaged the appraisal firm The Mentor Group, ("Mentor") to perform a third-party market value appraisal of the assets acquired in the transaction (Ethanol Plant and Elevator). Mentor inspected the facilities on April 13, 2007, and conducted its initial appraisal and evaluation based upon an orderly liquidation on an "as is" and "as completed" basis based on the leasehold improvements and integrated fixed equipment systems with a premised 12–18-month exposure and marketing period. Mentor updated their initial analysis and valuation performed on April 13, 2007, and at October 13, 2009, valued the facilities at $13,720,000 as of October 5, 2010.

For the purposes of determining the appropriate depreciation for the facilities, Mentor used the depreciation table provided by Marshall and Swift. As of July 14, 2009 (the acquisition date), Mentor determined the facilities had a 30-year useful life and an effective age of 10 years. This resulted in a 21% depreciation percentage was used. The company intends to continue using the Marshall and Swift tables depreciating the plant and elevator site by the percentage change in the table each year. Annual depreciation will be 3% of the asset value, with year 1 depreciation being $318,960, or $26,580 per month. Depreciation expense for the period ended October 31, 2009, was $93,000.

Evolution's accounting policy is to record depreciation on a straight-line basis over the estimated useful lives of the various assets as follows:

Furniture and fixtures	5–7 Years
Machinery and equipment	5–10 Years
Production facilities	20 Years

MULTIPLE-CHOICE QUESTIONS

1. An entity imported machinery to install in its new factory premises before year-end. However, due to circumstances beyond its control, the machinery was delayed by a few months but reached the factory premises before year-end. While this was happening, the entity learned from the bank that it was being charged interest on the loan it had taken to fund the cost of the plant. What is the proper treatment of freight and interest expense under ASC 360?

    (a) Both expenses should be capitalized.

    (b) Interest may be capitalized but freight should be expensed.

    (c) Freight charges should be capitalized but interest cannot be capitalized under these circumstances.

    (d) Both expenses should be expensed.

2. Which of the following costs should not be capitalized as part of the asset?

    (a) Import duties.

    (b) Repairs and maintenance.

    (c) Installation and setup costs.

    (d) Freight costs.

3. An entity installed a new production facility and incurred a number of expenses at the point of installation. The entity's accountant is arguing that most expenses do not qualify for capitalization. Included in those expenses are initial operating losses. These should be

    (a) Deferred and amortized over a reasonable period of time.

    (b) Expensed and charged to the income statement.

    (c) Capitalized as part of the cost of the plant as a directly attributable cost.

    (d) Taken to retained earnings since it is unreasonable to present it as part of the current year's income statement.

Chapter 11

FINANCIAL INSTRUMENTS (ASC 825)

INTRODUCTION

ASC 825, *Financial Instruments,* addresses the accounting for financial assets and financial liabilities. More specifically, ASC 825, along with additional guidance in ASC 320, contains requirements for

- When a financial asset or financial liability should first be recognized in the statement of financial position.
- When a financial asset or a financial liability should be derecognized (i.e., removed from the statement of financial position).
- How a financial asset or financial liability should be classified into one of the categories of financial assets or financial liabilities.
- How a financial asset or financial liability should be measured, including

    - When a financial asset or financial liability should be measured at amortized cost or fair value in the statement of financial position.
    - When to recognize and how to measure impairment of a financial asset or group of financial assets.
    - Special accounting rules for hedging relationships involving a financial asset or financial liability.

- How a gain or loss on a financial asset or financial liability should be recognized either in earnings or as a separate component of equity.

SCOPE

In general, ASC 825 applies to all entities in the accounting for both

- Financial instruments
- Other contracts that are specifically included in the scope

Financial Instruments

ASC 825 applies in the accounting for all financial instruments except for those financial instruments specifically exempted. A *financial instrument* is defined as any contract that gives rise to a financial asset of one entity and a financial liability or equity instrument of another entity. Thus, financial instruments include financial assets, financial liabilities, and equity instruments.

Examples

Financial assets within the scope of ASC 825 include

- Cash
- Deposits in other entities
- Receivables (e.g., trade receivables)
- Loans to other entities
- Investments in bonds and other debt instruments issued by other entities
- Investments in shares and other equity instruments issued by other entities

Financial liabilities within the scope of ASC 825 include

- Deposit liabilities
- Payables (e.g., trade payables)
- Loans from other entities
- Bonds and other debt instruments issued by the entity

CLASSIFICATION OF FINANCIAL ASSETS AND FINANCIAL LIABILITIES INTO CATEGORIES

In order to determine the appropriate accounting for a financial asset or financial liability, the asset or liability first must be classified into one of the categories specified by ASC 320. There are three categories of financial assets and financial liabilities. The classification of a financial asset or financial liability determines

- Whether the asset or liability should be measured at amortized cost or fair value in the statement of financial position.
- Whether a gain or loss should be recognized immediately in earnings or as accumulated other comprehensive income (with recognition in earnings at a later point in time).

Financial Assets and Liabilities

ASC 320 requires that all debt and equity securities with readily determinable fair values be placed into one of three categories:

1. Held-to-maturity debt securities
2. Trading securities
3. Available-for-sale securities

The first category, *held-to-maturity investments,* includes financial assets and liabilities with fixed or determinable payments and fixed maturity that the entity has the positive intention and ability to hold to maturity. This category is intended for investments in bonds and other debt instruments that the entity will not sell before their maturity date irrespective of changes in market prices or the entity's financial position or performance. For instance, a financial asset cannot be classified as held to maturity if the entity stands ready to sell the financial asset in response to changes in market interest rates or risks or liquidity needs. Since investments in shares and other equity instruments generally do not have a maturity date, such instruments cannot be classified as held-to-maturity investments.

If a security qualifies for held-to-maturity classification, it is to be measured and presented at amortized cost. In general, transfers to or from this category are not permitted.

Isolated, nonrecurring, and unusual events that could not have been reasonably anticipated may cause a sale or transfer without calling the originally determined intent or ability to hold into question. Other changes in circumstances that are not considered inconsistent include

- Material deterioration in creditworthiness of the issuer.
- Elimination or reduction of tax-exempt status of interest through a change in tax law.
- Major business disposition or combination.

- Statutory or regulatory changes that materially modify what a permissible investment is or regulatory changes that materially modify what a permissible investment is or the maximum level of the security to be held.
- Downsizing in response to a regulatory increase in the industry's capital requirements.
- A material increase in risk weights for regulatory risk-based capital purposes.

The sale of a security within three months of its maturity meets the requirement to hold to maturity as well since the interest rate risk is substantially diminished. Likewise, if a call is considered probable, a sale within three months of that date meets the requirement. The sale of a security after collection of at least 85% of the principal outstanding at acquisition also qualifies on the grounds that the "tail" portion no longer represents an efficient investment due to the economic costs of accounting for the remnants.

The second category, *trading securities,* includes debt and/or equity securities (with readily determinable fair value) that an entity intends to actively and frequently buy and sell for short-term profits. The securities in this category are required to be carried at fair value on the statement of financial position as current assets. All applicable interest and dividends, realized gains and losses, and unrealized gains and losses on changes in fair value are included in income from continuing operations.

The third category, *available-for-sale financial assets,* includes financial instruments that do not fall into any of the other categories of financial assets or that the entity otherwise has elected to classify into this category. For example, an entity could classify some of its investments in debt and equity instruments as available-for-sale financial assets and liabilities. Financial assets and liabilities that are held for trading, including derivatives, cannot be classified as available-for-sale financial assets or liabilities.

The securities in this category are required to be carried at fair value on the statement of financial position. The determination of current or noncurrent status for individual securities depends on whether the securities are considered working capital (ASC 210-10-45).

Other than the possibility of having some noncurrent securities on the statement of financial position, the major difference between trading securities and available-for-sale securities is the handling of unrealized gains and losses. Unlike trading securities, the unrealized gains and losses are excluded from net income. Instead, they are reported in other comprehensive income per ASC 220. All applicable interest (including premium and discount amortization) and any realized gains or losses from the sale of securities are included in income from continuing operations.

Case Study 1

Example of accounting for held-to-maturity investments

Facts

The 12/31/09 debt security portfolio categorized as held-to-maturity is

Security	Maturity value	Amortized cost	Assumed fair value
DEF 12% bond, due 12/31/10	$ 10,000	$10,320	$10,200
PQR mortgage-backed debt, due 12/31/12	100,000	92,000	90,000
JKL 8% bond, due 12/31/16	10,000	8,929	9,100

Required

Indicate how these investments would be reported on the statement of financial position as well as the treatment of interest income and realized gains and losses.

Solution

The statement of financial position would report all the securities in this category at amortized cost and would classify them as shown:

Security	Maturity date	Statement of financial position	Classification
DEF	12/31/10	$10,320	Current
PQR	12/31/12	92,000	Noncurrent
JKL	12/31/16	8,929	Noncurrent

Interest income, including premium and discount amortization, is included in income. Any realized gains or losses are also included in income.

Case Study 2

Example of accounting for trading securities

Facts

The year 1 current trading securities portfolio is

Security	Cost	Fair value	Difference (fair value minus cost)
ABC	$1,000	$ 900	$(100)
MNO calls	1,500	1,700	200
STU	2,000	1,400	(600)
XYZ 7% bond	2,500	2,600	100
	$7,000	$6,600	$(400)

Required

Calculate the adjustment and make the entry to recognize the decline in fair value.

Solution

A $400 adjustment is required in order to recognize the decline in fair value. The entry required is

Unrealized loss on trading securities	400	
Trading securities—MNO calls	200	
Trading securities—XYZ 7% bond	100	
Trading securities—ABC		100
Trading securities—STU		600

The unrealized loss would appear on the income statement as part of other expenses and losses. Dividend income and interest income (including premium and discount amortization) are included in income. Any realized gains or losses from the sale of securities are also included in income.

Case Study 3

Example of accounting for available-for-sale securities

Facts

Bonito Corporation purchases 2,500 shares of equity securities at $6 each, which it classifies as available-for-sale. At the end of one year, the quoted market price of the securities is $4, which rises to $9 at the end of the second year, when Bonito sells the securities. The company has an incremental tax rate of 25%. The calculation of annual gains and losses is

	Gain/(loss) before tax	Tax on gain/(loss)	Gain/(loss) net of tax
End of Year 1	(5,000)	(1,250)	(3,750)
End of Year 2	12,500	3,125	9,375
Net gain	7,500	1,875	5,625

Required

Determine the treatment of the gains and losses.

Solution

Bonito reports these gains and losses in net income and other comprehensive income in the indicated years as

	Year 1	Year 2
Net income:		
Gain on sale of securities		$7,500
Income tax expense		(1,875)
Net gain realized in net income		5,625
Other comprehensive income:		
Gain/(loss) on available-for-sale securities arising during period, net of tax	$(3,750)	9,375
Reclassification adjustment, net of tax		(5,625)
Other comprehensive income net gain/(loss)	(3,750)	3,750

Transfers between Categories

Fair value is used for transfers between categories. When the security is transferred, any unrealized holding gains and losses are accounted for in this manner:

1. *From trading.* Already recognized and not to be reversed.
2. *Into trading.* Recognize immediately in income.
3. *Available-for-sale debt security into held-to-maturity.* Continue to report the unrealized holding gain or loss at the transfer date as other comprehensive income and amortize the gain or loss over the investment's remaining life as an adjustment of yield in the same manner as a premium or discount. The transferred-in security probably will record a premium or discount since fair value is used. Thus, the two amortizations will tend to cancel each other on the income statement.
4. *Held-to-maturity debt security into available-for-sale.* Recognize in other comprehensive income per ASC 220. Few transfers are expected from the held-to-maturity category.

Summary

The next table summarizes the classification requirements and provides examples of financial instruments in the different categories.

Category	Classification requirements	Examples
Trading securities	Financial instruments that are either (1) held for trading or (2) electively designated into the category	Derivative instruments and investments in debt and equity securities that are held in a trading portfolio
Available-for-sale financial assets	Financial instruments that are either (1) electively designated into the category or (2) do not fall into any other category	Investments in debt and equity securities that do not fall into any other category
Held-to-maturity investments	Quoted financial instruments with fixed or determinable payments for which the entity has an intent and ability to hold to maturity	Investments in quoted debt securities for which the entity has an intent and ability to hold to maturity

RECOGNITION

The term *recognition* refers to when an entity should record an asset or liability initially on its statement of financial position.

The principle for recognition under ASC 825 is that an entity should recognize a financial asset or financial liability on its statement of financial position when, and only when, the entity becomes a party to the contractual provisions of the instrument. This means that an entity recognizes *all* its contractual rights and obligations that give rise to financial assets or financial liabilities on its statement of financial position.

A consequence of ASC 825's recognition requirement is that a contract to purchase or sell a financial instrument at a future date is itself a financial asset or financial liability that is recognized in the statement of financial position today. The contractual rights and obligations are recognized when the entity becomes a party to the contract *rather* than when the transaction is settled. Accordingly, derivatives are recognized in the financial statements even though the entity may have paid or received nothing on entering into the derivative.

Planned future transactions and other expected transactions, no matter how likely, are not recognized as financial assets or financial liabilities because the entity has not yet become a party to a contract. Thus, a forecast transaction is not recognized in the financial statements even though it may be highly probable. In the absence of any right or obligation, there is no financial asset or financial liability to recognize.

Case Study 4

This case illustrates the application of the principle for recognition of a financial asset or financial liability.

Facts

Entity A is evaluating whether each of the next items should be recognized as a financial asset or financial liability under ASC 825:

(a) An unconditional receivable.
(b) A forward contract to purchase a specified bond at a specified price at a specified date in the future.
(c) A planned purchase of a specified bond at a specified date in the future.
(d) A firm commitment to purchase a specified quantity of gold at a specified price at a specified date in the future. The contract cannot be net settled.
(e) A firm commitment to purchase a machine that is designated as a hedged item in a fair value hedge of the associated foreign currency risk.

Required

Help Entity A by indicating whether each of the above items should be recognized as an asset or liability under ASC 825.

Solution

(a) Entity A should recognize the unconditional receivable as a financial asset.
(b) In principle, Entity A should recognize the forward contract to purchase a specified bond at a specified price at a specified date in the future as a financial asset or financial liability. However, the initial carrying amount may be zero because forward contracts usually are agreed on terms that give them a zero fair value at inception.
(c) Entity A should not recognize an asset or liability for a planned purchase of a specified bond at a specified date in the future, because it does not have any present contractual right or obligation.
(d) Entity A should not recognize an asset or liability for a firm commitment to purchase a specified quantity of gold at a specified price at a specified date in the future. The contract is not a financial instrument but is instead an executory contract. Executory contacts are generally not recognized before they are settled under existing standards. (Firm commitments that are financial instruments or that are subject to net settlement, however, are recognized on the commitment date under ASC 825).
(e) Normally, a firm commitment to purchase a machine would not be recognized as an asset or liability because it is an executory contract. Under the hedge accounting provisions of ASC 825, however, Entity A would recognize an asset or liability for a firm commitment that is designated as a hedged item in a fair value hedge to the extent there have been changes in the fair value of the firm commitment attributable to the hedged risk (i.e., in this case, foreign currency risk).

DERECOGNITION

The term *derecognition* refers to when an entity should remove an asset or liability from its statement of financial position. The derecognition requirements in ASC 825 set out the conditions that must be met in order to derecognize a financial asset or financial liability and the computation of any gain or loss on derecognition. There are separate derecognition requirements for financial assets and financial liabilities.

Derecognition of Financial Assets

Derecognition of a financial asset is appropriate if either one of these two criteria is met:

1. The contractual rights to the cash flows of the financial asset have expired, *or*
2. The financial asset has been transferred (e.g., sold) and the transfer qualifies for derecognition based on an evaluation of the extent of transfer of the risks and rewards of ownership of the financial asset.

The first criterion for derecognition of a financial asset is usually easy to apply. The contractual rights to cash flows may expire, for instance, because a customer has paid off an obligation to the entity or an option held by the entity has expired worthless. In these cases, derecognition is appropriate because the rights associated with the financial asset no longer exist.

The application of the second criterion for derecognition of financial assets is often more complex. It relies on an assessment of the extent to which the entity has a loss of control over the asset.

More specifically, when an entity sells or otherwise transfers a financial asset to another party, the entity (transferor) must evaluate the extent to which it has transferred the *effective control* of the transferred financial asset to the other party (transferee).

Transfers of financial assets often occur in which the transferor has some continuing involvement either with the assets transferred or with the transferee, which raises issues about the circumstances under which the transfers should be considered as sales of all or part of the assets or as secured borrowings.

A transfer of an entire financial asset, a group of entire financial assets, or a participating interest in an entire financial asset in which the transferor surrenders control over those financial assets shall be accounted for as a sale if and only if all of these conditions are met:

1. The transferred financial assets have been isolated from the transferor—put presumptively beyond the reach of the transferor and its creditors, even in bankruptcy or other receivership. Transferred financial assets are isolated in bankruptcy or other receivership only if the transferred financial assets would be beyond the reach of the powers of a bankruptcy trustee or other receiver for the transferor or any of its consolidated affiliates included in the financial statements being presented.
2. Each transferee (or, if the transferee is an entity whose sole purpose is to engage in securitization or asset-backed financing activities and that entity is constrained from pledging or exchanging the assets it receives, each third-party holder of its beneficial interests) has the right to pledge or exchange the assets (or beneficial interests) it received, and no condition both constrains the transferee (or third-party holder of its beneficial interests) from taking advantage of its right to pledge or exchange and provides more than a trivial benefit to the transferor.
3. The transferor, its consolidated affiliates included in the financial statements being presented, or its agents do not maintain effective control over the transferred financial assets or third-party beneficial interests related to those transferred assets. Examples of a transferor's effective control over financial assets include, but are not limited to
   a. An agreement that both entitles and obligates the transferor to repurchase or redeem financial assets before their maturity when all of the following conditions are met:
      (1) The financial assets to be repurchased or redeemed are the same or substantially the same as those transferred.
      (2) The transferor is able to repurchase or redeem them on substantially the agreed terms, even in the event of default by the transferee.

(3) The agreement is to repurchase or redeem them before maturity, at a fixed or determinable price.

(4) The agreement is entered into contemporaneously with, or in contemplation of, the transfer.

b. An agreement that provides the transferor with both the unilateral ability to cause the holder to return specific financial assets and a more than trivial benefit attributable to that ability, other than through a cleanup call, *or*

c. An agreement that permits the transferee to require the transferor to repurchase the transferred financial assets at a price that is so favorable to the transferee that it is probable that the transferee will require the transferor to repurchase them.

On derecognition, if there is a difference between the consideration received and the carrying amount of the financial asset, the entity recognizes a gain or loss in earnings on the sale. For a derecognized financial asset classified as available for sale, the gain or loss is adjusted for any unrealized holding gains or losses that previously have been included in accumulated other comprehensive income for that financial asset.

Example

If the carrying amount of a financial asset is $26,300 and the entity sells it for cash of $26,500 in a transfer that qualifies for derecognition, an entity makes these entries:

Cash	26,500	
Asset		26,300
Gain on sale		200

If the asset sold was an AFS financial asset, the entries would look different. Changes in fair value of available-for-sale (AFS) financial assets are not recognized in earnings but as other comprehensive income until realized. If changes in fair value of $2,400 had previously been recognized as other comprehensive income, the entity would make these entries on derecognition, assuming the carrying amount was $26,300 and the sales price was $26,500:

Cash	26,500	
Available-for-sale gains recognized in equity	2,400	
Asset		26,300
Gain on sale		2,600

If the transfer of an entire financial asset, a group of entire financial assets, or a participating interest in an entire financial asset does not meet the conditions for a sale, or if a transfer of a portion of an entire financial asset does not meet the definition of a participating interest, the transferor and transferee shall account for the transfer as a secured borrowing with pledge of collateral. The transferor shall continue to report the transferred financial assets in its statement of financial position with no change in its measurement amount (basis of accounting).

Case Study 5

This case illustrates the application of the principle for derecognition of financial assets.

Facts

During the reporting period, Entity A has sold various financial assets:

(a) Entity A sells a financial asset for $10,000. There are no strings attached to the sale, and no other rights or obligations are retained by Entity A.

(b) Entity A sells an investment in shares for $10,000 but retains a call option to repurchase the shares at any time at a price equal to their current fair value on the repurchase date.

(c) Entity A sells a portfolio of short-term accounts receivable for $100,000 and promises to pay up to $3,000 to compensate the buyer if and when any defaults occur. Expected credit losses are significantly less than $3,000, and there are no other significant risks.

(d) Entity A sells an investment in shares for $10,000 and simultaneously enters into a total return swap with the buyer under which the buyer will return any increases in value to Entity A and Entity A will pay the buyer interest plus compensation for any decreases in the value of the investment.

Required

Help Entity A by evaluating the extent to which derecognition is appropriate in each of the above cases.

Solution

(a) Entity A should derecognize the transferred financial asset, because it has transferred control over the asset.

(b) Entity A should derecognize the transferred financial asset, because it has transferred control over the asset. While Entity A has retained a call option (i.e., a right that often precludes derecognition), the exercise price of this call option is the current fair value of the asset on the repurchase date. Therefore, the value of the call option should be close to zero. Accordingly, Entity A has not retained any significant control.

(c) Entity A should continue to recognize the transferred receivables because it has retained control of the receivables. It has kept all expected credit risk, and there are no other substantive risks.

(d) Entity A should continue to recognize the sold investment because it has retained control. The total return swap results in Entity A still being exposed to all increases and decreases in the value of the investment.

Derecognition of Financial Liabilities

The derecognition requirements for financial liabilities are different from those for financial assets. There is no requirement to assess the extent to which the entity has retained control in order to derecognize a financial liability. Instead, the derecognition requirements for financial liabilities focus on whether the financial liability has been extinguished. This means that derecognition of a financial liability is appropriate when the obligation specified in the contract is discharged or is canceled or expires. Absent legal release from an obligation, derecognition is not appropriate even if the entity were to set aside funds in a trust to repay the liability (so-called in-substance defeasance).

If a financial liability is repurchased (e.g., when an entity repurchases in the market a bond that it has issued previously), derecognition is appropriate even if the entity plans to reissue the bond in the future. If a financial liability is repurchased or redeemed at an amount different from its carrying amount, any resulting extinguishment gain or loss is recognized in earnings.

An extinguishment gain or loss is also recognized if an entity exchanges the original financial liability for a new financial liability with substantially different terms or substantially modifies the terms of an existing financial liability. In those cases, the extinguishment gain or loss equals the difference between the carrying amount of the old financial liability and the initial fair value (plus transaction costs) of the new financial liability. An exchange or modification is considered to have substantially different terms if the difference in present value of the cash flows under the old and new terms is at least 10%, discounted using the original effective interest rate of the original debt instrument.

Case Study 6

This case illustrates the application of the principle for derecognition of financial liabilities.

Facts

(a) A put option written by Entity A expires.

(b) Entity A owes Entity B $50,000 and has set aside that amount in a special trust that it will not use for any purpose other than to pay Entity B.

(c) Entity A pays Entity B $50,000 to discharge an obligation to pay $50,000 to Entity B.

Required

Evaluate the extent to which derecognition is appropriate in each of the above cases.

Solution

    (a) Derecognition is appropriate because the option liability has expired. Therefore, the entity no longer has an obligation and the liability has been extinguished.

    (b) Derecognition is not appropriate because Entity A still owes Entity B $50,000. It has not obtained legal release from paying this amount.

    (c) Derecognition is appropriate because Entity A has discharged its obligation to pay $50,000.

MEASUREMENT

The term *measurement* refers to the determination of the carrying amount of an asset or liability in the statement of financial position. The measurement requirements in ASC 825 also address whether gains and losses on financial assets and financial liabilities should be included in earnings or recognized directly in equity.

The next sections discuss these aspects of measurement of financial assets and financial liabilities:

- Initial measurement (measurement when a financial asset or financial liability is first recognized).
- Subsequent measurement (measurement subsequent to initial recognition). This subsection also discusses how to determine amortized cost and fair value.
- Impairment (adjustments to the measurement due to incurred losses).

The measurement of an asset or liability may also be adjusted because of a designated hedging relationship. Hedge accounting is discussed later in this chapter.

Initial Measurement

When a financial asset or financial liability is recognized initially in the statement of financial position, the asset or liability is measured at fair value (plus transaction costs in some cases). *Fair value* is the price that would be received to sell an asset or paid to transfer a liability in an orderly transaction between market participants at the measurement date.

Since fair value is a market transaction price, on initial recognition, fair value generally is assumed to equal the amount of consideration paid or received for the financial asset or financial liability. Accordingly, ASC 820 specifies that the best evidence of the fair value of a financial instrument at initial recognition generally is the transaction price. An entity may be able to overcome that presumption based on observable market data: In other words, if there is a difference between the transaction price and fair value as evidenced by comparison with other observable current market transactions in the same instrument or based on a valuation technique incorporating only observable market data, an immediate gain or loss on initial recognition results.

Transaction costs may arise in the acquisition, issuance, or disposal of a financial instrument. Transaction costs are incremental direct costs, such as fees and commissions paid to agents, advisors, brokers, and dealers; levies by regulatory agencies and securities exchanges; and transfer taxes and duties to sell an asset or transfer a liability in the most advantageous market for the asset or liability. Transaction costs are expensed as incurred for financial assets or financial liabilities measured at fair value, because the payment of transaction costs does not result in any increase in future economic benefits to the entity (i.e., you cannot sell a financial asset at a higher price because you have paid transaction costs on its acquisition).

There may be a difference between the fair value and the consideration received or paid for related-party transactions or transactions where the entity expects to obtain some other benefits. If there is a difference between the consideration paid or received and the initial amount recognized for the financial asset or financial liability, that difference is recognized in earnings (unless it qualifies as some other type of asset or liability).

Subsequent Measurement

Subsequent to initial recognition, financial assets and financial liabilities are measured using one of these two measurement attributes:

1. Amortized cost
2. Fair value

Whether a financial asset or financial liability is measured at amortized cost or fair value depends on its classification into one of the three categories of financial instruments defined by ASC 320 and whether its fair value can be reliably determined.

Amortized cost. *Amortized cost* is the cost of an asset or liability as adjusted, as necessary, to achieve a constant effective interest rate over the life of the asset or liability (i.e., constant interest income or constant interest expense as a percentage of the carrying amount of the financial asset or financial liability).

Example

If the amortized cost of an investment in a debt instrument for which no interest or principal payments are made during the year at the beginning of 20X4 is $100,000 and the effective interest rate is 12%, the amortized cost at the end of 20X4 is $112,000 [100,000 + (12% × 100,000)].

Subsequent to initial measurement, held-to-maturity financial assets and financial liabilities are measured at amortized cost in the statement of financial position.

It is not possible to compute amortized cost for instruments that do not have fixed or determinable payments, such as for equity instruments. Therefore, such instruments cannot be classified into these categories.

For held-to-maturity investments, income and expense items include interest income and impairment losses. In addition, if a held-to-maturity investment is sold, the realized gain or loss is recognized in earnings.

Financial liabilities measured at amortized cost are all financial liabilities other than those measured at fair value. For financial liabilities measured at amortized cost, the most significant item of expense is interest expense. In addition, if financial liabilities are repaid or repurchased before their maturity, extinguishment gains or losses will result if the repurchase price is different from the carrying amount.

In order to determine the amortized cost of an asset or liability, an entity applies the *effective interest rate method*. The effective interest rate method also determines how much interest income or interest expense should be reported in each period for a financial asset or financial liability.

The effective interest rate method allocates the contractual (or, when an asset or liability is prepayable, the estimated) future cash payments or receipts through the expected life of the financial instrument or, when appropriate, a shorter period, in order to achieve a *constant* effective interest rate (yield) in each period over the life of the financial instrument.

The *effective interest rate* is the internal rate of return of the cash flows of the asset or liability, including the initial amount paid or received, interest payments, and principal repayments.

PRACTICAL INSIGHT

The effective interest rate can be computed using a calculator or spreadsheet program. In mathematical terms, the effective interest is found by setting up this equation and solving for the interest rate (y) that equates (1) the initial carrying amount of the asset or liability (PV) with (2) the present value of the estimated future interest and principal cash flows (CF) in each period (i).

$$PV = \sum_{i=1}^{N} \frac{CF_i}{(1+y)^i}$$

In some cases, the effective interest rate will equal the stated interest rate of the asset or liability. This is often the case for loans and long-term note receivables or payables where the initial proceeds equal the principal and the entity was party to the contractual terms at its inception. For such assets, amortized cost equals cost and will be the same in each period. In other cases, the effective interest rate differs from the stated interest rate. This is the case when a debt

---

security is purchased or issued at a premium (higher price) or discount (lower price) to the stated principal (par) amount. In those cases, it is usually necessary to compute the effective interest rate and prepare an amortization schedule in order to determine amortized cost in each period.

Example

This amortization schedule example illustrates how the effective interest method allocates the estimated future cash payments or receipts in order to achieve a constant effective interest rate (yield) in each period over the life of a financial instrument.

Assume that a debt security has a stated principal amount of $100,000, which will be repaid by the issuer at maturity in five years, and a stated coupon interest rate of 6% per year payable annually at the end of each year until maturity (i.e., $6,000 per year). Entity A purchases the debt security in the market on January 1, 20X1, for $93,400 (including transaction costs of $100), that is, at a discount of $6,600 to its principal (par) amount of $100,000. Entity A classifies the debt security as held to maturity and makes this journal entry:

Held-to-maturity investments	93,400	
Cash		93,400

Based on the cash flows of the debt security (i.e., an initial outflow of $93,400, five annual interest cash inflows of $6,000, and one principal cash inflow at maturity of $100,000), it can be shown that the effective interest rate (internal rate of return) of the investment in the debt security is approximately 7.64%. This is the only discount rate that will give a present value of the future cash flows that equals the purchase price.

Based on the effective interest rate of 7.64%, the amortized cost and reported interest income in each year over the life of the financial asset can be computed as indicated in this amortization schedule:

Year	(A) Beginning-of-period amortized cost	(B) Interest cash inflows (at 6%) and principal cash inflow	(C) Reported interest income [=(A) × 7.64%]	(D) Amortization of debt discount [=(C) – (B)]	(E) End-of-period amortized cost [=(A)+(D)]
20X1	93,400	6,000	7,133	1,133	94,533
20X2	94,533	6,000	7,220	1,220	95,753
20X3	95,753	6,000	7,313	1,313	97,066
20X4	97,066	6,000	7,413	1,413	98,479
20X5	98,479	106,000	7,521	1,521	0.00

At the end of 20X1, Entity A makes this journal entry:

Cash	6,000	
Held-to-maturity investment	1,133	
Interest income		7,133

At the end of 20X2, Entity A makes this journal entry:

Cash	6,000	
Held-to-maturity investment	1,220	
Interest income		7,220

At the end of 20X3, Entity A makes this journal entry:

Cash	6,000	
Held-to-maturity investment	1,313	
Interest income		7,313

At the end of 20X4, Entity A makes this journal entry:

Cash	6,000	
Held-to-maturity investment	1,413	
Interest income		7,413

At the end of 20X5, Entity A makes this journal entry:

Cash	106,000	
Held-to-maturity investment	98,479	
Interest income		7,521

If the reporting period does not coincide with the interest payment dates (e.g., if interest is paid twice annually, on May 30 and November 30, while the reporting period ends on December 31), the amortization schedule is prepared using interest periods rather than reporting periods. The amounts computed as interest income in each interest period are then allocated to reporting periods.

Example

If interest income computed using the effective interest method for the interest period between November 30, 20X5, and May 30, 20X6, is $240,000, then one-sixth of that would be allocated to the 20X5 reporting period (i.e., $40,000) and five-sixths would be allocated to the 20X6 reporting period (i.e., $200,000).

On December 31, 20X5, this journal entry would be made:

Interest receivable	40,000	
Interest income		40,000

When interest is received on May 30, 20X6, this journal entry would be made:

Cash	240,000	
Interest income		200,000
Interest receivable		40,000

Case Study 7

This case illustrates how to determine the amortized cost of a financial instrument, including the preparation of an amortization schedule.

Facts

On January 1, 20X5, Entity A purchases a bond in the market for $53,993. The bond has a principal amount of $50,000 that will be repaid on December 31, 20X9. The bond has a stated rate of 10% payable annually, and the quoted market interest rate for the bond is 8%.

Required

Indicate whether the bond was acquired at a premium or a discount. Prepare an amortization schedule that shows the amortized cost of the bond at the end of each year between 20X5 and 20X9 and reported interest income in each period.

Solution

The bond was acquired at a premium to par because the purchase price is higher than the par amount. An amortization schedule that shows the amortized cost of the bond at the end of each year between 20X5 and 20X9 and reported interest income in each period follows.

Year	(A) Beginning-of-period amortized cost	(B) Interest cash inflows (at 10%) and principal cash inflow	(C) Reported interest income [= (A) × 8%]	(D) Amortization of debt premium [= (C) − (B)]	(E) End-of-period amortized cost [= (A) − (D)]
20X5	53,993	5,000	4,319	681	53,312
20X6	53,312	5,000	4,265	735	52,577
20X7	52,577	5,000	4,206	794	51,784
20X8	51,784	5,000	4,143	857	50,926
20X9	50,926	55,000	4,074	926	0

Fair value. As already indicated, *fair value* is defined as the price that would be received to sell an asset or paid to transfer a liability in an orderly transaction between market participants at the measurement date.

Two categories of financial assets and financial liabilities normally are measured at fair value in the statement of financial position:

1. Trading
2. Available for sale

Financial assets and financial liabilities in these categories include investments in debt instruments, investments in equity instruments, and issued debt instruments that are classified or designated into a category measured at fair value. However, there is one exception to fair value measurement in these categories. This exception applies to investments in equity instruments that are not quoted in an active market and cannot be reliably measured at fair value (or are derivatives that are linked to—and must be settled in—such an instrument). Such instruments are measured at cost instead of fair value.

The recognition of income and expense items in earnings differs among the categories measured at fair value.

- For trading securities, all changes in fair value are recognized in earnings when they occur. This includes unrealized holding gains and losses.
- For available-for-sale financial assets, unrealized holding gains and losses are reported in accumulated other comprehensive income until they are realized or impairment occurs. Only interest income and dividend income, impairment losses, and certain foreign currency gains and losses are recognized in earnings while available-for-sale financial assets are held. When gains or losses are realized (e.g., through a sale), the associated unrealized holding gains and losses that were previously reported in accumulated other comprehensive income are included in earnings.

ASC 820 establishes this hierarchy for determining fair value:

1. The existence of a *published price quotation* in an active market for identical assets or liabilities is the best evidence of fair value, and when such quotations exist, they are used to determine fair value. A financial instrument is regarded as quoted in an active market if quoted prices are readily and regularly available from an exchange, dealer, broker, industry group, pricing service, or regulatory agency, and those prices represent actual and regularly occurring market transactions on an arm's-length basis.

   Except for offsetting positions, assets are measured at the currently quoted bid price and liabilities are measured at the currently quoted asking price. When an entity has assets and liabilities with offsetting market risks, it may use midmarket prices for the offsetting positions. When current bid and asking prices are unavailable, the price of the most recent transaction provides evidence of fair value as long as there has not been a significant change in economic conditions since the time of the transaction. If circumstances have changed (e.g., a significant change in the risk-free interest rate) or the entity can demonstrate the last transaction does not reflect fair value (e.g., because it was not on arm's-length terms but a distress sale), the last transaction price is adjusted, as appropriate.

   The fair value of a portfolio of financial instruments is the product of the number of units of the instrument and its quoted market price. Therefore, portfolio factors are not considered in determining fair value. For instance, a control premium associated with holding a controlling interest or a liquidity discount associated with holding a large block of instruments that cannot be rapidly sold in the market would not be considered in determining fair value. Although such factors may affect the price that is paid for a group of instruments in an actual transaction, the effect of such factors is in practice difficult to quantify.

2. For assets or liabilities that are not quoted in active markets, fair value is determined using *valuation techniques*, such as discounted cash flow models or option pricing models. Such valuation techniques estimate the price that would have been paid in an arm's-length transaction motivated by normal business considerations on the date of the statement of financial position. If an entity uses a valuation technique to determine fair value, that technique should incorporate all factors that market participants would consider in setting a price, be consistent with accepted economic methodologies for pricing financial instruments, and maximize the use of market inputs.

   The fair value of financial liabilities incorporates the effect of the entity's own credit risk; that is, the higher the credit risk, the lower the fair value of the liability. However, the fair value of a financial liability that has a demand feature (e.g., a demand deposit liability) is not lower than the amount repayable on demand, discounted from the first date the amount could be required to be repaid.

PRACTICAL INSIGHT

Often the fair value of a debt instrument that does not have a quoted rate or price can be determined by scheduling the cash flows and discounting them using the applicable current market interest rate for debt instruments that have substantially the same terms and characteristics (similar remaining maturity, cash flow pattern, credit quality, currency risk, collateral, and interest basis) for which quoted rates in active markets exist. These and other techniques for determining fair value are discussed in finance and valuation textbooks.

Examples

Trading securities

Assume Entity A on December 15, 2009, acquires 1,000 shares in Entity B at a per share price of $55 for a total of $55,000 and classifies them as trading securities. On December 31, 2009, the quoted price of Entity B increases to $62, such that the fair value of all shares held in Entity B now equals $62,000. On January 1, 2010, Entity A sells the shares for a total of $62,000. In this case, the journal entries would be

December 15, 2009

Trading securities	55,000	
Cash		55,000

December 31, 2009

Trading securities	7,000	
Income from continuing operations		7,000

January 1, 2010

Cash	62,000	
Trading securities		62,000

Available-for-sale financial assets

If Entity A instead had classified the shares as available for sale, the journal entries would be

December 15, 2009

Available-for-sale financial assets	55,000	
Cash		55,000

December 31, 2009

Available-for-sale financial assets	7,000	
Accumulated other comprehensive income		7,000

January 1, 2010

Cash	62,000	
Accumulated other comprehensive income	7,000	
Available-for-sale financial assets		62,000
Gain on sale (available-for-sale financial asset)		7,000

Case Study 8

This case illustrates how to determine the fair value of a financial instrument.

Facts

Entity A is considering how to determine the fair value of these financial instruments:

(a) A share that is actively traded on a stock exchange
(b) A share for which no active market exists but for which quoted prices are available
(c) A loan asset originated by the entity
(d) A bond that is not actively traded but whose fair value can be determined by reference to quoted interest rates for government bonds
(e) A complex derivative that is tailor-made for the entity

Required

In each of these cases, discuss whether fair value would be determined using a quoted market price or a valuation technique under ASC 820.

Solution

(a) The fair value of a share that is actively traded on a stock exchange equals the quoted market price.

(b) The fair value of a share for which no active market exists, but for which quoted prices are available, would be determined using a valuation technique.

(c) The fair value of a loan asset originated by the entity would be determined using a valuation technique.

(d) The fair value of a bond that is not actively traded, but whose fair value can be determined by reference to quoted interest rates for government bonds, would be determined using a valuation technique.

(e) The fair value of a complex derivative that is tailor-made for the entity would be determined using a valuation technique.

Case Study 9

This case illustrates how to account for available-for-sale financial assets.

Facts

On August 1, 2007, Entity A purchased a two-year bond, which it classified as available for sale. The bond had a stated principal amount of $100,000, which Entity A will receive on August 1, 2009. The stated coupon interest rate was 10% per year, which is paid semiannually on December 31 and July 31. The bond was purchased at a quoted annual yield of 8% on a bond-equivalent yield basis.

Required

(a) What price did Entity A pay for the bond? (Hint: Compute the present value using a semiannual yield and semiannual periods.)

(b) Did Entity A purchase the bond at par, at a discount, or at a premium?

(c) Prepare the journal entry at the date Entity A purchased the bond. (Entity A paid cash to acquire the bond. Assume that no transaction costs were paid.)

(d) Prepare a bond amortization schedule for years 2007 to 2009. For each period, show cash interest receivable, recognized interest revenue, amortization of any bond discount or premium, and the carrying amount of the bond at the end of the period.

(e) Prepare the journal entries to record cash interest receivable and interest revenue on July 31, 2008.

(f) If the quoted market yield for the bond changes from 8% to 9% on December 31, 2008, should Entity A recognize an increase, a decrease, or no change in the carrying amount of the bond on that date? If you conclude that the carrying amount should change, compute the change and prepare the corresponding journal entries.

Solution

(a) Entity A paid a price of $103,629.90 for the bond. This price is determined by discounting the interest and principal cash flows using the yield at which the bond was purchased (i.e., 8%). More specifically, you can compute the price by

1. Computing the interest and principal cash flows and preparing a schedule showing the amounts and timing of the cash flows (column 1).

2. Determining the discount factors to use for a discount rate of 8% per year (column 2).

3. Multiplying each cash flow with its corresponding discount factor (column 3).

Since the stated coupon rate is 10% per year on a stated principal amount of $100,000, the total annual interest payment is $10,000 and the semiannual interest payment is half of that (i.e., $10,000/2 = $5,000).

On a bond-equivalent yield basis, the semiannual effective yield is simply half of the annual effective yield (i.e., 8% / 2 = 4%). In other words, the semiannual effective yield is not compounded, but doubled, to arrive at the quoted annual yield. This convention is commonly used in the marketplace.

Date	(1) Cash flow	(2) Discount factor	(3) Present value
12/31/2007	$5,000	$1 / (1 + 0.04) = 0.9615$	$ 4,807.69
7/31/2008	$5,000	$1 / (1 + 0.04)^2 = 0.9246$	$ 4,622.78
12/31/2008	$5,000	$1 / (1 + 0.04)^3 = 0.8890$	$ 4,444.98
7/31/2009	($100,000 + $5,000)	$1 / (1 + 0.04)^4 = 0.8548$	$ 89,754.44
Total			$103,629.89

Alternatively, you can use a discount factor for the principal payment and an annuity factor for the interest cash flows to compute the present value of the cash flows.

(b) Entity A purchased the bond at a premium. The amount of the premium is $3,629.90. When a bond is purchased at a price that is higher than its stated principal amount, it is said to be purchased at a premium. This occurs when the yield at which the bond is purchased is lower than the stated coupon yield, for instance, because market interest rates have declined since the bond was originally issued.

(c)   *January 1, 2007*

| Available-for-sale financial asset | 103,629.90 | |
| Cash | | 103,629.90 |

To record purchase of bond that is classified as available for sale

This amount is computed in question (a).

(d)

	(1) Cash interest receipts	(2) Interest revenue	(3) Amortization of premium	(4) Carrying amount
1/8/2007	—	—	—	103,629.90
12/31/2007	5,000.00	4,145.20	854.80	102,775.09
7/31/2008	5,000.00	4,111.00	889.00	101,886.09
12/31/2008	5,000.00	4,075.44	924.56	100,961.54
7/31/2009	5,000.00	4,038.46	961.54	100,000.00

Cash interest received (column 1) is computed as the stated nominal amount multiplied by the stated coupon interest rate for half a year (i.e., 100,000 × 10% × ½). Interest revenue reported in the income statement (column 2) is computed as the carrying amount in the previous period (column 4) times the effective interest rate (yield) at inception for half a year (i.e., previous carrying amount × 10% × ½). The amortization of the premium (column 3) is the difference between cash interest (column 1) and interest revenue (column 2). The carrying amount (column 4) equals the previous carrying amount (column 4) less the amortization of the premium during the period (column 3).

(e)   *July 31, 2008*

Interest receivable	5,000.00	
Available-for-sale financial asset		889.00
Interest revenue		4,111.00

To record interest revenue for the first half of 2008

(f) An increase in the current market yield of a bond results in a decrease in its fair value (an unrealized holding loss). Since the bond is classified as available for sale, Entity A should recognize this change in fair value as accumulated other comprehensive income, but not in earnings.

The new fair value is computed as the present value of the remaining cash flows discounted using the new quoted annual yield divided by half to obtain the semiannual yield (i.e., 9% / 2 = 4.5%):

$$($100,000 + $5,000) / 1.045 = $100,478.47$$

Since the carrying amount absent the change in interest rates would have been $100,961.54, an unrealized holding loss of $483.07 has occurred. The journal entries are

December 31, 2008

| Accumulated other comprehensive income | 483.07 | |
| Available-for-sale financial asset | | 483.07 |

To record the unrealized holding loss as a separate component of equity

Summary

Category	Type	Characteristics	Reported on statement of financial position	Reported in income
1. Held to maturity	Debt	Positive intent and ability to hold until maturity	Amortized cost	Interest Realized gains and losses
2. Trading	Debt or equity	Bought and held principally to sell short term	Fair value	Interest and dividends Realized gains and losses Unrealized gains and losses
3. Available for sale	Debt or equity	Neither held to maturity nor trading securities	Fair value Unrealized gains and losses to accumulated other comprehensive income (component of equity)	Interest and dividends Realized gains and losses

Impairment

ASC 320-10-35 establishes a multistep decision process to determine if an investment has been impaired, to evaluate whether the impairment is other than temporary (OTTI), and if OTTI is determined to have occurred, to measure the impairment loss.

Step 1. Determine whether the investment is impaired. An investment is impaired if its fair value is less than its cost. Cost as defined for this purpose includes adjustments made to the cost basis of an investment for accretion, amortization, previous other-than-temporary impairments, and hedging.

The unit of account used to determine impairment is the individual security level, defined as the level and method of aggregation that the reporting entity uses to measure realized and unrealized gains and losses on its debt and equity securities. For example, management may aggregate all equity securities of an issuer that have the same CUSIP number that were purchased in separate trade lots and use an average cost convention to compute realized or unrealized gains or losses.

In assessing impairment of debt securities, the investor is not permitted to combine separate contracts, such as guarantees or other credit enhancements.

The assessment of whether an investment is impaired is to be made for each interim and annual reporting period, subject to special provisions that apply to cost-method investments. After comparing fair value to cost, if cost exceeds fair value, the investment is considered impaired and the evaluator is to then proceed to step 2 to evaluate whether the impairment is considered to be other than temporary.

Step 2. Evaluate whether the impairment is other than temporary. If the fair value of the investment is less than its cost at the ending date of a reporting period (the date of the latest statement of financial position), management is tasked with evaluating whether the impairment is temporary or whether it is other than temporary. While the term *other than temporary* is not defined, the Financial Accounting Standards Board (FASB) affirmatively states that it does not mean permanent. Thus, a future recovery of all or a portion of the decline in fair value is not necessarily indicative that an assessment of OTTI made in prior periods was incorrect.

OTTI of available-for-sale equity securities. FASB does not provide specifics regarding how to make this determination. However, on April 13, 2009, the Staffs of the Division of Corporation Finance and the Office of the Chief Accountant of the U.S. Securities and Exchange Commission (SEC) issued Staff Accounting Bulletin (SAB) 111 (17 CFR Part 211) to amend Topic 5.M in the Codification of SABs (ASC 320-10-S99-1), which essentially carries forward previous guidance on OTTI of equity securities as well as making conforming amendments to exclude debt securities from the scope of the Topic. Topic 5M, *Other-Than-Temporary Impairment of Certain Investments in Debt and Equity Securities,* provides the next guidance, which, in the authors' opinion, represents the best thinking in the profession regarding impairment of equity securities.

When the fair value of an equity security declines, management is to start with a working premise that the decline may necessitate a write-down of the security. With that mind-set, management is to investigate the reasons for the decline by considering all available evidence to evaluate the AFS equity investment's realizable value. Many factors would be considered by management in performing the evaluation, and, of course, the evaluation will depend on the individual facts and circumstances. The SAB provides a few examples of factors that, when considered individually or in the aggregate, indicate that a decline in fair value of an AFS equity security is other than temporary and that an impairment write-down of the carrying value is required:

1. The period of time and the extent to which the fair value has been less than cost.
2. The financial condition and near-term prospects of the issuer, including any specific events that might influence the operations of the issuer, such as changes in technology that may impair the earnings potential of the investment or the discontinuance of a segment of the business that may affect the future earnings potential.
3. The intent or ability of the holder to retain its investment in the issuer for a period of time sufficient to allow for any anticipated recovery in fair value.

Unless there is existing evidence supporting a realizable value greater than or equal to the carrying value of the investment, a write-down to fair value accounted for as a realized loss is to be recorded. The loss is to be recognized as a charge to net income in the period in which it occurs, and the written-down value of the investment in investee becomes the new cost basis of the investment.

It is important to note that, if an investor has decided to sell an impaired AFS equity security, and the investor does not expect the fair value of the security to fully recover prior to the expected time of sale, the security is to be considered other-than-temporarily impaired in the period in which the investor decides to sell the security. However, even if a decision to sell the security has not been made, the investor is to recognize OTTI when that impairment has been determined to have been incurred.

OTTI of debt securities. If the fair value of a debt security is less than its amortized cost basis (ACB) at the date of the statement of financial position, management is to assess whether the impairment is an OTTI. If management intends to sell the security, then an OTTI is considered to have been incurred.

If management does not intend to sell the security, management is to consider all available evidence to assess whether, more likely than not (MLTN), it will be required to sell the security prior to recovery of its ACB (e.g., whether the entity's cash or working capital requirements; or contractual or regulatory obligations will require sale of the security prior to the occurrence of a forecasted recovery). If it is MLTN that sale will be required prior to recovery of the security's ACB, OTTI is considered to have been incurred.

If, at the measurement date, management does not expect to recover the entire ACB, this precludes an assertion that it will recover the ACB irrespective of whether management's intent is to continue holding the security or to sell the security. Therefore, when this is the case, OTTI is considered to have been incurred.

Expected recovery is computed by comparing the present value of cash flows expected to be collected (PVCF) from the security to the security's ACB.

If PVCF < ACB, the entire ACB of the security will not be recovered and a credit loss has occurred, and an OTTI has been incurred.

Amortized cost basis includes adjustments made to the original cost of the investment for such items as

1. Accretion.
2. Amortization.
3. Cash collections.
4. Previous OTTI recognized as charges to net income (less any cumulative-effect adjustments recognized in transitioning to the provisions of this FSP).
5. Fair value hedge accounting adjustments.

Step 3. Recognition of an other-than-temporary impairment. If, as a result of step 2, management judges the impairment to be other than temporary, the reporting entity recognizes an impairment loss as a charge to net income for the entire difference between the investment's cost and its fair value at the date of the statement of financial position. The impairment measurement is not to include any partial recoveries that might have occurred subsequent to the date of the statement of financial position but prior to issuance of the financial statements.

Example of other-than-temporary impairment of an available-for-sale security

In January 2010 new information comes to the attention of Neihaus Corporation management regarding the viability of Mitzen Corp. Based on this information, it is determined that the decline in Mitzen preferred stock is probably not a temporary one, but rather is other than temporary (i.e., the asset impairment requires financial statement recognition). ASC 320 prescribes that such a decline be reflected in net income and the written-down value be treated as the new cost basis. The fair value has remained at the amount last reported, $109,500. Accordingly, the entry to recognize the fact of the investment's permanent impairment is

Loss on holding equity securities	15,500	
Unrealized loss on securities—available for sale (other comprehensive income)		15,500

Any subsequent recovery in this value would not be recognized in net income unless realized through a sale of the investment to an unrelated entity in an arm's-length transaction, as long as the investment continues to be categorized as "available for sale," as distinct from "held for trading." However, if there is an increase in value (not limited to just a recovery of the amount of the loss just recognized, of course), the increase will be added to the investment account and shown in a separate account in stockholders' equity, since the asset is to be marked to fair value on the statement of financial position.

It should be noted that the issue of other-than-temporary impairment does not arise in the context of investments held for trading purposes, since unrealized holding gains and losses are immediately recognized without limitation. In effect, the distinction between realized and unrealized gains or losses does not exist for trading securities.

Example of temporary impairment

In March 2010 further information comes to management's attention that suggests that the decline in Mitzen preferred was indeed only a temporary decline; in fact, the value of Mitzen now rises to $112,000. Since the carrying value after the recognition of the impairment was $109,500, which is treated as the new cost basis for purposes of measuring further declines or recoveries, the increase to $112,000 will be accounted for as an increase to be reflected in the additional stockholders' equity account (accumulated other comprehensive income or AOCI):

Investment in equity securities—available for sale	2,500	
Unrealized gain on securities—available for sale (other comprehensive income)		2,500

Note that this increase in fair value is not recognized in current net income, since the investment is still considered to be available for sale rather than a part of the trading portfolio. Even though the previous decline in Mitzen stock was realized in current net income, because it was judged at the time to be an OTTI, the recovery is not permitted to be recognized in net income. Rather, the change in fair value will be included in other comprehensive income and then displayed in AOCI.

DERIVATIVES

Derivative financial instruments (DFI) are financial instruments whose fair value correlates to a specified benchmark, such as stock prices, interest rates, mortgage rates, currency rates, commodity prices, or some other agreed-on reference. (These are called "underlyings.") Option contracts and forward contracts are the two basic forms of derivatives, and they can be traded either publicly or privately. Forward contracts have symmetrical gain and loss characteristics—that is, they provide exposure to both losses and gains from market movements, although generally there is no initial premium to be paid. Forward contracts usually are settled on or near the delivery date by paying or receiving cash, rather than by physical delivery. Option contracts, however, have asymmetrical loss functions: They provide little or no exposure to losses (beyond the premium paid) from unfavorable market movements but can provide large benefits from favorable market movements.

Typical DFIs *include*

1. Option contracts
2. Interest rate caps
3. Interest rate floors
4. Fixed-rate loan commitments

5. Note issuance facilities
6. Letters of credit
7. Forward contracts
8. Forward interest rate agreements

9. Interest rate collars
10. Futures
11. Swaps
12. Instruments with similar characteristics

DFIs *exclude* all on-balance-sheet receivables and payables including

1. Mortgage-backed securities
2. Interest-only obligations
3. Principal-only obligations
4. Indexed debt
5. Other optional characteristics incorporated within those receivables and payables (such as convertible bond conversion or call terms)

In addition, DFI *exclude* contracts that either

- Require exchange for a nonfinancial commodity or
- Permit settlement by delivering a nonfinancial commodity.

Determining whether changes in fair value of a derivative should be recognized either in profit or loss or in equity depends in part on whether the entity uses the derivative to speculate or offset risk. As a general rule, changes in fair value of a derivative are recognized in earnings. However, when the derivative is used to offset risk and special hedge accounting conditions are met, some or all changes in fair value are recognized as a separate component of equity.

As discussed previously, there is an exception to the requirement to measure derivatives at fair value for derivatives that are linked to and must be settled by an investment in an unquoted equity instrument that cannot be reliably measured at fair value. For instance, an option to buy shares in a start-up entity that is not publicly traded may qualify for this exception. If the fair value cannot be reliably measured, such a derivative would be measured at cost instead of fair value (i.e., close to zero in many cases).

Case Study 10

This case illustrates how to account for derivatives.

Facts

On January 1, 2008, Entity A enters into a forward contract to purchase on January 1, 2010, a specified number of barrels of oil at a fixed price. Entity A is speculating that the price of oil will increase and plans to net settle the contract if the price increases. Entity A does not pay anything to enter into the forward contract on January 1, 2008. Entity A does not designate the forward contract as a hedging instrument. At the end of 2008, the fair value of the forward contract has increased to $400,000. At the end of 2009, the fair value of the forward contract has declined to $350,000.

Required

Prepare the appropriate journal entries on January 1, 2008, December 31, 2008, and December 31, 2009.

Solution

The journal entries are

> *January 1, 2008*
> No entry is required.

December 31, 2008		
Derivative asset	400,000	
Gain		400,000
December 31, 2009		
Loss	50,000	
Derivative asset		50,000

Embedded Derivatives

Sometimes derivatives are embedded in other types of contracts. For instance, one or more derivative features may be embedded in a loan, bond, share, lease, insurance contract, or purchase or sale contract. When a derivative feature is embedded in a nonderivative contract, the derivative is referred to as an *embedded derivative* and the contract in which it is embedded is referred to as a *host contract*.

Example

An entity may issue a bond with interest or principal payments that are indexed to the price of gold (e.g., the interest payments increase and decrease with the price of gold). Such a bond is a contract that combines a host debt instrument and an embedded derivative on the price of gold.

To achieve consistency in the accounting for derivatives (whether embedded or not) and to prevent entities from circumventing the recognition and measurement requirements for derivatives merely by embedding them in other types of contracts, entities are required to identify any embedded derivatives and account for them separately from their hosts contracts if these three conditions are met:

1. On a stand-alone basis, the embedded feature meets the definition of a derivative.
2. The combined (hybrid) contract is not required to be measured at fair value under generally accepted accounting principles (GAAP) with changes reported in earnings.
3. The economic characteristics and risks of the embedded feature are *not* closely related to the economic characteristics and risks of the host contract.

When any of these three conditions is not met, the embedded derivative is not separated (i.e., only if all conditions are met is an embedded derivative separated). When all of these conditions are met, the embedded derivative is separated (i.e., bifurcated) from the host contract and accounted for like any other derivative. The host instrument is accounted for under the accounting requirements that apply to the host instrument as if it had no embedded derivative.

The flowchart illustrates these three conditions.

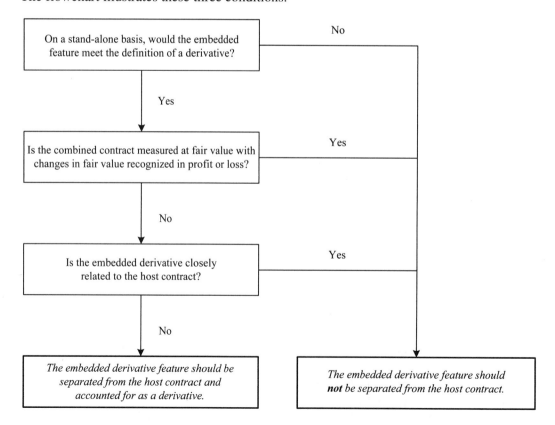

Example

A convertible bond is an instrument that combines both a host debt instrument and an equity conversion option (i.e., an option that enables the holder [investor] to convert the bond into a predetermined number of shares on specified conditions). In this case, the investor usually would be required to separate the equity conversion option from the investment in the host debt instrument and account for the equity conversion option separately as a derivative.

If an entity is required to separate an embedded derivative but is unable to reliably measure the embedded derivative, it is required to treat the entire hybrid instrument as a financial asset or financial liability and be measured at fair value.

Case Study 11

This case illustrates when to separate embedded derivatives.

Facts

Entity A is seeking to identify embedded derivatives that are required to be separated under ASC 815. It is considering whether these contracts contain embedded derivatives:

    (a) An investment in a bond whose interest payments are linked to the price of gold. The bond is classified as trading.

    (b) An investment in a bond whose interest payments are linked to the price of silver. The bond is classified as available for sale.

    (c) An investment in a convertible debt instrument that is classified as available for sale.

    (d) A lease contract that has a rent adjustment clause based on inflation.

    (e) An issued convertible debt instrument.

Required

Identify any embedded derivatives in these cases and, in each case, determine whether any identified embedded derivative requires separate accounting.

Solution

    (a) An investment in a bond whose interest payments are linked to the price of gold contains an embedded derivative on gold. However, because the bond is classified as trading, the embedded derivative should not be separated.

    (b) An investment in a bond whose interest payments are linked to the price of silver contains an embedded derivative on silver. Because the bond is not measured at fair value with changes in fair value recognized in earnings and a commodity derivative is not closely related to a host debt contract, the embedded derivative is separated and accounted for as a derivative.

    (c) An investment in a convertible debt instrument that is classified as available for sale contains an embedded equity conversion option. Because the bond is not measured at fair value with changes in fair value recognized in profit or loss and an equity conversion option is not closely related to a host debt contract, the embedded derivative is separated and accounted for as a derivative.

    (d) A lease contract that has a rent adjustment clause based on inflation contains an embedded derivative on inflation. However, the embedded derivative is not separated from the lease contract because a rent adjustment clause based on inflation is considered to be closely related to the host lease contract.

    (e) An issued convertible debt instrument contains an embedded equity conversion option. However, the equity conversion option generally is not accounted for as a derivative but is separated as an equity component and accounted for as own equity.

HEDGE ACCOUNTING

Hedging is a risk management technique that involves using one or more derivatives or other hedging instruments to offset changes in fair value or cash flows of one or more assets, liabilities, or future transactions. ASC 815 contains special accounting principles for hedging activities. When certain conditions are met, entities are permitted to depart from some of the ordinary accounting requirements and instead apply *hedge accounting* to assets and liabilities that form part of hedging relationships. These requirements are optional (i.e., entities are not required to apply hedge accounting unless they decide to do so). The effect of hedge accounting is that gains and losses on the hedging instrument and the hedged item are recognized in the same periods (i.e., gains and losses are matched).

Hedging Relationships

A *hedging relationship* has two components:

1. A *hedging instrument.* A hedging instrument is a derivative or, for a hedge of the risk of changes in foreign currency exchange rates, a nonderivative financial asset or nonderivative financial liability. To be designated as a hedging instrument, the fair value or cash flows of the hedging instrument should be expected to offset changes in the fair value or cash flows of the hedged item. In addition, the hedging instrument must be with an external party (i.e., an internal derivative with another division does not qualify as a hedging instrument) and not be a written option (or net written option).
2. A *hedged item.* A hedged item is an asset, liability, firm commitment, highly probable forecast transaction, or net investment in a foreign operation. To be designated as a hedged item, the designated hedged item should expose the entity to risk of changes in fair value or future cash flows.

ASC 815 identifies three types of hedging relationships:

1. Fair value hedges
2. Cash flow hedges
3. Net investment in a foreign operation

Accounting Treatment

Hedge accounting links the accounting for (1) the hedging instrument and (2) the hedged item to allow offsetting changes in fair value or cash flows to be recognized in the financial statements in the same time periods. Generally, hedge accounting involves either one of these two accounting treatments:

1. Changes in fair value of the *hedged item* are recognized in the current period to offset the recognition of changes in the fair value of the hedging instrument. This is the accounting treatment for fair value hedges.
2. Changes in fair value of the *hedging instrument* are *deferred* as accumulated other comprehensive income to the extent the hedge is effective and released to earnings in the time periods in which the hedged item impacts earnings. This is the accounting treatment for cash flow hedges and a net investment in a foreign operation.

PRACTICAL INSIGHT

Hedge accounting is not always necessary to reflect the effect of hedging activities in the financial statements. When consistent accounting principles apply to offsetting positions (e.g., when both the hedging instrument and the hedged item are accounted for at fair value or at amortized cost), there is no need for an entity to apply hedge accounting to achieve consistent accounting for the offsetting positions.

Hedge Accounting Conditions

As discussed, hedge accounting is optional and allows entities to defer or accelerate the recognition of gains and losses under otherwise applicable accounting requirements. To prevent abuse, therefore, ASC 815 limits the use of hedge accounting to situations where special hedge accounting conditions are met. To be eligible for designation as a hedged item, an asset or liability must meet all of these criteria:

1. There is formal designation and documentation of the hedging relationship and the entity's risk management objective and strategy for undertaking the hedge. Hedge accounting is permitted only from the date such designation and documentation is in place.
2. The hedging relationship is effective.

   a. The hedge is expected to be highly effective in achieving offsetting changes in fair value or cash flows attributable to the hedged risk ("prospective" effectiveness).
   b. The effectiveness of the hedge can be measured reliably.
   c. The hedge is assessed on an ongoing basis and determined actually to have been highly effective throughout the financial reporting periods for which the hedge was designated ("retrospective" effectiveness).

3. For cash flow hedges of forecast transactions, the hedged forecast transaction must be highly probable and must present an exposure to variations in cash flows that could ultimately affect earnings.

Example

The designation and documentation of a hedging relationship should include identification of

- The hedging relationship.
- The hedged item(s) or transaction(s).
- The nature of the risk(s) being hedged.
- The method that will be used to retrospectively and prospectively assess the hedging instrument's effectiveness in offsetting exposure to changes in the hedged item's fair value (if a fair value hedge) or hedged transaction's variability in cash flows (if a cash flow hedge) attributable to hedged risk.
- The method that will be used to measure hedge ineffectiveness.
- If the entity is hedging foreign currency risk on an after-tax basis, that assessment of effectiveness, including calculation of ineffectiveness, will be on an after-tax basis (rather than on a pretax basis).

Case Study 12

This case considers the reasons and conditions for hedge accounting.

Required

(1) Describe the three types of hedging relationships specified by ASC 815.
(2) Discuss in what circumstances entities may want to apply hedge accounting.
(3) Discuss the conditions for hedge accounting.

Solution

(1) ASC 815 identifies three types of hedging relationships:

(a) *Fair value hedges* are hedges of the exposure to changes in fair value of a recognized asset or liability or an unrecognized firm commitment that is attributable to a particular risk and that could affect earnings. Under fair value hedge accounting, if the hedged item is otherwise measured at cost or amortized cost, the measurement of the hedged item is adjusted for changes in its fair value attributable to the hedged risk. These changes are recognized in earnings. If the hedged item is an available-for-sale financial asset, changes in fair value that would otherwise have been included in equity are recognized in earnings.

(b) *Cash flow hedges* are hedges of the exposure to variability in cash flows that is attributable to a particular risk associated with a recognized asset or liability or a highly probable forecast transaction and could affect earnings. Under cash flow hedge accounting, changes in the fair value of the hedging instrument attributable to the hedged risk are deferred as a separate component of equity to the extent the hedge is effective (rather than being recognized immediately in earnings).

(c) *Hedges of net investments in foreign operations* are accounted for like cash flow hedges.

(2) Entities may want to use hedge accounting to avoid mismatches in the recognition of gains and losses on related transactions. When an entity uses a derivative (or other instrument measured at fair value) to hedge the value of an asset or liability measured at cost or amortized cost or not rec-

ognized at all, accounting that is not reflective of the entity's financial position and financial performance may result because of the different measurement bases used for the hedging instrument and the hedged item. The normally applicable accounting requirements would include the changes in fair value of a derivative in earnings but not the changes in fair value of the hedged item in earnings. In addition, when an entity uses a derivative (or other instrument measured at fair value) to hedge a future expected transaction, the entity would like to defer the recognition of the change in fair value of the derivative until the future transaction affects earnings. Otherwise, the changes in fair value of a derivative hedging instrument would be recognized in earnings without a corresponding offset associated with the hedged item.

(3) The hedge accounting conditions are listed next.

   (a) There is formal designation and documentation of the hedging relationship and the entity's risk management objective and strategy for undertaking the hedge. Hedge accounting is permitted only from the date such designation and documentation is in place.
   (b) The hedge is expected to be highly effective in achieving offsetting changes in fair value or cash flows attributable to the hedged risk.
   (c) The effectiveness of the hedge can be measured reliably.
   (d) The hedge is assessed on an ongoing basis and determined actually to have been highly effective throughout the financial reporting periods for which the hedge was designated.
   (e) For cash flow hedges, a hedged forecast transaction must be highly probable and must present an exposure to variations in cash flows that could ultimately affect earnings.

Fair Value Hedge

A *fair value hedge* is a hedge of the exposure to changes in fair value of a recognized asset or liability or an unrecognized firm commitment that is attributable to a particular risk and that could affect earnings. (A firm commitment is a binding agreement for the exchange of a specified quantity of resources at a specified price on a specified future date or dates.)

Fair value hedge accounting involves this accounting:

- The hedging instrument is measured at fair value with changes in fair value recognized in earnings.
- If the hedged item is an available-for-sale financial asset, changes in fair value that would otherwise have been included in accumulated other comprehensive income are recognized in earnings.

Under fair value hedge accounting, changes in the fair value of the hedging instrument and of the hedged item are recognized in earnings at the same time. The result is that there will be no (net) impact on earnings of the hedging instrument and the hedged item if the hedge is fully effective, because changes in fair value will offset each other. If the hedge is not 100% effective (i.e., the changes in fair value do not fully offset), such ineffectiveness is automatically reflected in earnings.

Example

Fair value hedges include

- A hedge of the exposure to changes in the fair value of a fixed interest rate loan due to changes in market interest rates. Such a hedge could be entered into by either the borrower or the lender.
- A hedge of the exposure to changes in the fair value of an available-for-sale investment.
- A hedge of the exposure to changes in the fair value of a nonfinancial asset (e.g., inventory).
- A hedge of the exposure to changes in the fair value of a firm commitment to purchase or sell a nonfinancial item (e.g., a contract to purchase or sell gold for a fixed price on a future date).

Example

On January 1, 20X5, Entity A purchases a five-year bond that has a principal amount of $100,000 and pays annually fixed interest rate of 5% per year (i.e., $5,000 per year). Entity A classifies the bond as an available-for-sale financial asset. Current market interest rates for similar five-year bonds are also 5% such that the fair value of the bond and the carrying amount of the bond on the acquisition date is equal to its principal amount of $100,000.

Because the interest rate is fixed, Entity A is exposed to the risk of declines in fair value of the bond. If market interest rates increase above 5%, for example, the fair value of the bond will decrease below $100,000. This is because the bond would pay a lower fixed interest rate than equivalent alternative investments available in the market (i.e., the present value of the principal and interest cash flows discounted using market interest rates would be less than the principal amount of the bond).

To eliminate the risk of declines in fair value due to increases in market interest rates, Entity A enters into a derivative to hedge (offset) this risk. More specifically, on January 1, 20X5, Entity A enters into an interest rate swap to exchange the fixed interest rate payments it receives on the bond for floating interest rate payments. If the derivative hedging instrument is effective, any declines in the fair value of the bond should offset by opposite increases in the fair value of the derivative instrument. Entity A designates and documents the swap as a hedging instrument of the bond.

On entering into the swap on January 1, 20X5, the swap has a net fair value of zero. (In practice, swaps usually are entered into at a zero fair value. This is achieved by setting the interest payments that will be paid and received such that the present value of the expected floating interest payments Entity A will receive exactly equals the present value of the fixed interest payments Entity A will pay because of the swap agreement.) Therefore, no journal entry is required on this date.

At the end of 20X5, the bond has accrued interest of $5,000. Entity A makes this journal entry:

Interest receivable	5,000	
Interest income		5,000

In addition, market interest rates have increased to 6%, such that the fair value of the bond has decreased to $96,535. Because the bond is classified as available for sale, the decrease in fair value would normally have been recorded directly in equity rather than in earnings. However, since the bond is classified as a hedged item in a fair value hedge of the exposure to interest rate risk, this change in fair value of the bond is instead recognized in earnings:

Hedging loss (hedged item)	3,465	
Available-for-sale financial asset		3,465

At the same time, Entity A determines that the fair value of the swap has increased by $3,465 to $3,465. Since the swap is a derivative, it is measured at fair value with changes in fair value recognized in earnings. Therefore, Entity A makes this journal entry:

Swap asset	3,465	
Hedging gain (hedging instrument)		3,465

Since the changes in fair value of the hedged item and the hedging instrument exactly offset, the hedge is 100% effective, and the net effect on earnings is zero.

Case Study 13

This case illustrates the accounting for a fair value hedge.

Facts

Entity A has originated a 5% fixed rate loan asset that is measured at amortized cost ($100,000). Because Entity A is considering whether to securitize the loan asset (i.e., to sell it in a securitization transaction), it wants to eliminate the risk of changes in the fair value of the loan asset. Thus, on January 1, 20X6, Entity A enters into a pay-fixed, receive-floating interest rate swap to convert the fixed interest receipts into floating interest receipts and thereby offset the exposure to changes in fair value. Entity A designates the swap as a hedging instrument in a fair value hedge of the loan asset.

Market interest rates increase. At the end of the year, Entity A receives $5,000 in interest income on the loan and $200 in net interest payments on the swap. The change in the fair value of the interest rate swap is an increase of $1,300. At the same time, the fair value of the loan asset decreases by $1,300.

Required

Prepare the appropriate journal entries at the end of the year. Assume that all conditions for hedge accounting are met.

Solution

Cash	5,000	
Interest income		5,000

To record interest income on the loan

Cash	200	
Interest income		200

To record the net interest settlement of the swap

Derivative	1,300	
Hedging gain		1,300

To record the increase in the fair value of the swap

Hedging loss	1,300	
Loan asset		1,300

To record the decrease in the fair value of the loan asset attributable to the hedged risk

Cash Flow Hedge

A *cash flow hedge* is a hedge of the exposure to variability in cash flows that

- Is attributable to a particular risk associated with a recognized asset or liability or a highly probable forecast transaction; *and*
- Could affect earnings.

A forecast transaction is an uncommitted but anticipated future transaction.
Cash flow hedge accounting involves this accounting:

- The effective portion of the gain or loss on a derivative instrument designated as a cash flow hedge is reported in other comprehensive income, and the ineffective portion is reported in earnings.
- The accounting for the hedged item is not adjusted.
- If a hedge of a forecast transaction subsequently results in the recognition of a financial asset or financial liability, the deferred gains and losses are reported in other comprehensive income.
- When the hedged item affects earnings (e.g., through depreciation or amortization), any corresponding amounts in accumulated other comprehensive income should be reclassified into earnings.

To the extent the cash flow hedge is not fully effective, the ineffective portion of the change in fair value of the derivative is recognized immediately in earnings.

Example

Cash flow hedges include

- A hedge of the exposure to variable interest cash flows on a bond that pays floating interest payments.
- A hedge of the cash flows from a forecast sale of an asset.
- A hedge of the foreign currency exposure associated with a firm commitment to purchase or sell a nonfinancial item.

Example

Entity A has the euro as its functional currency. It expects to purchase a machine for $10,000 on October 31, 20X6. Accordingly, it is exposed to the risk of increases in the dollar rate. If the dollar rate increases before the purchase takes place, the entity will have to pay more euros to obtain the $10,000 that it will have to pay for the machine. To offset the risk of increases in the dollar rate, the entity enters into a forward contract on April 30, 20X6, to purchase $10,000 in six months for a fixed amount (€8,000). Entity A designates the forward contract as a hedging instrument in a cash flow hedge of its exposure to increases in the dollar rate. At inception, the forward contract has a fair value of zero, so no journal entry is required.

On July 31, the dollar has appreciated, such that $10,000 for delivery on October 31, 20X6, costs €9,000 on the market. Therefore, the forward contract has increased in fair value to €1,000 (i.e., the difference between the committed price of €8,000 and the current price of €9,000 [ignoring, for simplicity, the effect of differences in interest rates between the two currencies]). Entity A still expects to purchase the machine for $10,000, so it concludes that the hedge is 100% effective. Because the hedge is fully effective, the entire change in the fair value of the hedging instrument is recognized directly in other comprehensive income. Entity A makes this entry:

Forward asset	1,000	
Accumulated other comprehensive income		1,000

On October 31, 20X6, the dollar rate has further increased, such that $10,000 costs €9,500 in the spot market. Therefore, the fair value of the forward contract has increased to €1,500 (i.e., the difference between the committed price of €8,000 and the spot price of €9,500). It still expects to purchase the machine for $10,000 and makes this journal entry:

Forward asset	500	
Accumulated other comprehensive income		500

The forward contract is settled and Entity A makes this entry:

Cash	1,500	
Forward asset		1,500

Entity A purchases the machine for $10,000 (€9,500) and makes this journal entry:

Machine	9,500	
Accounts payable		9,500

Depending on Entity A's accounting policy, the deferred gain or loss remaining in equity of €1,500 should either (1) remain in other comprehensive income and be released from equity as the machine is depreciated or otherwise affects earnings or (2) be deducted from the initial carrying amount of the machine. Assuming the latter treatment, Entity A would make this journal entry:

Accumulated other comprehensive income	1,500	
Machine		1,500

The net effect of the cash flow hedge is to lock in a price of €8,000 for the machine.

Example

At the beginning of 20X0, Entity B issues a 10-year liability with a principal amount of $100,000 for $100,000 (i.e., at par). The bond pays floating interest that resets each year as market interest rates change. Entity A measures the liability at amortized cost ($100,000). Because the interest rate regularly resets to market interest rates, the fair value of the liability remains approximately constant irrespective of how market interest rates change. However, Entity B wishes to convert the floating rate payments to fixed rate payments in order to hedge its exposure to changes in cash flows due to changes in market interest rates over the life of the liability.

To hedge the exposure, Entity B enters into a five-year interest rate swap under which the entity pays fixed rate payments (5%) and in return receives floating rate payments that exactly offset the floating rate payments it makes on the liability. Entity B designates and documents the swap as a cash flow hedge of its exposure to variable interest payments on the bond. On entering into the interest rate swap, it has a fair value of zero. The effect of that interest rate swap is to offset the exposure to changes in interest cash flows to be paid on the liability. In effect, the interest rate swap converts the liability's floating rate payments into fixed rate payments, thereby eliminating the entity's exposure to changes in cash flows attributable to changes in interest rates resulting from the liability.

At the end of 20X5, the bond has accrued interest of $6,000. Entity A makes this journal entry:

Interest expense	6,000	
Bond interest payable		6,000

At the same time, a net interest payment of $1,000 has accrued under the swap for the year. Therefore, Entity A makes this journal entry:

Swap interest receivable	1,000	
Interest expense		1,000

The net effect on earnings is fixed net interest expense of $5,000 (= 6,000 – 1,000).

Because the swap is a derivative, it is measured at fair value. Entity A determines that the fair value of the swap (excluding accrued interest) has increased by $5,200. As the swap is designated as a hedging instrument in a cash flow hedge, the change in fair value is not recognized in earnings but as accumulated other comprehensive income to the extent the swap is effective. In this case, Entity A determines that the swap is 100% effective. Therefore, Entity A makes this journal entry:

Swap asset	5,200	
Accumulated other comprehensive income		5,200

Because the fair value of the swap will converge to zero by its maturity, the hedging reserve for the swap will also converge to zero by its maturity to the extent the hedge remains in place and is effective.

Case Study 14

This case illustrates the accounting for a cash flow hedge.

Facts

Entity A is a producer of widgets. To hedge the risk of declines in the price of 100 widgets that it expects to sell on December 31, 20X9, Entity A on January 1, 20X8, enters into a net-settled forward contract on 100 widgets for delivery on December 31, 20X9. During 20X8, the change in the fair value of the forward contract is a decrease of $8,000. During 20X9, the change in the fair value of the forward contract is an increase of $2,000. On December 31, 20X9, Entity A settles the forward contract by paying $6,000. At the same time, it sells 100 widgets to customers for $93,000.

Required

Prepare the appropriate journal entries on January 1, 20X8, December 31, 20X9, and December 31, 20X9. Assume that all conditions for hedge accounting are met and that the hedging relationship is fully effective (100%).

Solution

January 1, 20X8
No entry required.

December 31, 20X8

Accumulated other comprehensive income	8,000	
Derivative liability		8,000

To record the decrease in fair value of the hedging instrument

December 31, 20X9

Derivative liability	2,000	
Accumulated other comprehensive income		2,000

To record the increase in fair value of the hedging instrument

Derivative liability	6,000	
Cash		6,000

To record the settlement of the hedging instrument

Cash	93,000	
Accumulated other comprehensive income		6,000
Sales revenue		87,000

To record the sale and the associated amount deferred in equity related to the hedge of the sale

Hedge of a Net Investment in a Foreign Operation

A foreign operation is an entity that is a subsidiary, associate, joint venture, or branch of a reporting entity, the activities of which are based or conducted in a country or currency other than those of the reporting entity. A net investment in a foreign operation is the amount of the reporting entity's interest in the net assets of that operation. A hedge of net investment in a foreign operation is accounted for like a cash flow hedge. In a hedge of a net investment, therefore, changes in fair value of the hedging instrument are reported in the cumulative translation adjustment section of other comprehensive income to the extent the hedge is effective (rather than being recognized immediately in earnings) and recognized in earnings on the disposal of the net investment.

Example

To hedge its net investment in a foreign operation that has the Japanese yen as its functional currency, Entity A borrows ¥100,000,000. Assuming all hedge accounting conditions are met, Entity A may designate its borrowing as a hedging instrument in a hedge of the net investment. As a result, foreign currency gains and losses on the borrowing that would otherwise have been included in earnings would be deferred in accumulated other comprehensive income to the extent the hedge is effective until the disposal of the net investment.

Hedge Effectiveness Assessment and Measurement

As mentioned, two of the conditions for hedge accounting are that the hedge is

1. Expected to be highly effective in achieving offsetting changes in fair value or cash flows during the period for which the hedge is designated (*prospective effectiveness*).
2. Determined actually to have been highly effective throughout the reporting period for which the hedge was designated (*retrospective effectiveness*).

ASC 815 does not define hedging effectiveness quantitatively. However, it is useful in this regard to contemplate the similar international financial reporting Standard, IAS 39. That Standard specifies that a hedge is normally regarded as highly effective if, at inception and throughout the life of the hedge, the enterprise can expect that the change in fair values of the hedging instrument and the hedged item will "almost fully offset." In addition, the Standard requires that actual results be within a range of 80% to 125%. Interpretive guidance to that Standard suggests that the appropriateness of any method of assessing hedge effectiveness depends on the nature of the risk being hedged and the type of hedging instrument used. Any method of assessing effectiveness must be reasonable and consistent with other similar hedges unless different methods are explicitly justified.

Logic suggests that the approach used under IAS 39 could also be applied under ASC 815, with a range of 80% to 125% being defined as effectiveness for hedge accounting purposes. This guidance has always appeared reasonable, particularly in the absence of any quantitative criteria for hedge effectiveness under U.S. GAAP.

Example

If actual results are such that the gain on the hedging instrument is $90 and the loss on the hedged item is $100, the degree of offset is 90% (= 90 / 100), or 111% (= 100 / 90). The hedge would be considered to be highly effective because the degree of offset is between 80% and 125%.

Hedge effectiveness is important not only as a condition for hedge accounting but also because the measurement of hedge effectiveness determines how much ineffectiveness will be reflected in earnings. To the extent the changes do not fully offset, such differences reflect ineffectiveness that generally should be included in earnings. Such ineffectiveness may exist even though a hedge is determined to be highly effective based on the prospective or retrospective hedge effectiveness assessment for purposes of continued qualification for hedge accounting.

Example

If, for a fair value hedge, the gain on the hedging instrument is $90 and the loss on the hedged item is $100, a net loss of $10 would be included in earnings.

For a qualifying cash flow hedge, ineffectiveness is included in earnings to the extent that the cumulative gain or loss on the hedging instrument exceeds the cumulative gain or loss on the hedged item since the inception of the hedging relationship (overhedging). If the cumulative gain or loss on the hedged item exceeds the cumulative gain or loss on the hedging instrument (underhedging), ineffectiveness also is reported in earnings. This is because—for a cash flow hedge—the hedged item is a future transaction that does not qualify for accounting recognition.

Discontinuation of Hedge Accounting

In any of these circumstances, an entity should discontinue hedge accounting prospectively:

- The hedging instrument expires or is sold, terminated, or exercised.

- The hedge no longer meets the hedge accounting conditions.
- The entity revokes the hedge designation.
- A hedged forecasted transaction is no longer expected to occur.

For discontinued fair value hedges, any previous hedge accounting adjustment to the carrying amount of hedged interest-bearing assets or liabilities are amortized over the remaining maturity of those assets and liabilities. Other hedge accounting adjustments to the carrying amount of hedged items remain in the carrying amount.

For discontinued cash flow hedges, hedging gains and losses that have been deferred in accumulated other comprehensive income remain there until the hedged item affects earnings unless a forecast transaction is no longer expected to occur, in which case the net gain or loss is recognized immediately in earnings.

DISCLOSURES

Fair Value Disclosures

Certain reporting entities are required to disclose the fair values of all (recognized and unrecognized) financial instruments that it is practicable to estimate, including liabilities. Pertinent descriptive information as to the fair value of the instrument is to be presented if an estimate of fair value cannot actually be made without incurring excessive costs.

These fair value disclosures are optional under ASC 825-10-50 for entities that

1. Have total assets less than $100 million at the date of the statement of financial position; and
2. Did not hold or issue any derivative financial instruments during the reporting period; and
3. Are not considered to be public enterprises under the definition in the ASC Master Glossary.

If the carrying amount for trade receivables and payables approximates their fair values (which is normally the case), no disclosure is required.

If an estimate of fair value cannot be made without incurring excessive costs, management is to disclose

1. Information pertinent to estimating fair value, such as carrying amount, effective interest rate, and maturities.
2. The reasons why estimating fair value is not practicable.

Derivatives Disclosures

ASC 815 imposes requirements for specific disclosures, for every annual and interim reporting period for which a statement of financial position is presented, about derivative instruments and nonderivative instruments designated and qualifying as hedging instruments. This disclosure requirement would also apply to hybrid instruments that have embedded credit derivatives. The purpose of the disclosures would enable users of financial statements to assess the potential effects of the credit derivatives on the financial position, financial performance, and cash flows of the entity. These items are required to be disclosed:

1. The nature of the credit derivative, including the terms, the objectives for using the derivative instruments, the circumstances that would require the seller to perform under the credit derivative, and the current status of the performance risk of the credit derivative.
2. The maximum potential of future payments the seller would be required to pay under the terms of the credit derivative. If the seller cannot determine an estimate of the maximum potential amount of future payments under the credit derivative, then the entity needs to disclose the reasons why it cannot estimate the maximum potential amount.
3. The fair value of the credit derivative as of the date of the financial position.
4. If the credit derivative provisions provide of the seller to recover from third parties or collateral, the seller shall indicate, if the amount can be estimated, the proceeds that it would expect to recover.

The disclosures should also provide insight to the statement users as to the reporting entity's objectives in using derivatives and the strategies for achieving them and the risk management policy followed by the entity. This information should enable the users to understand the volume of the entities activity involving derivative instruments.

The instruments should be distinguished between those used for risk management purposes and those used for other purposes. The disclosures should be segregated by major types of contracts. The descriptions of items or transactions that are hedged should be distinguished between each of the these:

1. Fair value hedges
2. Cash flow hedges
3. Foreign currency net investment hedges
4. All other derivatives

Derivative instruments not designated as hedges are to have the purpose of their activity disclosed. Qualitative disclosures concerning the use of derivative instruments are encouraged, particularly in a context of overall risk management strategies employed by the entity. The FASB also encourages disclosure of similar quantitative information about other nonderivative financial instruments or nonfinancial assets and liabilities related by activity to derivative instruments.

ASC 815 requires disclosing the fair values of derivative instruments and their gains and losses in a tabular format, which should provide a more complete picture of the location in the reporting entity's financial statements of both the derivative positions existing at period end and the effect of using derivatives during the reporting period. Also, disclosing information about credit risk–related contingent features is expected to provide information on the potential effect on an entity's liquidity from using derivatives. ASC 815 requires cross-referencing within the footnotes, which should help users of financial statements locate important information about derivative instruments.

Hedge Disclosures

In addition to the points just discussed, for every reporting period for which a complete set of financial statements is issued, there are required disclosures by hedge type.

Fair value hedges. For all designated and qualified instruments and the related hedged items that give rise to foreign currency transaction gains or losses under ASC 830, disclosure is required of the net gain or loss included in earnings, a description of where it is reported, and the amounts due to

1. Hedge ineffectiveness
2. Components that were excluded from the assessment of effectiveness
3. Hedged firm commitments that no longer qualify as hedges

Cash flow hedges. For all designated and qualified instruments and the related hedged items in cash flow hedges, these points are disclosed:

1. The net gain or loss in earnings, a description of where it is reported, and the amounts due to

   a. Hedge ineffectiveness.
   b. Components that were excluded from the assessment of effectiveness.

2. A description of events that will result in reclassification of amounts in accumulated other comprehensive income to earnings and the net amount expected to be reclassified during the next 12 months.
3. The maximum length of time of any cash flow hedges of forecasted transactions (excluding those relating to payment of variable interest on existing financial instruments).
4. The amount reclassified from accumulated other comprehensive income into earnings because a cash flow hedge was discontinued due to it being probable that the original forecasted transactions would not occur.

Foreign Currency Net Investment Hedges

For all such designated and qualified instruments that give rise to foreign currency transaction gains or losses under ASC 830, the net gain or loss that is included in the cumulative translation adjustment.

Comprehensive Income

The net gain or loss from cash flow hedges on derivative instruments reported in other comprehensive income must be shown as a separate classification. Accumulated other comprehensive income disclosures should show separately these items:

1. Beginning and ending accumulated derivative instrument gain or loss
2. Net change from current period hedging transactions
3. Net amount of reclassifications to earnings

EXTRACTS FROM FINANCIAL STATEMENTS

Provident New York Bancorp and Subsidiaries

For the fiscal year ended September 30, 2009

1. Basis of Financial Statement Presentation and Summary of Significant Accounting Policies

e. *Fair Values of Financial Instruments*

Fair values of financial instruments are estimated using relevant market information and other assumptions, as more fully disclosed in a separate note. Fair value estimates involve uncertainties and matters of significant judgment regarding interest rates, credit risk, prepayments, and other factors, especially in the absence of broad markets for particular items. Changes in assumptions or in market conditions could significantly affect the estimates.

g. *Securities*

Securities include U.S. Treasury, U.S. government agency and government-sponsored agencies, municipal and corporate bonds, mortgage-backed securities, collateralized mortgage obligations, and marketable equity securities.

The Company can classify its securities among three categories: held to maturity, trading, and available for sale. Management determines the appropriate classification of the Company's securities at the time of purchase.

Held-to-maturity securities are limited to debt securities for which management has the intent and the Company has the ability to hold to maturity. These securities are reported at amortized cost.

Trading securities are debt and equity securities held principally for the purpose of selling them in the near term. These securities are reported at fair value, with unrealized gains and losses included in earnings. The Company does not engage in security trading activities.

All other debt and marketable equity securities are classified as available for sale. These securities are reported at fair value, with unrealized gains and losses (net of the related deferred income tax effect) excluded from earnings and reported in a separate component of stockholders' equity (accumulated other comprehensive income or loss). Available-for-sale securities include securities that management intends to hold for an indefinite period of time, such as securities to be used as part of the Company's asset/liability management strategy or securities that may be sold in response to changes in interest rates, changes in prepayment risks, the need to increase capital, or similar factors.

Premiums and discounts on debt securities are recognized in interest income on a level-yield basis over the period to maturity. Amortization of premiums and accretion of discounts on mortgage-backed securities are based on the estimated cash flows of the mortgage-backed securities, periodically adjusted for changes in estimated lives, on a level-yield basis. The cost of securities sold is determined using the specific identification method. Unrealized losses are charged to earnings when management determines that the decline in fair value of a security is other than temporary.

Securities deemed to be other-than-temporarily impaired are permanently written down from their original cost basis to reflect the adjusted fair value subsequent to a measurement for impairment. The impairment is deemed other than temporary on an investment the Company does not expect to recover the amortized cost basis of that particular security. The Company assesses whether it intends to sell, or it is more likely than not that it will be required to sell a security in an unrealized loss position before recovery of its amortized cost basis. If either of these criteria is met, the entire difference between amortized cost and fair value is recognized in earnings. For securities that do not meet the aforementioned criteria, the amount of impairment recognized in earnings is limited to the amount related to credit losses, while impairment related to other factors is recognized in other comprehensive income or loss. There were no securities deemed to be other-than-temporarily impaired as of September 30, 2009.

o. Securities Repurchase Agreements

In securities repurchase agreements, the Company transfers securities to a counterparty under an agreement to repurchase the identical securities at a fixed price on a future date. These agreements are accounted for as secured financing transactions since the Company maintains effective control over the transferred securities and the transfer meets other specified criteria. Accordingly, the transaction proceeds are recorded as borrowings and the underlying securities continue to be carried in the Company's securities portfolio. Disclosure of the pledged securities is made in the consolidated statements of financial condition if the counterparty has the right by contract to sell or repledge such collateral.

Meta Financial Corp. for the Fiscal Year-End September 30, 2009

Note 1. Summary of Significant Accounting Policies

Securities

The Company classifies all securities as available for sale. Available-for-sale securities are those the Company may decide to sell if needed for liquidity, asset-liability management, or other reasons. Available-for-sale securities are reported at fair value, with net unrealized gains and losses reported as other comprehensive income or loss as a separate component of shareholders' equity, net of tax.

Gains and losses on the sale of securities are determined using the specific identification method based on amortized cost and are reflected in results of operations at the time of sale. Interest and dividend income, adjusted by amortization of purchase premium or discount over the estimated life of the security using the level-yield method, is included in income as earned.

Declines in the fair value of individual securities below their amortized cost that are deemed to be other than temporary are reflected in earnings as realized losses. In estimating other-than-temporary impairment losses, management considers (1) the length of time and the extent to which the fair value has been less than cost, (2) the financial condition and near-term prospects of the issuer, and (3) the intent and ability of the Company to retain its investment in the issuer for a period of time sufficient to allow for any anticipated recovery in fair value.

Loans Receivable

Loans receivable that management has the intent and ability to hold for the foreseeable future or until maturity or payoff are reported at their outstanding principal balances reduced by the allowance for loan losses and any deferred fees or costs on originated loans.

Interest income on loans is accrued over the term of the loans based on the amount of principal outstanding except when serious doubt exists as to the collectibility of a loan, in which case the accrual of interest is discontinued. Interest income is subsequently recognized only to the extent that cash payments are received until, in management's judgment, the borrower has the ability to make contractual interest and principal payments, in which case the loan is returned to accrual status.

Loan fees and certain direct loan origination costs are deferred, and the net fee or cost is recognized as an adjustment to interest income using the interest method.

Mortgage Servicing and Transfers of Financial Assets

The Bank regularly sells residential mortgage loans to others on a nonrecourse basis. Sold loans are not included in the consolidated financial statements. The Bank generally retains the right to service the sold loans for a fee. At September 30, 2009 and 2008, the Bank was servicing loans for others with aggregate unpaid principal balances of $26.8 million and $28.7 million, respectively.

Allowance for Loan Losses

Because some loans may not be repaid in full, an allowance for loan losses is recorded. The allowance for loan losses is increased by a provision for loan losses charged to expense and decreased by charge-offs (net of recoveries). Estimating the risk of loss and the amount of loss on any loan is necessarily subjective. Management's periodic evaluation of the adequacy of the allowance is based on the Company's past loan loss experience, known and inherent risks in the portfolio, adverse situations that may affect the borrower's ability to repay, the estimated value of any underlying collateral, and current economic conditions. While management may periodically allocate portions of the allowance for specific problem loan situations, the entire allowance is available for any loan charge-offs that occur.

Loans are considered impaired if full principal or interest payments are not anticipated in accordance with the contractual loan terms. Impaired loans are carried at the present value of expected future cash flows discounted at the loan's effective interest rate or at the fair value of the collateral if the loan is collateral dependent. A portion of the allowance for loan losses is allocated to impaired loans if the value of such loans is deemed to be less than the unpaid balance. If these allocations cause the allowance for loan losses to require an increase, such increase is reported as a component of the provision for loan losses.

The allowance consists of specific, general, and unallocated components. The specific component relates to loans that are classified as doubtful, substandard, or special mention. For such loans that are also classified as impaired, an allowance is established when the discounted cash flows (or collateral value or observable market price) of the impaired loan is lower than the carrying value of that loan. The general component covers loans not considered impaired and is based on historical loss experience adjusted for qualitative factors. An unallocated component is maintained to cover uncertainties that could affect management's estimate of probable losses. The unallocated component of the allowance reflects the margin of imprecision inherent in the underlying assumptions used in the methodologies for estimating specific and general losses in the portfolio.

Smaller-balance homogeneous loans are evaluated for impairment in total. Such loans include residential first-mortgage loans secured by one- to four-family residences, residential construction loans, and automobile, manufactured homes, home equity, and second-mortgage loans. Commercial and agricultural loans and mortgage loans secured by other properties are evaluated individually for impairment. When analysis of borrower operating results and financial condition indicates that underlying cash flows of the borrower's business are not adequate to meet its debt service requirements, the loan is evaluated for impairment. Often this is associated with a delay or shortfall in payments of 90 days or more. Nonaccrual loans are often also considered impaired. Impaired loans, or portions thereof, are charged off when deemed uncollectible.

Foreclosed Real Estate and Repossessed Assets

Real estate properties and repossessed assets acquired through, or in lieu of, loan foreclosure are initially recorded at the lower of cost or fair value less selling costs at the date of foreclosure, establishing a new cost basis. Any reduction to fair value from the carrying value of the related loan at the time of acquisition is accounted for as a loan loss and charged against the allowance for loan losses. Valuations are periodically performed by management, and valuation allowances are increased through a charge to income for reductions in fair value or increases in estimated selling costs.

Transfers of Financial Assets

Transfers of financial assets are accounted for as sales when control over the assets has been surrendered. Control over transferred assets is deemed to be surrendered when (1) the assets have been isolated from the Company, (2) the transferee obtains the right (free of conditions that constrain it from taking advantage of that right) to pledge or exchange the transferred assets, and (3) the Company does not maintain effective control over the transferred assets through an agreement to repurchase them before their maturity.

Financial Instruments with Off-Balance-Sheet Risk

The Company, in the normal course of business, makes commitments to make loans which are not reflected in the consolidated financial statements.

Assets and Liabilities Related to Discontinued Operations

Assets and liabilities related to discontinued operations are carried at the lower of cost or estimated market value in the aggregate.

Securities Sold under Agreements to Repurchase

The Company enters into sales of securities under agreements to repurchase with primary dealers only, which provide for the repurchase of the same security. Securities sold under agreements to repurchase identical securities are collateralized by assets which are held in safekeeping in the name of the Bank or by the dealers who arranged the transaction. Securities sold under agreements to repurchase are treated as financings, and the obligations to repurchase such securities are reflected as a liability. The securities underlying the agreements remain in the asset accounts of the Company.

MULTIPLE-CHOICE QUESTIONS

1. The scope of ASC 825 includes all of the following items **except:**
    (a) Financial instruments that meet the definition of a financial asset.
    (b) Financial instruments that meet the definition of a financial liability.
    (c) Financial instruments issued by the entity that meet the definition of an equity instrument.
    (d) Contracts to buy or sell nonfinancial items that can be settled net.

2. Which of the following is **not** a category of financial assets defined in ASC 320?
    (a) Trading securities.
    (b) Available-for-sale financial assets.
    (c) Held-for-sale investments.
    (d) Held-to-maturity investments.

3. All of the following are characteristics of financial assets classified as held-to-maturity investments **except:**
    (a) They have fixed or determinable payments and a fixed maturity.
    (b) The holder can recover substantially all of its investment (unless there has been credit deterioration).
    (c) They are quoted in an active market.
    (d) The holder has a demonstrated positive intention and ability to hold them to maturity.

4. Which of the following items is **not** precluded from classification as a held-to-maturity investment?
    (a) An investment in an unquoted debt instrument.
    (b) An investment in a quoted equity instrument.
    (c) A quoted derivative financial asset.
    (d) An investment in a quoted debt instrument.

5. What is the principle for recognition of a financial asset or a financial liability?
    (a) A financial asset is recognized when, and only when, it is probable that future economic benefits will flow to the entity and the cost or value of the instrument can be measured reliably.
    (b) A financial asset is recognized when, and only when, the entity obtains control of the instrument and has the ability to dispose of the financial asset independent of the actions of others.
    (c) A financial asset is recognized when, and only when, the entity obtains the risks and rewards of ownership of the financial asset and has the ability to dispose of the financial asset.

    (d) A financial asset is recognized when, and only when, the entity becomes a party to the contractual provisions of the instrument.

6. In which of the following circumstances is derecognition of a financial asset **not** appropriate?
    (a) The contractual rights to the cash flows of the financial assets have expired.
    (b) The financial asset has been transferred and effective control of the asset has also been transferred.
    (c) The financial asset has been transferred and the entity has retained substantially all the risks and rewards of ownership of the transferred asset.
    (d) The financial asset has been transferred, and the entity has neither retained nor transferred substantially all the risks and rewards of ownership of the transferred asset. In addition, the entity has lost control of the transferred asset.

7. Which of the following transfers of financial assets qualifies for derecognition?
    (a) A sale of a financial asset where the entity retains an option to buy the asset back at its current fair value on the repurchase date.
    (b) A sale of a financial asset where the entity agrees to repurchase the asset in one year for a fixed price plus interest.
    (c) A sale of a portfolio of short-term accounts receivable where the entity guarantees to compensate the buyer for any losses in the portfolio.
    (d) A loan of a security to another entity (i.e., a securities lending transaction).

8. Which of the following is **not** a relevant consideration when evaluating whether to derecognize a financial liability?
    (a) Whether the obligation has been discharged.
    (b) Whether the obligation has been cancelled.
    (c) Whether the obligation has expired.
    (d) Whether substantially all the risks and rewards of the obligation have been transferred.

9. At what amount is a financial asset or financial liability measured on initial recognition?
    (a) The consideration paid or received for the financial asset or financial liability.
    (b) Acquisition cost. Acquisition cost is the consideration paid or received plus any directly attributable transaction costs to the acquisition or issuance of the financial asset or financial liability.

(c) Fair value.

(d) Zero.

10. In addition to trading securities, which of the following categories of financial assets is measured at fair value in the statement of financial position?

   (a) Available-for-sale financial assets.

   (b) Held-to-maturity investments.

   (c) Loans and receivables.

   (d) Investments in unquoted equity instruments.

11. What is the best evidence of the fair value of a financial instrument?

   (a) Its cost, including transaction costs directly attributable to the purchase, origination, or issuance of the financial instrument.

   (b) Its estimated value determined using discounted cash flow techniques, option pricing models, or other valuation techniques.

   (c) Its quoted price, if an active market exists for the financial instrument.

   (d) The present value of the contractual cash flows less impairment.

12. What is the effective interest rate of a bond or other debt instrument measured at amortized cost?

   (a) The stated coupon rate of the debt instrument.

   (b) The interest rate currently charged by the entity or by others for similar debt instruments (i.e., similar remaining maturity, cash flow pattern, currency, credit risk, collateral, and interest basis).

   (c) The interest rate that exactly discounts estimated future cash payments or receipts through the expected life of the debt instrument or, when appropriate, a shorter period to the net carrying amount of the instrument.

   (d) The basic, risk-free interest rate that is derived from observable government bond prices.

13. Which of the following is **not** objective evidence of impairment of a financial asset?

   (a) Significant financial difficulty of the issuer or obligor.

   (b) A decline in the fair value of the asset below its previous carrying amount.

   (c) A breach of contract, such as a default or delinquency in interest or principal payments.

   (d) Observable data indicating that there is a measurable decrease in the estimated future cash flows from a group of financial assets although the decrease cannot yet be associated with any individual financial asset.

14. All of the following are characteristics of a derivative **except:**

   (a) It is acquired or incurred by the entity for the purpose of generating a profit from short-term fluctuations in market factors.

   (b) Its value changes in response to the change in a specified underlying (e.g., interest rate, financial instrument price, commodity price, foreign exchange rate, etc.).

   (c) It requires no initial investment or an initial net investment that is smaller than would be required for other types of contracts that would be expected to have a similar response to changes in market factors.

   (d) It is settled at a future date.

15. Is a derivative (e.g., an equity conversion option) that is embedded in another contract (e.g., a convertible bond) accounted for separately from that other contract?

   (a) Yes. All derivatives (both freestanding and embedded) are to be accounted for as derivatives.

   (b) No. Entities are precluded from splitting financial instruments and accounting for the components separately.

   (c) It depends. ASC 815 requires embedded derivatives to be accounted for separately as derivatives if, and only if, the entity has embedded the derivative in order to avoid derivatives accounting and has no substantive business purpose for embedding the derivative.

   (d) It depends. ASC 815 requires embedded derivatives to be accounted for separately if, and only if, the economic characteristics and risks of the embedded derivative and the host contract are not closely related and the combined contract is not measured at fair value with changes in fair value recognized in profit or loss.

16. Which of the following is **not** a condition for hedge accounting?

   (a) Formal designation and documentation of the hedging relationship and the entity's risk management objective and strategy for undertaking the hedge at inception of the hedging relationship.

   (b) The hedge is expected to be highly effective in achieving offsetting changes in fair value or cash flows attributable to the hedged risk, the effectiveness of the hedge can be reliably measured, and the hedge is assessed on an ongoing basis and determined actually to have been effective.

    (c)   For cash flow hedges, a forecast transaction must be highly probable and must present an exposure to variations in cash flows that could ultimately affect profit or loss.

    (d)   The hedge is expected to reduce the entity's net exposure to the hedged risk, and the hedge is determined actually to have reduced the net entity-wide exposure to the hedged risk.

17. What is the accounting treatment of the hedging instrument and the hedged item under fair value hedge accounting?

    (a)   The hedging instrument is measured at fair value, and the hedged item is measured at fair value with respect to the hedged risk. Changes in fair value are recognized in earnings.

    (b)   The hedging instrument is measured at fair value, and the hedged item is measured at fair value with respect to the hedged risk. Changes in fair value are recognized directly in equity to the extent the hedge is effective.

    (c)   The hedging instrument is measured at fair value with changes in fair value recognized directly in equity to the extent the hedge is effective. The accounting for the hedged item is not adjusted.

    (d)   The hedging instrument is accounted for in accordance with the accounting requirements for the hedged item (i.e., at fair value, cost or amortized cost, as applicable), if the hedge is effective.

18. What is the accounting treatment of the hedging instrument and the hedged item under cash flow hedge accounting?

    (a)   The hedged item and hedging instrument are both measured at fair value with respect to the hedged risk, and changes in fair value are recognized in earnings.

    (b)   The hedged item and hedging instrument are both measured at fair value with respect to the hedged risk, and changes in fair value are recognized directly in equity.

    (c)   The hedging instrument is measured at fair value with changes in fair value recognized directly in equity to the extent the hedge is effective. The accounting for the hedged item is not adjusted.

    (d)   The hedging instrument is accounted for in accordance with the accounting requirements for the hedged item (i.e., at fair value, cost or amortized cost, as applicable), if the hedge is effective.

Chapter 12

EQUITY METHOD INVESTMENTS AND JOINT VENTURES (ASC 323)

BACKGROUND AND INTRODUCTION

This Standard is to be applied to all accounting for investments in associates but does not apply to investments in associates held by a venture capital organization, a mutual fund, a unit trust, and a similar entity, including investment-linked insurance funds, where these investments upon initial recognition are designated at fair value through profit or loss or classified as held for trading and accounted for in accordance with ASC 815.

DEFINITIONS OF KEY TERMS
(in accordance with ASC 323)

Corporate joint ventures. A corporation formed, owned, and operated by two or more businesses (venturers) as a separate and discrete business or project (venture) for their mutual benefit.

Equity method. A method of accounting by which an investment is initially recognized at cost and adjusted thereafter to reflect the postacquisition change in the investor's share of the net assets of the investee. The profit or loss attributable to the investment in the investee is included in the investor's income statement.

Joint venture. A legal entity owned and operated by two or more businesses referred to as the venturers, organized for the purpose of a separate business activity or project that mutually benefits the venturers.

Significant influence. The power to participate in the financial and operating policy decisions of the investee but not to control them; that control includes joint control over those policies.

EQUITY METHOD

The equity method, sometimes referred to as "one-line consolidation," permits an entity (investor) owning a percentage of the common stock of another entity (investee) to incorporate its pro rata share of the investee's operating results into its net income. However, rather than include its share of each component (e.g., sales, cost of sales, operating expenses, etc.) in its financial statements, the investor includes only its share of the investee's net income as a separate line item in its income.

Note that there are exceptions to this one-line rule. The investor's share of investee extraordinary items and prior period adjustments are to retain their identities in the investor's income and retained earnings statements and are to be separately reported, if material in relation to the investor's income. It should be noted that the final bottom-line impact on the investor's financial statements is identical whether the equity method or full consolidation is employed; only the amount of detail presented within the financial statements will differ.

The equity method is not a substitute for consolidation; it is employed where the investor has significant influence over the operations of the investee but lacks control. In general, significant influence is inferred when the investor owns between 20% and 50% of the investee's voting common stock. Any ownership percentage over 50% presumably gives the investor actual voting control, making full consolidation of financial statements necessary. The 20% threshold stipulated in ASC 323 is not absolute; circumstances may suggest that significant influence exists even though the investor's level of ownership is less than 20%, or that it is absent despite a level of ownership above 20%.

In considering whether significant influence exists, ASC 323-10-15 identifies these five factors:

1. Opposition by the investee
2. Agreements under which the investor surrenders shareholder rights
3. Majority ownership by a small group of shareholders
4. Inability to obtain desired information from the investee
5. Inability to obtain representation on investee board of directors, and so on

Whether sufficient contrary evidence exists to negate the presumption of significant influence is a matter of judgment. Judgment requires a careful evaluation of all pertinent facts and circumstances, over an extended period of time in some cases.

Initial Measurement

The investor is to measure its initial equity method investment at cost. Generally, the acquisition of an equity method investment is recorded at the cost to the investor. When the consideration is in the form of cash, the cost of the acquisition is measured as the amount of cash paid to acquire the investment, including transaction costs associated with the acquisition.

In some transactions, noncash consideration is surrendered by the investor. This can take the form of noncash assets, liabilities incurred or assumed, or equity interests issued. The measurement of consideration in these transactions is based on either the cost to the acquirer or the fair value of the assets (or net assets) acquired, whichever is considered more reliably measurable. No gain or loss is recognized by the investor, unless the value of noncash assets surrendered as consideration differs from their carrying amounts in the investor's accounting records.

It is highly unlikely that the cost of the investment to the investor would be equal to the fair value of the investor's proportionate share of the investee's net assets. ASC 323-10-35-13 requires these differences to be accounted for in the same manner as if the investee were a consolidated subsidiary. Doing this requires analysis to determine whether the differences are attributable to (a) specific tangible assets whose fair values exceed their carrying values as recorded in the accounting records of the investee, or (b) specifically identifiable intangible assets that are not recognized in the accounting records of the investee because they were internally developed.

Any excess remaining after allocating the differences to (a) and/or (b) is analogous to goodwill in a business combination accounted for under the former *purchase method* or, commencing in 2009, the *acquisition method*. Since the ultimate income statement effects of applying the equity method of accounting generally must be the same as full consolidation, an adjustment must be made to account for these differentials.

Subsequent Accounting

In periods subsequent to the initial acquisition of the investment, the investor recognizes increases to the carrying value of the investment for the investor's proportionate share of the investee's net income and recognizes decreases in the carrying value of the investment for the investor's proportionate share of the investee's net losses and by dividends received.

Example of the equity method

A simple case ignoring deferred income taxes

On January 2, 2010, R Corporation (the investor) acquired 40% of E Company's (the investee) voting common stock from the former owner for $100,000. Unless demonstrated otherwise, it is assumed that R Corporation can exercise significant influence over E Company's operating and financing policies. On January 2, E's stockholders' equity consists of

Common stock, $1.00 par value per share; 100,000 shares authorized, 50,000 shares issued and outstanding	$ 50,000
Additional paid-in capital	150,000
Retained earnings	50,000
Total stockholders' equity	$250,000

Note that, although improbable in practice, for this simple example, the cost of E Company common stock was exactly equal to 40% of the book value of E's net assets. Assume also that there is no difference between the book value and the fair value of E Company's assets and liabilities. Accordingly, the balance in the investment account in R's records represents exactly 40% of E's stockholders' equity (net assets). Assume further that E Company reported net income for 2010 of $30,000 and paid cash dividends of $10,000. Its stockholders' equity at year-end would be

Common stock, $1.00 par value per share; 100,000 shares authorized, 50,000 shares issued and outstanding	$ 50,000
Additional paid-in capital	150,000
Retained earnings	70,000
Total stockholders' equity	$270,000

R Corporation would record its share of the increase in E Company's net assets during 2010 in this way:

Investment in E Company	12,000	
Equity in E income		12,000
($30,000 × 40%)		
Cash	4,000	
Investment in E Company		4,000
($10,000 × 40%)		

When R's statement of financial position is prepared at December 31, 2010, the balance reported as the carrying value of the equity-method investment in E Company would be $108,000 (= $100,000 + $12,000 – $4,000). This amount continues to represent 40% of the book value of E's net assets at the end of the year (40% × $270,000). Note also that the equity in E income is reported as a separate caption in R's income statement, typically as a component of income from continuing operations before income taxes.

Deferred Income Tax Accounting

The equity method is not a recognized accounting method for federal income tax purposes under the U.S. Internal Revenue Code (IRC). For income tax purposes, the investor's share of the investee's net income is not recognized until it is realized through either the investor's receipt of dividends from the investee or the investor's sale of the investment. Thus, when the investor, under the equity method, recognizes its proportionate share of the net income of the investee as an increase to the carrying value of the investment, a future taxable temporary difference between the carrying value of the equity method investment for financial reporting purposes and the income tax basis of the investment will arise. The temporary difference will give rise to recognition of a deferred income tax liability.

In computing the deferred income tax effects of income recognized by applying the equity method, the investor must make an assumption regarding the means by which the undistributed earnings of the investee will be realized. The earnings can be realized either through later dividend receipts or by disposition of the investment at a gain. The former assumption would result in income taxes at the investor's marginal income tax rate on ordinary income (net of the 80% dividends received deduction permitted by the Internal Revenue Code for intercorporate investments of less than 80% but at least 20%; a lower deduction of 70% applies if ownership is below 20%). The latter option would be treated as a capital gain, which is currently taxed at the full corporate income tax rate, since the preferential corporate capital gains rate was eliminated by the 1986 Tax Reform Act.

Example of the equity method

A simple case including deferred income taxes

Assume the same information as in the example above. In addition, assume that R Corporation has a combined (federal, state, and local) marginal income tax rate of 34% on ordinary income and that it anticipates realization of E Company earnings through future dividend receipts.

R Corporation's current income tax expense associated with its investment is computed based on its current dividends received less the dividends received deduction under IRC §243. Since R owns a 40% interest in E, the applicable percentage for the dividends received deduction is 80%. Note that the dividends received deduction constitutes a permanent difference under ASC 740 that never reverses. The provision for income taxes currently payable is computed as:

Dividends received	$4,000
Less dividends received deduction (80%)	(3,200)
Taxable income from investment in E	800
× Current combined federal and state tax rate	× 34%
Income taxes currently payable	$ 272

To compute deferred income taxes under the liability method used in ASC 740, at each reporting date we must determine the temporary difference between the carrying amount of the investment for financial reporting purposes and its income tax basis. In this case, this is done as follows:

Carrying value of equity-method investment for financial reporting purposes	
Original cost	$100,000
Equity method earnings	12,000
Dividends	(4,000)
Income tax basis	
Original cost	100,000
Temporary difference	$ 8,000

Since R expects to realize this difference in the future through the receipt of dividends, it adjusts the difference for the permanent difference that arises from benefit of the dividends received deduction of 80% of $8,000, or $6,400, thus leaving $1,600 that would be subject to the effective rate that R expects to apply to reversal of the temporary difference, which, as provided in the assumptions above, is 34%. Applying the 34% expected future effective tax rate to the $1,600 taxable portion of the temporary difference would yield a deferred income tax expense (and related liability) of $544. The entry to record these items at December 31, 2010, is

Income tax expense—Current	272	
Income tax expense—Deferred	544	
Income taxes currently payable		272
Deferred income tax liability		544

To record provision for income taxes for the year ended 12/31/2010 attributable to equity-method investment in E

Differences in Fiscal Year

If the investor and investee have different fiscal years, ASC 323-10-35-6 permits the investor to use the most recent financial statements available as long as the lag in reporting is consistent from period to period. Analogizing from ASC 810, the lag period is not to exceed three months.

If the investee changes its fiscal year-end to reduce or eliminate the lag period, ASC 810-10-45 stipulates that the change be treated as a voluntary change in accounting principle under ASC 250. Although ASC 250 requires such changes to be made by retrospective application to all periods presented, it provides an exception if it is not practical to do so.

Accounting for a differential between cost of an equity method investment and the investor's proportionate share of net assets. The preceding examples ignored one of the major complexities of the equity method; namely, the ASC 323 requirement that the investor account for any differential between its cost and its proportionate share of the fair value of the investee's net identifiable assets consistent with the accounting for a business combination under the acquisition method prescribed by ASC 805.

In almost all instances, the price paid by an investor to acquire shares of an investee will differ from the corresponding underlying book value (i.e., the investee's net assets per its generally accepted accounting principles [GAAP]–basis financial statements). The differential can be broken down into four components from the authoritative literature on business combinations:

1. Tangible and intangible assets recognized in the accounting records of the investee at carrying values that are below their fair values.
2. Identifiable intangible assets not recognized in the accounting records of the investee because of the long-standing prohibition in GAAP against recognizing internally developed intangibles (with the notable exception of internal-use software). These might include in-process research and development assets, customer lists, and other amortizable or nonamortizable intangibles.
3. Contingent consideration.
4. Goodwill.

This means that premiums or discounts versus underlying book values must be identified, analyzed, and dealt with in the accounting for the investment under the equity method. It also means that assets or liabilities not recognized by the investee must be identified and assigned, on a memo basis, the appropriate shares of the investor's purchase cost.

Under ASC 323, any premium paid by the investor that cannot be identified as being attributable to appreciated recognized tangible and intangible assets or unrecognized internally developed intangible assets of the investee is analogous to goodwill. Although under prior rules this goodwill component would have been amortized, under ASC 350-20-35-58 and 35-59, this component is subject not to amortization but rather to impairment testing. The impairment testing regime to be applied is not, however, that specified in ASC 350, which pertains only to testing by entities that actually record an asset explicitly as goodwill (i.e., the acquirer in a business combination accounted for under ASC 805). Equity method investors will continue to assess impairment of investments in investees by considering whether declines in the fair values of those investments, versus the carrying values of the underlying assets, may be other than temporary in nature.

Investor Share of Investee Losses in Excess of the Carrying Value of the Investment

As demonstrated in the foregoing paragraphs, the carrying value of an investment that is accounted for by the equity method is increased by the investor's share of investee earnings and reduced by its share of investee losses and by dividends received from the investee. Sometimes the losses are so large that the carrying value is reduced to zero, and this raises the question of whether the investment account should be allowed to "go negative" or whether losses in excess of the investment account should be recognized in some other manner.

In general, an equity-method investment would not be permitted to have a negative (i.e., credit) balance, since this would imply that it represented a liability. In the case of normal corporate investments, the investor would enjoy limited liability and would not be held liable to the investee's creditors should, for instance, the investee become insolvent. For this reason, excess losses of the investee would not be reflected in the financial statements of the investor. The practice is to discontinue application of the equity method when the investment account reaches a zero balance, with adequate disclosure being made of the fact that further investee losses are not being reflected in the investor's earnings. If the investee later returns to profitability, the investor ignores its share of earnings until the previously ignored losses have been fully offset; thereafter, normal application of the equity method is resumed.

In some cases, after the recognition of investee losses is suspended, the investor will make a further investment in the investee, and the question arises whether recognition of some or all of the previously unrecognized investee losses should be given recognition immediately, up to the amount of the additional investment.

ASC 323-10-35-29 holds that recognition of some or all of the previously unrecognized ("suspended") losses is conditioned on whether the new investment represents funding of prior investee losses. To the extent that it does, the previously unrecognized share of prior losses will be given recognition (i.e., reported in the investor's current period net income). Making this determination requires the use of judgment and is fact specific, but some of the considerations would be

- Whether the additional investment is acquired from a third party or directly from the investee, since it is unlikely that funding of prior losses occurs unless funds are infused into the investee.
- The fair value of the consideration received in relation to the value of the consideration paid for the additional investment, with an indicated excess of consideration paid over that received being suggestive of a funding of prior losses.
- Whether the additional investment results in an increase in ownership percentage of the investee, with investments being made without a corresponding increase in ownership or other interests (or, alternatively, a pro rata equity investment made by all existing investors) being indicative of the funding of prior losses.
- The seniority of the additional investment relative to existing equity of the investee, with investment in subordinate instruments being suggestive of the funding of prior losses.

Intercompany Transactions between Investor and Investee

In preparing consolidated financial statements, all intercompany (parent-subsidiary) transactions are eliminated. However, when the equity method is used to account for investments, only the profit component of intercompany (investor-investee) transactions is eliminated. This is because the equity method does not result in the combining of all income statement accounts (such as sales and cost of sales) and therefore will not cause the financial statements to contain redundancies. In contrast, consolidated statements would include redundancies if the gross amounts of all intercompany transactions were not eliminated.

Another distinction between the consolidation and equity method situations pertains to the percentage of intercompany profit to be eliminated. In the case of consolidated statements, the entire intercompany profit is eliminated, regardless of the percentage ownership of the subsidiary. However, according to ASC 323-10-35-11, only the investor's pro rata share of intercompany profit is to be eliminated in equity accounting, whether the transaction giving rise to the profit is "downstream" (a sale to the investee) or "upstream" (a sale to the investor). An exception is made when the transaction is not "arm's length" or if the investee company was created by or for the benefit of the investor. In these cases, 100% profit elimination would be required, unless realized through a sale to a third party before year-end.

Case Study 1

Facts

Company A sells inventory to its 30% owned investee, B. The inventory had cost A $200,000 and was sold for $300,000. B also has sold inventory to A. The cost of this inventory to B was $100,000, and it was sold for $120,000.

Required

How would the intercompany profit on these transactions be dealt with in the financial statements if none of the inventory had been sold at year-end?

Solution

Company A to Company B

	$000
The intergroup profit is $(300 − 200)	100
Profit reported would be 100 × 70/100 =	70

The remaining profit would be deferred until the sale of the inventory.

Company B to Company A

The profit made by B would be $(120 − 100) = 20

An amount of 20 × 30/100 would be eliminated from the carrying value of the investment, that is, $6,000.

The alternative is to eliminate the whole of the profit from B's profit for the period and then calculate the profit attributable to the investee.

Eliminating entries for intercompany profits in fixed assets are similar to those in the previous examples. However, intercompany profit is realized only as the assets are depreciated by the purchasing entity. In other words, if an investor buys or sells fixed assets from or to an investee at a price above book value, the gain would be realized only piecemeal over the asset's remaining depreciable life. Accordingly, in the year of sale the pro rata share (based on the investor's percentage ownership interest in the investee, regardless of whether the sale is upstream or downstream) of the unrealized portion of the intercompany profit would have to be eliminated. In each subsequent year during the asset's life, the pro rata share of the gain realized in the period would be added to income from the investee.

Investee Income Items Separately Reportable by the Investor

In the examples thus far, the investor has reported its share of investee income, and the adjustments to this income, as a single item described as equity in investee income. However, when the investee has extraordinary items and/or prior period adjustments that are material, the investor is to report its share of these items separately on its statements of income and retained earnings.

Example of accounting for separately reportable items

Assume that both an extraordinary item and a prior period adjustment reported in an investee's income and retained earnings statements are individually considered material from the investor's viewpoint.

Statement of income	
Income before extraordinary item	$ 80,000
Extraordinary loss from earthquake (net of income taxes of $12,000)	(18,000)
Net income	$ 62,000

Statement of changes in retained earnings	
Retained earnings at January 1, 2009, as originally reported	250,000
Add restatement for prior period adjustment—correction of an error made in 2008 (net of income taxes of $10,000)	20,000
Retained earnings at January 1, 2009, restated	$270,000

If an investor owned 30% of the voting common stock of this investee, the investor would make these journal entries in 2009:

1.   Investment in investee company   24,000
         Equity in investee income before extraordinary item   24,000
      $80,000 × 30%

2.   Equity in investee extraordinary loss   5,400
         Investment in investee company   5,400
      $18,000 × 30%

3.   Investment in investee company   6,000
         Equity in investee prior period adjustment   6,000
      $20,000 × 30%

The equity in the investee's prior period adjustment should be reported on the investor's statement of changes in retained earnings, which is often presented in a more all-encompassing format with the statement of changes in stockholders' equity. The equity in the extraordinary loss is reported separately in the appropriate section on the investor's statement of income.

Investor Accounting for Investee Capital Transactions

According to ASC 323-10-35-15, investee transactions of a capital nature that affect the investor's share of the investee's stockholders' equity are accounted for as if the investee were a consolidated subsidiary. These transactions principally include situations where the investee purchases treasury stock from, or sells unissued shares or reissues treasury shares it holds to, outside shareholders. (If the investor participates in these transactions on a pro rata basis, its percentage ownership will not change and no special accounting will be necessary.) Similar results are obtained when holders of outstanding options or convertible securities acquire investee common shares.

When the investee engages in one of the foregoing types of capital transactions, the investor's ownership percentage is changed. This gives rise to a gain or loss, depending on whether the price paid (for treasury shares acquired) or received (for shares issued) is greater or lesser than the per share carrying value of the investor's interest in the investee. However, since no gain or loss can be recognized on capital transactions, these purchases or sales will affect additional paid-in capital and/or retained earnings directly, without being reflected in the investor's income statement. This method is consistent with the treatment that would be accorded to a consolidated subsidiary's capital transaction. An exception is that, under certain circumstances, the Securities and Exchange Commission (SEC) will permit income recognition based on the concept that the investor is essentially selling part of its investment.

Case Study 2

Example of accounting for an investee capital transaction

Facts

Assume R Corp. purchases, on 1/2/09, 25% (2,000 shares) of E Corp.'s outstanding shares for $80,000. The cost is equal to both the book and fair values of R's interest in E's underlying net assets (i.e., there is no differential to be accounted for). One week later, E Corp. buys 1,000 shares of its stock from other shareholders for $50,000. Since the price paid ($50/share) exceeded R Corp.'s per share carrying value of its interest, $40, R Corp. has in fact suffered an economic loss by the transaction. Also, its percentage ownership of E Corp. has increased as the number of shares held by third parties has been reduced.

Required

What is the effect of this transaction on R Corp.? Calculate R Corp.'s interest in E's net assets.

Solution

Since the price paid ($50/share) exceeded R Corp.'s per share carrying value of its interest, $40, R Corp. has in fact suffered an economic loss by the transaction. Also, its percentage ownership of E Corp. has increased as the number of shares held by third parties has been reduced.

R Corp.'s new interest in E's net assets is

$$\frac{2{,}000 \text{ shares held by R}}{7{,}000 \text{ shares outstanding}} \times \text{E Corp. net assets}$$

$$.2857 \times (\$320{,}000 - \$50{,}000) = \$77{,}143$$

The interest held by R Corp. has thus been diminished by $80,000 – $77,143 = $2,857.

Therefore, R Corp. should make this entry:

Additional paid-in capital (or retained earnings)	2,857	
Investment in E Corp.		2,857

R Corp. charges the loss against additional paid-in capital if such amounts have accumulated from past transactions of a similar nature; otherwise, the debit is to retained earnings. Had the transaction given rise to a gain, it would have been credited to additional paid-in capital only (never to retained earnings) following the rule that transactions in one's own shares cannot produce net income.

Note that the amount of the charge to additional paid-in capital (or retained earnings) in the previous entry can be verified in this way: R Corp.'s share of the posttransaction net equity (2/7) times the "excess" price paid ($50 – $40 = $10) times the number of shares purchased = 2/7 × $10 × 1,000 = $2,857.

Investor's Proportionate Share of Other Comprehensive Income Items

ASC 323-10-35-37 holds that an investor's proportionate share of an investee's equity adjustments for other comprehensive income items (e.g., fair value adjustments to available-for-sale investments) is to be offset against the carrying value of the investment in the investee entity at the time significant influence is lost. To the extent that the offset results in a carrying value of the investment that is less than zero, an investor will (1) reduce the carrying value of the investment to zero and (2) record the remaining balance in income.

Change in Level of Ownership or Degree of Influence

An equity method investor is to account for an issuance of shares by the investee as if the investor had sold a proportionate share of its investment. Any gain or loss to the investor that results from the investee's share issuance is to be recognized in net income.

Significant Influence in the Absence of Ownership of Voting Common Stock

ASC 323-10-15-13 states that a reporting entity that has the ability to exercise significant influence over the operating and financial policies of an investee is to apply the equity method only when it has an investment(s) in common stock and/or an investment that is in-substance common stock. In-substance common stock is an investment in an entity that has risk and reward characteristics that are substantially similar to the investee's common stock. Whether significant influence is wielded is a fact question, and suggested criteria are not provided in the ASC.

Management is to consider certain characteristics when determining whether an investment in an entity is substantially similar to an investment in that entity's common stock. These are conjunctive constraints; thus, if the entity determines that any one of the next three characteristics indicates that an investment in an entity is not substantially similar to an investment in that entity's common stock, the investment is not in-substance common stock.

1. *Subordination.* It must be determined whether the investment has subordination characteristics substantially similar to the investee's common stock. If there are substantive liquidation preferences, the instrument would not be deemed substantially similar to common stock. However, certain liquidation preferences are not substantive (e.g., when the stated liquidation preference is not significant in relation to the purchase price of the investment) and would be discounted in this analysis.
2. *Risks and rewards of ownership.* A reporting entity must determine whether the investment has risks and rewards of ownership that are substantially similar to an investment in the investee's common stock. If an investment is not expected to participate in the earnings (and losses) and capital appreciation (and depreciation) in a manner that is substantially similar to common stock, this condition would not be met. Participating and convertible preferred stocks likely would meet this criterion, however.
3. *Obligation to transfer value.* An investment is not substantially similar to common stock if the investee is expected to transfer substantive value to the investor and the common shareholders do not participate in a similar manner. For example, if the investment has a substantive redemption provision (e.g., a mandatory redemption provision or a non–fair value put option) that is not available to common shareholders, the investment is not substantially similar to common stock.

In some instances, it may be difficult to assess whether the foregoing characteristics are present or absent. ASC 323-10-15-13 suggests that, in such circumstances, management of the reporting entity (the investor) is also to analyze whether the future changes in the fair value of the investment are expected to be highly correlated with the changes in the fair value of the investee's common stock. If the changes in the fair value of the investment are not expected to be highly correlated with the changes in the fair value of the common stock, then the investment is not in-substance common stock.

According to ASC 323-10-15-13, the determination of whether an investment vehicle is in-substance common stock must be made upon acquisition, if the entity has the ability to exercise significant influence. The assessment is to be revisited if one or more of these occur:

1. The contractual terms of the investment are changed resulting in a change to any of its characteristics described above.
2. There is a significant change in the capital structure of the investee, including the investee's receipt of additional subordinated financing.
3. The reporting entity obtains an additional interest in an investment in which the investor has an existing interest. As a result, the method of accounting for the cumulative interest is based on the characteristics of the investment at the date at which the entity obtains the additional interest (i.e., the characteristics that the entity evaluated in order to make its invest-

ment decision) and will result in the reporting entity applying one method of accounting to the cumulative interest in an investment of the same issuance.

The mere fact that the investee is suffering losses is not a basis for reconsideration of whether the investment is in-substance common stock.

Upon implementation of ASC 323-10-15-13, for investments in which the entity has the ability to exercise significant influence over the operating and financial policies of the investee, the reporting entity is to make an initial determination about whether existing investments are in-substance common stock. The initial determination is to be based on circumstances that existed on the date of adoption rather than on the date that the investment was made.

EQUITY INVESTMENTS IN CORPORATE JOINT VENTURES AND NONCORPORATE ENTITIES

Corporate Joint Ventures

Venturers are to account for their investments in corporate joint ventures using the equity method (ASC 323-10-05-4; ASC 970-323-25-9).

General Partnerships

There is a rebuttable presumption that a general partner that has a majority voting interest is in control of the partnership. If voting rights are indeterminate under the provisions of the partnership agreement or applicable law, the general partner with a majority of the financial interests in the partnership's profits or losses would be presumed to have control. If this presumption is not overcome, the general partner with voting control or the majority financial interest would consolidate the partnership in its financial statements and the other noncontrolling general partners would use the equity method (ASC 323, ASC 970-323).

Limited Partnerships

The structure of many limited partnerships consists of one investor serving as general partner and having only a small equity interest and the other investors holding limited partnership (or equivalent) interests. The proper accounting for such structures is ASC 970-323, *Real Estate Investments—Equity Method and Joint Ventures,* which formally deals only with certain real estate investments but has been applied by analogy to other investments. ASC 810-10-25 provides expanded guidance to the appropriate accounting in those circumstances where the majority owner lacks control due to the existence of "substantial participating rights" by minority owners.

If the investor/holder is an entity that is required under GAAP to measure its investment in the limited partnership (LP) at fair value with changes in fair value reported in the income statement, then it follows that applicable specialized guidance with respect to accounting for its investment.

If the investee entity is a variable interest entity (VIE) under the provisions of ASC 810, the holders of interests in the entity are to use the GAAP applicable to those interests. If the investor has a controlling financial interest in the VIE, the investor is deemed to be the entity's primary beneficiary (analogous to a parent company) and is required to consolidate the investee in its financial statements.

Noncontrolling interest holders in an LP that is a VIE are to account for their interests using the equity method or the cost method. Limited partner interests that are so minor that the LP has virtually no influence over operating and financial policies of the partnership would be accounted for using the cost method (ASC 970-323). In order to be considered to be this minor, the SEC Staff has indicated that an interest would not be permitted to exceed 3% to 5% (ASC 323-30-S99). In practice, this benchmark is also generally accepted for non-SEC registrants since it represents the most authoritative guidance currently available with respect to making this determination.

If the LP is not a VIE and the partners are not subject to specialized industry fair value accounting rules, a determination is made as to whether a single general partner or multiple general partners control the LP. If a single general partner controls the LP, that partner is to consolidate the LP, all other general partners are to apply the equity method of accounting to their investments, and the LPs will use either the cost method (for minor investments) or the equity method.

If the LPs have the *substantive ability* to dissolve (liquidate) the limited partnership or otherwise remove the general partners without cause—which is referred to as "kick-out rights"—then the general partners will be deemed to lack control over the partnership. In such cases, consolidated financial reporting would not be appropriate, but equity method accounting would almost inevitably be warranted. To qualify, the kick-out rights must be exercisable by a single LP or a simple majority (or fewer) of limited partners. Thus, if a supermajority of LP votes is required to remove the general partner(s), this would not constitute a substantive ability to dissolve the partnership and would not thwart control by the general partner(s).

Limited Partnerships Controlled by the General Partners

As previously stated, the general partners are collectively presumed to be in control of the limited partnership. If this is substantively the case, the accounting for the general partners depends on whether control of the entity rests with a single general partner. If a single general partner controls the limited partnership, that general partner consolidates the limited partnership in its financial statements. If no single general partner controls the limited partnership, each general partner applies the equity method to account for its interest (ASC 810-20).

Noncontrolling LPs are to account for their interests using the equity method or by the cost method. As previously discussed, LP interests that are so minor (not to exceed 3%–5%) that the LP has virtually no influence over operating and financial policies of the partnership would be accounted for using the cost method (ASC 970-323).

Limited Partnerships Controlled by the Limited Partners

If the presumption of control by the general partners is overcome by applying ASC 810-20 and the LPs control the partnership, the general partners would use the equity method to account for their interests in the partnership.

If there is a controlling LP, that partner would consolidate the limited partnership in its financial statements. Noncontrolling LPs would follow the same guidance provided earlier that applies when the general partners control the partnership (i.e., use the equity method unless the interest is minor—in which case the cost method would be used).

Limited Liability Companies that Maintain a Specific Ownership Account for Each Investor

When a limited liability company (LLC) maintains individual equity accounts for each member, similar to the structure of a limited partnership, the investor/member is to analogize to the previous guidance that applies to accounting for investments in limited partnerships using either the cost method or equity method (ASC 272 and, by reference, ASC 970-323 and ASC 323-30-S99). In the discussion of ASC 272, it was indicated that it might be appropriate to apply this guidance by analogy to other entities that have similar specifically identifiable ownership account structures.

ASC 272 provides an exception to this general rule. Its scope does not include investments in LLCs used as securitization vehicles under ASC 860 that continue to be held by a transferor in a securitization transaction accounted for as a sale. These interests are accounted for as debt securities and categorized as either available-for-sale or trading securities under ASC 320 and are subject to specialized requirements regarding recognition of interest income and impairment (ASC 325-40).

Limited Liability Companies that Are Functionally Equivalent to Corporations ("Analogous Entities")

Some LLCs have governance structures that have characteristics that closely resemble those of corporations. These LLCs are not included in the scope of ASC 272 summarized earlier. Instead, membership interests in these LLCs are subject to different criteria to determine the proper accounting treatment to be used in the investor/member's financial statements.

The applicable GAAP relative to LLCs that are analogous entities is ASC 810-10-25. Under ASC 810-10-25, there is a similar rebuttable presumption that the majority voting interest holder(s) are in control of the investee. Management is to exercise judgment based on the relevant facts and circumstances as to whether one or more minority shareholders or members possess rights that individually or in the aggregate provide them with effective participation in the significant decisions expected to be made in the "ordinary course of business." If the minority owner or owners possess substantive participating rights, the presumption of control by the majority owners is overcome, and the minority owner or owners are considered to be in control.

Again, the controlling interest holder would be required to consolidate, and the noncontrolling interest holders would apply either the equity method or cost method, depending on the extent of their respective holdings.

Display in the Reporting Entity's Financial Statements When the Investee Is Not a Corporation

Under some circumstances, investor-venturers account for undivided interests in assets by means of pro rata consolidation, including a fraction of each asset category of the investee in the investor's statement of financial position, typically commingled with the investor's own assets. This has occurred most commonly in the case of construction joint ventures and is not a procedure formally defined under GAAP. In ASC 810-10-45, the issue addressed is whether proportional consolidation can be used to account for an investment in a partnership or a joint venture, as an alternative to full consolidation, equity method accounting, or historical cost.

The standard states that the pro rata method of consolidation is not appropriate for an investment in an unincorporated legal entity, except when the investee is in either the construction industry or an extractive industry, where there is a long-standing practice of its use. An entity is considered to be in an extractive industry only if its activities are limited to the extraction of mineral resources (such as oil and gas exploration and production) and not if its activities involve such related pursuits as refining, marketing, or transporting the extracted mineral resources.

MULTIPLE-CHOICE QUESTIONS

1. How is goodwill arising on the acquisition of an investee dealt with in the financial statements?
  (a) It is amortized.
  (b) It is impairment tested individually.
  (c) It is written off against profit or loss.
  (d) Impairment is assessed to determine whether declines in fair value of investments are temporary in nature.

2. What should happen when the financial statements of an investee are not prepared as of the same date as the investor's accounts?
  (a) The investor is allowed to use the most recent financial statements of the investee as long as they are within three months of the investor's year-end.
  (b) The financial statements of the investee prepared up to a different accounting date will be used as normal.
  (c) Any major transactions between the date of the financial statements of the investor and that of the investee should be accounted for.

3. An investor sells inventory for cash to a 25% associate. The inventory cost the investor $6 million and is sold to the associate for $10 million. None of the inventory has been sold at year-end. How much of the profit on the transaction would be reported in the group accounts?
  (a) $4 million
  (b) $1 million
  (c) $3 million
  (d) Zero

4. A company has a 40% share in a joint venture and loans the venture $2 million. What figure will be shown for the loan in the statement of financial position of the venturer?
  (a) $2 million
  (b) $800,000
  (c) $1.2 million
  (d) Zero

5. When the investor's share of investee losses are in excess of the carrying value of the investment
  (a) The investment account should be shown as a negative.
  (b) The equity method investment should be shown as a liability.
  (c) The investor is required to make a contribution to the investee in order to bring the investment account up to zero.
  (d) The investor should discontinue application of the equity method when the investment account reaches a zero balance and resume the equity method once previously ignored losses have been offset with profits.

6. Which of the following would **not** be accounted for under the equity method?
  (a) An investment in a corporate joint venture.
  (b) The controlling limited partners' share of a limited partnership.
  (c) The noncontrolling limited partners' share of a limited partnership.

Chapter 13

INTANGIBLE ASSETS (ASC 350)

INTRODUCTION AND BACKGROUND

The purpose of this Standard is to prescribe the financial accounting and reporting related to intangible assets other than the accounting at acquisition. Subtopics 805-20 and 805-30 address the financial accounting and reporting of intangibles acquired in a business combination at acquisition.

The principal issues involved relate to the nature and recognition of intangible assets, determining their costs, and assessing the amortization and impairment losses that need to be recognized.

DEFINITIONS OF KEY TERMS

Asset. A resource controlled by an entity as a result of past events and from which future economic benefits are expected to flow to the entity.

Cost. The amount paid or fair value of other consideration given to acquire or construct an asset.

Depreciable amount. The cost of an asset less its residual value.

Depreciation. The systematic allocation of the depreciable amount of an asset over its expected useful life.

Development. The application of research findings or other knowledge to a plan or design for the production of new or substantially improved materials, devices, products, processes, systems, or services before the start of commercial production or use.

Fair value. The amount for which an asset could be exchanged between knowledgeable, willing parties in an arm's-length transaction.

Intangible asset. An identifiable, nonmonetary asset without physical substance. The term *intangible assets* is used to refer to intangible assets other than goodwill.

Research. Original and planned investigation undertaken with the prospect of gaining new scientific or technical knowledge and understanding.

Useful life. The period over which an asset is expected to be utilized, or the number of production units expected to be obtained from the use of the asset.

Residual value of an asset. The estimated amount, less estimated disposal costs, that could currently be realized from the asset's disposal if the asset was already of an age and condition expected at the end of its useful life.

INTANGIBLE ASSETS

The range of intangibles is perhaps more clearly understood today than it was in the past, and there is more pressure to improve the relevance of financial reporting in light of changing business and economic conditions.

For manufacturing companies, the primary assets typically are tangible, such as buildings and equipment. For financial institutions, the major assets are financial instruments. For high-technology, knowledge-based companies, however, the primary assets are more commonly intangible (e.g., patents and copyrights). For professional service firms, the key assets may be "soft" resources, such as knowledge bases and client relationships, which, to the extent given financial statement recognition, are also intangibles. Overall, enterprises for which intangible assets constitute a large and growing component of total assets are a rapidly growing part of the economy.

Intangible assets are defined as both current and noncurrent assets that lack physical substance. Specifically excluded, however, are financial instruments and deferred income tax assets.

Goodwill is not considered an identifiable intangible asset. Accordingly, under ASC 350-20, it is accounted for differently from identifiable intangibles. Goodwill is the preeminent unidentifiable intangible, and this characteristic (i.e., the lack of identifiability) has been determined by the Financial Accounting Standards Board (FASB) to be the critical element in the definition of goodwill. Accordingly, identifiable intangible assets that are reliably measurable are recognized and reported separately from goodwill.

Defensive Intangible Assets

In connection with a business combination or asset acquisition, management of the acquirer may acquire intangible assets that it does not intend to actively use but, rather, wishes to hold in order to prevent other parties from employing them or obtaining access to them. These intangibles often are referred to as defensive assets or as locked-up assets.

To qualify as a defensive intangible asset, the asset must either be

1. Acquired with the intent to not use it, *or*
2. Used by the acquirer with the intent to discontinue its use after completion of a transition period.

Upon being characterized as a defensive intangible, the asset is precluded from being considered abandoned upon acquisition, regardless of the fact that it is not being used.

Subsequent to the asset being characterized as a defensive intangible, management may decide to actively employ the asset. If so, the asset would cease to be considered a defensive intangible.

At acquisition, defensive intangibles are subject to the same fair value valuation principles as any other acquired intangible asset, including that they be measured considering exit price to marketplace participants that would put them to their highest and best use. In making the measurement, defensive intangibles are accounted for as a separate unit of accounting and are not to be grouped with other intangibles.

Defensive intangible assets are, in theory, to be assigned a useful life representing how (and for how long) the entity expects to consume the expected benefits related to them in the form of direct and indirect cash flows that would result from the prevention of others from realizing any value from them. In practice, however, such estimates would be difficult to make and highly subjective. Consequently, FASB substituted what it believed to be a more workable determination of useful life based on management's estimate of the period over which the defensive intangible asset diminishes in fair value.

Leasehold Improvements

Leasehold improvements result when tangible physical enhancements are made to property by or on behalf of the lessee of real estate. By law, when improvements are made to real property and those improvements are permanently affixed to the property, the title to those improvements automatically transfers to the owner of the property. The rationale behind this is that the improvements, when permanently affixed, are inseparable from the rest of the real estate, which is not owned by the lessee.

As a result of this automatic title transfer, the lessee's interest in the improvements is not a direct ownership interest but rather an intangible right to use and benefit from the improvements during the term of the lease. Consequently, the capitalized costs incurred by a lessee in constructing improvements to property that it leases represent an intangible asset analogous to a license to use them. Thus, when allocating the costs of leasehold improvements to the periods benefited, the expense is referred to as amortization (as used in the context of amortization of intangibles) and not depreciation.

A frequently encountered issue with respect to leasehold improvements relates to determination of the period over which they are to be amortized. Normally, the cost of long-lived assets is charged to expense over the estimated useful lives of the assets. However, the right to use a leasehold improvement expires when the related lease expires, irrespective of whether the physical improvement has any remaining useful life. Thus, the appropriate useful life for a leasehold improvement is the lesser of the useful life of the improvement or the term of the underlying lease. ASC 840-10-35-9 reinforces this concept by requiring that leasehold improvements acquired in a business combination or leasehold improvements completed well after commencement of a lease agreement be amortized over the lesser of the useful life of the leasehold improvement or a time period that includes required lease periods as well as reasonably assured lease renewal periods.

Some leases contain a fixed, noncancelable term and additional renewal options. When considering the term of the lease for the purposes of amortizing leasehold improvements, normally only the initial fixed noncancelable term is included. There are exceptions to this general rule that arise out of the application of GAAP to the lessee's accounting for the lease. If a renewal option is a bargain renewal option, then it is probable at the inception of the lease that it will be exercised; therefore, the option period is included in the lease term for purposes of determining the amortizable life of the leasehold improvements.

Additionally, under the definition of the lease term, there are other situations where it appears probable that an option to renew for an additional period would be exercised. These situations include periods for which failure to renew the lease imposes a penalty on the lessee in such amount that a renewal appears, at the inception of the lease, to be reasonably assured. Other situations of this kind arise when an otherwise excludable renewal period precedes a provision for a bargain purchase of the leased asset or when, during periods covered by ordinary renewal options, the lessee has guaranteed the lessor's debt on the leased property.

In deciding whether to include the period covered by a renewal option in the calculation of the amortizable life of the leasehold improvements, management of the lessee must be consistent with its own interpretation of renewal options that it included in the minimum lease payment calculations made to determine whether the lease is a capital or operating lease.

Example

Dozzy Corporation occupies a warehouse under a five-year operating lease commencing January 1, 2010, and expiring December 31, 2014. The lease contains three successive options to renew for additional five-year periods. The options are not bargain renewals as they call for fixed rentals at the prevailing fair market rents that will be in effect at the time of exercise. When the initial calculation was made to determine whether the lease is an operating lease or a capital lease, only the initial noncancelable term of five years was included in the calculation. Consequently, for the purpose of determining the amortizable life of any leasehold improvements made by Dozzy Corporation, only the initial five-year term is used. If Dozzy Corporation decides, at the beginning of year 4 of the lease, to make a substantial amount of leasehold improvements to the leased property, it could be argued that it would now be probable that Dozzy would exercise one or more of the renewal periods, since not doing so would impose the substantial financial penalty of abandoning expensive leasehold improvements. This would trigger accounting for the lease as if it were a new agreement and would require testing to determine whether the lease, prospectively, qualifies as a capital or operating lease.

The Securities and Exchange Commission (SEC) has provided the following guidance on the proper accounting treatment by a lessee for incentives or allowances provided by a lessor to a lessee under an operating lease.[1]

1. The incentives are not permitted to be netted against the leasehold improvements they were intended to subsidize. Instead, they are to be recorded as deferred rent and amortized as reductions to lease expense over the lease term.
2. The leasehold improvements are to be recorded gross, at their cost, and amortized as discussed above.
3. The lessee's cash flow statement is to reflect the cash received from the lessor as an incentive or allowance as cash provided by operating activities and the acquisition of the leasehold improvements as cash used for investing activities.

Note that this guidance is a reasonable interpretation of generally accepted accounting principles (GAAP) and thus should be applied to all entities, not just those subject to the jurisdiction of the SEC.

Software Developed for Internal Use

ASC 350-40 provides guidance on accounting for the costs of software developed for internal use. Software must meet two criteria to be accounted for as internal-use software.

1. The software's specifications must be designed or modified to meet the reporting entity's internal needs, including costs to customize purchased software.
2. During the period in which the software is being developed, there can be no plan or intent to market the software externally, although development of the software can be jointly funded by several entities that each plan to use the software internally.

In order to justify capitalization of related costs, it is necessary for management to conclude that it is probable that the project will be completed and that the software will be used as intended. Absent that level of expectation, costs must be expensed currently as research and development (R&D) costs. Entities that engage in both R&D of software for internal use and for sale to others must carefully identify costs with one or the other activity, since the former is (if all conditions are met) subject to capitalization, while the latter is expensed as R&D costs until technological feasibility is demonstrated, per ASC 985-20.

Costs subject to capitalization. Cost capitalization commences when an entity has completed the conceptual formulation, design, and testing of possible project alternatives, including the process of vendor selection for purchased software, if any. These early-phase costs (referred to as "preliminary project stage" in ASC 350-40) are analogous to R&D costs and must be expensed as incurred. These cannot be later restored as assets, even if the development proves to be successful.

Costs incurred subsequent to the preliminary project stage that meet the criteria under GAAP as long-lived assets are capitalized and amortized over the asset's expected economic life. Capitalization of costs begins when both of two conditions are met:

1. Management having the relevant authority authorizes and commits to funding the project and believes that it is probable that it will be completed and that the resulting software will be used as intended.
2. The conceptual formulation, design, and testing of possible software project alternatives (i.e., the preliminary project stage) have all been completed.

Costs capitalized include those of the application development stage of the software development process. These include coding and testing activities and various implementation costs. These costs are limited to

1. External direct costs of materials and services consumed in developing or obtaining internal-use computer software.

---

[1]   *Letter from SEC Chief Accountant to the chairman of the AICPA Center for Public Company Audit Firms (CPCAF) dated February 7, 2005; www.sec.gov/info/accountants/staffletters/ cpcaf020705.htm.*

2. Payroll and payroll-related costs for employees who are directly associated with and who devote time to the internal-use computer software project to the extent of the time spent directly on the project.
3. Interest cost incurred while developing internal-use computer software, consistent with the provisions of ASC 835-20.

General and administrative costs, overhead costs, and training costs are expensed as incurred. Even though these may be costs that are associated with the internal development or acquisition of software for internal use, under GAAP, those costs relate to the period in which they are incurred. The issue of training costs is particularly important, since internal-use computer software purchased from third parties often includes, as part of the purchase price, training for the software (and often fees for routine maintenance as well). When the amount of training or maintenance fees is not specified in the contract, entities are required to allocate the cost among training, maintenance, and amounts representing the capitalizable cost of computer software. Training costs are recognized as expense as incurred. Maintenance fees are recognized as expense ratably over the maintenance period.

ASC 350-40 provides examples of computer software acquired or developed for internal use. Some of these are

- When modifications are made to software controlling robots acquired for use in the manufacturing process.
- Software is developed for cash management, payroll processing, or accounts payable system purposes.
- A bank develops an online account status inquiry system for customers to utilize.
- A travel agency invests in software to give it access to an airline reservation system.
- A communications provider develops computerized systems to manage customer services such as voice mail.
- When a publisher invests in computerized systems to produce a product that is then sold to customers.

Software that does not qualify as being for internal use includes

- Software sold by a robot manufacturer to purchasers of its products.
- The cost of developing programs for microchips used in automobile electronic systems.
- Software developed for both sale to customers and internal use.
- Computer programs written for use in R&D efforts.
- Costs of developing software under contract with another entity.

In some cases internal-use software is later sold or licensed to third parties, notwithstanding the original intention of management that the software was acquired or developed solely for internal use. In such cases, ASC 350-40 provides that any proceeds received are to be applied first as a reduction of the carrying amount of the software. No profit is recognized until the aggregate proceeds from sales exceed the carrying amount of the software. After the carrying value is fully recovered, any subsequent proceeds are recognized in revenue as earned.

Impairment. Impairment of capitalized internal-use software is recognized and measured in accordance with the provisions of ASC 360 in the same manner as tangible long-lived assets and other amortizable intangible assets.

Circumstances that might suggest that impairment has occurred and that would trigger a recoverability evaluation include

1. A realization that the internal-use computer software is not expected to provide substantive service potential.
2. A significant change in the extent or manner in which the software is used.
3. A significant change has been made or is being anticipated to the software program.
4. The costs of developing or modifying the internal-use computer software significantly exceed the amount originally expected.

In some instances, ongoing software development projects will become troubled before being discontinued. ASC 350-40 provides that management needs to assess the likelihood of successful completion of projects in progress. When it becomes no longer probable that the computer software being developed will be completed and placed in service, the asset is to be written down to the lower of the carrying amount or fair value, if any, less costs to sell. Importantly, it is a rebuttable presumption that any uncompleted software has a zero fair value.

ASC 350-40 provides indicators that the software is no longer expected to be completed and placed in service. These include

1. A lack of expenditures budgeted or incurred for the project.
2. Programming difficulties that cannot be resolved on a timely basis.
3. Significant cost overruns.
4. Information indicating that the costs of internally developed software will significantly exceed the cost of comparable third-party software or software products, suggesting that management intends to obtain the third-party software instead of completing the internal development effort.
5. The introduction of new technologies which increase the likelihood that management will elect to obtain third-party software instead of completing the internal project.
6. A lack of profitability of the business segment or unit to which the software relates or actual or potential discontinuation of the segment.

Amortization. As for other long-lived assets, the cost of computer software developed or obtained for internal use should be amortized in a systematic and rational manner over its estimated useful life. The intangible nature of the asset contributes to the difficulty of developing a meaningful estimate, however. Among the factors to be weighed are the effects of obsolescence, new technology, and competition. Management would need to consider, in particular, whether rapid changes are occurring in the development of software products, software operating systems, or computer hardware and whether it intends to replace any technologically obsolete software or hardware.

Amortization commences for each module or component of a software project when the software is ready for its intended use, without regard to whether the software is to be placed in service in planned stages that might extend beyond a single reporting period. Computer software is deemed ready for its intended use after substantially all testing has been completed.

Example of Software Developed for Internal Use

The Da Vinci Invention Company employs researchers based in countries around the world. The far-flung nature of its operations makes it extremely difficult for the payroll staff to collect time sheets, so the management team authorizes the design of an in-house, Web-based timekeeping system. The project team incurs these costs:

Cost type	Charged to expense	Capitalized
Concept design	$ 2,500	
Evaluation of design alternatives	3,700	
Determination of required technology	8,100	
Final selection of alternatives	1,400	
Software design		$ 28,000
Software coding		42,000
Quality assurance testing		30,000
Data conversion costs	3,900	
Training	14,000	
Overhead allocation	6,900	
General and administrative costs	11,200	
Ongoing maintenance costs	6,000	
Totals	$57,700	$100,000

Thus, the total capitalized cost of this development project is $100,000. The estimated useful life of the timekeeping system is five years. As soon as all testing is completed, Da Vinci's controller begins amortizing using a monthly charge of $1,666.67. The calculation is

$$\$100,000 \text{ capitalized cost} \div 60 \text{ months} = \$1,666.67 \text{ amortization charge}$$

Once operational, management elects to construct another module for the system that issues an e-mail reminder for employees to complete their time sheets. This represents significant added functionality, so the design cost can be capitalized. These costs are incurred:

Labor type	Labor cost	Payroll taxes	Benefits	Total cost
Software developers	$11,000	$ 842	$1,870	$13,712
Quality assurance testers	7,000	536	1,190	8,726
Totals	$18,000	$1,378	$3,060	$22,438

The full $22,438 amount of these costs can be capitalized. By the time this additional work is completed, the original system has been in operation for one year, thereby reducing the amortization period for the new module to four years. The calculation of the monthly straight-line amortization is

$22,438 capitalized cost ÷ 48 months = $467.46 incremental amortization charge

The Da Vinci management then authorizes the development of an additional module that allows employees to enter time data into the system from their cell phones using text messaging. Despite successfully passing through the concept design stage, the development team cannot resolve interface problems on a timely basis. Management elects to shut down the development project, requiring the charge of all $13,000 of programming and testing costs to expense in the current period.

After the system has been operating for two years, a Da Vinci customer sees the timekeeping system in action and begs management to sell it as a stand-alone product. The customer becomes a distributor and lands three sales in the first year. From these sales Da Vinci receives revenues of $57,000 and incurs these related expenses:

Expense type	Amount
Distributor commission (25%)	$14,250
Service costs	1,900
Installation costs	4,300
Total	$20,450

Thus, the net proceeds from the software sale is $36,550 ($57,000 revenue less $20,450 related costs). Rather than recording these transactions as revenue and expense, the $36,550 net proceeds are offset against the remaining unamortized balance of the software asset with this entry:

Revenue	57,000	
Fixed assets—software		36,550
Commission expense		14,250
Service expense		1,900
Installation expense		4,300

At this point, the remaining unamortized balance of the timekeeping system is $40,278, which is calculated as

Original capitalized amount	$100,000
+ Additional software module	22,438
– 24 months amortization on original capitalized amount	(40,000)
– 12 months amortization on additional software module	(5,610)
– Net proceeds from software sales	(36,550)
Total unamortized balance	$40,278

Immediately thereafter, Da Vinci's management receives a sales call from an application service provider that manages an Internet-based timekeeping system. The terms offered are so good that the company abandons its in-house system at once and switches to the ASP system. As a result of this change, the company writes off the remaining unamortized balance of its timekeeping system with this entry:

Accumulated amortization	45,610	
Loss on asset disposal	40,278	
Fixed assets—software		85,888

Web Site Development Costs

The costs of developing a Web site, including the costs of developing services that are offered to visitors (e.g., chat rooms, search engines, blogs, social networking, e-mail, calendars, etc.), are often quite significant. The SEC staff had expressed the opinion that a large portion of those costs should be accounted for in accordance with ASC 350-50, *Web Site Development Costs,* which sets forth certain conditions that must be met before costs may be capitalized.

Per ASC 350-50, costs incurred in the planning stage must be expensed as incurred. The cost of software used to operate a Web site must be accounted for consistent with ASC 350-50, unless a plan exists to market the software externally, in which case ASC 985-20 governs. Costs incurred to develop graphics (broadly defined as the "look and feel" of the Web page) are included in software costs, and thus accounted for under ASC 350-50 or ASC 985-20, as noted in the foregoing. Costs of operating Web sites are accounted for in the same manner as other operating costs analogous to repairs and maintenance. ASC 350-50-55 includes a detailed exhibit stipulating how a variety of specific costs are to be accounted for under its requirements.

INITIAL RECOGNITION AND MEASUREMENT OF INTANGIBLES

Intangibles acquired individually or with a group of other assets are initially recognized and measured based on their fair values. Fair value, consistent with ASC 820, is determined based on the assumptions that market participants would use in pricing the asset. Even if the reporting entity does not intend to use an intangible asset in a manner that is its highest and best use, the intangible is nevertheless measured at its fair value.

This principle extends even to defensive intangible assets (sometimes referred to as "locked-up assets"), assets that management has acquired expressly to prevent others from using or obtaining access to and that management does not intend to use.

The aggregate amount assigned to a group of assets acquired is to be allocated to the individual assets acquired based on their relative fair values. Goodwill is prohibited from being recognized in an asset acquisition. (It may, of course, be recognized in business acquisitions that also involve the purchase of intangibles.)

Although a reporting entity can purchase intangibles that were developed by others, U.S. GAAP continues to maintain a strict prohibition against capitalizing costs of internally developing, maintaining, or restoring intangibles, including goodwill. The only exceptions to this general rule are leasehold improvements, software developed for internal use, and Web site development costs, as discussed previously in this chapter.

Amortization and Impairment Considerations

Many intangible assets are based on rights that are conveyed legally by contract, statute, or similar means. For example, governments grant franchises or similar rights to taxi companies, cable companies, and hydroelectric plants. Companies and other private-sector organizations grant franchises to automobile dealers, fast-food outlets, and professional sports teams. Other rights, such as airport landing rights, are granted by contract. Some of those franchises or similar rights are for finite terms, while others are perpetual. Many of those with finite terms are routinely renewed, absent violations of the terms of the agreement, and the costs incurred for renewal are minimal. Many such assets are also transferable, and the prices at which they trade reflect expectations of renewal at minimal cost. However, for others, renewal is not assured, and their renewal may entail substantial cost.

Trademarks, service marks, and trade names may be registered with the government for a period of 20 years and are renewable for additional 20-year periods as long as the trademark, service mark, or trade name is used continuously. (Brand names, often used synonymously with trademarks, are typically not registered and thus the required attribute of control will be absent.) The U.S. government now grants copyrights for the life of the creator plus 50 years. Patents are granted by the government for a period of 17 years but may be effectively renewed by adding minor modifications that are patented for additional 17-year periods. Such assets also are commonly transferable.

If no legal, regulatory, contractual, competitive, economic, or other factors limit the useful life of an intangible asset to the reporting entity, the useful life of the asset is considered to be indefinite (which is not, of course, the same as unlimited or infinite).

Identifiable intangible assets having indefinite useful economic lives supported by clearly identifiable cash flows are not subject to regular periodic amortization. Instead, the carrying amount of the intangible is tested for impairment annually and again between annual tests if events or circumstances warrant such a test. An impairment loss is recognized if the carrying amount exceeds the fair value. Furthermore, amortization of the asset commences when evidence suggests that its useful economic life is no longer deemed indefinite.

Under the ASC 350-30-35-3, the reporting entity is to consider its own historical experience in renewing or extending similar arrangements in determining the assumptions regarding renewal or extension, in particular

1. The entity's expected use of the asset.
2. The expected useful life of another asset or asset group to which the useful life of the intangible asset may be related.
3. Any provisions contained in applicable law, regulation, or contract that may limit the useful life.
4. The entity's own historical experience in renewing or extending similar arrangements if such experience is consistent with the intended use of the intangible asset by the reporting entity, and irrespective of whether those similar arrangements contained explicit renewal or extension provisions. In the absence of such historical experience, management is to consider the assumptions that market participants would use about the renewal or extension consistent with their highest and best use of the asset, and adjusted for relevant entity-specific factors.
5. The effects of obsolescence, demand, competition, and other economic factors, such as

   a. Stability of the industry.
   b. Known technological advances.
   c. Legislative action that results in an uncertain or changing regulatory environment.
   d. Expected changes in distribution channels.

6. The level of maintenance expenditures that would be required to obtain the expected future cash flows from the asset.

An income approach is commonly used to measure the fair value of an intangible asset. The period of expected cash flows used to measure fair value of the intangible, adjusted for applicable entity-specific factors, is to be considered by management in determining the useful life of the intangible for amortization purposes.

ASC 350-30-35 provides guidance about when it is appropriate to combine into a single "unit of accounting" for impairment testing purposes, separately recorded indefinite-life intangibles, whether acquired or internally developed.

The assets may be combined into a single unit of accounting for impairment testing if they are operated as a single asset and, as such, are inseparable from one another. The following indicators are to be used in evaluating the individual facts and circumstances to enable the exercise of judgment.

Indicators that Indefinite-Lived Intangibles Are to Be Combined as a Single Unit of Accounting

1. The intangibles will be used together to construct or enhance a single asset.
2. If the intangibles had been part of the same acquisition, they would have been recorded as a single asset.
3. The intangibles, as a group, represent "the highest and best use of the assets" (e.g., they could probably realize a higher sales price if sold together than if they were sold separately). Indicators pointing to this situation are

   a. The unlikelihood that a substantial portion of the assets would be sold separately; or
   b. The fact that, should a substantial portion of the intangibles be sold individually, there would be a significant reduction in the fair value of the remaining assets in the group.

4. The marketing or branding strategy of the entity treats the assets as being complementary (e.g., a trademark and its related trade name, formulas, recipes, and patented or unpatented technology can all be complementary to an entity's brand name).

Indicators that Indefinite-Lived Intangibles Are Not to Be Combined as a Single Unit of Accounting

1. Each separate intangible generates independent cash flows.
2. In a sale, it would be likely that the intangibles would be sold separately. If the entity had previously sold similar assets separately, this would constitute evidence that combining the assets would not be appropriate.
3. The entity is either considering or has already adopted a plan to dispose of one or more of the intangibles separately.
4. The intangibles are used exclusively by different asset groups (as defined in the ASC Master Glossary).
5. The intangibles have differing useful economic lives.

ASC 350-30-35 provides guidance regarding the "unit of accounting" determination:

1. Goodwill and finite-lived intangibles are not permitted to be combined in the "unit of accounting" since they are subject to different impairment rules.
2. A defensive intangible asset (discussed earlier) is to be accounted for as a separate unit of accounting.
3. If the intangibles collectively constitute a business, they may not be combined into a unit of accounting.
4. If the unit of accounting includes intangibles recorded in the separate financial statements of consolidated subsidiaries, it is possible that the sum of impairment losses recognized in the separate financial statements of the subsidiaries will not equal the consolidated impairment loss.

   NOTE: Although counterintuitive, this situation can occur when

   1. *At the **separate subsidiary level,** an intangible asset is impaired since the cash flows from the other intangibles included in the unit of accounting that reside in other subsidiaries cannot be considered in determining impairment.*
   2. *At the **consolidated level,** when the intangibles are considered as a single unit of accounting, they are not impaired.*

5. Should a unit of accounting be included in a single reporting unit, that same unit of accounting and associated fair value is to be used in computing the implied fair value of goodwill for measuring any goodwill impairment loss.

Useful Life and Residual Value Considerations

Identifiable intangible assets, such as franchise rights, customer lists, trademarks, patents and copyrights, and licenses are to be amortized over their expected useful economic life with required impairment reviews of their recoverability when necessitated by changes in facts and circumstances in the same manner as set forth in ASC 360 for tangible long-lived assets.

ASC 360 also requires consideration of the intangible's residual value (analogous to salvage value for a tangible asset) in determining the amount of the intangible to amortize. Residual value is defined as the value of the intangible to the entity at the end of its (entity-specific) useful life reduced by any estimated disposition costs. The residual value of an amortizable intangible is assumed to be zero unless the intangible will continue to have a useful life to another party after the end of its useful life to its current holder, and one or both of these criteria are met:

1. The current holder has received a third-party commitment to purchase the intangible at the end of its useful life, *or*
2. A market for the intangible exists and is expected to continue to exist at the end of the asset's useful life as a means of determining the residual value of the intangible by reference to marketplace transactions.

EXTRACTS FROM PUBLISHED FINANCIAL STATEMENTS

General Electric Company, December 31, 2008

Note 1. Summary of Significant Accounting Policies

Intangible Assets

We do not amortize goodwill, but test it at least annually for impairment using a fair value approach at the reporting unit level. A reporting unit is the operating segment, or a business one level below that operating segment (the component level) if discrete financial information is prepared and regularly reviewed by segment management. However, components are aggregated as a single reporting unit if they have similar economic characteristics. We recognize an impairment charge if the carrying amount of a reporting unit exceeds its fair value and the carrying amount of the reporting unit's goodwill exceeds the implied fair value of that goodwill. We use discounted cash flows to establish fair values. When available and as appropriate, we use comparative market multiples to corroborate discounted cash flow results. When all or a portion of a reporting unit is disposed of, goodwill is allocated to the gain or loss on disposition based on the relative fair values of the business disposed of and the portion of the reporting unit that will be retained.

We amortize the cost of other intangibles over their estimated useful lives unless such lives are deemed indefinite. The cost of intangible assets is generally amortized on a straight-line basis over the asset's estimated economic life, except that individually significant customer-related intangible assets are amortized in relation to total related sales. Amortizable intangible assets are tested for impairment based on undiscounted cash flows and, if impaired, written down to fair value based on either discounted cash flows or appraised values. Intangible assets with indefinite lives are tested annually for impairment and written down to fair value as required.

Note 15. Goodwill and Other Intangible Assets

December 31 (In millions)	*2008*	*2007*
Other intangible assets		
GE		
Intangible assets subject to amortization	**$9,010**	$9,278
Indefinite-lived intangible assets[a]	**2,354**	2,355
	11,364	11,633
GECS		
Intangible assets subject to amortization	**3,613**	4,509
Total	**$14,977**	$16,142

[a] *Indefinite-lived intangible assets principally comprised trademarks, tradenames, and U.S. Federal Communications Commission licenses.*

Intangible Assets Subject to Amortization

December 31 (In millions)	*Gross carrying amount*	*Accumulated amortization*	*Net*
GE			
2008			
Customer-related	**$4,551**	**$(900)**	**$3,651**
Patents, licenses, and trademarks	**4,751**	**(1,690)**	**3,061**
Capitalized software	**4,706**	**(2,723)**	**1,983**
All other	**470**	**(155)**	**315**
Total	**$14,478**	**$(5,468)**	**$9,010**
2007			
Customer-related	4,526	(698)	3,828
Patents, licenses, and trademarks	4,561	(1,369)	3,192
Capitalized software	4,573	(2,589)	1,984
All other	436	(162)	274
Total	$14,096	$(4,818)	$9,278

December 31 (In millions)	Gross carrying amount	Accumulated amortization	Net
GECS			
2008			
Customer-related	**1,746**	**(613)**	**1,133**
Patents, licenses, and trademarks	**589**	**(460)**	**129**
Capitalized software	**2,170**	**(1,476)**	**694**
Lease valuations	**1,805**	**(594)**	**1,211**
Present value of future profits	**831**	**(401)**	**430**
All other	**181**	**(165)**	**16**
Total	**$7,322**	**$(3,709)**	**$3,613**
2007			
Customer-related	2,395	(869)	1,526
Patents, licenses and trademarks	428	(309)	119
Capitalized software	1,832	(1,095)	737
Lease valuations	1,841	(360)	1,481
Present value of future profits	818	(364)	454
All other	347	(155)	192
Total	$7,661	$(3,152)	$4,509

During 2008, we recorded additions to intangible assets subject to amortization of $2,029 million. The components of finite-lived intangible assets acquired during 2008 and their respective weighted-average amortizable period are: $756 million—Customer-related (17.1 years); $382 million—Patents, licenses, and trademarks (17.4 years); $765 million—Capitalized software (4.4 years); $38 million—Lease valuations (8.7 years); and $88 million—All other (9.4 years).

Consolidated amortization related to intangible assets subject to amortization was $2,091 million and $2,071 million for 2008 and 2007, respectively. We estimate that annual pretax amortization for intangible assets subject to amortization over the next five calendar years to be as follows: 2009—$1,772 million; 2010—$1,541 million; 2011—$1,326 million; 2012—$1,145 million; 2013—$957 million.

MULTIPLE-CHOICE QUESTIONS

1. Which item listed below does **not** qualify as an intangible asset?
   (a) Computer software.
   (b) Registered patent.
   (c) Copyrights that are protected.
   (d) Notebook computer.

2. Which of the following items qualify as an intangible asset under ASC 350?
   (a) Advertising and promotion on the launch of a huge product.
   (b) College tuition fees paid to employees who decide to enrol in an executive MBA program at Harvard University while working with the company.
   (c) Operating losses during the initial stages of the project.
   (d) Legal costs paid to intellectual property lawyers to register a patent.

3. Once recognized, intangible assets can be carried at:
   (a) Cost less accumulated depreciation.
   (b) Cost less accumulated depreciation and less accumulated amortization.
   (c) Fair value less accumulated depreciation.
   (d) Cost plus a notional increase in fair value since the intangible asset is acquired.

4. Which of the following is **not** a cost of internally developed software that may be capitalized?
   (a) External direct costs of material and services consumed in developing the software.
   (b) Payroll and payroll-related costs for employees who are directly associated with the development of the software.
   (c) Interest cost incurred while developing the software.
   (d) Indirect overhead cost related to production of the internally developed software.

5. In connection with a business combination or asset acquisition, management of the acquirer may acquire intangible assets that it does not intend to actively use but, rather, wishes to hold in order to prevent other parties from employing them or obtaining access to them. Which of the following is **not** true?
   (a) Because it is a defensive intangible asset, the asset may be considered abandoned upon acquisition because it is not intended to be used.
   (b) Subsequent to the asset being characterized as a defensive intangible, management may decide to actively employ the asset.
   (c) Defensive intangibles are accounted for as a separate unit of accounting and not to be grouped with other intangibles interest cost incurred while developing the software.
   (d) The useful life is based on management's estimate of the period over which the defensive intangible asset diminishes in fair value.

Chapter 14

CONSOLIDATED AND SEPARATE FINANCIAL STATEMENTS (ASC 810)

SCOPE

This chapter focuses on the Standard to be applied in preparing the consolidated financial statements of groups of companies controlled by a parent entity.

DEFINITIONS OF KEY TERMS
(in accordance with ASC 810)

Consolidated financial statements. The financial statements of a parent and all of its subsidiaries presented as a single economic entity.

Control (or controlling financial interest). Control of an entity can be obtained either (1) by obtaining ownership of a majority of its outstanding voting interests (the controlled entity being referred to as a voting interest entity), or (2) by obtaining contractual rights to receive the majority of the financial benefits and/or by assuming contractual obligations to bear the majority of the financial consequences that occur in the future from the entity outperforming or underperforming its expectations. (The controlled entity being referred to is a variable interest entity [VIE].) These conditions are mutually exclusive (i.e., an entity is either a voting interest entity controlled by the holders of a voting majority of its equity or is a variable interest entity controlled individually or collectively by one or more other parties referred to as holders of variable interests). In the latter instance, when a single party has control, the party is referred to as the primary beneficiary of the VIE.

Entities that might otherwise be considered voting interest entities nevertheless might not be controlled by the holders of the majority of the voting interests in situations where, for example, the entity is in legal reorganization, subject to bankruptcy proceedings, or operating subject to governmental restrictions (e.g., foreign exchange restrictions or other controls) that impose uncertainties on the entity whose severity casts significant doubt regarding the voting owner's ability to control the entity.

Equity interests. In an investor-owned entity, instruments evidencing rights of ownership. In a mutual entity, instruments evidencing ownership, membership, or participation rights.

More likely than not (MLTN). A likelihood or probability of more than 50%.

Noncontrolling interest. The equity or net assets in a subsidiary not directly or indirectly attributable to its parent. Noncontrolling interests were formerly referred to in accounting literature as minority interests.

Owners. Holders of ownership interests (equity interests) in investor-owned or mutual entities. Owners include parties referred to as shareholders, partners, proprietors, members, or participants.

Parent. An entity that possesses a controlling financial interest in one or more subsidiaries including an entity that is the primary beneficiary of a variable interest entity.

Primary beneficiary. A variable interest holder that is required to consolidate a variable interest entity (VIE). Under ASC 805, this party is also referred to as a "parent" and the VIE is also referred to as a "subsidiary."

Consolidation is required when the holder of one or more variable interests would absorb a majority of the VIE's expected losses, receive a majority of the VIE's expected residual returns, or both. If one holder would absorb a majority of the VIE's expected losses and another holder would receive a majority of the VIE's expected residual returns, the holder absorbing the majority of the expected losses is the primary beneficiary and is thus required to consolidate the VIE.

Subsidiary. An entity, including unincorporated entities such as partnerships or trusts, in which another entity, referred to as its parent, holds a controlling financial interest. A variable interest entity that is consolidated by a primary beneficiary is also included in this definition.

Variable interest. Ownership, contractual, or other monetary interests in an entity that either are entitled to receive expected positive variability (referred to as expected residual returns) or obligated to absorb expected negative variability (referred to as expected losses).

Variable interest entity. An entity for which an analysis of the at-risk investments of the holders of its voting interests would not be effective in establishing the party or parties that hold a controlling financial interest in the entity. This situation arises either (1) because the entity is not adequately capitalized by at-risk equity sufficient to absorb its expected losses or (2) because the at-risk equity holders do not receive or bear all of the financial benefits or detriments that would provide those holders with a controlling financial interest in the entity.

PRESENTATION OF FINANCIAL STATEMENTS

Financial statements should be presented by the parent entity unless these four conditions are met:

1. Sale by the parent of all or a portion of its ownership interest in the subsidiary resulting in the parent no longer holding a controlling financial interest.
2. Expiration of a contract that granted control of the subsidiary to the parent.
3. Issuance by the subsidiary of stock that reduces the ownership interest of the parent to a level not representing a controlling financial interest.
4. Loss of control of the subsidiary by the parent because the subsidiary becomes subject to control by a governmental body, court, administrator, or regulator.

CONSOLIDATED FINANCIAL STATEMENTS

All subsidiaries of the parent should be consolidated. Control is presumed to exist when the parent owns a majority of the voting rights of the entity.

In exceptional circumstances, if it can be demonstrated that such ownership does not constitute control, then the parent/subsidiary relationship does not exist. Even if less than half or even half of the voting rights are acquired, it is still possible for control to exist where there is power

- Over more than half of the voting rights because of an agreement with other investors.
- To govern the financial and operating policies of the entity by law or by agreement.
- To appoint or remove the majority of the members of the board of directors and control of the entity is by that board.

- To cast the majority of votes at a meeting of the board of directors and control is exercised by that board.

PRACTICAL INSIGHT

Payton Industries, Inc. (PI) discloses in its financial statements that it has a 66% subsidiary; the remaining 34% is held by another party. PI had the right to nominate four out of six members of the subsidiary's management board, although the minority shareholder had a blocking right in various circumstances. The articles were changed so that members of the board were nominated equally by PI and the minority shareholder. The view taken by PI was that the blocking rights were not intended to deprive it of its ability to control the subsidiary and have never been used as such. PI considers that it continues to exercise control under ASC 810 and continues to consolidate the subsidiary.

A subsidiary cannot be excluded from consolidation because its business is dissimilar from that of the other entities within the group.

An entity loses control when it loses the power to govern its financial and operating policies. This could occur, for example, where a subsidiary becomes subject to the control of the government, a regulator, a court of law, or as a result of a contractual agreement.

A subsidiary that is operating under severe long-term restrictions that impair its ability to transfer funds to the parent should not be excluded from consolidation. The parent entity must lose control of the subsidiary in order for the exclusion to happen.

Case Study 1

Facts

There are currently severe restrictions on the repatriation of dividends from a subsidiary located in Country A. As a result, the directors of the U.S. parent entity wish to deconsolidate the subsidiary, as they feel that this restriction may be in place for several years. Two subsidiaries located in the country are individually immaterial but collectively material. The directors of the U.S. parent also wish to deconsolidate these entities.

Required

Can the results of these subsidiaries be deconsolidated?

Solution

Control must be lost for deconsolidation to occur. However, the impairment of the ability to transfer funds would not result in a loss of control. Therefore, the subsidiary should still be consolidated. Additionally, generally accepted accounting principles (GAAP) is not applicable to immaterial items, but since the two subsidiaries taken as a whole are material, GAAP must be adhered to.

ACCOUNTING PROCEDURES

Under U.S. GAAP, the parent company and its subsidiaries are not required to use uniform accounting policies for reporting transactions.

Noncontrolling interests in a consolidated subsidiary can be presented in liabilities, in equity, or in a special category.

The financial statements of the parent and its subsidiaries should be prepared using the same reporting date. If the reporting dates are different, the subsidiary should prepare additional financial statements for consolidation purposes as of the same date of the parent entity, unless it is impracticable to do so. In this case, adjustments must be made for the effects of significant transactions that have occurred between the date of the financial statements of the subsidiary and the parent entity. The difference between these dates should never be more than three months.

PRACTICAL INSIGHT

Coulter Co. states that those subsidiaries' financial statements with different year-ends all fell within the three-month window. In the year ended November 30, 2010, the statements of financial position of all subsidiaries have been harmonized to the end of November. A note in the financial statements cautions that this should be taken into account for comparability purposes and discloses an increase in revenue of $40 million and an increase in profit after tax of $2 million.

Investments in subsidiaries, associates, and jointly controlled entities should be accounted for by either measuring the investments at cost or in accordance with the equity method. Any such items that are classified as held for sale should be measured at acquisition date fair value less cost to sell consistent with ASC 360.

VARIABLE INTEREST ENTITIES

Variable interests are identified by thoroughly analyzing the assets, liabilities, and contractual arrangements of an entity to determine whether each item being analyzed creates variability or absorbs/receives variability.

Each of the next six items is potentially an explicit or implicit variable interest in an entity or in specified assets of an entity. This list is not all-inclusive.

1. At-risk equity investments in a VIE
2. Investments in subordinated debt instruments issued by a VIE
3. Investments in subordinated beneficial interests issued by a VIE
4. Guarantees of the value of VIE assets or liabilities
5. Written put options on the assets of a VIE or similar obligations that protect senior interests from suffering losses
6. Forward contracts to sell assets owned by the entity at a fixed price

Whether an entity qualifies as a VIE is initially determined when an entity obtains its variable interest in that entity. This determination is based on the circumstances existing at that date, taking into account future changes that are required in existing governing documents and contractual arrangements.

A holder of a variable interest initially determines whether it is the primary beneficiary of a VIE in conjunction with the initial determination that the entity is a VIE (i.e., when the holder initially obtains its interest in the entity).

This initial determination of whether an interest holder is the primary beneficiary (irrespective of whether the holder is or is not considered to be the primary beneficiary) needs to be reconsidered when changes are made to the entity's governing documents or contractual arrangements that result in a reallocation of the obligation to absorb expected losses or the right to receive expected residual returns of the VIE between the existing primary beneficiary and other unrelated parties.

An entity must consolidate a VIE of which it is the primary beneficiary. The variable interest holder that is the primary beneficiary of a VIE holds a variable interest (or combination of variable interests) that will absorb a majority of the entity's expected losses, receive a majority of the entity's expected residual returns, or both.

Absorbing losses is more important than receiving residual returns. If one entity will absorb a majority of a VIE's expected losses and another (unrelated) entity will receive a majority of the VIE's expected residual returns, the entity absorbing a majority of the losses must consolidate the VIE.

If there are other (noncontrolling) interests, which are analogous to minority interests, these are shown in the consolidated statement of financial position just as minority interests are under GAAP. Likewise, a share of the operating results of the VIE are allocated to the noncontrolling interests in the consolidated statements of income (operations).

If the primary beneficiary of a VIE and the VIE itself are under common control, the primary beneficiary (parent) is to initially measure the assets, liabilities, and noncontrolling interests of the newly consolidated reporting entity at their preexisting carrying amounts.

Absent common control, the rules governing the initial measurement of the assets and liabilities of a newly consolidated VIE differ depending on the date on which the VIE is initially consolidated.

ASC 810-10-45-18 specifies that the elimination of intra-entity profit or loss is not affected by the existence of a noncontrolling interest and that the elimination may be allocated between the parent (the controlling interest) and the noncontrolling interests.

DISCLOSURES

Consolidated financial statements should disclose the consolidation policy that is being followed. The requirements under this Standard are quite extensive. A parent having one or more less-than-wholly-owned subsidiaries shall disclose these points in each reporting period:

1. Separately, on the face of the consolidated financial statements, both the

    a. Amounts of consolidated net income and consolidated comprehensive income.
    b. The related amounts of each attributable to the parent and the noncontrolling interest should be disclosed.

2. If reported in the consolidated financial statements, amounts attributable to the parent for income from continuing operations, discontinued operations, and extraordinary items should be disclosed in the notes or on the face of the consolidated income statement.
3. Either in the consolidated statement of changes in equity (if presented), or in the notes to consolidated financial statements, a reconciliation should be prepared separately disclosing net income, transactions with owners acting in their capacity as owners, and each component of comprehensive income.
4. The effects of any changes in a parent's ownership interest in a subsidiary on the equity attributable to the parent.

Three disclosures are required when a subsidiary is deconsolidated:

1. The amount of any gain or loss recognized in accordance with paragraph 810-10-40-5.
2. The portion of any gain or loss related to the remeasurement of any retained investment in the former subsidiary to its fair value.
3. The caption in the income statement in which the gain or loss is recognized unless separately presented on the face of the income statement.

Case Study 2

Facts

Entity X is preparing its group accounts for the year ended December 31, 2010, and has acquired investments in three companies. The details are set out next.

(a) Entity Y

The whole of the share capital of Y was acquired on July 1, 2010, with a view to selling the subsidiary within a year. At the date of acquisition, the estimated fair value less cost to sell of Y is $27 million. (The fair value of the liabilities is $8 million.) At year-end (December 31, 2010), the estimated fair value less costs to sell is $26 million. (The fair value of the liabilities is $7 million.)

(b) Entity Z

X has acquired, on August 1, 2010, 48% of Z, which is a major supplier of X. X has a written agreement with another major shareholder, which owns 30% of the share capital of Z, whereby X can receive as much of Z's production as it wishes. X has also made a substantial loan to Z, which is repayable on demand. If repaid currently, Z would be insolvent.

(c) Entity W

X has acquired 45% of the voting shares of W on September 1, 2010. The other shares are owned by V (25%) and T (30%). V and T are both institutional investors and have representation on the board of directors. X can appoint four members of the board; V and T appoint three each. The effective power to set W's operating policies lies with the four directors appointed by X. However, if there is to be any change in the capital structure of the company, then the full board (10 directors) must vote in favor of the proposal.

Required

Discuss how these three investments should be treated in the consolidated financial statements of X group for the year ended December 31, 2010.

Solution

Entity Y, which was acquired on July 1, 2010, will have to be accounted for under ASC 360. It will meet the criteria as being held for sale and, therefore, must be accounted for in this way.

Initially, the fair value of the assets would be recorded at $27 million plus $8 million, which is $35 million. The fair value of the liabilities would be recorded at $8 million. At the first statement of financial position date, X will have to remeasure the investment in entity Y at the lower of its cost and fair value less cost to sell, which will be $26 million. The assets and liabilities will have to be presented separately in the consolidated financial statements from any other assets and liabilities. The total assets at year-end December 31 will be shown separately as $33 million, and the total liabilities will be shown separately as $7 million. Obviously the subsidiary is not consolidated as such.

X owns 48% of the voting shares and has the power to control who has access to the operating capacity of Z by virtue of a written agreement with another shareholder that owns 30% of the share capital. There will be a presumption that X will have significant influence over Z through its ability to demand repayment of a substantial loan. Therefore, X should consolidate Z. X has the power to govern the financial and operating policies of the entity through agreement and through its relationship with Z.

Regarding entity W, X has 45% of the voting power, V has 25%, and T has 30%, but V and T are institutional investors, and the directors who represent these investors have no effective power. Substantial power lies with the four directors of W. Although the full board retains some powers, these powers are limited. The four directors representing W have effective control over most of the financing and operating policies, which would represent a significant part of the decision making. X has effective control over V through its control over the board of directors and decision making. Therefore, W should be consolidated.

EXTRACT FROM PUBLISHED FINANCIAL STATEMENT

Nokia, Annual Report 2008

Notes to the Financial Statements

Principles of consolidation

The consolidated financial statements include the accounts of Nokia's parent company ("Parent Company"), and each of those companies over which the Group exercises control. Control over an entity is presumed to exist when the Group owns, directly or indirectly through subsidiaries, over 50% of the voting rights of the entity, the Group has the power to govern the operating and financial policies of the entity through agreement or the Group has the power to appoint or remove the majority of the members of the board of the entity.

The Group's share of profits and losses of associated companies is included in the consolidated profit and loss account in accordance with the equity method of accounting. An associated company is an entity over which the Group exercises significant influence. Significant influence is generally presumed to exist when the Group owns, directly or indirectly through subsidiaries, over 20% of the voting rights of the company.

All intercompany transactions are eliminated as part of the consolidation process. Minority interests are presented separately as a component of net profit and they are shown as a component of shareholders' equity in the consolidated statement of financial position.

Profits realized in connection with the sale of fixed assets between the Group and associated companies are eliminated in proportion to share ownership. Such profits are deducted from the Group's equity and fixed assets and released in the Group accounts over the same period as depreciation is charged.

The companies acquired during the financial periods presented have been consolidated from the date on which control of the net assets and operations was transferred to the Group. Similarly, the result of a Group company divested during an accounting period is included in the Group accounts only to the date of disposal.

MULTIPLE-CHOICE QUESTIONS

1. X has control over the composition of Y's board of directors. X owns 49% of Y and is the largest shareholder. X has an agreement with Z, which owns 10% of Y, whereby Z will always vote in the same way as X. Can X exercise control over Y?

    (a) X cannot exercise control because it owns only 49% of the voting rights.

    (b) X cannot exercise control because it can control only the makeup of the board and not necessarily the way the directors vote.

    (c) X can exercise control solely because it has an agreement with Z for the voting rights to be used in whatever manner X wishes.

    (d) X can exercise control because it controls more than 50% of the voting power, and it can govern the financial and operating policies of Y through its control of the board of directors.

2. X owns 50% of Y's voting shares. The board of directors consists of six members; X appoints three of them, and Y appoints the other three. The casting vote at meetings always lies with the directors appointed by X. Does X have control over Y?

    (a) No, control is equally split between X and Z.

    (b) Yes, X holds 50% of the voting power and has the casting vote at board meetings in the event that there is not a majority decision.

    (c) No, X owns only 50% of the entity's shares and therefore does not have control.

    (d) No, control can be exercised only through voting power, not through a casting vote.

3. Z has sold all of its shares to the public. The company was formerly a state-owned entity. The national regulator has retained the power to appoint the board of directors. An overseas entity acquires 55% of the voting shares, but the regulator still retains its power to appoint the board of directors. Who has control of the entity?

    (a) The national regulator.

    (b) The overseas entity.

    (c) Neither the national regulator nor the overseas entity.

    (d) The board of directors.

4. A manufacturing group has just acquired a controlling interest in a football team that is listed on a stock exchange. The management of the manufacturing group wishes to exclude the football team from the consolidated financial statements on the grounds that its activities are dissimilar. How should the football team be accounted for?

    (a) The entity should be consolidated as there is no exemption from consolidation on the grounds of dissimilar activities.

    (b) The entity should not be consolidated using the purchase method but should be consolidated using equity accounting.

    (c) The entity should not be consolidated and should appear as an investment in the group accounts.

    (d) The entity should not be consolidated; details should be disclosed in the financial statements.

5. Where should noncontrolling interests be presented in the consolidated statement of financial position?

    (a) Within long-term liabilities.

    (b) In between long-term liabilities and current liabilities.

    (c) Within the parent shareholders' equity.

    (d) Within equity but separate from the parent shareholders' equity.

6. Which of the items below is potentially an explicit or implicit variable interest in an entity or in specified assets of an entity?

    (a) At-risk equity investments in a VIE.

    (b) Investments in subordinated beneficial interests issued by a VIE.

    (c) Guarantees of the value of VIE assets or liabilities.

    (d) All of the above.

7. When should a holder of a variable interest initially determine whether it is the primary beneficiary of a VIE?

    (a) At the end of the reporting period (i.e., statement of financial position date) in which the holder obtains interest in the entity.

    (b) In conjunction with the initial determination that the entity is a VIE (i.e., when the holder initially obtains its interest in the entity).

    (c) One year after the holder obtains its interest in the entity.

    (d) The holder is not required to determine whether or not it is the primary beneficiary of the VIE.

Chapter 15

BUSINESS COMBINATIONS (ASC 805)

BACKGROUND AND INTRODUCTION

The U.S. generally accepted accounting standards (GAAP) assume that an acquirer can be determined and identified in nearly all business combinations. ASC 805 applies to all business combinations except joint venture operations, the acquisition of an asset or a group of assets that does not constitute a business, combinations of entities under common control, and combinations between not-for-profit entities (NFPs) or the acquisition of a for-profit business by an NFP.

DEFINITIONS OF KEY TERMS

Acquiree. One or more businesses in which an acquirer obtains control in a business combination.

Acquirer. An entity that obtains control over one or more businesses in a business combination. When the acquiree is a variable interest entity (VIE), the primary beneficiary of the VIE is always the acquirer.

Acquisition date. The date on which control of the acquiree is obtained by the acquirer.

Acquisition method. The required method of accounting for business combinations where the acquisition date occurs during fiscal years ending on or after December 31, 2009. The application of the acquisition method will normally result in substantive differences in the types of assets and liabilities recognized by the acquirer as well as the measurements of the amounts recognized for those items in the consolidated financial statements of the acquirer.

Acquisition-related costs. Expenses incurred by an acquirer to enter into a business combination.

Business combination. A transaction or event that results in an acquirer obtaining control over one or more businesses.

Closing date. The day on which an acquirer legally transfers consideration, acquires the assets, and assumes the liabilities of an acquiree.

Combined financial statements. Financial statements that present the collective results of operations and financial position of a group of entities under common management or control as if the group were a single economic entity. The presentation of the combined group excludes the party or parties that control or manage it.

Control. The power to govern the financial and operating policies of an entity so as to obtain benefits from its activities.

Purchase method. Looks at the business combination from the perspective of the acquiring company. It measures the cost of the acquisition and allocates the cost of the acquisition to the net assets acquired.

Business Combination

If a business combination involves the purchase of net assets, including goodwill of another entity, rather than the purchase of the equity of the other entity, this does not result in a parent/subsidiary relationship. All business combinations within the scope of ASC 805 have to be accounted by for using the acquisition method. The pooling and purchase methods of accounting for business combinations are no longer acceptable (although the current acquisition method shares many features of the superseded purchase method), and an acquirer must be identified for all business combinations.

Acquisition Method

The *acquisition method* is a new term to GAAP and was introduced to emphasize that a business combination can occur even when a purchase transaction is not involved. Eight steps are required for the acquisition method to be applicable:

1. Identify the acquirer.
2. Determine the acquisition date.
3. Identify the assets and liabilities, if any, requiring separate accounting because they result from transactions that are not part of the business combination, and account for them in accordance with their nature and the applicable GAAP.
4. Identify assets and liabilities that require acquisition date classification or designation decisions to facilitate application of GAAP in postcombination financial statements and make those classifications or designations based on (a) contractual terms, (b) economic conditions, (c) acquirer operating or accounting policies, and (d) other pertinent conditions existing at the acquisition date.
5. Recognize and measure the identifiable tangible and intangible assets acquired and liabilities assumed.
6. Recognize and measure any noncontrolling interest in the acquiree.
7. Measure the consideration transferred.
8. Recognize and measure goodwill or, if the business combination results in a bargain purchase, recognize a gain.

Control

There is a presumption that control is obtained when an entity acquires more than half of the other entity's voting rights unless it can be shown otherwise. It is possible not to hold more than half of the voting rights of the other entity and still obtain control of that entity where

- An entity has power over more than half of the voting rights because of an agreement with other investors; *or*
- It has power to control the financial and operating policies of another entity because of a law or an agreement; *or*
- It has the power to appoint or remove the majority of the board of directors; *or*
- It has the power to cast the majority of votes at board meetings or equivalent bodies within the entity.

Case Study 1

Facts

A, a public limited company, owns 50% of B and 49% of C. There is an agreement with the shareholders of C that the group will control the board of directors.

Required

Should C be consolidated as a subsidiary in the group accounts?

Solution

C will be consolidated on the basis of actual dominant influence and control exercised by the group because of the control contract.

IDENTIFYING AN ACQUIRER

ASC 805 emphasizes the concept that every business combination has an acquirer. The determination of the acquirer is based on the provisions outlined in ASC 810 regarding the party that possesses a controlling financial interest in another entity. ASC 810 provides that in general, direct or indirect ownership of a majority of the outstanding voting interests in another entity "is a condition pointing toward consolidation"; however, the Standard also notes there are some exceptions. One such exception is that majority-owned entities are not to be consolidated if the majority owner does not hold a controlling financial interest in the entity. Occasionally it may be difficult to identify an acquirer, but normally there will be indications that one exists; for example, when entities combine, the fair value of one of the entities is likely to be significantly greater than that of the other entity, or one entity may provide the bulk of the management expertise. In this case, the entity with the greater fair value and that provides the management expertise is probably the acquirer. Similarly, if the combination results in the management of one of the entities being able to dominate the composition of the management team of the combined entity, then the entity whose management is dominating the composition of the management team is likely to be the acquirer.

Case Study 2

Facts

X, a public limited company, is to merge its operations with Z, a public limited company. The terms of the merger will be that Z will offer two of its shares for every one share of X. There will be no cash consideration. Z's market capitalization is $500 million and X's is $250 million. After the issue of shares, the board of directors will be comprised of only directors from Z. The group is to be named Z Group. Three months after the acquisition, 20% of X is sold.

Required

Is it possible to identify an acquirer?

Solution

It seems obvious that Z is the acquirer of X and not vice versa. Z is a much larger company and will dominate the business combination because of its control of the board of directors. Also, the group is to be named the Z Group, which really confirms that Z is the acquirer. Additionally, part of X is sold after the acquisition, which again seems to indicate that Z acquired X.

Generally speaking, the entity that issues the equity shares in exchange for the net assets of the other entity normally can be designated the acquirer. However, in some business combinations that are referred to as reverse acquisitions, the acquirer could be the entity whose equity interests are acquired and the issuing entity is the acquiree. This can be the case where a private entity decides to have itself "acquired" by a smaller public entity in order to obtain a stock exchange listing. The entity issuing the shares will be regarded as the parent, and the private entity will be regarded as the subsidiary. The legal subsidiary will be deemed to be the acquirer if it has the power to govern the financial and operation policies of the legal parent.

PRACTICAL INSIGHT

Alliance Pharmaceutical ("Alliance") was "acquired" by Peerless Technology ("Peerless") on December 23, 2009. Peerless became the legal parent of Alliance but, due to the relative values of the companies, the former shareholders of Alliance became the majority shareholder with 67% of the combined company. The management of the new group was that of Alliance, and Peerless changed its name to Alliance Pharmaceutical. This was a reverse acquisition.

As a result of this reverse acquisition, the financial statements would comprise those of Alliance plus those of Peerless from the date of acquisition, and the comparative results of Alliance.

COST OF ACQUISITION

The cost of the acquisition has to be measured. Under ASC 805, acquisition-related costs are to be charged to expense of the period in which the costs are incurred and the related services received. The costs to be expensed include professional fees (i.e., accounting, legal, consulting, etc.); advisory, valuation, and finder's fees; and costs incurred by the internal acquisitions department.

An exception is made in ASC 805 for costs to register and issue equity or debt securities. These costs are to be recognized in accordance with other applicable GAAP; stock issuance costs are normally charged against the gross proceeds of the issuance and debt issuance costs (under CON 6) are to be treated either as a reduction of the amount borrowed or treated as an expense of the period in which they are incurred; however, some reporting entities have treated these costs as deferred charges and amortized them to income during the term of the debt.

The cost of the business combination could be subject to adjustment because it may be contingent on certain future events. The amount of that adjustment should be included in the cost of the business combination if the adjustment is probable and can be measured reliably. Such an adjustment might be, for example, where the cost is contingent on a specified level of profit being maintained or achieved in future or on the market price of the equity shares that are issued being maintained. If, however, the contingent payment is either not probable or not capable of being measured reliably, it is not included as part of the initial cost of the business combination. When the amount subsequently becomes probable and can be measured reliably, the additional consideration can be treated as an adjustment to the cost of acquisition.

PRACTICAL INSIGHT

Newmark Security acquired a subsidiary in the year ended April 30, 2009. The company paid an initial amount with a further sum, not exceeding $3.5 million, being due over the next four years. The deferred consideration is payable subject to the subsidiary achieving an agreed level of average profit over the period. Newmark felt that it would be payable in full and, therefore, included the additional amount in the initial cost of acquisition.

NET ASSETS ACQUIRED

The acquirer must recognize separately at the date of acquisition the acquiree's identifiable assets, liabilities, and contingent liabilities that satisfy the recognition criteria at that date set out in GAAP. These net assets must be recognized irrespective of whether they have previously been recognized in the acquiree's financial statements. The criteria used are

- Assets other than intangible assets must be recognized if it is probable that the future economic benefits will go to the acquirer and their fair value can be measured reliably.
- A liability other than a contingent liability must be recognized if it is probable that there will be an outflow of resources required to settle the obligation and the fair value can be measured reliably.

- A contingent liability or an intangible asset must be recognized if its fair value can be recognized reliably.

Any noncontrolling interest is stated at the noncontrolling interest's proportion of the net fair value of the above items.

Any agreed restructuring provisions would not be recognized. These costs would be recognized in postcombination financial statements in accordance with ASC 420, *Exit or Disposal Cost Obligations*. Identifiable assets, liabilities, and contingent liabilities must be measured initially at full fair value, which includes any noncontrolling interest share of those items. The acquirer should not recognize any liabilities for future losses or other costs expected to be incurred as a result of the acquisition. If the acquiree's restructuring plan is conditional on it being acquired, then just before the acquisition, the provision does not represent a present obligation, nor is it a contingent liability.

Intangible assets acquired must be recognized as assets separately from goodwill. These intangible assets must meet the definition of an asset in that they should be controlled and provide economic benefits and are

1. Either separable or arise from contractual or other legal rights; *and*
2. Their fair value can be measured reliably.

Thus, such items as trademarks, trade names, customer lists, order or production backlogs, customer contracts, artistic-related intangible assets, and contract-based intangible assets such as licensing and royalty agreements and lease agreements may meet the definition of an intangible asset for the purpose of ASC 350.

Similarly, all contingent liabilities assumed must be recognized if their fair value can be measured reliably.

The contingent liabilities are to be accounted for subsequently in the same manner as contingent consideration arrangements entered into between the acquirer and acquiree as a part of the business combination:

1. If additional information is obtained during the measurement period that pertains to facts and circumstances that existed at the acquisition date and affects the acquisition date fair value (ADFV) of the contingency, the acquirer is to reflect the effects of the new information on ADFV as a measurement period adjustment.
2. Changes in the fair value of the contingency resulting from postacquisition events, such as meeting a targeted level of earnings, reaching a specified stock price, or successfully meeting a milestone of a research and development project, are not to be reflected as measurement period adjustments.

Case Study 3

Facts

Boxwood Company	$m
Cost of acquisition	700
less fair value of net assets	300
less restructuring provision	(70)
Goodwill	470
Income statement at year end	
Profit before amortization	140
Amortization of goodwill	(47)
	93
Interest	(13)
Profit before tax	80

This information relates to the acquisition of Boxwood Co., a public limited company, by Yearling, a public limited company. At the date of acquisition, the fair value of the intangible assets and the contingent liabilities of Boxwood Co. were $100 million and $30 million respectively. At the date of the preparation of the financial statements, the value of the net assets of Boxwood Co. had increased significantly. The intangible assets have a life of 10 years.

Required

How would the acquisition be accounted for under GAAP?

Solution

	$m
Cost of acquisition	700
Less fair value of net assets	(300)
Less fair value of intangibles	(100)
Contingent liabilities	30
Goodwill	330
Income statement at year-end	
Profit before amortization	140
Amortization of intangibles	(10)
Goodwill impairment	0
	130
Interest	(13)
Profit before tax	117

The restructuring provision is not allowed under GAAP. The intangibles will have to be tested annually for impairment. The contingent liabilities will need recording also. The net assets of Boxwood Co. have increased significantly, and, therefore, it is unlikely that goodwill will be impaired at the financial year-end.

GOODWILL

At the acquisition date, management of the acquirer is required to document the basis for and method of determining the fair value of the acquiree as well as other related factors, such as the underlying rationale for making the acquisition and management's expectations with respect to dilution, synergies, and other financial measurements.

The benchmark assessment for goodwill involves identifying the valuation model to be used, documenting key assumptions, and measuring the fair value of the reporting unit. In general, goodwill is assigned consistent with previous recognition of goodwill and with the reporting units to which the acquired assets and liabilities had been assigned.

Goodwill assigned to a reporting unit is measured by the difference between the fair value of the entire reporting unit and the collective sum of the fair values of the reporting unit's assets, net of its liabilities. Goodwill may also be split among two or more reporting units of the acquirer. Any allocation method used is to be consistently applied and the logic for doing so documented.

Although it may be costly to accomplish, this benchmark assessment is necessary to ensure that the entity has identified and documented all key assumptions and tested the outputs of the selected valuation model for reasonableness prior to actually testing goodwill for impairment. Furthermore, measuring the fair value of the reporting unit as part of the benchmark assessment will provide management with a reality check on whether the amount of goodwill assigned to the reporting unit is reasonable, by comparing the fair value of the reporting unit with its carrying (book) value.

Goodwill is required to be tested for impairment on an annual basis, although interim testing also remains necessary when an event or circumstance occurs between annual tests that suggests that the fair value of a reporting unit might have declined below its carrying value.

Goodwill is also required to be tested for impairment on an interim basis when it is deemed "more likely than not" that a reporting unit or a significant portion of a reporting unit will be sold or otherwise disposed of, and furthermore, when a significant asset group within a reporting unit is required to be reviewed for recoverability because of the events and circumstances triggers included in ASC 360.

Goodwill impairment testing is a two-step process. The first step is application of a threshold test: Is the fair value of the reporting unit greater than, or less than, its carrying value? If the fair value is lower than the carrying value, impairment is suggested. The impairment, however, is not validly measured by the shortfall computed in step 1, because to do so would effectively be to adjust the carrying value of the entire reporting unit to the lower of cost or market.

The second step of the process is performed in this way:

1. Management assigns the fair value of the reporting unit to all of its assets and liabilities and to any unrecognized intangibles as if the reporting unit had been acquired at the measurement date. Any excess of fair value over amounts assigned to net assets is the implied fair value of goodwill.
2. Management compares the implied fair value of goodwill to its carrying amount (book value). If the carrying amount of the goodwill is greater than its implied fair value, a write-down of the carrying amount is required. Once written down, goodwill cannot later be written back up, even if later tests show that the fair value has recovered and exceeds carrying value.

INITIAL ACCOUNTING

The accounting for a business combination initially involves the identification of the fair values to be given to the acquiree's net assets, contingent liabilities, and the cost of the acquisition.

Sometimes the initial accounting can be determined only provisionally by the time the first accounts are drawn up after the acquisition. If this is the case, then the acquiring entity should use those provisional values. However, any adjustments to those provisional values should be made within 12 months of the acquisition and from the date of the acquisition. Any further adjustments to the values given to the net assets and contingent liabilities and cost of the combination after the initial accounting has been completed should be made only to correct an error, in accordance with ASC 250.

Case Study 4

Facts

JCE, a public limited company, acquired LZE, a public limited company, on December 31, 2008. LZE has among its net assets customer lists of information in the form of a database. LZE has two such databases: one where the nature of the information is subject to national laws regarding confidentiality and another where the information can be sold or leased. LZE also has contracts for the supply of maintenance services for computer systems. These contracts have another five years left to run. The company insures computer systems against potential disasters, and these contracts are renewable every year.

Additionally, JCE requested an official valuation of the computer equipment of LZE. By the time of the 2008 annual financial statements, the valuation had not been completed and a provisional value for the assets was included in the financial statements. The final valuation was received on June 30, 2009. On March 1, 2010, the auditors discover an error in the valuation of property, plant, and equipment as at December 31, 2008. A piece of equipment had been omitted from the valuation listing.

Required

Describe the implications of the preceding information for accounting for the acquisition of LZE.

Solution

The customer lists meet the definition of an intangible asset and should be accounted for separately. However, the customer list that is subject to national laws regarding confidentiality would not meet the criteria for an intangible asset, as the laws would prevent the entity from disseminating the information about its customers. The contract-based intangibles—the contracts for the supply of maintenance services—would meet the definition of an intangible asset. These intangibles will be recognized separately from goodwill, provided that the fair value can be measured reliably. In deciding on the fair value of a customer relationship, for example, JCE will consider assumptions such as the expected renewal of the supply agreement. The insurance contracts that it already has with its customers meet the contractual legal criterion for identification as an intangible asset and will be recognized separately from goodwill, providing the fair value can be measured reliably.

In determining the fair value of the liability relating to these insurance contracts, the holding company will bear in mind potential estimates of cancellations by policyholders. Currently ASC 944-20, *Financial Services—Insurance*, deals with the accounting for such contracts. Also, the number of policyholders that are expected to renew their contracts each year must be borne in mind when assessing the accounting for these contracts.

Regarding the computer equipment that has been acquired, at year-end, the entity has not determined the value of this equipment. Therefore, a provisional value will be placed on the computer equipment. Any adjustment to this provisional value will be made from the acquisition date and have to be made within 12 months of that acquisition date. The valuation was received on June 30; as a result, goodwill at December 31, 2008, will be recalculated. In the 2009 accounts, an adjustment will be made to the opening carrying value of the computer equipment less any depreciation for the period. The carrying value of goodwill will be adjusted for the reduction in value at the acquisition date, and the 2008 comparative information will be restated to reflect the adjustment. In the 2008 accounts, the financial statements should disclose that the initial accounting for the business combination has been determined only provisionally and explain why this is so. In the 2009 accounts, there should be an explanation of what adjustments have been made to the provisional values during the period.

The error in 2010 regarding the omission of a piece of plant and equipment should be accounted for under ASC 250-10-45-23. ASC 250-10-45 requires the correction of an error to be accounted for retrospectively and for the financial statements to be presented as if the error had never occurred by correcting the prior period's information. In the 2010 financial statements, an adjustment will be made to the opening value of property, plant, and equipment. The adjustment will be the fair value of the equipment at December 31, 2008, less any amounts that should have been recognized for the depreciation of that equipment. The carrying value of goodwill is also adjusted for the reduction in value. Also, the comparative information for the year to December 31, 2009, will be restated, and any additional depreciation relating to that period will be charged.

DISCLOSURES

For each business combination, this information should be disclosed:

1. Names and descriptions of the combining entities
2. The acquisition date
3. The percentage of voting equity instruments acquired
4. The cost of the combination and a description of the components of that cost
5. Amounts recognized at the acquisition date for each class of the acquiree's assets, liabilities, and contingent liabilities and the carrying amounts of each of those classes immediately before the acquisition unless that is impracticable
6. The amount of any negative goodwill that has been shown in the income statement
7. The factors that contributed to the recognition of goodwill
8. The amount of the acquiree's profit or loss since acquisition that has been included in the acquirer's profit or loss for the period, unless this is, again, impracticable
9. The revenue of the combined entity for the period, as if the combination had occurred at the beginning of that period
10. The profit or loss of the combined entity for the period as if the combination had been effected at the beginning of the period

EXTRACTS FROM PUBLISHED FINANCIAL STATEMENTS

The Walt Disney Company Annual Report 2009 for the Fiscal Year Ended October 3, 2009

Note 4. Acquisition

2009 Acquisitions

A&E/Lifetime

On September 15, 2009, the Company and the Hearst Corporation (Hearst) both contributed their 50% interests in Lifetime Entertainment Services LLC (Lifetime) to A&E Television Networks, LLC (AETN) in exchange for an increased interest in AETN. Prior to this transaction, the Company and Hearst each held 37.5% of AETN while NBC Universal (NBCU) held 25%. The Company accounted for the transaction as a sale of a portion of its interest in Lifetime which resulted in a $228 million noncash pretax gain ($142 million after-tax) reflecting the difference between the Company's carrying amount of the Lifetime interest sold and the fair value of the incremental AETN interest received. Following the transaction the Company's ownership interest in the combined AETN/Lifetime is approximately 42%. Under the terms of the agreement, NBCU may elect or be required to exit the combined AETN/Lifetime over a period of up to 15 years, in which event the Company and Hearst would each own 50%. The Company will account for its interest in the combined AETN/Lifetime as an equity-method investment consistent with how it previously accounted for AETN and Lifetime.

Marvel

On August 31, 2009, the Company announced an agreement to acquire Marvel Entertainment, Inc. (Marvel) in a cash and stock transaction. Under the terms of the agreement Marvel shareholders would receive $30 per share in cash and 0.7452 Disney shares for each Marvel share they own. At closing, the amount of cash and stock will be adjusted if necessary so that the total value of the Disney stock issued as merger consideration based on its trading value at that time is not less than 40% of the total merger consideration. Based upon Disney's stock price as of November 20, 2009, the acquisition purchase price would be approximately $4 billion. The acquisition is subject to the effectiveness of a registration statement with respect to Disney shares to be issued in the transaction and other customary closing conditions. The acquisition is also subject to the approval of Marvel shareholders.

Jetix Europe

In December 2008, the Company acquired an additional 26% interest in Jetix Europe N.V., a publicly traded pan-European kids' entertainment company, for approximately $354 million (bringing our total ownership interest to over 99%). The Company intends to acquire the remaining outstanding shares through statutory buy-out proceedings.

UTV

On May 9, 2008, the Company acquired a 24% interest (bringing its fully undiluted interest to 37%) in UTV Software Communications Limited (UTV), a media company headquartered and publicly traded in India, for approximately $197 million. In accordance with Indian securities regulations, the Company was required to make an open tender offer to purchase up to an additional 23% of UTV's publicly traded voting shares for a price equivalent to the May 9, 2008, Indian rupee purchase price. In November 2008, the Company completed the open offer and acquired an incremental 23% of UTV's voting shares for approximately $138 million bringing its undiluted interest to 60%. Due to the change in the exchange rate between the U.S. dollar and the Indian rupee from May to November, the U.S. dollar price per share was lower in November than in May. UTV's founder has a four-year option to buy all or a portion of the shares acquired by the Company during the open offer period at a price no less than the Company's open offer price. If the trading price upon exercise of the option exceeds the price paid by the Company, then the option price is capped at the Company's open offer price plus a 10% annual return. The Company does not have the right to vote the shares subject to the option until the expiration of the option and accordingly the Company's ownership interest in voting shares is 48%. In addition to the acquisition of UTV, on August 5, 2008, the Company invested $28 million in a UTV subsidiary, UTV Global Broadcasting Limited (along with UTV, the "UTV Group"). The Company's investment in the UTV Group is accounted for under the equity method.

Although UTV's operating performance to date has generally been consistent with our expectations, in light of recent economic conditions we have tempered our future expectations. Based on the Company's internal valuation of the UTV business, which was estimated using a discounted cash flow model, we recorded noncash impairment charges totaling $65 million in fiscal 2009. The Company's carrying value of its investment in the UTV Group of $298 million significantly exceeds the current trading value, and the Company will continue to monitor its investment in the UTV Group. UTV has recently announced that it is considering raising additional capital which could consist of equity shares of UTV stock, debentures or foreign currency convertible bonds. If UTV issued additional shares, depending upon the price of the issuance, an incremental impairment of our investment in UTV Group could be required.

The Disney Stores North America

On April 30, 2008, the Company acquired certain assets of the Disney Stores North America for approximately $64 million in cash from, and terminated its long-term licensing arrangement for the Disney Stores with, The Children's Place, the former licensee. The Company acquired the inventory, leasehold improvements, and certain fixed assets of, and assumed the leases on 229 stores. The Company conducted the wind-down and closure of an additional 88 stores but did not assume the leases on these stores.

In connection with the acquisition, the Company waived its rights to certain claims against The Children's Place and in accordance with the applicable accounting guidance recorded an $18 million noncash gain for the estimated fair value of the claims. The gain is classified in "Other income (expense)" in the Consolidated Statement of Income.

Club Penguin

On August 1, 2007, the Company acquired all of the outstanding shares of Club Penguin Entertainment, Inc. (Club Penguin), a Canadian company that operates clubpenguin.com, an online virtual world for children. The purchase price included up-front cash consideration of approximately $350 million and additional consideration of up to $350 million payable if Club Penguin achieved predefined earnings targets in calendar years 2008 and 2009. There have been no additional payments of consideration for Club Penguin. Remaining additional consideration of up to $175 million is potentially payable based on calendar year 2009 results.

NASN

On February 1, 2007, the Company acquired all the outstanding shares of NASN, an Irish company that operates cable television networks in Europe dedicated to North American sporting events and related programming, for consideration valued at $112 million consisting of cash and assumption of debt. In February, 2009, NASN was rebranded as ESPN America.

The changes in the carrying amount of goodwill for the years ended October 3, 2009, and September 27, 2008, are as follows:

	Media networks	Parks and resorts	Studio entertainment	Consumer products	Interactive media	Total
Balance at September 29, 2007	$15,456	$173	$4,788	$425	$557	$21,399
Acquisitions	30	—	—	—	61	91
Other, net	14	(1)	(37)	(2)	1	(25)
Balance at September 27, 2008	15,500	$172	$4,751	$423	$619	$21,465
Acquisitions	258	—	—	—	20	278
Impairments	—	—	—	—	(29)	(29)
Other, net	(14)	—	(14)	(1)	(2)	(31)
Balance at October 3, 2009	**$15,744**	**$172**	**$4,737**	**$422**	**$608**	**$21,683**

Nike, Inc. Annual Report 2009 for the fiscal year ended May 31, 2009

Note 4. Acquisition, Identifiable Intangible Assets, Goodwill, and Umbro Impairment

Acquisition

On March 3, 2008, the Company completed its acquisition of 100% of the outstanding shares of Umbro, a leading United Kingdom–based global soccer brand, for a purchase price of 290.5 million British pounds sterling in cash (approximately $576.4 million), inclusive of direct transaction costs. This acquisition is intended to strengthen the Company's market position in the United Kingdom and expand Nike's global leadership in soccer, a key area of growth for the Company. This acquisition also provides positions in emerging soccer markets such as China, Russia, and Brazil. The results of Umbro's operations have been included in the Company's consolidated financial statements since the date of acquisition as part of the Company's "Other" operating segment.

The acquisition of Umbro was accounted for as a purchase business combination in accordance with SFAS 141, *Business Combinations*. The purchase price was allocated to tangible and identifiable intangible assets acquired and liabilities assumed based on their respective estimated fair values on the date of acquisition, with the remaining purchase price recorded as goodwill.

Based on our preliminary purchase price allocation at May 31, 2008, identifiable intangible assets and goodwill relating to the purchase approximated $419.5 million and $319.2 million, respectively. Goodwill recognized in this transaction is deductible for tax purposes. Identifiable intangible assets include $378.4 million for trademarks that have an indefinite life, and $41.1 million for other intangible assets consisting of Umbro's sourcing network, established customer relationships, and the United Soccer League Franchise. These intangible assets will be amortized on a straight-line basis over estimated lives of 12 to 20 years.

During the quarter ended February 28, 2009, the Company finalized the purchase-price accounting for Umbro and made revisions to preliminary estimates, including valuations of tangible and intangible assets and certain contingencies, as further evaluations were completed and information was received from third parties subsequent to the acquisition date. These revisions to preliminary estimates resulted in a $12.4 million decrease in the value of identified intangible assets, primarily Umbro's sourcing network, and an $11.2 million increase in noncurrent liabilities, primarily related to liabilities assumed for certain contingencies and adjustments made to deferred taxes related to the fair value of assets acquired. These changes in assets acquired and liabilities assumed affect the amount of goodwill recorded.

The following table summarizes the allocation of the purchase price, including transaction costs of the acquisition, to the assets acquired and liabilities assumed at the date of acquisition based on their estimated fair values, including final purchase accounting adjustments (in millions):

	May 31, 2008 Preliminary	Adjustments	May 31, 2009 Final
Current assets	$ 87.2	—	$ 87.2
Noncurrent assets	90.2	—	90.2
Identified intangible assets	419.5	(12.4)	407.1
Goodwill	319.2	23.6	342.8
Current liabilities	(60.3)	—	(60.3)
Noncurrent liabilities	(279.4)	(11.2)	(290.6)
Net assets acquired	$ 576.4	$ —	$ 576.4

The pro forma effect of the acquisition on the combined results of operations for fiscal 2008 was not material.

Umbro Impairment

In accordance with FAS 142, *Goodwill and Other Intangible Assets*, the Company performs annual impairment tests on goodwill and intangible assets with indefinite lives in the fourth quarter of each fiscal year, or when events occur or circumstances change that would, more likely than not, reduce the fair value of a reporting unit or intangible assets with an indefinite life below its carrying value. As a result of a significant decline in global consumer demand and continued weakness in the macroeconomic environment, as well as decisions by Company management to adjust planned investment in the Umbro brand, the Company concluded that sufficient indicators of impairment existed to require the performance of an interim assessment of Umbro's goodwill and indefinite-lived intangible assets as of February 1, 2009. Accordingly, the Company performed the first step of the goodwill impairment assessment for Umbro by comparing the estimated fair value of Umbro to its carrying amount, and determined there was a potential impairment of goodwill as the carrying amount exceeded the estimated fair value. Therefore, the Company performed the second step of the assessment, which compared the implied fair value of Umbro's goodwill to the book value of goodwill. The implied fair value of goodwill is determined by allocating the estimated fair value of Umbro to all of its assets and liabilities, including both recognized and unrecognized intangibles, in the same manner as goodwill was determined in the original business combination.

The Company measured the fair value of Umbro by using an equal weighting of the fair value implied by a discounted cash flow analysis and by comparisons with the market values of similar publicly traded companies. The Company believes the blended use of both models compensates for the inherent risk associated with either model if used on a stand-alone basis, and this combination is indicative of the factors a market participant would consider when performing a similar valuation. The fair value of Umbro's indefinite-lived trademark was estimated using the relief from royalty method, which assumes that the trademark has value to the extent that Umbro is relieved of the obligation to pay royalties for the benefits received from the trademark. The assessments of the Company resulted in the recognition of impairment charges of $199.3 million and $181.3 million related to Umbro's goodwill and trademark, respectively, during the third quarter ended February 28, 2009. A deferred tax benefit of $54.5 million was recognized as a result of the trademark impairment charge. In addition to the above impairment analysis, the Company determined an equity investment held by Umbro was impaired, and recognized a charge of $20.7 million related to the impairment of this investment. These charges are included in the Company's "Other" category for segment reporting purposes.

The discounted cash flow analysis calculated the fair value of Umbro using management's business plans and projections as the basis for expected cash flows for the next 12 years and a 3% residual growth rate thereafter. The Company used a weighted-average discount rate of 14% in its analysis, which was derived primarily from published sources as well as our adjustment for increased market risk given current market conditions. Other significant estimates used in the discounted cash flow analysis include the rates of projected growth and profitability of Umbro's business and working capital effects. The market valuation approach indicates the fair value of Umbro based on a comparison of Umbro to publicly traded companies in similar lines of business. Significant estimates in the market valuation approach include identifying similar companies with comparable business factors such as size, growth, profitability, mix of revenue generated from licensed and direct distribution and risk of return on investment.

Holding all other assumptions constant at the test date, a 100 basis point increase in the discount rate would reduce the adjusted carrying value of Umbro's net assets by 12%.

Identified Intangible Assets and Goodwill

All goodwill balances are included in the Company's "Other" category for segment reporting purposes. The following table summarizes the Company's goodwill balance as of May 31, 2009 and 2008 (in millions):

Goodwill, May 31, 2007	$130.8
Acquisition of Umbro Plc	319.2
Other[1]	(1.2)
Goodwill, May 31, 2008	448.8
Purchase price adjustments	23.6
Impairment charge	(199.3)
Other[1]	(79.6)
Goodwill, May 31, 2009	$193.5

[1] Other consists of foreign currency translation adjustments on Umbro goodwill.

The following table summarizes the Company's identifiable intangible asset balances as of May 31, 2009 and 2008.

	Gross carrying amount	Accumulated amortization	Net carrying amount	Gross carrying amount	Accumulated amortization	Net carrying amount
Amortized intangible assets:						
Patents	$56.6	$(17.2)	$39.4	$47.5	$(14.4)	$33.1
Trademarks	37.5	(10.9)	26.6	13.2	(7.8)	5.4
Other	40.0	(19.6)	20.4	65.2	(19.7)	45.5
Total	$134.1	$(47.7)	$86.4	$125.9	$(41.9)	$84.0
Unamortized intangible assets —						
Trademarks			381.0			659.1
Identifiable intangible assets, net			467.4			743.1

The effect of foreign exchange fluctuations for the year ended May 31, 2009, reduced unamortized intangible assets by approximately $98.2 million, resulting from the strengthening of the U.S. dollar in relation to the British pound sterling.

Amortization expense, which is included in selling and administrative expense, was $11.9 million, $9.2 million, and $9.9 million for the years ended May 31, 2009, 2008, and 2007, respectively. The estimated amortization expense for intangible assets subject to amortization for each of the years ending May 31, 2010 through May 31, 2014 are 2010: $12.6 million; 2011: $12.2 million; 2012: $11.5 million; 2013: $9.6 million; 2014: $7.6 million.

During the year ended May 31, 2008, the gross carrying amount of unamortized and amortized trademarks were reduced by $59.6 million and $37.5 million, respectively, as a result of the Company's divestitures of the Starter brand business and Nike Bauer Hockey during the year ended May 31, 2008. See Note 17—Divestitures for more information the Company's divestitures.

Dell Inc.

Notes to the Consolidated Financial Statements for the Fiscal Year Ended January 30, 2009

Note 8. Goodwill and Intangible Assets

Goodwill

Goodwill allocated to Dell's business segments as of January 30, 2009, and February 1, 2008, and changes in the carrying amount of goodwill for the fiscal year ended January 30, 2009, were

(in millions)	Americas commercial	EMEA commercial	APJ commercial	Global consumer	Total
Balance at February 1, 2008	$822	$412	$127	$287	$1,648
Goodwill acquired	78	37	21	—	136
Adjustments to goodwill	(31)	(14)	(10)	8	(47)
Balance at January 30, 2009	$869	$435	$138	$295	$1,737

(in millions)	January 30, 2009	February 1, 2008
Balance at beginning of the year	$1,648	$110
Goodwill acquired during the year	136	1,538
Adjustments to goodwill	(47)	—
Balance at end of the year	$1,737	$1,648

Goodwill is tested annually during the second fiscal quarter and whenever events or circumstances indicate an impairment may have occurred. If the carrying amount of goodwill exceeds its fair value, estimated based on discounted cash flow analyses, an impairment charge would be recorded. Based on the results of its annual impairment tests, Dell determined that no impairment of goodwill existed at August 1, 2008, and for the fiscal years ended January 30, 2009, and February 1, 2008. The goodwill adjustments are primarily the result of purchase price allocation adjustments related to the finalization of deferred tax calculations and the effects of foreign currency adjustments where the purchase price was recorded in entities where the local currency is the functional currency. In the fourth quarter of fiscal 2009, Dell updated its annual analysis of potential triggering events for goodwill and indefinite lived intangible asset impairments. Based on this analysis, Dell concluded that there was no evidence that would indicate an impairment of goodwill or indefinite lived intangible assets.

Intangible Assets

Dell's intangible assets associated with completed acquisitions at January 30, 2009, and February 1, 2008, are

(in millions)	January 30, 2009			February 1, 2008		
	Gross	Accumulated amortization	Net	Gross	Accumulated amortization	Net
Technology	$524	$(82)	$442	$492	$(16)	$476
Customer relationships	243	(38)	205	231	(9)	222
Tradenames	41	(9)	32	39	(6)	33
Covenants not to compete	26	(6)	20	23	(1)	22
Amortizable intangible assets	$834	$(135)	$699	$785	$(32)	$753
Indefinite lived intangible assets	25	—	25	27	—	27
Total intangible assets	$859	$(135)	$724	$812	$(32)	$780

During fiscal 2009 and fiscal 2008, Dell recorded additions to intangible assets of $64 million and $762 million, respectively. Amortization expense related to finite-lived intangible assets was approximately $103 million and $27 million in fiscal 2009 and in fiscal 2008. During the year ended January 30, 2009, Dell did not record any impairment charges as a result of its analysis of its intangible assets.

Estimated future annual pretax amortization expense of finite-lived intangible assets as of January 30, 2009, over the next five fiscal years and thereafter is

Fiscal Years	(in millions)
2010	$159
2011	144
2012	124
2013	100
2014	69
Thereafter	103
Total	$699

MULTIPLE-CHOICE QUESTIONS

1. Which of the following accounting methods must be applied to all business combinations under ASC 805, *Business Combinations*?
- (a) Pooling of interests method.
- (b) Equity method.
- (c) Acquisition method.
- (d) Purchase method.

2. Acquisition accounting requires an acquirer and an acquiree to be identified for every business combination. Where a new entity (H) is created to acquire two preexisting entities, S and A, which of these entities will be designated as the acquirer?
- (a) H.
- (b) S.
- (c) A.
- (d) A or S.

3. ASC 805 requires all identifiable intangible assets of the acquired business to be recorded at their fair values. Under ASC 805, when would an intangible asset be "identifiable"?
- (a) When it meets the definition of an asset in the *Framework* document only.
- (b) When it meets the definition of an intangible asset under GAAP, and its fair value can be measured reliably.
- (c) Intangible assets should be recorded along with goodwill. They are not required to be separately identified.
- (d) Where it has been acquired in a business combination.

4. Which of the following examples is unlikely to meet the definition of an intangible asset arising from business combinations accounted for under ASC 805?
- (a) Marketing related, such as trademarks and internet domain names.
- (b) Customer related, such as customer lists and contracts.
- (c) Technology based, such as computer software and databases.
- (d) Pure research based, such as general expenditure on research.

5. An intangible asset with an indefinite life is one where
- (a) There is no foreseeable limit on the period over which the asset will generate cash flows.
- (b) The length of life is over 20 years.
- (c) The directors feel that the intangible asset will not lose value in the foreseeable future.
- (d) There is a contractual or legal arrangement that lasts for a period in excess of five years.

6. An intangible asset with an indefinite life is accounted for in this way:
- (a) No amortization but annual impairment test.
- (b) Amortized and impairment tests annually.
- (c) Amortize and impairment tested if there is a "trigger event."
- (d) Amortized and no impairment test.

7. An acquirer should at the acquisition date recognize goodwill acquired in a business combination as an asset. Goodwill should be accounted for in this way:
- (a) Recognize as an intangible asset and amortize over its useful life.
- (b) Write off against retained earnings.
- (c) Recognize as an intangible asset and impairment test when a trigger event occurs.
- (d) Recognize as an intangible asset and annually impairment test (or more frequently if impairment is indicated).

8. If the impairment of the value of goodwill is seen to have reversed, then the company may
- (a) Reverse the impairment charge and credit income for the period.
- (b) Reverse the impairment charge and credit retained earnings.
- (c) Not reverse the impairment charge.
- (d) Reverse the impairment charge only if the original circumstances that led to the impairment no longer exist and credit retained earnings.

9. On acquisition, all identifiable assets and liabilities, including goodwill, will be allocated to reporting units within the business combination. Goodwill impairment is assessed within the reporting units. If the combined organization has reporting units significantly below the level of an operating segment, then the risk of an impairment charge against goodwill as a result of ASC 805 is
- (a) Significantly decreased because goodwill will be spread across many cash-generating units.
- (b) Significantly increased because poorly performing units can no longer be supported by those that are performing well.
- (c) Likely to be unchanged from previous accounting practice.
- (d) Likely to be decreased because goodwill will be a smaller amount due to the greater recognition of other intangible assets.

10. The management of an entity is unsure how to treat a restructuring provision that it wishes to set up on the acquisition of another entity. Under ASC 805, the treatment of this provision will be

(a) A charge in the income statement in the postacquisition period.

(b) To include the provision in the allocated cost of acquisition.

(c) To provide for the amount and, if the provision is overstated, to release the excess to the income statement in the postacquisition period.

(d) To include the provision in the allocated cost of acquisition if the acquired entity commits itself to a restructuring within a year of acquisition.

11. ASC 805 requires that the contingent liabilities of the acquired entity should be recognized in the statement of financial position at fair value. The existence of contingent liabilities is often reflected in a lower purchase price. Recognition of such contingent liabilities will

(a) Decrease the value attributed to goodwill, thus decreasing the risk of impairment of goodwill.

(b) Decrease the value attributed to goodwill, thus increasing the risk of impairment of goodwill.

(c) Increase the value attributed to goodwill, thus decreasing the risk of impairment of goodwill.

(d) Increase the value attributed to goodwill, thus increasing the risk of impairment of goodwill.

12. Entity A purchases 30% of the ordinary share capital of Entity B for $10 million on January 1, 2008. The fair value of the assets of Entity B at that date was $20 million. On January 1, 2009, Entity A purchases a further 40% of Entity B for $15 million, when the fair value of Entity B's assets was $25 million. On January 1, 2008, Entity A does not have significant influence over Entity B. What value would be recognized for goodwill (before any impairment test) in the consolidated financial statements of A for the year ended December 31, 2009?

(a) $11 million

(b) $7.5 million

(c) $9 million

(d) $14 million

13. Corin, a private limited company, has acquired 100% of Coal, a private limited company, on January 1, 2008. The fair value of the purchase consideration was 10 million ordinary shares of $1 of Corin, and the fair value of the net assets acquired was $7 million. At the time of the acquisition, the value of the ordinary shares of Corin and the net assets of Coal were only provisionally determined. The value of the shares of Corin ($11 million) and the net assets of Coal ($7.5 million) on January 1, 2008, were finally determined on November 30, 2008. However, the directors of

Corin have seen the value of the company decline since January 1, 2008, and as of February 1, 2009, wish to change the value of the purchase consideration to $9 million. What value should be placed on the purchase consideration and net assets of Coal as at the date of acquisition?

(a) Purchase consideration $10 million, net asset value $7 million.

(b) Purchase consideration $11 million, net asset value $7.5 million.

(c) Purchase consideration $9 million, net asset value $7.5 million.

(d) Purchase consideration $11 million, net asset value $7 million.

14. Mask, a private company, has arranged for Man, a public company, to acquire it as a means of obtaining a stock exchange listing. Man issues 15 million shares to acquire the whole of the share capital of Mask (6 million shares). The fair value of the net assets of Mask and Man are $30 million and $18 million respectively. The fair value of each of the shares of Mask is $6 and the quoted market price of Man's shares is $2. The share capital of Man is 25 million shares after the acquisition. Calculate the value of goodwill in this acquisition.

(a) $16 million

(b) $12 million

(c) $10 million

(d) $ 6 million

Chapter 16

INCOME TAXES (ASC 740)

BACKGROUND AND INTRODUCTION

The Standard Applies to the Accounting for Income Taxes

ASC 740 uses the liability method and adopts a statement of financial position approach. Instead of accounting for the timing differences between the accounting and tax consequences of revenue and expenses, it accounts for the temporary differences between the accounting and tax bases of assets and liabilities. The accounting standard adopts a full-provision statement of financial position approach to accounting for tax.

It is assumed that the recovery of all assets and the settlement of all liabilities have tax consequences and that these consequences can be estimated reliably and will be unavoidable.

The main reason why deferred tax has to be provided is that generally accepted accounting principles (GAAP) recognition criteria often are different from those that are set forth in tax law. Thus, there will be income and expenditures in financial statements that will not be allowed for taxation purposes in the same reporting periods.

A deferred tax liability or asset is recognized for future tax consequences of past transactions. There are some limited exemptions to this general rule.

DEFINITIONS OF KEY TERMS

Deferred income tax asset. The asset recognized to reflect the expected future benefit available to be realized upon the reversal of deductible temporary differences.

Deferred income tax liability. The liability recognized to reflect the expected future income taxes that will be payable upon the reversal of taxable temporary differences.

Effective settlement. A conclusion reached by applying criteria specified in ASC 740-10-25 that a taxing authority has, in effect, made its final determination with respect to the portion of a tax position, if any, that it will accept and that management considers the possibility of further examination or reexamination of any aspect of the position to be remote.

Future deductible temporary difference. The difference between the GAAP carrying amount and income tax basis of an asset or liability that will reverse in the future and result in future income tax deductions; these give rise to deferred income tax assets.

Future taxable temporary difference. Temporary differences that result in future taxable amounts that give rise to deferred income tax liabilities.

Highly certain income tax position. An income tax position that, based on clear and unambiguous tax law, rulings, regulations, and interpretations, has a remote likelihood of being disallowed by the applicable taxing jurisdiction examining it with full possession of all relevant facts.

Income tax position. Each judgment that management makes on an income tax return that has been or will be filed that affects the measurement of current or deferred income tax assets and liabilities at an interim or year-end date. The effects of taking an income tax position can result in a permanent reduction of income taxes payable or deferral of the payment of income taxes to a future year. The taking of an income tax position can also affect management's estimate of the valuation allowance sufficient to reflect the amount of deferred income tax assets that it believes will be realizable.

Permanent differences. Differences between pretax accounting income and taxable income as a result of the treatment accorded certain transactions by the income tax laws and regulations that differ from the accounting treatment. Permanent differences will not reverse in subsequent periods.

Temporary differences. In general, differences between income tax and financial reporting bases of assets and liabilities that will result in taxable or deductible amounts in future periods. Temporary differences include "timing differences" as defined by prior GAAP as well as certain other differences, such as those arising from business combinations. Some temporary differences cannot be associated with particular assets or liabilities but nonetheless do result from events that received financial statement recognition and will have income tax effects in future periods.

Valuation allowance. The contra asset that is to be reflected to the extent that, in management's judgment, it is "more likely than not" that the deferred income tax asset will not be realized.

The presumption is that the reporting entity will settle its liabilities and recover its assets eventually, over time, and at that point the tax consequences will crystallize. For example, if a machine has a carrying value in the financial statements of $5 million and its tax basis is $2 million, then there is a taxable temporary difference of $3 million.

The tax base of a liability is normally its carrying amount less amounts that will be deductible for tax in the future. The tax base of an asset is the amount that will be deductible for tax purposes against future profits generated by the asset.

The Standard sets out two kinds of temporary differences: a *taxable temporary difference* and a *deductible temporary difference*.

A taxable temporary difference results in the payment of tax when the carrying amount of the asset or liability is settled.

In simple terms, this means that a deferred tax liability will arise when the carrying value of the asset is greater than its tax base or when the carrying value of the liability is less than its tax base.

Deductible temporary differences are differences that result in amounts being deductible in determining taxable profit or loss in future periods when the carrying value of the asset or liability is recovered or settled. When the carrying value of the liability is greater than its tax base or when the carrying value of the asset is less than its tax base, a deferred tax asset may arise.

This means, for example, that when an accrued liability is paid in future periods, part or all of that payment may become allowable for tax purposes.

Benefit of uncertain tax positions can be recognized only to the extent that there is at least a 50% likelihood ("more likely than not") of being sustained on exam.

GAAP prohibits the recognition of effects of temporary differences when they are related to foreign currency nonmonetary assets when the reporting currency is the functional currency, and intercompany transfers of inventory or other assets remaining within the company.

Case Study 1

Facts

An entity has these assets and liabilities recorded in its statement of financial position at December 31, 2010:

	Carrying value $ million
Property	10
Plant and equipment	5
Inventory	4
Trade receivables	3
Trade payables	6
Cash	2

The value for tax purposes of property and for plant and equipment are $7 million and $4 million, respectively. The entity has made a provision for inventory obsolescence of $2 million, which is not allowable for tax purposes until the inventory is sold. Further, an impairment charge against trade receivables of $1 million has been made. This charge does not relate to any specific trade receivable but to the entity's assessment of the overall collectibility of the amount. This charge will not be allowed in the current year for tax purposes but will be allowed in the future. Income tax paid is at 30%.

Required

Calculate the deferred tax provision at December 31, 2010.

Solution

	Carrying value $m	Tax base $m	Temporary difference $m
Property	10	7	3
Plant and equipment	5	4	1
Inventory	4	6	(2)
Trade receivables	3	4	(1)
Trade payables	6	6	-
Cash	2	2	-
			1

The deferred tax provision will be $1 million × 30%, or $300,000.

Because the provision against inventory and the impairment charge are not currently allowed, the tax base will be higher than the carrying value by the respective amounts.

Every asset or liability is assumed to have a tax base. Normally this tax base will be the amount that is allowed for tax purposes.

Some items of income and expenditure may not be taxable or tax deductible, and they will never enter into the computation of taxable profit. These items sometimes are called permanent differences.

Generally speaking, these items will have the same tax base as their carrying amount; that is, no temporary difference will arise.

For example, if an entity has on its statement of financial position interest receivable of $2 million that is not taxable, then its tax base will be the same as its carrying value, or $2 million. There is no temporary difference in this case. Therefore, no deferred taxation will arise.

Case Study 2

Facts

An entity acquired plant and equipment for $1 million on January 1, 2010. The asset is depreciated at 25% a year on the straight-line basis, and local tax legislation permits the management to depreciate the asset at 30% a year for tax purposes.

Required

Calculate any deferred tax liability that might arise on the plant and equipment at December 31, 2010, assuming a tax rate of 30%.

Solution

$15,000 (30% of the temporary difference of $50,000). The carrying value of the plant and equipment is $750,000 and the tax written down value will be $700,000, thus giving a taxable temporary difference of $50,000.

CURRENT TAX LIABILITIES AND ASSETS

The Standard also deals with current tax liabilities and current tax assets.

An entity should recognize a liability in the statement of financial position in respect of its current tax expense both for the current and prior years to the extent that it is not yet paid.

An entity should recognize an asset in the statement of financial position in respect of its current tax expense (credit) both for the current and prior years to the extent that it is not yet collected via a tax refund.

ACCOUNTING FOR DEFERRED TAX

To account for deferred tax under ASC 740, first prepare a statement of financial position that shows all the assets and liabilities in the accounting statement of financial position and their tax base.

Also show any other items that may not have been recognized as assets or liabilities in the accounting statement of financial position but that may have a tax base. Then take the difference between these values and the accounting values, and calculate the deferred tax based on these differences.

Deferred tax assets and liabilities are classified as current or noncurrent based on the classification of the related asset or liability for financial reporting.

Most taxable differences arise because of differences in the timing of the recognition of the transaction for accounting and tax purposes.

Examples

(a) Accumulated depreciation that differs from accumulated tax depreciation
(b) Employee expenditure recognized when incurred for accounting purposes and when paid for tax purposes
(c) Costs of research and development, which may be expensed in one period for accounting purposes but allowed for tax purposes in later periods

Situations exist where assets and liabilities are valued at fair value for accounting purposes but there is no equivalent measurement for tax purposes.

To the extent that deferred income tax assets are of doubtful realizability—that is, are not "more likely than not to be realized"—a valuation allowance is provided, analogous to the allowance for uncollectible receivables.

Summary of Accounting for Deferred Tax

The process of accounting for deferred tax is

1. Determine the tax base of the assets and liabilities in the statement of financial position.
2. Compare the carrying amounts in the statement of financial position with the tax base. Any differences will normally affect the deferred taxation calculation.
3. Identify the temporary differences that have not been recognized due to exceptions in GAAP.
4. Apply the tax rates to the temporary differences.
5. Determine the movement between opening and closing deferred tax balances.

6. Decide whether the offset of deferred tax assets and liabilities between different companies is acceptable in the consolidated financial statements.
7. Recognize the net change in deferred taxation.

Case Study 3

Facts

An entity has spent $600,000 in developing a new product. These costs meet the definition of an intangible asset under ASC 350 and have been recognized in the statement of financial position. Local tax legislation allows these costs to be deducted for tax purposes when they are incurred. Therefore, they have been recognized as an expense for tax purposes. At the year-end the intangible asset is deemed to be impaired by $50,000.

Required

Calculate the tax base of the intangible asset at the accounting year-end.

Solution

Zero, because the tax authority has already allowed the intangible asset costs to be deducted for tax purposes.

CONSOLIDATED FINANCIAL STATEMENTS

Temporary differences can also arise from adjustments on consolidation.

The tax base of an item is often determined by the value in the entity accounts, that is, for example, the subsidiary's accounts.

Deferred tax is determined on the basis of the consolidated financial statements and not the individual entity accounts.

Therefore, the carrying value of an item in the consolidated accounts can be different from the carrying value in the individual entity accounts, thus giving rise to a temporary difference.

An example is the consolidation adjustment that is required to eliminate unrealized profits and losses on intergroup transfer of inventory. Such an adjustment will give rise to a temporary difference, which will reverse when the inventory is sold outside the group.

Case Study 4

Facts

A subsidiary sold goods costing $10 million to its parent for $11 million, and all of these goods are still held in inventory at the year-end. Assume a tax rate of 30%.

Required

Explain the deferred tax implications.

Solution

The unrealized profit of $1 million will have to be eliminated from the consolidated income statement and from the consolidated statement of financial position in group inventory. The sale of the inventory is a taxable event, and it causes a change in the tax base of the inventory. The carrying amount in the consolidated financial statements of the inventory will be $10 million, but the tax base is $11 million. This gives rise to a deferred tax asset of $1 million at the tax rate of 30%, which is $300,000 (assuming that both the parent and subsidiary are residents in the same tax jurisdiction).

Case Study 5

Facts

An entity has acquired a subsidiary on January 1, 2009. Goodwill of $2 million has arisen on the purchase of this subsidiary. The subsidiary has deductible temporary differences of $1 million, and it is probable that future taxable profits are going to be available for the offset of this deductible temporary difference. The tax rate during 2009 is 30%. The deductible temporary difference has not been taken into account in calculating goodwill.

Required

What is the figure for goodwill that should be recognized in the consolidated statement of financial position of the parent?

Solution

$1.7 million. A deferred tax asset of $1 million × 30%, or $300,000, should be recognized because it is stated that future taxable profits will be available for offset. Thus, at the time of acquisition, there is an additional deferred tax asset that has not as yet been taken into account. The result of this will be to reduce goodwill from $2 million to $1.7 million.

TEMPORARY DIFFERENCES NOT RECOGNIZED FOR DEFERRED TAX

Some temporary differences are not recognized for deferred tax purposes. These arise

1. From goodwill.
2. From the initial recognition of certain assets and liabilities.
3. From investments when certain conditions apply.

GAAP does not allow a deferred tax liability for goodwill on initial recognition or where any reduction in the value of goodwill is not allowed for tax purposes. Because goodwill is the residual amount after recognizing assets and liabilities at fair value, recognizing a deferred tax liability in respect of goodwill would simply increase the value of goodwill; therefore, the recognition of a deferred tax liability in this regard is not allowed. Deferred tax liabilities for goodwill could be recognized to the extent that they do not arise from initial recognition.

Case Study 6

Facts

An entity has acquired a subsidiary, and goodwill arising on the transaction amounts to $20 million. Goodwill is not allowable for tax purposes in the entity's jurisdiction. Tax rate for the entity is 30% and the subsidiary is 60% owned.

Required

Calculate the deferred tax liability relating to goodwill, and explain whether a taxable temporary difference would arise if goodwill was allowable for tax purposes on an amortized basis.

Solution

Zero. A deferred tax liability should not be recognized for any taxable temporary difference that arises on the initial recognition of goodwill. Where goodwill is deductible for tax purposes on an amortized basis, a taxable temporary difference will arise in future years being the difference between the carrying value in the entity's accounts and the tax base.

The second temporary difference not recognized is on the initial recognition of certain assets and liabilities that are not fully deductible or liable for tax purposes. For example, if the cost of an asset is not deductible for tax purposes, then this has a tax base of zero.

Generally speaking, this gives rise to a taxable temporary difference. However, the Standard does not allow an entity to recognize any deferred tax that occurs as a result of this initial recognition. Thus, no deferred tax liability or asset is recognized where the carrying value of the item on initial recognition differs from its initial tax base. An example of this is a nontaxable government grant that is related to the acquisition of an asset. Note, however, that if the initial recognition occurs on a business combination, or an accounting or taxable profit or loss arises, then deferred tax should be recognized.

Case Study 7

Facts

An entity purchases plant and equipment for $2 million. In the tax jurisdiction, there are no tax allowances available for the depreciation of this asset; neither are any profits or losses on disposal taken into account for taxation purposes. The entity depreciates the asset at 25% per annum. Taxation is 30%.

Required

Explain the deferred tax position of the plant and equipment on initial recognition and at the first year-end after initial recognition.

Solution

The asset would have a tax base of zero on initial recognition, and this would normally give rise to a deferred tax liability of $2 million @ 30%, or $600,000. This would mean that an immediate tax expense has arisen before the asset was used. ASC 740 prohibits the recognition of this expense. This could be classified as a permanent difference.

At the date of the first accounts, the asset would have been depreciated by, say, 25% of $2 million, or $500,000. As the tax base is zero, this would normally cause a deferred tax liability of $1.5 @ 30%, or $450,000. However, this liability has arisen from the initial recognition of the asset and therefore is not provided for.

A further temporary difference not recognized relates to investments in subsidiaries, associates, and joint ventures. Normally deferred tax assets and liabilities should be recognized on these investments. Such temporary differences often will be as a result of the undistributed profits of such entities. However, where the parent or the investor can control the timing of the reversal of a taxable temporary difference and it is probable that the temporary difference will not reverse in the foreseeable future, then a deferred tax liability should not be recognized. This would be the case where the parent is able to control when and if the retained profits of the subsidiary are to be distributed.

Similarly, a deferred tax asset should not be recognized if the temporary difference is expected to continue into the foreseeable future and there are no taxable profits available against which the temporary difference can be offset.

In the case of a joint venture or an associate, normally a deferred tax liability would be recognized, because normally the investor cannot control the dividend policy. However, if there is an agreement between the parties that the profits will not be distributed, then a deferred tax liability would not be provided for.

DEFERRED TAX ASSETS

Deductible temporary differences give rise to deferred tax assets. Examples of this are tax losses carried forward or temporary differences arising on provisions that are not allowable for taxation until the future.

These deferred tax assets can be recognized if it is probable that the asset will be realized.

Realization of the asset will depend on whether there are sufficient taxable profits available in the future.

Sufficient taxable profits can arise from three different sources:

1. They can arise from existing taxable temporary differences. In principle, these differences should reverse in the same accounting period as the reversal of the deductible temporary difference or in the period in which a tax loss is expected to be used.
2. If there are insufficient taxable temporary differences, the entity may recognize the deferred tax asset where it feels that there will be future taxable profits, other than those arising from taxable temporary differences. These profits should relate to the same taxable authority and entity.
3. The entity may be able to prove that it can create tax planning opportunities whereby the deductible temporary differences can be utilized.

Wherever tax planning opportunities are considered, management must have the capability and ability to implement them.

Similarly, an entity can recognize a deferred tax asset arising from unused tax losses or credits when it is probable that future taxable profits will be available against which these can be offset. However, the existence of current tax losses is probably evidence that future taxable profit will not be available.

The evidence to suggest that future taxable profits are available must be relevant and reliable. For example, the existence of signed sales contracts and a good profit history may provide such evidence. The period for which these tax losses can be carried forward under the tax regulations must be taken into account also.

Where an entity has not been able to recognize a deferred tax asset because of insufficient evidence concerning future taxable profit, it should review the situation at each subsequent date of the statement of financial position to see whether some, or all, of the unrecognized asset can be recognized.

ACCOUNTING FOR UNCERTAINTY IN INCOME TAXES

The term *tax position* is used in ASC 740-10 to refer to *each* judgment that management makes on an income tax return that has been or will be filed that affects the measurement of current or deferred income tax assets and liabilities at the date of each interim or year-end statement of financial position.

Tax positions include

1. Deductions claimed
2. Deferrals of current income tax to one or more future periods
3. Income tax credits applied
4. Characterization as capital gain versus ordinary income
5. Whether to report income on an income tax return or not
6. Whether to file an income tax return in a particular jurisdiction or not

ASC 740-10 uses a two-step approach to recognition and measurement:

1. *Initial recognition.* Management is to evaluate each tax position as to whether, based on the position's technical merits, it is "more likely than not" that the position would be sustained upon examination by the taxing authority.
2. *Initial measurement.* If a tax position meets the initial recognition threshold, it is then measured to determine the amount to recognize in the financial statements.

Tax liabilities resulting from applying ASC 740-10 are current tax obligations. They are *not* to be classified as deferred income tax liabilities unless they are recognized as the result of a future taxable temporary difference created by a tax position that meets the more-likely-than-not criterion.

TAX RATES

The tax rates that should be used to calculate deferred tax are the ones that are expected to apply in the period when the asset is realized or the liability settled. The best estimate of this tax rate is the rate that has been enacted or substantially enacted at the date of the statement of financial position.

The tax rate to be used should be that which was applicable to the particular tax that has been levied. For example, if tax is going to be levied on a gain on a particular asset, then the rate of tax relating to those types of gain should be used in order to calculate the deferred taxation amount.

DISCOUNTING

Deferred tax assets and liabilities should not be discounted, as this has never been permitted by GAAP. The reason for this is generally because it is difficult to accurately predict the timing of the reversal of each temporary difference.

Case Study 8

Facts

An entity operates in a jurisdiction where the tax rate is 30% for retained profits and 40% for distributed profits. Management has declared a dividend of $10 million, which is payable after the year-end. A liability has not been recognized in the financial statements at the year-end. The taxable profit before tax of the entity was $100 million.

Required

Calculate the current income tax expense for the entity for the current year.

Solution

$30 million (30% of $100 million). The tax rate that should be applied should be that relating to retained profits.

CURRENT AND DEFERRED TAX RECOGNITION

Current and deferred tax should both be recognized as income or expense and included in the net profit or loss for the period.

However, to the extent that the tax arises from a transaction or event that is recognized directly in equity, then the tax that relates to these items that are credited or charged to equity should also be charged or credited directly to equity.

Any tax arising from a business combination should be recognized as an identifiable asset or liability at the date of acquisition.

Current tax assets and current tax liabilities should be offset in the statement of financial position only if the enterprise has the legal right and the intention to settle these on a net basis and they are levied by the same taxation authority.

The tax expense relating to profit or loss for the period should be presented on the face of the income statement, and the principal elements of the expense should also be disclosed.

DIVIDENDS

There are certain tax consequences of dividends.

ASC 740 requires disclosure of the potential tax consequences of the payment of dividends.

Effect of Share-Based Payment Transactions

In some jurisdictions, tax relief is given on share-based payment transactions. A deductible temporary difference may arise between the carrying amount, which will be zero, and its tax base, which will be the tax relief in future periods. A deferred tax asset may therefore be recognized.

Case Study 9

Facts

A parent has recognized in its own financial statements a dividend receivable of $500,000 from an 80%-owned subsidiary. The dividend is not taxable in the country in which the entity operates.

Required

Calculate the temporary difference arising from the recognition of the dividend receivable in the accounts of the parent.

Solution

Zero. There is no temporary difference arising in respect of the dividend as the carrying amount of $500,000 is the same as the tax base.

DISCLOSURE: KEY ELEMENTS

For disclosure, requirements to the standard are quite extensive. For example:

(a) A reporting entity is required to disclose these components of the net deferred income tax liability or asset recognized in the statement of financial position:

1. Total of all deferred income tax liabilities.
2. Total of all deferred income tax assets.
3. Total valuation allowance.
4. Net change in the valuation allowance for the period.
5. Narrative description of the types of temporary differences and carryforwards that cause significant portions of deferred income tax assets and liabilities. Public enterprises additionally are required to disclose the approximate income tax effect (not the separate effect for each jurisdiction) of each temporary difference and carryforward (gross, without consideration of any necessary valuation allowance).

(b) When deferred income tax liabilities are not recognized because of the exceptions provided under ASC 740-30, this information is to be provided:

1. The types of temporary differences and the events that would cause those temporary differences to become taxable
2. The cumulative amount of each type of temporary difference
3. The amount of unrecognized deferred income tax liability for any undistributed foreign earnings, or a statement that such a determination is not practicable
4. The amount of unrecognized deferred income tax liability for other temporary differences that arose prior to the period for which application of this statement was first required for each of those particular differences

(c) All significant components of income taxes associated with continuing operations (i.e., current and deferred income tax expense or benefit, general business credits, investment tax credits, government grants, the benefits of net operating loss carryforwards, etc.) are required to be disclosed for each period for which an income statement is presented.

(d) The amounts of income tax expense or benefit allocated to financial statement elements other than continuing operations.

(e) The amounts and expiration dates of net operating loss and tax credit carryforwards under the currently enacted tax law.

(f) The amount of the valuation allowance for which subsequently recognized income tax benefits will be allocated to contributed capital and, if the pre-ASC 805 effective date accounting was still applicable, tax benefits that were allocated to reduce goodwill or other noncurrent intangible assets of an acquired entity.

(g) A narrative description of the nature of significant reconciling items between income tax expense or benefit computed on pretax income from continuing operations by applying the statutory federal income tax rate and the actual amount of such expense or benefit reflected in the financial statements. For the purpose of this disclosure, the federal statutory rate is the regular marginal rate to which ordinary taxable income is subjected (currently 34%) without consideration of the effect of graduated rates, alternative minimum tax rates, or income taxes from other state, local, or foreign taxing jurisdictions.

(h) ASC 740 sets out many other disclosure requirements.

Case Study 10

Facts

East is a private entity, and it has recently acquired two 100%-owned subsidiaries, West and North. West and North are themselves private entities. East has a business plan whereby in a few years it is going to acquire a stock exchange listing for its shares and capital. East acquired West on July 1, 2009. When East acquired West, it had unused tax losses. On July 1, 2009, it seemed that West would have sufficient taxable profit in the future to realize the deferred tax asset created by these losses. However, subsequent events have shown that the future taxable profit will not be sufficient to realize all of the unused tax losses.

West has made a general impairment charge of $4 million against its total accounts receivable. West gets tax relief on impairment of specific accounts receivable. Because of the current economic situation, West feels that impairment charges will increase in the future.

West has investments that are valued at fair value in the statement of financial position and any gain or loss is taken to the income statement. The gains and losses become taxable when the investments are sold.

East acquired North on July 1, 2009, for $10 million, when the fair value of the net assets was $8 million. The tax base of the net assets acquired was $7 million. Any impairment loss on goodwill is not allowed as a deduction in determining taxable profit.

During the current year, North has sold goods to East of $10 million. North has made a profit of 20% on the selling price on the transaction. East has $5 million worth of these goods recorded in its statement of financial position at the current year-end.

The directors of East have decided that during the period up to the date they intend to list the shares of the entity, they will realize the earnings of the subsidiary, North, through dividend payments. Tax is payable on any remittance of dividends to the holding entity. In the current year no dividends have been declared or paid.

Taxation is payable for listed entities at 40% and for private entities at 35% in the jurisdiction.

Required

Prepare a memorandum that sets out the deferred tax implications of the above information for the East Group.

Solution

The creation of a group through the purchase of subsidiaries during the period has a major impact on the deferred taxation charge. Deferred taxation is looked at from the point of view of the group as a whole. Individual companies may not have sufficient future taxable profits to offset any unused tax losses, but in the group situation, a deferred tax asset may be recognized if there are sufficient taxable profits within the group.

Differences arise between the fair values of the net assets being recognized and their tax bases. In the case of the acquisition of North, deferred taxation will be calculated on the basis of the difference between the fair value of the net assets of $8 million and the tax base of $7 million, giving taxable temporary differences of $1 million.

No provision is required for deferred taxation regarding the temporary difference arising on the recognition of non-tax-deductible goodwill of $2 million, but goodwill will increase by the deferred tax arising on the acquisition of North.

East is hoping to achieve a stock exchange listing of its shares in the near future. This may affect the tax rate used to calculate deferred tax. The current tax rate for private companies is 35%; for public companies, it is 40%. Therefore, a decision will have to be made as to whether the temporary differences are going to reverse at the higher tax rate; if so, deferred tax will be provided for at this rate.

In the case of West, the entity has investments that are stated at fair value in the statement of financial position. The gains and losses are taxed when the investments are sold; therefore, a temporary difference will arise as the tax treatment is different from the accounting treatment. The tax base is not adjusted for any surplus on the investments. Therefore, the difference between the carrying amount of the investments and the tax base will give rise to a deferred tax liability. The resultant deferred tax expense will be charged against the income statement, not equity, as the surplus on the investments has already gone to the income statement.

In the case of the impairment of trade receivables, because the tax relief is available only on the specific impairment of an account, a deductible temporary difference arises that represents the difference between the carrying amount of the trade receivables and their tax base, which in this case will be zero. It appears that the impairment loss is likely to increase in the future. Therefore, it is unlikely that the temporary difference will actually reverse soon. It does not affect the fact that a provision for deferred tax ought to be made. A deferred tax asset will arise at the value of the difference between the tax base and carrying value of the trade receivables at the tax rate applicable for the East Group of companies. This is subject to the general rule in ASC 740 that there will be sufficient taxable profits available in the future against which this deductible temporary difference can be offset.

East has unused tax losses brought forward. These can create a deferred tax asset. However, deferred tax assets should be recognized only to the extent that they can be recovered in the future. Thus, the deferred tax assets must be capable of being realized. If a deferred tax asset can be realized, then it can be recognized for that amount. Generally speaking, the future realization of the deferred tax asset is dependent on the existence of sufficient taxable profit of the appropriate type being available in the future. The appropriate type normally would be taxable operating profit or taxable gain. In general, suitable taxable profits will be created only in the same taxable entity and will be assessed by the same taxation authority as the income. It is possible that tax planning opportunities may be available to the group in order that these unrelieved tax losses may be utilized. Tax planning opportunities should be considered only in determining the extent to which a deferred tax asset will be realized. They should never be used to reduce a deferred tax liability. Any asset recognized as a result of implementing a tax planning strategy should be reduced by the costs of implementing it. In this case, any deferred tax asset arising should be recognized together with the corresponding adjustment to goodwill.

Intergroup profits are eliminated on consolidation. Therefore, $1 million should be taken from the value of inventory in the consolidated statement of financial position at year-end. However, because an equivalent adjustment has not been made for tax purposes, a temporary difference will arise between the carrying amount of the inventory in the group accounts and its value in East's statement of financial position. The tax base of the inventory will be $5 million and the carrying value will be $4 million, giving rise to a temporary difference of $1 million.

Temporary differences can arise between the carrying amount of the parent's investment in a subsidiary and its tax base. Often this difference is caused by the undistributed earnings in the subsidiary. ASC 740 requires recognition of all taxable temporary differences associated with the parent's investments in its subsidiaries, except when the parent actually can control the timing of the reversal of the temporary difference and it is probable that the temporary difference will not reverse in the near future. The provision is required if the parent entity cannot control the timing of the remittance of undistributed profits or it is probable a remittance will take place in the near future.

The parent, East, appears to be recovering the carrying value of its investment in North through the payment of dividends. The method of recovering the value of the investment in the subsidiary is obviously under control of the parent entity. Because the payment of dividends is under the control of East, ASC 740 would not require the recognition of a deferred tax liability in respect of the undistributed profits of North.

EXTRACTS FROM PUBLISHED FINANCIAL STATEMENTS

Lowe's Companies, Inc. 2008 Annual Report to Shareholders

Note 10. Income Taxes

The following is a reconciliation of the effective tax rate to the federal statutory tax rate:

	2008	2007	2006
Statutory federal income tax rate	35.0%	35.0%	35.0%
State income taxes, net of federal tax benefit	2.9	3.0	3.3
Other, net	(0.5)	(0.3)	(0.4)
Effective tax rate	**37.4**	**37.7%**	**37.9%**

The components of the income tax provision are as follows:

(In millions)	2008	2007	2006
Current:			
Federal	$1,070	$1,495	$1,657
State	166	207	242
Total current	**1,236**	**1,702**	**1,899**
Deferred:			
Federal	82	(1)	(11)
State	(7)	1	5
Total deferred	**75**	**—**	**(6)**
Total income tax provision	**$1,311**	**$1,702**	**$1,893**

The tax effect of cumulative temporary differences that gave rise to the deferred tax assets and liabilities is as follows:

(In millions)	January 30, 2009	February 1, 2008
Deferred tax assets:		
Self-insurance	$221	$189
Share-based payment expense	95	81
Other, net	223	205
Total deferred tax assets	**$539**	**$475**
Valuation allowance	(42)	(22)
Net deferred tax assets	**$497**	**$453**
Deferred tax liabilities:		
Property	$(977)	$(834)
Other, net	(14)	(42)
Total deferred tax liabilities	**$(991)**	**$(876)**
Net deferred tax liability	**$(494)**	**$(423)**

The Company operates as a branch in various foreign jurisdictions and cumulatively has incurred net operating losses of $130 million and $63 million as of January 30, 2009, and February 1, 2008, respectively. The net operating losses are subject to expiration in 2017 through 2028. Deferred tax assets have been established for these net operating losses in the accompanying consolidated balance sheets. Given the uncertainty regarding the realization of the foreign net deferred tax assets, the Company recorded cumulative valuation allowances of $42 million and $22 million as of January 30, 2009, and February 1, 2008, respectively.

The Company adopted FASB Interpretation (FIN) 48, *Accounting for Uncertainty in Income Taxes, an Interpretation of FASB Statement No. 109*, effective February 3, 2007. The cumulative effect of applying this Interpretation was recorded as a decrease of $8 million to retained earnings, a decrease of $158 million to the net deferred tax liability, an increase of $146 million to the reserve for unrecognized tax benefits, an increase of $13 million to accrued interest, and an increase of $7 million to accrued penalties.

A reconciliation of the beginning and ending balances of unrecognized tax benefits is as follows:

(In millions)	2008	2007
Unrecognized tax benefits, beginning of year	$138	$186
Additions for tax positions of prior years	82	11
Reductions for tax positions of prior years	(16)	(81)

(In millions)	2008	2007
Additions based on tax positions related to the current year	16	23
Settlements	(19)	(1)
Reductions due to a lapse in applicable statute of limitations	(1)	—
Unrecognized tax benefits, end of year	$200	$138

The amounts of unrecognized tax benefits that, if recognized, would favorably impact the effective tax rate were $40 million and $46 million as of January 30, 2009, and February 1, 2008, respectively.

The Company includes interest related to tax issues as part of net interest in the consolidated financial statements. The Company records any applicable penalties related to tax issues within the income tax provision. For the year ended January 30, 2009, the Company recognized $10 million of interest expense and a $3 million reduction in penalties related to uncertain tax positions on the consolidated statement of earnings. As of January 30, 2009, the Company had $30 million of accrued interest and $9 million of accrued penalties. For the year ended February 1, 2008, the Company recognized $3 million of interest expense and $5 million of penalties related to uncertain tax positions in the consolidated statement of earnings. As of February 1, 2008, the Company had $24 million of accrued interest and $12 million of accrued penalties.

The Company does not expect any changes in unrecognized tax benefits over the next 12 months to have a significant impact on the results of operations, the financial position or the cash flows of the Company.

The Company is subject to examination in the U.S. federal tax jurisdiction for fiscal years 2004 forward. The Company is subject to examination in major state tax jurisdictions for fiscal years 2002 forward. The Company believes appropriate provisions for all outstanding issues have been made for all jurisdictions and all open years.

Nike, Inc., Annual Report for the year ended May 31, 2009

Note 9. Income Taxes

Income before income taxes is as follows:

	Year ended May 31		
(In millions)	2009	2008	2007
Income before income taxes:			
United States	$ 845.7	$713.0	$ 805.1
Foreign	1,110.8	1,789.9	1,394.8
	$1,956.5	$2,502.9	$2,199.9

The provision for income taxes is as follows:

	Year ended May 31		
(In millions)	2009	2008	2007
Current:			
United States			
Federal	$410.1	$469.9	$352.6
State	46.1	58.4	59.6
Foreign	307.7	391.8	261.9
	763.9	920.1	674.1
Deferred:			
United States			
Federal	(251.4)	(273.0)	38.7
State	(7.9)	(5.0)	(4.8)
Foreign	(34.8)	(22.6)	0.4
	(294.1)	(300.6)	34.3
	$469.8	$619.5	$708.4

Deferred tax assets and (liabilities) are comprised of the following:

	May 31	
	2009	*2008*
(In millions)		
Deferred tax assets:		
Allowance for doubtful accounts	$ 17.9	$ 13.1
Inventories	52.8	49.2
Sales return reserves	52.8	49.2
Deferred compensation	160.9	158.4
Stock-based compensation	93.7	55.2
Reserves and accrued liabilities	66.7	57.0
Property, plant, and equipment	—	7.9
Foreign loss carry-forwards	31.9	40.1
Foreign tax credit carry-forwards	32.7	91.9
Hedges	1.1	42.9
Undistributed earnings of foreign subsidiaries	272.9	—
Other	46.2	40.5
Total deferred tax assets	829.6	605.4
Valuation allowance	(26.0)	(40.7)
Total deferred tax assets after valuation allowance	803.6	564.7
Deferred tax liabilities:		
Undistributed earnings of foreign subsidiaries	—	(113.2)
Property, plant, and equipment	(92.2)	(67.4)
Intangibles	(100.7)	(214.2)
Hedges	(86.6)	(1.3)
Other	(4.2)	(0.7)
Total deferred tax liability	(283.7)	(396.8)
Net deferred tax asset	$ 519.9	$ 167.9

At the end of fiscal 2009, the Company reported a net deferred tax asset of $272.9 million associated with its investment in certain non-U.S. subsidiaries. Prior to fiscal 2009, the Company reported a net deferred tax liability for book to tax differences in its investment in non-U.S. subsidiaries. The change to a deferred tax asset position at the end of fiscal 2009 is due primarily to the impact of the impairment of Umbro's goodwill, intangible and other assets as described in Note 4—Acquisition, Identifiable Intangible Assets, Goodwill, and Umbro Impairment.

A reconciliation from the U.S. statutory federal income tax rate to the effective income tax rate follows:

	Year ended May 31		
	2009	*2008*	*2007*
Federal income tax rate	35.0%	35.0%	35.0%
State taxes, net of federal benefit	1.2%	1.4%	1.6%
Foreign earnings	–14.9%	–12.9%	–4.1%
Other, net	2.7%	1.3%	–0.3%
Effective income tax rate	24.0%	24.8%	32.2%

The effective tax rate for the year ended May 31, 2009, of 24.0% decreased from the fiscal 2008 effective tax rate of 24.8%. The effective tax rate for the year ended May 31, 2009, was favorably impacted by a benefit associated with the impairment of goodwill, intangible, and other assets of Umbro (see Note 4—Acquisition, Identifiable Intangible Assets, Goodwill, and Umbro Impairment), the impact of the resolution of audit items and the retroactive reinstatement of the research and development tax credit. The Tax Extenders and Alternative Minimum Tax Relief Act of 2008, which was signed into law during the second quarter of fiscal 2009, reinstated the U.S. federal research and development tax credit retroactive to January 1, 2008. The effective tax rate for the year ended May 31, 2008, of 24.8% decreased from the fiscal 2007 effective tax rate of 32.2%. Over the few years preceding fiscal 2008, a number of international entities generated losses for which the Company did not recognize offsetting tax benefits because the realization of those benefits was uncertain. The necessary steps to realize these benefits were taken in the first quarter of fiscal 2008, resulting in a one-time reduction of the effective tax rate for the year ended May 31, 2008. Also reflected in the effective tax rate for the years ended May 31, 2009, and May 31, 2008, is a reduction in our ongoing effective tax rate resulting from our operations outside of the United States, as our tax rates on those operations are generally lower than the U.S. statutory rate.

The Company adopted FASB Interpretation 48, *Accounting for Uncertainty in Income Taxes* ("FIN 48") effective June 1, 2007. Upon adoption, the Company recognized an additional long-term liability of $89.4 million for unrecognized tax benefits, $15.6 million of which was recorded as a reduction to the Company's beginning retained earnings, and the remaining $73.8 million was recorded as a reduction to the Company's noncurrent deferred tax liability. In addition, the Company reclassified $12.2 million of unrecognized tax benefits from income taxes payable to other long term liabilities in conjunction with the adoption of FIN 48.

At the adoption date of June 1, 2007, the Company had $122.5 million of gross unrecognized tax benefits, excluding related interest and penalties, $30.7 million of which would affect the Company's effective tax rate if recognized in future periods. Including related interest and penalties and net of federal benefit of interest and unrecognized state tax benefits, at June 1, 2007, the Company had $135.0 million of total unrecognized tax benefits, $52.0 million of which would affect the Company's effective tax rate if recognized in future periods. As of May 31, 2009, the total gross unrecognized tax benefits, excluding related interest and penalties, were $273.9 million, $110.6 million of which would affect the Company's effective tax rate if recognized in future periods. Total gross unrecognized tax benefits, excluding interest and penalties, as of May 31, 2008, was $251.1 million, $60.6 million of which would affect the Company's effective tax rate if recognized in future periods. The Company does not anticipate total unrecognized tax benefits will change significantly within the next 12 months.

The following is a reconciliation of the changes in the gross balance of unrecognized tax benefits:

	May 31	
	2009	*2008*
(In millions)		
Unrecognized tax benefits, as of the beginning of the period	$251.1	$122.5
Gross increases related to prior period tax positions	53.2	71.6
Gross decreases related to prior period tax positions	(61.7)	(23.1)
Gross increases related to current period tax positions	71.5	87.7
Settlements	(29.3)	(13.4)
Lapse of statute of limitations	(4.1)	(0.7)
Changes due to currency translation	(6.8)	6.5
Unrecognized tax benefits, as of the end of the period	$273.9	$251.1

The Company recognizes interest and penalties related to income tax matters in income tax expense. Upon adoption of FIN 48 at June 1, 2007, the Company had $32.0 million (excluding federal benefit) accrued for interest and penalties related to uncertain tax positions. The liability for payment of interest and penalties increased $2.2 million and $41.2 million during the years ended May 31, 2009 and 2008, respectively. As of May 31, 2009 and 2008, accrued interest and penalties related to uncertain tax positions was $75.4 million and $73.2 million, respectively (excluding federal benefit).

The Company is subject to taxation primarily in the United States, China, and the Netherlands as well as various state and other foreign jurisdictions. The Company has concluded substantially all U.S. federal income tax matters through fiscal year 2006. The Company is currently subject to examination by the Internal Revenue Service for the 2007, 2008, and 2009 tax years. The Company's major foreign jurisdictions, China and the Netherlands, have concluded substantially all income tax matters through calendar year 1998 and fiscal year 2002, respectively.

The Company has indefinitely reinvested approximately $2.6 billion of the cumulative undistributed earnings of certain foreign subsidiaries. Such earnings would be subject to U.S. taxation if repatriated to the United States. Determination of the amount of unrecognized deferred tax liability associated with the permanently reinvested cumulative undistributed earnings is not practicable.

Deferred tax assets at May 31, 2009 and 2008, respectively, were reduced by a valuation allowance relating to tax benefits of certain foreign subsidiaries with operating losses where it is more likely than not that the deferred tax assets will not be realized. The net change in the valuation allowance was a decrease of $14.7 million during fiscal 2009 and a decrease of $1.6 million during fiscal 2008.

The Company does not anticipate any foreign tax credit carryforwards will expire. A benefit was recognized for foreign loss carryforwards of $13.1 million at May 31, 2009. Such losses will expire as follows:

(In millions)	Year ending May 31, 2014	Indefinite
Net Operating Losses	$2.2	$10.9

During the years ended May 31, 2009, 2008, and 2007, income tax benefits attributable to employee stock-based compensation transactions of $25.4 million, $68.9 million, and $56.6 million, respectively, were allocated to shareholders' equity.

Whirlpool Corporation Annual Report 2009

12. Income Taxes

Income tax expense is as follows:

	Year ended December 31		
(In millions)	2008	2007	2006
Current:			
Federal	$ 9	$ (28)	$125
State and local	14	8	(7)
Foreign	66	128	68
	89	108	186
Deferred:			
Federal	(309)	28	(112)
State and local	(31)	3	1
Foreign	50	(22)	51
	(290)	9	(60)
Total income tax (benefit) expense	$(201)	$117	$126

Domestic and foreign earnings (loss) before income taxes and other items are as follows:

	Year ended December 31		
(In millions)	2008	2007	2006
Domestic	$(433)	$103	$231
Foreign	679	701	388
Total earnings (loss) from continuing operations before income tax and other items	$246	$804	$619

Reconciliations between tax expense at the U.S. federal statutory income tax rate of 35% and the consolidated effective income tax rate for earnings from continuing operations before income taxes and other items are as follows:

	Year ended December 31		
	2008	2007	2006
Income tax rate computed at U.S. federal statutory rate	35.0	35.0	35.0
U.S. foreign tax credits	(73.9)	(2.2)	(5.3)
U.S. tax on foreign dividends and subpart F income	66.6	0.7	2.9
U.S. government tax incentives	(42.6)	(3.7)	(10.2)
Foreign government tax incentive	(34.5)	(7.6)	(2.7)
Deductible interest on capital	(13.4)	(2.7)	(3.1)
Foreign tax rate differential	(9.4)	(1.4)	1.6
Settlement of global tax audits	(8.6)	2.7	2.6
State and local taxes, net of federal tax benefit	(6.7)	1.0	0.3
Real estate donations	—	(1.1)	—
Medicare Part D subsidy	—	(0.6)	(1.1)
Impact of tax rate changes	0.7	1.9	—
Valuation allowances	2.1	(7.1)	0.3
Foreign withholding taxes	4.7	1.9	2.3
Other items, net	(1.7)	(2.3)	(2.2)
Effective tax rate	(81.7)	14.5	20.4

Deferred income taxes reflect the net tax effects of temporary differences between the carrying amounts of assets and liabilities used for financial reporting purposes and the amounts used for income tax purposes.

Significant components of our deferred tax liabilities and assets from continuing operations are as follows:

	December 31	
	2008	*2007*
(In millions)		
Deferred tax liabilities		
Property, plant, and equipment	$229	$262
Financial services leveraged leases	22	25
Pensions	17	17
Software costs	12	17
LIFO inventory	86	81
Intangibles	633	633
Other	164	163
Total deferred tax liabilities	1,163	1,198
Deferred tax assets		
Postretirement obligations	470	492
Inventory prepayments	323	—
Pensions	439	189
Restructuring costs	28	30
Product warranty accrual	75	85
Receivable and inventory allowances	57	46
Capital loss carryforwards	—	19
Loss carryforwards	306	286
Employee payroll and benefits	87	128
Foreign tax credit carryforwards	4	102
U.S. general business credit carryforwards	175	88
Hedging	109	2
Accrued expenses	68	128
Other	218	135
Total deferred tax assets	2,359	1,730
Valuation allowances for deferred tax assets	(147)	(72)
Deferred tax assets, net of valuation allowances	2,212	1,658
Net deferred tax assets	$1,049	$460

At December 31, 2008, we have net operating loss carryforwards of $1,380 million, $789 million of which do not expire, with substantially all of the remaining expiring in various years through 2013. As of December 31, 2008, we had $4 million of foreign tax credit carryforwards and $175 million of U.S. general business credit carryforwards available to offset future payments of federal income taxes, expiring between 2016 and 2028.

We routinely review the future realization of deferred tax assets based on projected future reversal of taxable temporary differences, available tax planning strategies, and projected future taxable income. We have recorded a valuation allowance to reflect the net estimated amount of certain deferred tax assets associated with net operating loss and other deferred tax assets we believe will be realized. Our recorded valuation allowance of $147 million at December 31, 2008, consists of $86 million of net operating loss carryforwards and $61 million of other deferred tax assets. We believe that it is more likely than not that we will realize the benefit of existing deferred tax assets, net of valuation allowances mentioned above.

We have historically reinvested all unremitted earnings of our foreign subsidiaries and affiliates. We plan to distribute approximately $147 million of foreign earnings over the next several years. This distribution is forecasted to result in tax benefits which have not been recorded because of their contingent nature. There has been no deferred tax liability provided on the remaining amount of unremitted earnings of $1.8 billion at December 31, 2008. Should we make a distribution out of the $1.8 billion of unremitted earnings, we would be subject to additional U.S. taxes (subject to an adjustment for foreign tax credits) and withholding taxes payable to the various foreign countries. It is not practicable to estimate the amount of the deferred tax liability associated with these unremitted earnings.

On October 3, 2008, the Emergency Economic Stabilization Act of 2008 (the "Act") was signed into law. The Act includes a wide range of provisions that are intended to ensure that conservation and efficiency are a central component to the United States energy strategy. Among the many provisions of this legislation are manufacturers' tax credits for the accelerated U.S. production of super-efficient clothes washers, refrigerators, and dishwashers that meet or exceed certain Energy Star thresholds for energy and water conservation levels as set by the U.S. Department of Energy ("Energy Credit"). The tax credits apply to eligible production during the 2008 to 2010 calendar years provided the production of qualifying product in any individual year exceeds a rolling two-year baseline of production. We have historically, and will continue to, invest over 2% of our annual sales in research and development to provide innovative and energy efficient products that meet these standards for our customers. As a result, during the December 2008 quarter and in future periods through 2010 we expect to record a tax credit benefit under the provisions of the Act related to the production of qualifying appliances. Including the Energy Credit, total general business tax credits recorded during 2008 reduced our effective tax rate by 43%.

We are in various stages of audits by certain governmental tax authorities. We establish liabilities for the difference between tax return provisions and the benefits recognized in our financial statements. Such amounts represent a reasonable provision for taxes ultimately expected to be paid, and may need to be adjusted over time as more information becomes known.

We adopted FIN 48, *Accounting for Uncertainty in Income Taxes—an Interpretation of FASB 109* (FIN 48) on January 1, 2007, at which time the total amount of gross unrecognized tax benefit on the Consolidated Balance Sheet was $166 million. Upon adoption of FIN 48, we recognized a $2 million increase in the liability for unrecognized tax benefits and a $2 million decrease in federal benefit related to state uncertain tax positions. The increase has been accounted for as a reduction to retained earnings in the amount of $8 million and a reduction to goodwill in the amount of $4 million. A reconciliation of the beginning and ending amount of unrecognized tax benefits is as follows:

(In millions)	2008	2007
Balance, January 1	$189	$166
Additions for tax positions of the current year	4	36
Additions for tax positions of the prior year	2	20
Reductions for tax positions of prior years for		
Changes in judgment	(39)	(28)
Settlements during the period	(37)	(4)
Lapses of applicable statute of limitation	—	(1)
Balance, December 31	$119	$189

Included in the liability for unrecognized tax benefits at December 31, 2008 and 2007 are $119 and $141 million, respectively, of unrecognized tax benefits that if recognized would impact the effective tax rate, net of $16 million and $16 million, respectively, of federal benefits related to state uncertain tax positions.

We recognize charges related to interest and penalties for unrecognized tax benefits as a component of income tax expense. As of December 31, 2008 and 2007, we have accrued interest and penalties of $25 and $40 million, respectively. Interest and penalties are not included in the tabular roll-forward of unrecognized tax benefits above.

We file income tax returns in the U.S. federal, various state, local, and foreign jurisdictions. We are no longer subject to any significant U.S. federal, state, local, or foreign income tax examinations by tax authorities for years before 2006. The Internal Revenue Service commenced an examination of our U.S. income tax returns for 2006 and 2007 in the fourth quarter of 2008 that is anticipated to be completed during early 2010. It is reasonably possible that certain unrecognized tax benefits of $1 million could be settled with the related jurisdictions during the next 12 months.

MULTIPLE-CHOICE QUESTIONS

1. A subsidiary has sold goods costing $1.2 million to its parent for $1.4 million. All of the inventory is held by the parent at year-end. The subsidiary is 80% owned. The parent pays taxation at 30%, and the subsidiary pays taxation at 30%. Calculate any deferred tax asset that arises on the sale of the inventory from the subsidiary entity to the parent.

   (a) $ 60,000
   (b) $200,000
   (c) $ 48,000
   (d) $ 80,000

2. An entity issued a convertible bond on January 1, 2010, that matures in five years. The bond can be converted into ordinary shares at any time. The entity has calculated that the liability and equity components of the bond are $3 million for the liability component and $1 million for the equity component, giving a total amount of the bond of $4 million. The interest rate on the bond is 6%, and local tax legislation allows a tax deduction for the interest paid in cash. Calculate the deferred tax liability arising on the bond as at the year ending December 31, 2010. The tax rate is 30%.

   (a) $1.2 million
   (b) $900,000
   (c) $300,000
   (d) $4 million

3. An entity is undertaking a reorganization. Under the plan, part of the entity's business will be demerged and will be transferred to a separate entity, Entity Z. This also will involve a transfer of part of the pension obligation to Entity Z. Because of this, Entity Z will have a deductible temporary difference at its year-end of December 31, 2010. It is anticipated that Entity Z will be loss making for the first four years of its existence, but thereafter it will become a profitable entity. The future forecasted profit is based on estimates of sales to intergroup companies. Should Entity Z recognize the deductible temporary difference as a deferred tax asset?

   (a) The entity should recognize a deferred tax asset.
   (b) Management should not recognize a deferred tax asset as future profitability is not certain.
   (c) The entity should recognize a deferred tax asset if the authenticity of the budgeted profits can be verified.
   (d) The entity should recognize a deferred tax asset if the intergroup profit in the budgeted profit is eliminated.

4. The current liabilities of an entity include fines and penalties for environmental damage. The fines and penalties are stated at $10 million. The fines and penalties are not deductible for tax purposes. What is the tax base of the fines and penalties?

   (a) $10 million
   (b) $3 million
   (c) $13 million
   (d) Zero

Chapter 17

CURRENT LIABILITIES AND CONTINGENCIES (VARIOUS SECTIONS UNDER THE ASC)

BACKGROUND AND INTRODUCTION

Presenting a statement of financial position that classifies assets and liabilities into current and noncurrent categories enables the reader of the financial statements to readily compute important measures of liquidity and solvency, such as working capital (defined as current assets minus current liabilities) and current ratio (current assets divided by current liabilities). The amount of working capital, which is the relatively liquid portion of total entity capital, is closely monitored to gauge the ability of an entity to repay its obligations as they become due. Working capital assumes a going-concern concept. If the entity is to be liquidated in the near future, this mode of statement of financial position classification of assets and liabilities is generally inappropriate.

Although measurement of current liabilities is generally straightforward, some liabilities are difficult to measure because of uncertainties. Uncertainties regarding whether an obligation exists, how much of an entity's assets will be needed to settle the obligation, and when the settlement will take place can impact whether, when, and for how much an obligation will be recognized in the financial statements.

DEFINITIONS OF KEY TERMS
(in accordance with the ASC Master Glossary)

Contingency. An existing condition, situation, or set of circumstances involving uncertainty as to possible gain or loss that ultimately will be resolved when one or more future events occur or fail to occur.

Contingent asset. A possible asset arising from past events and whose existence will be confirmed only by the occurrence or nonoccurrence of one or more uncertain future events that are not completely within the control of the entity.

Liability. Probable future sacrifices of economic benefits arising from present obligations of an enterprise to transfer assets or provide services to others in the future as a result of past transactions.

Operating cycle. The average length of time necessary for a reporting entity to purchase goods and/or services, produce or construct salable finished goods, sell the goods and/or services, and collect cash from customers to pay for the goods and services.

CURRENT LIABILITIES

In general, obligations classified on the statement of financial position as current liabilities are to include debts that management of the reporting entity expects to settle in cash within one year of the statement of financial position date, or within one operating cycle, if that period is longer than one year. Current liabilities can be categorized into several different types, each with certain distinguishing characteristics that will be discussed and illustrated in this chapter.

These obligations can be divided into those where

1. Both the amount and the payee are known.
2. The payee is known but the amount may have to be estimated.
3. The payee is unknown and the amount may have to be estimated.
4. The liability has been incurred due to a loss contingency.

Amount and Payee Known

Accounts payable are obligations that the reporting entity owes to its vendors and suppliers for the purchase of products and services on credit. ASC 835-30, *Imputation of Interest*, states that accounts payable that arise from transactions with suppliers in the normal course of business and that are due in customary trade terms not to exceed one year may be stated at their face amount rather than at the present value of the required future cash flows.

Notes payable are more formalized obligations, evidenced by an executed promissory agreement between the reporting entity (the borrower or debtor) and a lender, a financial institution, or, in many cases in privately held enterprises, a related party. The proceeds may be used to repay other debts, to provide liquidity, to finance operations, or for other purposes.

Dividends payable represent an obligation of the reporting entity to distribute accumulated profits to its stockholders. Cash dividends become a liability of the reporting entity on the declaration date, the date that the board of directors passes a resolution declaring the dividend. Since declared dividends usually are paid within a short period of time after the declaration date, they are classified as current liabilities.

Unearned revenues (sometimes referred to as "deferred revenue") or *advances* result from customer prepayments for either performance of services or delivery of product. They may be required by the seller as a condition of the sale or may be made by the buyer as a means of ensuring that the seller will perform the desired service or deliver the product. Unearned revenues and advances are classified as current liabilities at the statement of financial position date if the services are to be performed or the products are to be delivered within one year or the operating cycle, whichever is longer.

Refundable deposits (or security deposits) may be received to cover possible future damage to property. Many utility companies require security deposits. A deposit may be required for the use of a reusable container, or a lessor may require a security deposit to protect against any damage to the leased property. Refundable deposits are classified as current liabilities if the firm expects to refund them during the current operating cycle or within one year, whichever is longer.

Accrued liabilities have their origin in the end-of-period adjustment process required by accrual accounting. They represent an estimate of services performed or benefits received during the reporting period for which payment will be made in a later reporting period. Commonly accrued liabilities include wages and salaries payable (including incentive bonuses), accrued rents, accrued interest, accrued real estate taxes, and accrued profit-sharing contributions.

The *currently maturing portion of long-term debt or of capital lease obligations* are classified as current liabilities if the obligations are to be liquidated by using assets classified as current. However, if the currently maturing debt is to be liquidated by using noncurrent assets (i.e., by using a sinking fund that is properly classified as a noncurrent investment), then these obligations are to be classified as long-term liabilities.

Short-Term Obligations Expected to Be Refinanced

Short-term obligations that arise in the normal course of business and are due under customary trade terms are to be classified as current liabilities. Under certain circumstances, however, the reporting entity is permitted to exclude all or a portion of these obligations from current liabilities. In order to qualify for this treatment, however, management must have both the intent and ability to refinance the obligation on a long-term basis. Management's intent is to be supported by either of these two rules (ASC 470-10-45-14):

1. *Post–statement of financial position date issuance of a long-term obligation or equity securities.* After the date of the entity's statement of financial position but before that statement of financial position is issued, a long-term obligation is incurred or equity securities are issued for the purpose of refinancing the short-term obligations on a long-term basis.
2. *Financing agreement.* Before the statement of financial position is issued, the entity has entered into a financing agreement that clearly enables the entity to refinance its short-term obligation on a long-term basis on readily determinable terms that meet all of these requirements:

   a. The agreement is noncancelable by the lender (or prospective lender) or investor and will not expire within one year (or one operating cycle, if longer) of the statement of financial position date.
   b. The replacement debt will not be callable during that period except for violation of a provision of the financing agreement with which compliance is objectively determinable or measurable.
   c. At the date of the statement of financial position, the reporting entity is not in violation of the terms of the financing agreement and there is no information that a violation occurred subsequent to the statement of financial position and before issuance of the financial statements, unless such a violation was waived by the lender.
   d. The actual or prospective lender or investor is expected to be financially capable of honoring the financing agreement.

Payee Known but Amount May Have to Be Estimated

Income taxes payable includes federal, state, and local income taxes. The amount of income taxes payable is an estimate because the income tax laws and rates in effect when the accrual is determined may differ from the laws and rates in effect when the income taxes are eventually paid. Temporary differences in recognition and measurement between accounting standards and income tax laws create deferred income tax liabilities (and deferred income tax assets). The portion deemed currently payable must be classified as a current liability. The remaining amount is classified as a long-term liability.

Accrued real estate and personal property taxes represent the unpaid portion of an entity's obligation to a state, county, or other taxing authority that arises from the ownership of real or personal property, respectively. ASC 720-30, *Real and Personal Property Taxes*, indicates that the most acceptable method of accounting for property taxes is a monthly accrual of property tax expense during the fiscal period of the taxing authority for which the taxes are levied. The fiscal period of the taxing authority is the fiscal period that includes the assessment or lien date.

A liability for property taxes payable arises when the fiscal year of the taxing authority and the fiscal year of the entity do not coincide or when the assessment or lien date and the actual payment date do not fall within the same fiscal year.

Example of accrued real estate taxes

Rohlfs Corporation is a calendar-year corporation that owns real estate in a state that operates on a June 30 fiscal year. In this state, real estate taxes are assessed and become a lien against real property on July 1. These taxes, however, are payable in arrears in two installments due on April 1 and August 1 of the next calendar year. Real estate taxes assessed were $18,000 and $22,000 for the years ended 6/30/2010 and 6/30/11, respectively. Rohlfs computes its accrued real estate taxes at December 31, 2010, as follows:

Fiscal year-end of tax jurisdiction	Assessment date/lien date	Installment due dates		Annual assessment	2010 Expense	Portion of expense paid in 2010	Accrued real estate tax at 12/31/10
		April 1	*August 1*				
6/30/2010	7/1/2009	2010	2010	$18,000	$ 9,000	$ 9,000	$ —
6/30/2011	7/1/2010	2011	2011	22,000	11,000	—	11,000
					$20,000	$ 9,000	$ 11,000

Proof of the accrual computation is as follows:

Annual assessment—year-end 6/30/11 of $22,000 ÷ 12 = $1,833/month × 6 months ≈ $11,000

Bonus payments may require estimation since the amount of the bonus may be affected by the entity's net income for the year, by the income taxes currently payable, or by other factors. Additional estimation is necessary if bonus payments are accrued on a monthly basis for purposes of interim financial reporting but are determinable only annually by using a formula whose values are uncertain until shortly before payment.

Compensated absences refer to paid vacation, paid holidays, paid sick leave, and other paid leaves of absence. ASC 710-10-25 requires an employer to accrue a liability for employee's compensation for future absences if all of these four conditions are met:

1. The employee's right to receive compensation for future absences is attributable to employee services already rendered.
2. The right vests or accumulates.
3. Payment of the compensation is probable.
4. The amount of the payment can be reasonably estimated.

Vesting

If an employer is required to compensate an employee for unused vacation, holidays, or sick days even if employment is terminated, then the employee's right to this compensation is said to vest. Accrual of a liability for nonvesting rights depends on whether the unused rights expire at the end of the year in which earned (often referred to as a use-it-or-lose-it policy) or accumulate and are carried forward to succeeding years. If the rights expire, a liability for future absences is not accrued at year-end because the benefits to be paid in subsequent years would not be attributable to employee services rendered in prior years. If all or a portion of the unused rights accumulate and increase the benefits otherwise available in subsequent years, a liability is accrued at year-end to the extent that it is probable that employees will be paid in subsequent years for the increased benefits attributable to the accumulated rights and the amount can be reasonably estimated.

Sick Pay

ASC 710-10-25-7 allows an exception for employee paid sick days that accumulate but do not vest. No accrued liability is required for sick days that only accumulate. However, an employer is permitted to accrue these benefits if the four conditions are met. The required accounting is to be determined by the employer's actual administration of sick pay benefits. If the employer routinely lets employees take time off when they are not ill and allows that time to be charged as sick pay, then an accrual is required.

Other Types of Paid Time Off

Pay for other employee leaves of absence that represent time off for past services (jury duty, personal days) are considered compensation subject to accrual. Pay for employee leaves of absence that will provide future benefits and that are not attributable to past services rendered are not subject to accrual.

ASC 710-10-25-4 et seq. govern the accounting for sabbatical leaves or other similar benefit arrangements that require the completion of a minimum service period and for which the benefit does not increase with additional years of service. Under these arrangements, the individual continues to be a compensated employee and is not required to perform duties for the entity during their absence. Assuming the four conditions set forth earlier are met, the compensation cost associated with a sabbatical or other similar arrangement must be ratably accrued over the presabbatical periods of service

Payee Unknown and the Amount May Have to Be Estimated

Sales incentives usually are offered by a vendor to its customers as an inducement to increase sales. The consideration offered to the customer can take many forms, such as discounts, coupons, rebates, and offers to receive free products or services. They may or may not require the payment of a cash amount. If the incentive offer terminates at the end of the current period but has not been completely settled, or if it extends into the next accounting period, a current liability for the estimated number of redemptions that are expected in the future period would be recorded. If the incentive offer extends for more than one operating cycle, the estimated liability must be divided into a current portion and a long-term portion.

Product warranties providing for repair or replacement of defective products may be sold separately or may be included in the sale price of the product. If the warranty extends into the next accounting period, a current liability for the estimated amount of warranty expense expected in the next period must be recorded. If the warranty spans more than the next period, the estimated liability must be partitioned into a current and long-term portion.

Entities are required to disclose this information:

1. The nature of the product warranty, including how the warranty arose and the events or circumstances in which the entity must perform under the warranty.
2. The entity's accounting policy and methodology used to determine its liability for the product warranty, including any liability (such as deferred revenue) associated with an extended warranty.
3. A reconciliation of the changes in the aggregate product warranty liability for the reporting period. The reconciliation must include five components:

   a. The beginning aggregate balance of the liability
   b. The reductions in the liability caused by payments under the warranty
   c. The increase in the liability for new warranties issued during the period
   d. The change in the liability for adjustments to estimated amounts to be paid under preexisting warranties
   e. The ending aggregate balance of the liability

4. The nature and extent of any recourse provisions or available collateral that would enable the entity to recover the amounts paid under the warranties, and an indication (if estimable) of the approximate extent to which the proceeds from recovery or liquidation would be expected to cover the maximum potential amount of future payments under the warranty.
5. The disclosures required by ASC 850, *Related-Party Disclosures*, if the warranties are granted to benefit related parties.

Example of product warranty expense

The Churnaway Corporation manufactures clothes washers. It sells $900,000 of washing machines during its most recent month of operations. Based on its historical warranty claims experience, it records an estimated warranty expense of 2% of revenues with this entry:

Warranty expense	18,000	
Accrued warranty claims		18,000

During the following month, Churnaway incurs $10,000 of actual labor and $4,500 of actual materials expenses to perform repairs required under warranty claims, which it charges to the warranty claims accrual with this entry:

Accrued warranty claims	14,500	
Labor expense		10,000
Materials expense		4,500

Churnaway also sells three-year extended warranties on its washing machines that begin once the initial one-year manufacturer's warranty expires. During one month, it sells $54,000 of extended warranties, which it records with this entry:

| Cash | 54,000 | |
| Unearned warranty revenue | | 54,000 |

This liability is unaltered for one year from the purchase date, after which the extended warranty servicing period begins. Churnaway recognizes the warranty revenue on a straight-line basis over the 36 months of the warranty period, using this entry each month:

| Unearned warranty revenue | 1,500 | |
| Warranty revenue | | 1,500 |

Future product returns are accrued if a buyer has a right to return the product purchased and the sale is recognized currently. An accrual for returns must reduce both revenue and the associated cost of sales (ASC 605-15). In the relatively unlikely situation where the reporting entity is unable to make a reasonable estimate of the amount of future returns, the sale cannot be recognized until the return privilege has expired or conditions permit the loss to be estimated, at which point it would become reportable. Four examples of factors that might impair the ability to reasonably estimate a loss are

1. Susceptibility of the product to technological or other obsolescence.
2. A lengthy period over which returns are permitted.
3. Absence of experience with returns on similar products sold to similar markets.
4. Sales are few, significant, and have unique terms (rather than a large number of relatively homogeneous sales of small dollar amounts).

Environmental Remediation Liabilities

Obligations arising from pollution of the environment have become a major cost for businesses. ASC 410-30, *Environmental Obligations*, sets forth a very detailed description of relevant laws, remediation provisions, and other pertinent information, which is useful to auditors as well as to reporting entities. In terms of accounting guidance, ASC 450-20, *Loss Contingencies*, contains the principal rules with respect to accounting for environmental obligations (e.g., determining the threshold for accrual of a liability, etc.) and its sets "benchmarks" for liability recognition. The benchmarks for the accrual and evaluation of the estimated liability (i.e., the stages that are deemed to be important to ascertaining the existence and amount of the liability) are

1. The identification and verification of an entity as a potentially responsible party (PRP), since ASC 410-30 stipulates that accrual is to be based on the premise that expected costs will be borne by only the "participating potentially responsible parties" and that the "recalcitrant, unproven and unidentified" PRP will not contribute to costs of remediation.
2. The receipt of a "unilateral administrative order."
3. Participation, as a PRP, in the remedial investigation/feasibility study (RI/FS).
4. Completion of the feasibility study.
5. Issuance of the record of decision (RoD).
6. The remedial design through operation and maintenance, including postremediation monitoring.

The amount of the liability that is to be accrued is affected by the entity's allocable share of liability for a specific site and by its share of the amounts related to the site that will not be paid by the other PRP or the government. The categories of costs to be included in the accrued liability include incremental direct costs of the remediation effort itself, as well as the costs of compensation and benefits for employees directly involved in the remediation effort. The Statement of Position indicates that costs are to be estimated based on existing laws and technologies and are not to be discounted to estimated present values unless timing of cash payments is fixed or reliably determinable.

Incremental direct costs include such items as

- Fees paid to outside law firms for work related to the remediation effort.
- Costs relating to completing the RI/FS.
- Fees to outside consulting and engineering firms for site investigations and development of remedial action plans and remedial actions.

- Costs of contractors performing remedial actions, government oversight costs and past costs.
- The cost of machinery and equipment dedicated to the remedial actions that do not have an alternative use.
- Assessments by a PRP group covering costs incurred by the group in dealing with a site.
- The costs of operation and maintenance of the remedial action, including costs of post remediation monitoring required by remedial action plan.

CONTINGENCIES

ASC 450 defines a contingency as an existing condition, situation, or set of circumstances involving uncertainty as to possible gain or loss. The uncertainty ultimately will be resolved when one or more future events occur or fail to occur. ASC 450 defines the different levels of probability as to whether or not future events will confirm the existence of a loss in this way:

1. *Probable.* The future event or events are likely to occur.
2. *Reasonably possible.* The chance of the future event or events occurring is more than remote but less than likely.
3. *Remote.* The chance of the future event or events occurring is slight.

Professional judgment is required to classify the likelihood of the future events occurring. All relevant information that can be acquired concerning the uncertain set of circumstances needs to be obtained and used to determine the classification.

ASC 450 states that a loss must be accrued if *both* of these conditions are met:

1. It is probable that an asset has been impaired or a liability has been incurred at the date of the financial statements.
2. The amount of loss can be reasonably estimated.

Loss Contingency

Loss contingencies are recognized only if there is an impairment of an asset or the incurrence of a liability as of the date of the statement of financial position. Examples of possible loss contingencies include

- Collectability of receivables
- Warranty liabilities and product defects
- Loss due to fire, explosion, or other hazards
- Expropriation of assets
- Litigation, claims, and assessments
- Incurred but not reported (IBNR) claims if the entity insures its risk of loss with a claims-made policy
- Exposures under multiple-year retrospectively rated insurance contacts
- Catastrophic losses by insurance and reinsurance entities
- The contingent obligations under guarantees
- Obligations under standby letters of credit
- Repurchase agreements
- Withdrawal from a multiemployer plan
- Consideration for a failed registration statement

Events that give rise to loss contingencies that occur after the date of the statement of financial position (i.e., bankruptcy or expropriation) but before issuance of the financial statements may require disclosure so that statement users are not misled. Note disclosures or pro forma financial statements may be prepared as supplemental information to show the effect of the loss.

It is not necessary that a single amount be identified. A range of amounts is sufficient to indicate that some amount of loss has been incurred and is required to be accrued. The amount accrued is the amount within the range that appears to be the best estimate. If there is no best estimate, the minimum amount in the range is accrued since it is probable that the loss will be at least that amount (ASC 450-20). The maximum amount of loss is required to be disclosed. If future events indicate that the minimum loss originally accrued is inadequate, an additional loss is to be accrued in the period when this fact becomes known. This accrual is a change in estimate, not a prior period adjustment.

When a loss is probable and no estimate is possible, these facts also are to be disclosed in the current period. The accrual of the loss is to be made in the earliest period in which the amount of the loss can be estimated. Accrual of that loss in future periods is a change in estimate. It is not treated as a restatement (prior period adjustment).

If the occurrence of the loss is reasonably possible, the facts and circumstances of the possible loss and an estimate of the amount, if determinable, are to be disclosed. If the occurrence of the loss is remote, no accrual or disclosure is usually required.

When a public company cannot estimate the reasonably likely impact of a contingent liability, but a range of amounts are determinable, the Securities and Exchange Commission (SEC) requires disclosure of those amounts. Disclosure of contingencies for public companies is also to include quantification of the related accruals and adjustments, costs of legal defense, and reasonably likely exposure to additional loss as well as the assumptions that management has made about those amounts and the extent to which the resulting estimates of loss are sensitive to changes in those assumptions.

Unasserted Claims or Assessments

It is not necessary to disclose loss contingencies for an unasserted claim or assessment where there has been no manifestation of an awareness of possible claim or assessment by a potential claimant unless it is deemed probable that a claim will be asserted and a reasonable possibility of an unfavorable outcome exists.

Estimate versus Contingency

Distinguishing between an estimate and a contingency can be difficult because both involve an uncertainty that will be resolved by future events. However, an estimate exists because of uncertainty about the amount of a loss resulting from an event requiring an acknowledged accounting recognition. The event has occurred and the effect is known, but the amount itself is uncertain.

In a contingency, the amount also is usually uncertain, although that is not an essential characteristic. Instead, the uncertainty lies in whether the event has occurred (or will) and what the effect, if any, on the enterprise would be. Collectability of receivables is a contingency because it is uncertain whether a customer will not pay at a future date, although it is probable that some customers will not pay. Similar logic would hold for obligations related to product warranties. That is, it is uncertain whether a product will fail, but it is probable that some will fail within the warranty period.

The most difficult area of contingencies is litigation. Accountants must rely on attorneys' assessments concerning the likelihood of such events. Unless the attorney indicates that the risk of loss is remote or slight, or that the loss if it occurs would be immaterial to the company, disclosure in financial statements is necessary and an accrual may also be necessary. In cases where judgments have been entered against the reporting entity, or where the attorney gives a range of expected losses or other amounts and indicates that an unfavorable outcome is probable, accruals of loss contingencies for at least the minimum point of the range must be made. In most cases, however, an estimate of the contingency is unknown and the contingency is reflected only in footnotes.

Guarantees

While disclosures of at least some guarantees had been common under GAAP, the economic significance of such arrangements had rarely been measured or disclosed in the past. ASC 460, *Guarantees*, significantly altered past practice by requiring that the fair value of guarantees be recognized as a liability.

ASC 460 applies to guarantee contracts that contingently require the guarantor to make payments (in cash, financial instruments, shares of its stock, other assets, or in services) to the guaranteed party based on any of these four circumstances:

1. Changes in a specified interest rate, security price, commodity price, foreign exchange rate, index of prices or rates, or any other variable, including the occurrence or nonoccurrence of a specified event that is related to an asset or liability of the guaranteed party. For example, the provisions apply to these, as cited by ASC 460:

   a. A financial standby letter of credit.
   b. A market value guarantee on either securities (including the common stock of the guaranteed party) or a nonfinancial asset owned by the guaranteed party.
   c. A guarantee of the market price of the common stock of the guaranteed party.
   d. A guarantee of the collection of the scheduled contractual cash flows from individual financial assets held by a variable interest entity (VIE).
   e. A guarantee granted to a business or its owners that the revenue received by the business will equal or exceed some stated amount.
   f. One common example of this type of situation is where a hospital lures a doctor to open a practice in an underserved community with a guarantee of fee income for an initial period. ASC 460 explicitly states that these types of assurances are guarantees and must be given accounting recognition.

2. Another entity's failure to perform under an obligating agreement. For example, the provisions apply to a performance standby letter of credit, which obligates the guarantor to make a payment if the specified entity fails to perform its nonfinancial obligation.
3. The occurrence of a specified event or circumstance (an indemnification agreement), such as an adverse judgment in a lawsuit or the imposition of additional taxes due to either a change in the tax law or an adverse interpretation of the tax law, provided that the guarantor is an entity other than an insurance or reinsurance company.
4. The occurrence of specified events under conditions whereby payments are legally available to creditors of the guaranteed party and those creditors may enforce the guaranteed party's claims against the guarantor under the agreement (an indirect guarantee of the indebtedness of others).

ASC 460 does *not* apply to

1. Commercial letters of credit and other loan commitments.
2. Subordination on arrangements in securitization transactions where, for example, investors (or creditors) in one subordinated class (or tranche) of an entity's securities might not be entitled to receive any cash flows until the investors in another higher-priority class or tranche of securities are paid in full.
3. A lessee's guarantee of the residual value of leased property.
4. A guarantee contract or an indemnification agreement that is issued by either an insurance or a reinsurance company.
5. Contingent rents.
6. Vendor rebates (by the guarantor) based on either the sales revenues of or the number of units sold by the guaranteed party.
7. Guarantees that prevent the guarantor from recognizing either the sale of the asset underlying the guarantee or the profits from that sale.
8. Guarantees arising from pension plans, vacation pay arrangement, deferred compensation contracts, and stock issued to employees.
9. A registration payment arrangement within the scope of ASC 825-20-15, *Financial Instruments, Registration Payment Arrangements.*
10. A guarantee accounted for as a credit derivative instrument at fair value under ASC 815-10-50-4J through 4L.

ASC 460's requirement to recognize an initial liability does not apply to these types of guarantees (i.e., these guarantees are subject only to ASC 460's disclosure requirements):

1. A guarantee, other than a credit derivative, that is accounted for as a derivative instrument at fair value under ASC 815, *Derivatives and Hedging.*

2. A contract that guarantees the functionality of nonfinancial assets that are owned by the guaranteed party (product warranties).

3. Contingent consideration in a business combination or an acquisition of a business or non-profit activity by a not-for-profit entity.

4. A guarantee that requires the guarantor to issue its own equity shares.

5. A guarantee by an original lessee that has become secondarily liable under a new lease that relieved the original lessee of the primary obligation under the original lease.

6. A guarantee issued between parents and their subsidiaries or between corporations under common control.

7. A parent's guarantee of a subsidiary's debt to a third party (irrespective of whether the parent is a corporation or an individual).

8. A subsidiary's guarantee of a parent's debt to a third party or the debt of another subsidiary of the parent.

9. Software licenses that contain an "indemnification clause" protecting the licensee from liabilities and damages that might arise if the licensor's software is subject to a claim of patent, copyright, or trade secret infringement.

ASC 460 establishes the notion that a guarantee actually consists of two distinct components. These two obligations have quite different accounting implications. The first of these is a noncontingent obligation, namely, the obligation to stand ready to perform over the term of the guarantee in the event that the specified triggering events or conditions occur. This stand-ready obligation is unconditional and thus is not considered a contingent obligation. The second element, which is a contingent obligation, is the obligation to make future payments if those triggering events or conditions occur. At the inception of a guarantee, the guarantor would recognize a liability for both the noncontingent and contingent obligations at their fair values. However, in the unusual circumstance that a liability is recognized under ASC 450-20 for the contingent obligation (i.e., because it is deemed probable of occurrence and reasonable of estimation that the guarantor will pay), the liability to be recognized initially for the noncontingent obligation would only be the portion, if any, of the guarantee's fair value not already recognized to comply with ASC 450-20.

In practice, if the likelihood that the guarantor will have to perform is judged to be only "reasonably possible" or "remote," the only amount to be recorded will be the fair value of the noncontingent obligation to stand ready to perform. If, however, the contingency is probable of occurrence and can be reasonably estimated under ASC 450-20, that amount must be recognized and the liability under the guarantee arrangement will be the greater of (1) the fair value computed as explained above, or (2) the amount computed in accordance with ASC 450-20's provisions.

Example of estimating the fair value of a guarantee using CON 7 when recognition of a loss contingency under ASC 450 would not be otherwise required

Big Red Company guarantees a $1,000,000 debt of Little Blue Company for the next three years in conjunction with selling equipment to Little Blue. Big Red evaluates its risk of payment in this way:

(1) There is no possibility that Big Red will pay during year 1.

(2) There is a 15% chance that Big Red will pay during year 2. If it has to pay, there is a 30% chance that it will have to pay $500,000 and a 70% chance that it will have to pay $250,000.

(3) There is a 20% chance that Big Red will pay during year 3. If it has to pay, there is a 25% chance that it will have to pay $600,000 and a 75% chance that it will have to pay $300,000.

The expected cash flows are computed as

Year 1   100% chance of paying $0 = $0
Year 2   85% chance of paying $0 and a 15% chance of paying (.30 × $500,000 + .70 × $250,000 =) $325,000 = $48,750
Year 3   80% chance of paying $0 and a 20% chance of paying (.25 × $600,000 + .75 × $300,000 =) $375,000 = $75,000

The present value of the expected cash flows is computed as the sum of the years' probability-weighted cash flows, here assuming an appropriate discount rate of 8%.

Year 1	$0 × 1/1.08 =	$	0
Year 2	$48,750 × 1/(1.08)^2 =		41,795
Year 3	$75,000 × 1/(1.08)^3 =		59,537
Fair value of the guarantee			$101,332

Based on the foregoing, a liability of $101,332 would be recognized at inception. This would reduce the net selling price of the equipment sold to Little Blue, thereby reducing the profit to be reported on the sale transaction.

Example of estimating the fair value of a guarantee using CON 7 when recognition of a loss contingency under ASC 450 is also required

Assume the same basic facts as in the foregoing example, but now also assume that it has been determined that there is a 60% likelihood that the buyer eventually will default and, after legal process, Big Red will have to repay debt amounting to $400,000 at the end of the fifth year. Assume also that a likelihood of 60% is deemed to make this contingent obligation "probable" under ASC 450. The present value of that payment is $272,233, but ASC 450 does not address or seemingly anticipate the application of present value methods. Thus, it would appear that accrual of the full $400,000 expected loss is required, unaffected by expected timing or by the probability (60%, in this example) that it will occur. Since this amount exceeds the amount computed under ASC 460, no additional amount would be recognized in connection with the noncontingent obligation to stand ready to perform.

If, instead of the immediate foregoing facts, the probable repayments were estimated to be $75,000, then the liabilities to be recognized would total $101,322, of which $75,000 would be required to satisfy the provisions of ASC 450, and the incremental amount, $26,332, would be attributed to the noncontingent obligation.

Disclosure requirements. A guarantor is now required to disclose the next six points about each guarantee, or each group of similar guarantees, even if the likelihood of the guarantor's having to make any payments under the guarantee was deemed remote:

1. The nature of the guarantee, including its approximate term, how the guarantee arose, and the events or circumstances that would require the guarantor to perform under the guarantee, and the current status of the guarantee as of the date of the statement of financial position of the payment/performance risk of the guarantee. The current status could, for example, be based either on recently issued external credit ratings or on current internal groupings used by the guarantor to manage its risk. If the reporting entity uses internal groupings, management is to disclose how those groupings are determined and used for managing risk.
2. The maximum potential amount of future payments (undiscounted) under the guarantee.
3. The carrying amount of the liability, if any, for the guarantor's obligations under the guarantee, including any contingent loss amount recognized under ASC 450-20.
4. The nature and extent of any recourse provisions or available collateral that would enable the guarantor to recover the amounts paid under the guarantee, and an indication of the approximate extent to which the proceeds from recoveries or liquidation would be expected to cover the maximum potential amount of future payments under the guarantee.
5. The fair value of financial guarantees issued, if the entity is required to disclose the fair value of financial instruments under the provisions of ASC 825.
6. The disclosures required by ASC 850 if the guarantees are made to benefit related parties.

EXTRACTS FROM PUBLISHED FINANCIAL STATEMENTS

Beacon Enterprise Solutions Group, Annual Report September 30, 2009

Notes to the Consolidated Financial Statements

Note 13. Commitments and Contingencies

Employment agreements. The Company has entered into at will employment agreements with seven of its key executives with no specific expiration dates that provide for aggregate annual compensation of $1,170,000 and up to $1,263,000 of severance payments for termination without cause.

Operating leases. The Company has entered into operating leases for office facilities in Louisville, KY, Columbus, OH, and Cincinnati, OH. A summary of the minimum lease payments due on these operating leases exclusive of the Company's share of operating expenses and other costs is

Fiscal year ending September 30, 2010	$123,423
Fiscal year ending September 30, 2011	19,400
	$142,823

Engagement of investor relations firm. On January 20, 2009, we engaged an investor relations firm to aid us in developing a marketing plan directed at informing the investing public as to our business and increasing our visibility to FINRA registered broker/dealers, the investing public, and other institutional and fund managers. In exchange for providing such services, the firm will receive $10,000 per month for the duration of the agreement, 10,000 shares of our restricted common stock per month for the first six months, and 15,000 shares of our restricted common stock per month for the remaining six months for an aggregate of 150,000 shares of restricted stock. For the year ended September 30, 2009, we paid $50,000 and issued 50,000 shares of restricted common stock, with aggregate fair value of $43,800, under the terms of this agreement. The common stock issued under this agreement was recorded as professional fees expense using the measurement principles enumerated under ASC 505, *Equity-Based Payment to Non-Employee.* The contract has a 12-month term and can be terminated upon 30 days' notice.

On June 5, 2009, our Board of Directors authorized us to issue an additional 150,000 shares of common stock to the same investor relations firm subject to the attainment of certain performance conditions, to be performed within a six-month time period ending November 5, 2009. The performance-based share arrangement supersedes the previous agreement. As of September 30, 2009, 20,000 shares with an aggregate fair value of $40,300 were deemed to have been earned as of the date of issuance. The common stock issued was recorded as professional fees expense using the measurement principles enumerated under ASC 505.

On March 13, 2009, we engaged an investor relations firm to further aid us in developing a marketing plan directed at informing the investing public as to our business and increasing our visibility to FINRA registered broker/dealers, the investing public and other institutional and fund managers. In exchange for providing such services, the firm will receive $10,000 per month for the duration of the agreement. Concurrent with executing the agreement, we paid $10,000 and issued 200,000 shares of fully vested and nonforfeitable restricted common stock with a fair value of $80,000 on date of grant recorded as professional fees expense using the measurement principles enumerated under ASC 505. We recorded $560,850 of expense including cash in the amount of $480,850 and shares with a fair value of $80,000.

Engagement for advisory services. On January 1, 2009, we entered into a three-year advisory agreement with an outside party whereby the party will provide corporate finance and business strategy advisory services pertaining to Beacon's business affairs in the areas of business combinations, financing, etc. The agreement provides for compensation of $25,000 per month, any part of which can be prepaid. For the year-end September 30, 2009, we have recognized $225,000 of professional fees expense under this agreement and have recorded a prepayment of $320,000 for future services, which has been classified as prepaid expense in the accompanying Consolidated Balance Sheet as of September 30, 2009.

Onstream Media Corporation, Annual Report September 30, 2009

Notes to the Consolidated Financial Statements

Note 5: Commitments and Contingencies

Narrowstep acquisition termination and litigation. On May 29, 2008, we entered into an Agreement and Plan of Merger (the "Merger Agreement") to acquire Narrowstep, Inc. ("Narrowstep"), which Merger Agreement was amended twice (on August 13, 2008, and on September 15, 2008). The terms of the Merger Agreement, as amended, allowed that if the acquisition did not close on or prior to November 30, 2008, the Merger Agreement could be terminated by either us or Narrowstep at any time after that date provided that the terminating party was not responsible for the delay. On March 18, 2009, we terminated the Merger Agreement and the acquisition of Narrowstep.

As a result of this termination, we recorded the write-off of certain acquisition-related costs in our operating results for the year ended September 30, 2009 (see note 1—Effects of Recent Accounting Pronouncements). In addition, we may incur additional future costs and expenses not included in this write-off, as follows: (1) satisfaction of a claim by Narrowstep for certain equipment alleged to be in our custody and (2) satisfaction of certain other damages asserted by Narrowstep. These items are discussed below.

In November 2008, Narrowstep invoiced us approximately $372,000 for their equipment alleged to be in our custody as of that date, and in June 2009 a letter issued by their counsel demanded that we pay $400,000 related to this matter. Although we acknowledged possession of at least some of this equipment, we have not agreed to a payment for that equipment and believe that if a payment were made, it would be substantially less than the Narrowstep demand. Accordingly, this matter is not reflected as a liability on our financial statements, nor have we included any related assets on our financial statements. However, we received approximately $32,000 in merchandise credit for certain of this equipment, which was recorded as a reduction of our acquisition cost write-off for the year ended September 30, 2009, and is considered to be a valid offset to amounts included in that write-off but that we believe should have been paid by Narrowstep. In addition to these costs, we believe that we could seek reimbursement from Narrowstep of certain general and administrative costs reflected in our operating expenses for the years ended September 30, 2009 and 2008 (i.e., not segregated as part of the specific write-off of acquisition costs), since they were incurred in direct support of Narrowstep operations.

On April 16, 2009, Narrowstep issued a press release announcing that it was seeking $14 million and other damages (including the above matter) from us, as a result of our alleged actions in connection with the termination of the agreement to acquire Narrowstep. This demand was made in the form of a letter issued at about the same time by Narrowstep's counsel. After reviewing the demand letter issued by Narrowstep's counsel, we determined that Narrowstep had no basis in fact or in law for any claim, and, accordingly, this matter was not reflected as a liability on our financial statements.

On December 1, 2009, Narrowstep filed a complaint against us in the Court of Chancery of the State of Delaware, alleging breach of contract, fraud, and three additional counts and is seeking (1) $14 million in damages; (2) reimbursement of an unspecified amount for all of its costs associated with the negotiation and drafting of the Merger Agreement, including but not limited to attorney and consulting fees; (3) the return of Narrowstep's equipment alleged to be in our possession; (4) reimbursement of an unspecified amount for all of its attorneys fees, costs, and interest associated with this action; and (5) any further relief determined as fair by the court. After reviewing the complaint document, we have again determined that Narrowstep has no basis in fact or in law for any claim and accordingly, this matter has not been reflected as a liability on our financial statements. On December 18, 2009, we were served with a summons, and we intend to file the required response on or before the required deadline and to vigorously defend against all claims. Furthermore, we do not expect the ultimate resolution of this matter to have a material impact on our financial position or results of operations.

Other legal proceedings. On May 26, 2009, we were served with a summons and complaint filed in Broward County, Florida, containing a breach of contract claim against us by a firm seeking compensation for legal services allegedly rendered to us, plus court costs, in the amount of approximately $383,000. We have accrued approximately $115,000 related to this matter on our financial statements as of September 30, 2009, which was included in the write-off of certain acquisition-related costs included in our operating results for the year then ended (see note 1—Effects of Recent Accounting Pronouncements). Certain discovery activities by the parties are in process, mediation has been set for January 26, 2010, and trial has been set for March 8, 2010. We believe that the ultimate resolution of the matter will not have a material adverse effect on our financial position or results of operations.

We are involved in other litigation and regulatory investigations arising in the ordinary course of business. While the ultimate outcome of these matters is not presently determinable, it is the opinion of our management that the resolution of these outstanding claims will not have a material adverse effect on our financial position or results of operations.

NASDAQ letter regarding minimum share price listing requirement. We received a letter from NASDAQ dated January 4, 2008, indicating that we had 180 calendar days, or until July 2, 2008, to regain compliance with what is now Listing Rule 5550(a)(2)—formerly Marketplace Rule 4310(c)(4) (the "Rule"), which is necessary in order to be eligible for continued listing on the NASDAQ Capital Market. The NASDAQ letter indicated that our noncompliance with the Rule was as a result of the bid price of ONSM common stock closing below $1.00 per share for the preceding 30 consecutive business days. On July 3, 2008, we received a letter from NASDAQ stating that we were not considered compliant with the Rule as of that date, but because we met all other initial NASDAQ listing criteria, we were granted an additional 180 calendar days, or until December 30, 2008, to regain compliance with the Rule. On October 22, 2008, we received a letter from NASDAQ stating that NASDAQ had suspended enforcement of the bid price listing requirement through January 19, 2009, which suspension NASDAQ extended several more times. Since we were in a bid price compliance period at the time of the initial suspension, we remained at the same stage of the process we were in when the NASDAQ first announced the suspension until that suspension was terminated on July 31, 2009. Accordingly, we were subsequently notified by NASDAQ that as a result of the termination of the suspension, we had until October 16, 2009, to regain compliance with the Rule. On October 19, 2009, we received a letter from NASDAQ stating that since we had not regained compliance with the Rule as of October 16, 2009, our common stock was subject to delisting. However, such delisting would not occur if we requested a hearing with the NASDAQ Listing Qualifications Panel ("the "Panel") and pending the Panel's decision subsequent to that hearing.

We requested such a hearing with the Panel, which we attended on December 3, 2009, and at which time we presented our plan for regaining compliance with the Rule and requested that our securities be allowed to remain listed pending the completion of that plan. Based on the Panel's consideration of that plan, as well as any other relevant factors, the Panel has the ability to grant us a period of up to 180 days (counting from the date of the October 19, 2009, letter) to regain compliance with the Rule. As of December 29, 2009, the Panel had not informed us of their decision, and there can be no assurance that the Panel will grant our request for continued listing.

We might be considered compliant with the Rule, subject to the NASDAQ staff's discretion, if our common stock closes at $1.00 per share or more for a minimum of ten consecutive business days. The closing ONSM share price was $0.28 per share on December 24, 2009. Although we have not decided on such action, we have been advised that as a Florida corporation, we may implement a reverse split of our common shares without shareholder approval, provided a proportionate reduction is made in the number of our authorized common shares and we provide appropriate advance notice to NASDAQ and other applicable authorities.

The terms of the 8% Senior Convertible Debentures and the 8% Subordinated Convertible Debentures (and the related warrants), which we issued from December 2004 through April 2006, as well as the common shares we issued in connection with the April 2007 Infinite Merger, contain penalty clauses if our common stock is not traded on NASDAQ or a similar national exchange—see further discussion below.

Registration payment arrangements. We included the 8% Subordinated Convertible Debentures and the related $1.50 warrants on a registration statement which was declared effective by the SEC on July 26, 2006. We are only required to expend commercially reasonable efforts to keep the registration statement continuously effective. However, in the event the registration statement or the ability to sell shares thereunder lapses for any reason for 30 or more consecutive days in any 12-month period or more than twice in any 12-month period, the purchasers of the 8% Subordinated Convertible Debentures may require us to redeem any shares obtained from the conversion of those notes and still held, for 115% of the market value for the previous five days. The same penalty provisions apply if our common stock is not listed or quoted, or is suspended from trading on an eligible market for a period of 20 or more trading days (which need not be consecutive). Due to the fact that that there is no established mechanism for reporting to us changes in the ownership of these shares after they are originally issued, we are unable to quantify how many of these shares are still held by the original recipient and thus subject to the above provisions. Regardless of the above, we believe that the applicability of these provisions would be limited by equity and/or by statute to a certain time frame after the original security purchase. All of these debentures were converted to common shares on or before March 31, 2007.

The $1.50 warrants provide that, starting one year after issuance, in the event the shares are not subject to an effective registration statement at the time of exercise, the holder could elect a "cashless exercise" whereby we would issue shares equal in value to the excess of the market price at the time of the exercise over the warrant exercise price. 403,650 of these warrants were still outstanding as of September 30, 2009, and will expire in March and April of 2011—see note 8.

We included the common shares underlying the 8% Senior Convertible Debentures, including the Additional 8% Convertible Debentures (AIR), and the related $1.65 warrants, on a registration statement declared effective by the SEC on June 29, 2005. These debentures provide cash penalties of 1% of the original purchase price for each month that (a) our common shares are not listed on the NASDAQ Capital Market for a period of three (3) trading days (which need not be consecutive) or (b) the common shares underlying those securities and the related warrants are not salable subject to an S-3 or other registration statement then effective with the SEC. The latter penalty only applies for a five-year period beginning with the June 29, 2005, registration statement effective date and does not apply to shares salable under Rule 144(k). Regardless of the above, we believe that the applicability of these provisions would be limited by equity and/or by statute to a certain time frame after the original security purchase—all of these debentures were converted to common shares on or before March 31, 2007.

The $1.65 warrants provide that if the shares are not subject to an effective registration statement on the date required in relation to the initial and/or subsequent issuance of shares under the related transactions and at the time of warrant exercise, the holder could elect a "cashless exercise" whereby we would issue shares equal in value to the excess of the market price at the time of the exercise over the warrant exercise price. Although 1,128,530 of these warrants were still outstanding as of September 30, 2009, 737,114 of that total expired on December 23, 2009, and the remainder will expire on February 15, 2010—see note 8.

During March and April 2007, we sold an aggregate of 4,888,889 restricted common shares at $2.25 per share for total gross proceeds of approximately $11.0 million. This private equity financing was arranged by us to partially fund the Infinite Merger—see note 2. These shares were included in a registration statement declared effective by the SEC on June 15, 2007. We are required to maintain the effectiveness of this registration statement until the earlier of the date that (1) all of the shares have been sold, (2) all the shares have been transferred to persons who may trade such shares without restriction (including our delivery of a new certificate or other evidence of ownership for such securities not bearing a restrictive legend), or (3) all of the shares may be sold at any time, without volume or manner of sale limitations pursuant to Rule 144(k) or any similar provision (in the opinion of our counsel). In the event such effectiveness is not maintained or trading in the shares is suspended or if the shares are delisted for more than five (5) consecutive trading days, then we are liable for a compensatory payment (prorated on a daily basis) of one and one-half percent (1.5%) per month until the situation is cured, such payment based on the purchase price of the shares still held and provided that such payments may not exceed ten percent (10%) of the initial purchase price of the shares with respect to any one purchaser. Regardless of the above, we believe that the applicability of these provisions would be limited by equity and/or by statute to a certain time frame after the original security purchase.

We have concluded that the arrangements discussed in the preceding five paragraphs are registration payment arrangements, as that term is defined in the Derivatives and Hedging topic (Contracts in Entity's own Entity subtopic) of the ASC. Based on our satisfactory recent history of maintaining the effectiveness of our registration statements and our NASDAQ listing, as well as stockholders' equity in excess of the NASDAQ listing standards as of September 30, 2009, we have concluded that material payments under these registration payment arrangements are not probable and that no accrual related to them is necessary under the requirements of the Contingencies topic of the ASC. However, the $0.28 quoted market price of our common shares was below the $1.00 NASDAQ requirement as of December 24, 2009, which condition could eventually affect our NASDAQ listing status, as discussed above.

Registration rights. We granted a major shareholder demand registration rights, effective six months from the January 2007 modification date of a certain convertible note, for any unregistered common shares issuable thereunder. Upon such demand, we would have 60 days to file a registration statement, using our best efforts to promptly obtain the effectiveness of such registration statement. 784,592 of the 2,789,592 shares issued in March 2007 and subject to these rights were included in a registration statement declared effective by the SEC on June 15, 2007, and as of December 24, 2009, we have not received any demand for the registration of the balance. As the note does not provide for damages or penalties in the event we do not comply with these registration rights, we have concluded that these rights do not constitute registration payment arrangements. Furthermore, since the unregistered shares were originally issued in March 2007, they may be salable, in whole or in part, under Rule 144. In any event, we have determined that material payments in relation to these rights are not probable and therefore no accrual related to them is necessary under the requirements of the Contingencies topic of the ASC.

We granted demand registration rights, effective six months from the date of a certain October 2006 convertible note, for any unregistered common shares issuable thereunder. Upon such demand, we would have 60 days to file a registration statement, using our best efforts to promptly obtain the effectiveness of such registration statement. 1,000,000 of the 1,694,495 total principal and interest shares subject to these rights were included in a registration statement declared effective by the SEC on June 15, 2007, and as of December 24, 2009, we have not received any demand for the registration of the balance. As the note does not provide for damages or penalties in the event we do not comply with these registration rights, we have concluded that these rights do not constitute registration payment arrangements. Furthermore, since the unregistered shares were originally issued in November and December 2006, they may be salable, in whole or in part, under Rule 144. In any event, we have determined that material payments in relation to these rights are not probable and therefore no accrual related to them is necessary under the requirements of the Contingencies topic of the ASC.

We granted piggyback registration rights in connection with 100,000 shares and 220,000 options issued to consultants prior to June 15, 2007, which shares and options were not included on the registration statement declared effective by the SEC on that date. As these options and shares do not provide for damages or penalties in the event we do not comply with these registration rights, we have concluded that these rights do not constitute registration payment arrangements. In any event, we have determined that material payments in relation to these rights are not probable and therefore no accrual related to them is necessary under the requirements of the Contingencies topic of the ASC.

We granted piggyback registration rights in connection with 285,000 shares and 350,000 options issued to consultants subsequent to June 15, 2007. We have not filed a registration statement with the SEC since that date. As the 285,000 shares do not provide for damages or penalties in the event we do not comply with these registration rights, we have concluded that these rights do not constitute registration payment arrangements. Although 150,000 of the 350,000 options include cashless exercise rights until they are registered, and therefore do constitute registration payment arrangements, since the exercise price of $1.73 per share is significantly in excess of the market price of $0.41 per share as of September 30, 2009, we have concluded that no accrual related to these rights is necessary as of that date under the requirements of the Contingencies topic of the ASC. Although 200,000 of the 350,000 options include cashless exercise rights starting one year after issuance until they are registered, and therefore do constitute registration payment arrangements, since the exercise prices of $0.50, $0.75, and $1.00 per share are significantly in excess of the market price of $0.41 per share as of September 30, 2009, we have concluded that no accrual related to these rights is necessary as of that date under the requirements of the Contingencies topic of the ASC.

Employment contracts and severance. On September 27, 2007, our Compensation Committee and Board of Directors approved three-year employment agreements with Messrs. Randy Selman (President and CEO), Alan Saperstein (COO and Treasurer), Robert Tomlinson (Chief Financial Officer), Clifford Friedland (Senior Vice President Business Development), and David Glassman (Senior Vice President Marketing), collectively referred to as "the Executives." On May 15, 2008, and August 11, 2009, our Compensation Committee and Board approved certain corrections and modifications to those agreements, which are reflected in the discussion of the terms of those agreements below.

The agreements provide initial annual base salaries of $253,000 for Mr. Selman, $230,000 for Mr. Saperstein, $207,230 for Mr. Tomlinson, and $197,230 for Messrs. Friedland and Glassman, and allow for 10% annual increases through December 27, 2008, and 5% per year thereafter. In addition, each of the Executives receives an auto allowance payment of $1,000 per month, a "retirement savings" payment of $1,500 per month, and an annual $5,000 allowance for the reimbursement of dues or charitable donations. We also pay insurance premiums for the Executives, including medical, life, and disability coverage. These employment agreements contain certain nondisclosure and noncompetition provisions, and we have agreed to indemnify the Executives in certain circumstances.

As part of the above employment agreements, and in accordance with the terms of the "2007 Equity Incentive Plan" approved by our shareholders in their September 18, 2007, annual meeting, our Compensation Committee and Board of Directors granted Plan Options to each of the Executives to purchase an aggregate of 400,000 shares of ONSM common stock at an exercise price of $1.73 per share, the fair market value at the date of the grant, which shall be exercisable for a period of four (4) years from the date of vesting. The options vest in installments of 100,000 per year, starting on September 27, 2008, and they automatically vest upon the happening of the following events on a date more than six (6) months after the date of the agreement: (1) change of control (2) constructive termination, and (3) termination other than for cause, each as defined in the employment agreements. Unvested options automatically terminate upon (1) termination for cause or (2) voluntary termination. In the event the agreement is not renewed or the Executive is terminated other than for cause, the Executives shall be entitled to require us to register the vested options.

As part of the above employment agreements, the Executives were eligible for a performance bonus, based on meeting revenue and cash flow objectives. In connection with this bonus program, our Compensation Committee and Board of Directors granted Plan Options to each of the Executives to purchase an aggregate of 220,000 shares of ONSM common stock at an exercise price of $1.73 per share, the fair market value at the date of the grant, which shall be exercisable for a period of four (4) years from the date of vesting. Up to one-half of these shares were eligible for vesting on a quarterly basis and the rest annually, with the total grant allocable over a two-year period ending September 30, 2009. Vesting of the quarterly portion was subject to achievement of increased revenues over the prior quarter as well as positive and increased net cash flow per share (defined as cash provided by operating activities per our statement of cash flow, measured before changes in working capital components and not including investing or financing activities) for that quarter. Vesting of the annual portion was subject to meeting the above cash flow requirements on a year-over-year basis, plus a revenue growth rate of at least 30% for the fiscal year over the prior year. In the event of quarter to quarter decreases in revenues and/or cash flow, the options did not vest for that quarter but the unvested quarterly options were added to the available options for the year, vested subject to achievement of the applicable annual goal. In the event options did not vest based on the quarterly or annual goals, they immediately expired. In the event the agreement is not renewed or the Executive is terminated other than for cause, the Executives shall be entitled to require us to register the vested options.

We have determined that the above performance objectives were met for the quarter ended December 31, 2007, but that they were not met for the remaining three quarters of fiscal 2008 nor were they met for the fiscal year ended September 30, 2008. We have also determined that the performance objectives were met for the quarter ended June 30, 2009, but that they were not met for the remaining three quarters of fiscal 2009 nor were they met for the fiscal year ended September 30, 2009. Therefore, 13,750 options out of a potential 110,000 performance options vested for each executive during each fiscal year 2008 and 2009, and as a result we recognized total aggregate compensation expense of approximately $80,000 for each fiscal year, related to the vested portion of these options.

On August 11, 2009, our Compensation Committee agreed to extend the above bonus program for two years under substantially the same terms, except that the annual revenue growth rate will be 20%, we will negotiate with the Executives in good faith as to how revenue increases from specific acquisitions are measured, and one-half of the applicable quarterly or annual bonus options will be earned/vested if the cash flow target is met but the revenue target is not met. Implementation of this program is subject only to the approval by our shareholders of a sufficient increase in the number of authorized 2007 Plan options, at which time the performance bonus options will be granted and priced—it is anticipated that the request for shareholder authorization will be submitted at time of the next annual Shareholder Meeting, expected to be held in February or March 2010. We have also agreed that this bonus program will continue after this additional two-year period, with the specific bonus parameters to be negotiated in good faith between the parties at least ninety (90) days before the expiration of the program then in place.

Under the terms of the above employment agreements, upon a termination subsequent to a change of control, termination without cause or constructive termination, each as defined in the agreements, we would be obligated to pay each of the Executives an amount equal to three times the Executive's base salary plus full benefits for a period of the lesser of (1) three years from the date of termination or (2) the date of termination until a date one year after the end of the initial employment contract term. We may defer the payment of all or part of this obligation for up to six months, to the extent required by Internal Revenue Code Section 409A. In addition, if the five-day average closing price of the common stock is greater than or equal to $1.00 per share on the date of any termination or change in control, all options previously granted the Executive(s) will be cancelled, with all underlying shares (vested or unvested) issued to the executive, and we will pay all related taxes for the Executive(s). If the five-day average closing price of the common stock is less than $1.00 per share on the date of any termination or change in control, the options will remain exercisable under the original terms.

Under the terms of the above employment agreements, we may terminate an Executive's employment upon his death or disability or with or without cause. To the extent that an Executive is terminated for cause, no severance benefits are due him. If an employment agreement is terminated as a result of the Executive's death, his estate will receive one year base salary plus any bonus or other compensation amount or benefit then payable or that would have been otherwise considered vested or earned under the agreement during the one-year period subsequent to the time of his death. If an employment agreement is terminated as a result of the Executive's disability, as defined in the agreement, he is entitled to compensation in accordance with our disability compensation for senior executives to include compensation for at least 180 days, plus any bonus or other compensation amount or benefit then payable or that would have been otherwise considered vested or earned under the agreement during the one-year period subsequent to the time of his disability.

As part of the above employment agreements, our Compensation Committee and Board of Directors agreed that in the event we are sold for a Company Sale Price that represents at least $1.00 per share (adjusted for recapitalization including but not limited to splits and reverse splits), the Executives will receive, as a group, cash compensation of twelve percent (12.0%) of the Company Sale Price, payable in immediately available funds at the time of closing such transaction. The Company Sale Price is defined as the number of Equivalent Common Shares outstanding at the time we are sold multiplied by the price per share paid in such Company Sale transaction. The Equivalent Common Shares are defined as the sum of (1) the number of common shares issued and outstanding, (2) the common stock equivalent shares related to paid for but not converted preferred shares or other convertible securities, and (3) the number of common shares underlying "in-the-money" warrants and options, such sum multiplied by the market price per share and then reduced by the proceeds payable upon exercise of the "in-the-money" warrants and options, all determined as of the date of the above employment agreements but the market price per share used for this purpose to be no less than $1.00. The 12.0% is allocated in the employment agreements as two and one-half percent (2.5%) each to Messrs. Selman, Saperstein, Friedland, and Glassman and two percent (2.0%) to Mr. Tomlinson.

Our general policy is to not include severance or minimum employment periods in employment contracts, with the exception of the above employment contracts with the Executives. However, as of September 30, 2009, we have entered into arrangements with three (3) employees that would require minimum payments of approximately $320,000 for wages, taxes and benefits over the approximately 14-month period after that date.

Other compensation. In addition to the 12% allocation of the Company Sale Price to the Executives, as discussed above, on August 11, 2009, our Compensation Committee determined that an additional three percent (3.0%) of the Company Sale Price would be allocated, on the same terms, with two percent (2.0%) allocated to the four outside Directors (0.5% each), as a supplement to provide appropriate compensation for ongoing services as a director and as a termination fee, one-half percent (0.5%) allocated to one additional executive-level employee and the remaining one-half percent (0.5%) to be allocated by the Board and our management at a later date, which will be primarily to compensate other executives not having employment contracts, but may also include additional allocation to some or all of these five senior Executives.

Consultant contracts. We have entered into a consulting contract, effective June 1, 2009, with an individual for executive management services to be performed for our Infinite division. This contract calls for base compensation of $175,000 per year, plus $25,000 commission per year provided certain current revenue levels are maintained. In addition we have agreed to pay a travel allowance of $3,000 to $5,000 per month for up to the first 13 months of the contract, plus a one-time $15,000 moving expenses reimbursement. Termination of the contract without cause before the end of the two-year contract term requires six months' notice (which includes a three-month severance period) from the terminating party, although termination with cause requires no notice. The contract is renewable by mutual agreement of the parties with six months' notice to the other. As part of the contract, a new four-year term (from vesting) option grant was made for the purchase of 400,000 common ONSM shares, vesting over four years at 100,000 per year, exercisable at the fair market value at the date of grant, but no less than $0.50 per share. See notes 6 and 8.

We have entered into various agreements for financial consulting and advisory services which, if not terminated as allowed by the terms of such agreements, will require the issuance after September 30, 2009, of approximately 110,000 unregistered shares and 800,000 options to purchase common shares at exercise prices from $0.50 to $1.00 per share. The options would include piggyback registration rights as well as cashless exercise rights starting one year after issuance until the options are registered. The services related to these shares and options will be provided over a 12-month period, and will result in a professional fees expense of approximately $145,000 over that service period, based on the current $0.28 market value of an ONSM common share as of December 24, 2009—see notes 6 and 8.

Bandwidth and co-location facilities purchase commitments. Effective July 1, 2008, we entered into a two-year long-distance bandwidth rate agreement with a national CDN (content delivery network) company, which includes a minimum purchase commitment of approximately $200,000 per year. We are in compliance with this agreement, based on comparing our purchases through September 30, 2009, to the corresponding pro rata share of that commitment. We have also entered into various agreements for our purchase of bandwidth and use of co-location facilities, for an aggregate minimum purchase commitment of approximately $570,000, such agreements expiring at various times through December 2011.

Long distance purchase commitment. Effective January 15, 2006, our EDNet division entered into a two-year long distance telephone rate agreement with a national telecommunications company, which included a telephone services purchase commitment of approximately $120,000 per year. On September 13, 2007, this agreement was extended to add another two years, for a total term of four years. We are in compliance with this agreement, based on comparing our purchases through September 30, 2009, to the corresponding pro rata share of that commitment.

Lease commitments. We are obligated under operating leases for our five offices (one each in Pompano Beach, Florida; San Francisco, California; and Colorado Springs, Colorado and two in the New York City area), which call for monthly payments totaling approximately $57,500. The leases have expiration dates ranging from 2010 to 2012 (after considering our rights of termination) and in most cases provide for renewal options. Most of the leases have annual rent escalation provisions. Future minimum lease payments required under these noncancelable leases as of September 30, 2009, excluding the capital lease obligations discussed in note 4, total approximately $968,000.

The three-year operating lease for our principal executive offices in Pompano Beach, Florida, expires September 15, 2010. The monthly base rental is currently approximately $22,500 (including our share of property taxes and common area expenses) with annual five percent (5%) increases. The lease provides for one two-year renewal option with 5% annual increases.

The five-year operating lease for our office space in San Francisco expires April 30, 2014. The monthly base rental (including month-to-month parking) is approximately $16,800 with annual increases up to 4.4%. The lease provides one five-year renewal option at 95% of fair market value and also provides for early cancellation at any time after April 30, 2010, at our option, with six (6) months' notice and a payment of no more than approximately $44,000.

The three-year operating lease for our Infinite Conferencing location in New Jersey expires October 31, 2012. The monthly base rental is approximately $10,800 with five percent (5%) annual increases. The lease provides one two-year renewal option, with no rent increase.

Our operating lease for office space in New York City expires January 31, 2010. The monthly base rental is approximately $6,600. During the second quarter of fiscal 2010, we expect to replace this month-to-month lease with a multiyear lease commitment at another location for no more than the monthly rental amount being incurred at the current location.

The future minimum lease payments required under the noncancelable leases, plus the capital leases included in Notes Payable and more fully discussed in note 4, are as follows:

Year Ending September 30:	Operating leases	Capital leases	All leases
2010	$616,093	$121,825	$ 737,918
2011	197,715	9,938	207,653
2012	142,615	9,938	152,553
2013	11,932	9,938	21,870
2014	—	3,313	3,313
Total minimum lease payments	$968,355	$154,952	$1,123,307
Less: amount representing interest		(12,028)	
Present value of net minimum lease payments		$142,924	
Less: current portion		(115,635)	
Long-term portion		$ 27,289	

Total rental expense (including executory costs) for all operating leases was approximately $849,000 and $776,000 for the years ended September 30, 2009, and 2008, respectively.

Software purchase and royalty commitment. On March 31, 2008, we agreed to pay $300,000 (plus a $37,500 annual support fee) for a perpetual license for software we utilize to provide automatic meta-tagging and other DMSP services. An initial $56,250 payment was paid in July 2008 with the $281,250 balance included in payables at September 30, 2009 and 2008. In connection with this license, we agreed to pay a 1% royalty on revenues from the use, licensing or offering of the functionality of this software to our customers, if such revenue exceeds certain levels, subject to a minimum amount per transaction and to the extent the calculated royalty exceeds the license payment. We are not yet liable for payments under this agreement.

On August 5, 2009, the vendor of the above software stated that the license would be terminated if $305,718.75 (balance plus interest) was not paid by September 4, 2009, and that our obligation to pay would not be affected by such termination. We believe that this termination would not have a material effect on our ongoing operations, since the licenses are the basis for new products being developed for which there are not yet significant revenues, are being used to provide excess capacity over our current operational needs, or are being used to provide noncore services with an insignificant net contribution to our operating results. Furthermore, we believe that we have meritorious defenses supporting our lack of payment to date, including product performance and integration issues.

SAIC contract. As part of the Onstream Merger, we became obligated under a contract with SAIC, under which SAIC would build a platform that eventually, after further design and reengineering by the Company, became the DMSP. The contract terminated by mutual agreement of the parties on June 30, 2008. Although cancelation of the contract among other things releases SAIC to offer what is identified as the "Onstream Media Solution" directly or indirectly to third parties, our management does not expect this right to result in a material adverse impact on future DMSP sales.

Auction Video Japan office. On December 5, 2008, we entered into an agreement whereby one of the former owners of Auction Video Japan, Inc. agreed to shut down the Japan office of Auction Video as well as assume all of our outstanding assets and liabilities connected with that operation, in exchange for nonexclusive rights to sell our products in Japan and be compensated on a commission-only basis. As a result, we recognized other income of approximately $45,000 for the year ended September 30, 2009, which is the difference between the assumed liabilities of approximately $84,000 and the assumed assets of approximately $39,000. It is the opinion of our management that any further developments with respect to this shutdown or the above agreement will not have a material adverse effect on our financial position or results of operations. See note 2.

MULTIPLE-CHOICE QUESTIONS

1. Which of the following is **not** a requirement for accrual of compensated absences?
- (a) Payment of the compensation is reasonably possible.
- (b) The right vests or accumulates.
- (c) The amount of the payment can be reasonably estimated.
- (d) The employee's right to receive compensation for future absences is attributable to employee services already rendered.

2. If the occurrence of a loss contingency is remote,
- (a) Disclosure of the facts and circumstances regarding the contingency is to be made but no accrual is necessary in the financial statements.
- (b) Accrual of the contingency is to be made in the financial statements.
- (c) No accrual or disclosure is necessary.

3. A competitor has sued an entity for unauthorized use of its patented technology. The amount that the entity may be required to pay to the competitor if the competitor succeeds in the lawsuit is determinable with reliability, and according to legal counsel, it is reasonably possible that an outflow of the resources would be needed to meet the obligation. The entity that was sued should at year-end
- (a) Recognize a liability for this possible obligation.
- (b) Make a disclosure of the possible obligation in footnotes to the financial statements.
- (c) Make no provision or disclosure and wait until the lawsuit is finally decided and then expense the amount paid on settlement, if any.
- (d) Set aside, as an appropriation, a contingency reserve, an amount based on the best estimate of the possible liability.

4. A factory owned by XYZ Inc. was destroyed by fire. XYZ Inc. lodged an insurance claim for the value of the factory building, plant, and an amount equal to one year's net profit. During the year there were a number of meetings with the representatives of the insurance company. Finally, before year-end, it was decided that XYZ Inc. would receive compensation for 90% of its claim. XYZ Inc. received a letter that the settlement check for that amount had been mailed, but it was not received before year-end. How should XYZ Inc. treat this in its financial statements?
- (a) Disclose the contingent asset in the footnotes.
- (b) Wait until next year when the settlement check is actually received and not recognize or disclose this receivable at all since at year-end it is a contingent asset.
- (c) Because the settlement of the claim was conveyed by a letter from the insurance company that also stated that the settlement check was in the mail for 90% of the claim, record 90% of the claim as a receivable as it is virtually certain that the contingent asset will be received.
- (d) Because the settlement of the claim was conveyed by a letter from the insurance company that also stated that the settlement check was in the mail for 90% of the claim, record 100% of the claim as a receivable at year-end as it is virtually certain that the contingent asset will be received, and adjust the 10% next year when the settlement check is actually received.

5. Which of the following is **not** required to be recorded in the financial statements?
- (a) Product warranties that extend into the next accounting period.
- (b) Security deposits that are expected to be refunded during the current operating cycle.
- (c) A probably unfavourable outcome related to litigation where the attorney has provided a range of losses.
- (d) An unasserted claim where a range of possible outcomes exists and it has been deemed reasonably possible that a claim will be asserted.

Chapter 18

LONG-TERM LIABILITIES (ASC 480 AND 835)

INTRODUCTION

Long-term (or noncurrent) liabilities are liabilities that will be paid or otherwise settled over a period of more than one year or, if longer, greater than one operating cycle. This chapter discusses accounting for bonds, long-term notes payable, mandatorily redeemable shares, and obligations to issue or repurchase the entity's own shares.

DEFINITIONS OF KEY TERMS

Bond. A written agreement whereby a borrower agrees to pay a sum of money at a designated future date plus periodic interest payments at the stated rate.

Effective interest method. Amortizing the discount or premium to interest expense so as to result in a constant rate of interest when applied to the amount of debt outstanding at the beginning of any given period.

Mandatorily redeemable shares. Any of various financial instruments issued in the form of shares that embody an unconditional obligation requiring the issuer to redeem the instrument by transferring its assets at a specified or determinable date (or dates) or upon an event that is certain to occur.

Market rate. The current rate of interest available for obligations issued under the same terms and conditions by an issuer of similar credit standing.

NOTES AND BONDS

Notes are a common form of exchange in business transactions for cash, property, goods, and services. Notes represent debt issued to a single investor without intending for the debt to be broken up among many investors. A note's maturity, usually lasting one to seven years, tends to be shorter than that of a bond.

Bonds are primarily used to borrow funds from the general public or institutional investors when a contract for a single amount (a note) is too large for any one lender to supply. Dividing up the amount needed into $1,000 or $10,000 units makes it easier to sell the bonds. Bonds also result from a single agreement.

Notes and bonds share common characteristics. They both are promises to pay sums of money at designated maturity dates, plus periodic interest payments at stated rates. They each feature written agreements stating the amounts of principal, the interest rates, when the interest and principal are to be paid, and the restrictive covenants, if any, that must be met.

The interest rate is affected by many factors, including the cost of money, the business risk factors, and general and industry-specific inflationary expectations. The stated rate on a note or bond often differs from the market rate at the time of issuance. When this occurs, the present value of the interest and principal payments will differ from the maturity, or face value.

If the market rate exceeds the stated rate, the cash proceeds will be less than the face value of the debt because the present value of the total interest and principal payments discounted back to the present yields an amount that is less than the face value. Because an investor rarely is willing to pay more than the present value, the bonds must be issued at a discount. The discount is the difference between the issuance price (present value) and the face, or stated, value of the bonds.

This discount is then amortized over the life of the bonds to increase the recognized interest expense so that the total amount of the expense represents the actual bond yield.

When the stated rate exceeds the market rate, the bond will sell for more than its face value (at a premium) to bring the effective rate to the market rate. Amortization of the premium over the life of the bonds will decrease the total interest expense.

When the market and stated rates are equivalent at the time of issuance, no discount or premium exists, and the instrument will sell at its face value. Changes in the market rate subsequent to issuance are irrelevant in determining the discount or premium or its amortization.

All commitments to pay (and receive) money at a determinable future date are subject to present value techniques and, if necessary, interest imputation with the exception of

1. Normal accounts payable due within one year.
2. Amounts to be applied to purchase price of goods or services or that provide security to an agreement (e.g., advances, progress payments, security deposits, and retentions).
3. Transactions between parent and subsidiary.
4. Obligations payable at some indeterminable future date (e.g., warranties).
5. Lending and depositor savings activities of financial institutions whose primary business is lending money.
6. Transactions where interest rates are affected by prescriptions of a governmental agency (e.g., revenue bonds, tax-exempt obligations, etc.).

Notes Issued Solely for Cash

When a note is issued solely for cash, its present value is assumed to be equal to the cash proceeds. The interest rate is that rate equating the cash proceeds to the amounts to be paid in the future. For example, a $1,000 note due in three years that sells for $889 has an implicit rate of 4% (= $1,000 × .889, where .889 is the present value factor at 4% for a lump sum due three years hence). This implicit rate, 4%, is to be used when amortizing the discount.

In most situations, a bond will be issued at a price other than its face value. The amount of the cash exchanged is equal to the total of the present values of all the future interest and principal payments. The difference between the cash proceeds and the face value is recorded as a premium if the cash proceeds are greater than the face value or a discount if they are less. The journal entry to record a bond issued at a premium is shown next.

Cash	(proceeds)	
Bonds payable		(face value)
Premium on bonds payable		(difference)

Case Study 1

Facts

Example of bonds issued for cash

Lola Inc. issues $100,000 of 10-year bonds bearing interest at 10%, paid semiannually, at a time when the market demands a 12% return from issuers with similar credit standings.

Required

Calculate the proceeds of the bond issuance and record the journal entry for the issuance of the bond.

Solution

The proceeds of the bond issuance would be $88,500, which is computed as

Present value of 20 semiannual interest payments of $5,000 discounted at 12% (6% semiannually: factor = 11.4699)	$57,300
Present value of $100,000 due in 10 years, discounted at 12% compounded semiannually (factor = .31180)	31,200
Present value of bond issuance	$88,500

The journal entry would be

Cash	88,500	
Discount on bonds payable	11,500	
Bonds payable		100,000

Notes Issued for Cash and a Right or Privilege

Often when a note bearing an unrealistic rate of interest is issued in exchange for cash, an additional right or privilege is granted, such as the issuer agreeing to sell merchandise to the purchaser at a reduced rate. The difference between the present value of the receivable and the cash loaned is regarded as an addition to the cost of the products purchased for the purchaser/lender and as unearned revenue to the seller/issuer.

This treatment stems from an attempt to match revenue and expense in the proper periods and to differentiate between those factors that affect income from operations and income or expense from nonoperating sources.

In the situation just described, the purchaser/lender will amortize the discount (difference between the cash loaned and the present value of the note) to interest income over the life of the note, and the contractual right to purchase inventory at a reduced rate will be allocated to inventory (or cost of sales) as the right expires. The seller/issuer of the note will amortize the discount to interest expense over the life of the note, and the unearned revenue will be recognized in sales as the products are sold to the purchaser/lender at the reduced price. Because the discount is amortized on a different basis from the contractual right, net income for the period is also affected.

Case Study 2

Facts

Example of accounting for a note issued for both cash and a contractual right

1. Lola borrows $10,000 via a non-interest-bearing three-year note from Jefferson.
2. Lola agrees to sell $50,000 of merchandise to Jefferson at less than the ordinary retail price for the duration of the note.
3. The market rate of interest on a note with similar payment terms and a borrower of similar creditworthiness is 10%.

Required

Make the necessary entries to record the transaction for both Lola and Jefferson.

Solution

According to ASC 835-30, the difference between the present value of the note and the face value of the loan is to be regarded as part of the cost of the products purchased under the agreement. The present value factor for an amount due in three years at 10% is .75132. Therefore, the present value of the note is $7,513 (= $10,000 × .75132). The $2,487 (= $10,000 – $7,513) difference between the face value and the present value is to be recorded as a discount on the note payable and as unearned revenue on the future purchases by the debtor. The next entries would be made by the debtor (Lola) and the creditor (Jefferson) to record the transaction:

Lola			*Jefferson*		
Cash	10,000		Note receivable	10,000	
Discount on note payable	2,487		Contract right with supplier	2,487	
Note payable		10,000	Cash		10,000
Unearned revenue		2,487	Discount on note receivable		2,487

The discount on note payable (and note receivable) is to be amortized using the effective interest method, while the unearned revenue account and contract right with supplier account are amortized on a pro rata basis as the right to purchase merchandise is used up. Thus, if Jefferson purchased $20,000 of merchandise from Lola in the first year, these entries would be necessary:

Lola			*Jefferson*		
Unearned revenue	995		Inventory (or cost of sales)	995	
[$2,487 × (20,000/50,000)]			Contract right with supplier		995
Sales		995			
Interest expense	751		Discount on note receivable	751	
Discount on note payable			Interest revenue		751
($7,513 × 10%)		751			

The amortization of unearned revenue and contract right with supplier accounts will fluctuate with the amount of purchases made. If there is a balance remaining in the account at the end of the loan term, it is amortized to the appropriate account in that final year.

Noncash Transactions

When a note is issued for consideration such as property, goods, or services, and the transaction is entered into at arm's length, the stated interest rate is presumed to be fair unless (1) no interest rate is stated; (2) the stated rate is unreasonable; or (3) the face value of the debt is materially different from the consideration involved or the current market value of the note at the date of the transaction. According to ASC 835-30, when the rate on the note is not considered fair, the note is to be recorded at the "fair market value of the property, goods, or services received or at an amount that reasonably approximates the market value of the note, whichever is the more clearly determinable." When this amount differs from the face value of the note, the difference is to be recorded as a discount or premium and amortized to interest expense.

Case Study 3

Facts

Example of accounting for a note exchanged for property

1. Brie sells Morache a machine that has a fair market value of $7,510.
2. Brie receives a three-year non-interest-bearing note having a face value of $10,000.

Required

Make the necessary entries to record the transaction for Morache.

Solution

In this situation, the fair market value of the consideration is readily determinable and, thus, represents the amount at which the note is to be recorded. This entry by Brett is necessary:

Machine	7,510	
Discount on notes payable	2,490	
Notes payable		10,000

The discount will be amortized to interest expense over the three-year period using the interest rate implied in the transaction. The interest rate implied is 10%, because the factor for an amount due in three years is .75132, which when applied to the $10,000 face value results in an amount equal to the fair value of the machine.

If the fair market value of the consideration or note is not determinable, then the present value of the note must be determined using an imputed interest rate. This rate will then be used to establish the present value of the note by discounting all future payments on the note at this rate. General guidelines for imputing the interest rate, which are provided by ASC 835-30, include the prevailing rates of similar instruments from creditors with similar credit ratings and the rate the debtor could obtain for similar financing from other sources. Other determining factors include any collateral or restrictive covenants involved, the current and expected prime rate, and other terms pertaining to the instrument. The objective is to approximate the rate of interest that would have resulted if an independent borrower and lender had negotiated a similar transaction under comparable terms and conditions. This determination is as of the issuance date, and any subsequent changes in interest rates would be irrelevant.

Case Study 4

Facts

Example of accounting for a note exchanged for property

1. Brie sells Morache a used machine. The fair market value is not readily determinable.
2. Brie receives a three-year non-interest-bearing note having a face value of $20,000. The market value of the note is not known.
3. Morache could have borrowed the money for the machine's purchase from a bank at a rate of 10%.

Required

Make the necessary entries to record the transaction for Morache.

Solution

In this situation, the fair market value of the consideration is not readily determinable, so the present value of the note is determined using an imputed interest rate. The rate used is the rate at which Morache could have borrowed the money: 10%. The factor for an amount due in three years at 10% is .75132, so the present value of the note is $15,026. This entry by Brett is necessary:

Machine	15,026	
Discount on notes payable	4,974	
Notes payable		20,000

MANDATORILY REDEEMABLE SHARES AND SIMILAR INSTRUMENTS

ASC 480 requires that shares of stock (typically, but not necessarily, preferred shares) that are issued with mandatory redemption features be reported as liabilities rather than equity instruments. Payments or accruals of "dividends" and other amounts to be paid to holders of such shares are to be reported as interest expense. The only exception to those rules is for shares that are required to be redeemed only upon the liquidation or termination of the issuer, since the fundamental "going concern assumption" underlying generally accepted accounting principles (GAAP) financial statements means that such an eventuality is not given recognition.

Shares are mandatorily redeemable if the issuer has an unconditional obligation to redeem the shares by transferring its assets at a specified or determinable date (or dates) or upon an event certain to occur (e.g., the death of the holder). The obligation to transfer assets must be unconditional—that is, there is no specified event that is outside the control of the issuer that will release the issuer from its obligation. Thus, callable preferred shares, which are redeemable at the issuer's option, and convertible preferred shares, which are redeemable at the holder's option, are not mandatorily redeemable shares.

Example of mandatorily redeemable preferred shares

On June 1, 2010, Verde Corporation issues 1,000 shares of mandatorily redeemable 5% preferred stock with a par value $100 for $110,330. The shares are redeemable at $150 on May 31, 2017. At issuance, Verde Corporation recognizes a liability of $110,330.

Some corporations and partnerships, primarily closely held ones, issue shares or units that are redeemed at the death of the holder. If those shares or units represent the only shares or units in the entity, the entity reports those instruments as liabilities and describes them in its statement of financial position as shares (or units) subject to mandatory redemption, to distinguish them from other liabilities. The classification is unaffected by any insurance policies that the entity may have on the holders' lives. The entity presents interest expense and payments to holders of those instruments separately, apart from interest and payments to other creditors in its statements of income and cash flows. The entity also discloses that the instruments are mandatorily redeemable upon the death of the holders.

Example of shares that are mandatorily redeemable at the death of the holder

Mike and Ike are equal shareholders in M&I's Auto Repair, Inc. Upon the death of either shareholder, the corporation will redeem shares of the deceased for half of the book value of the corporation. The next information would be disclosed in the notes to the financial statements:

All of the corporation's shares are subject to mandatory redemption upon death of the shareholders, and are thus reported as a liability. The liability amount consists of

Common stock: 100 par value, 1,000 shares authorized, issued and outstanding	$100,000
Undistributed earnings attributable to those shares	50,000
Accumulated other comprehensive income	(2,000)
Total liability	$148,000

After issuance, the amount of the liability for the mandatorily redeemable shares should be adjusted using the effective interest method if both the amount to be paid and the settlement date are fixed. If either the amount to be paid or the settlement date varies based on specified conditions, the liability is measured subsequently at the amount of cash that would be paid under the conditions specified in the contract if settlement occurred at the reporting date, recognizing the resulting change in that amount from the previous reporting date as interest cost.

The effective interest rate, calculated as described in the "Effective Interest Method" section of this chapter, is 8.5%. Continuing the previous example of Verde Corporation, it would recognize these annual interest expense and liability amounts:

	Cash paid	*Interest at 8.5% annually*	*Change in liability*	*Ending liability*
06/01/10				110,330
05/31/11	5,000	9,378	4,378	114,708
05/31/12	5,000	9,750	4,750	119,458
05/31/13	5,000	10,154	5,154	124,612
05/31/14	5,000	10,592	5,592	130,204
05/31/15	5,000	11,067	6,068	136,271
05/31/16	5,000	11,583	6,583	142,854
05/31/17	155,000	12,146	(142,854)	0

The entry to record the first "dividend" payment would be

Interest expense	9,378	
Liability		4,378
Cash		5,000

If shares have a conditional redemption feature, which requires the issuer to redeem the shares by transferring its assets upon an event not certain to occur, the shares become mandatorily redeemable—and, therefore, become a liability—if that event occurs, the event becomes certain to occur, or the condition is otherwise resolved. The fair value of the shares is reclassified as a liability, and equity is reduced by that amount, recognizing no gain or loss.

Note that when redemption value is based on a notion of fair value, defined in the underlying agreement, the initial recognition of the difference between this computed amount and the corresponding book value will almost inevitably result in a surplus or deficit. In other words, the promised redemption amounts, measured at transition and again at the date of each statement of financial position, will not equal the book value of the equity that is subject to redemption. This discrepancy must be reflected in stockholders' equity, even though the redeemable equity is reclassified to a liability. In effect, the redemption arrangement will result in either a residual in equity (assuming that a redemption was to fully occur at the date of the statement of financial position) or a deficit, because the agreement provides that redeeming shareholders are entitled to more or less than their respective pro rata shares of the book value of their equity claims.

If the redemption price of mandatorily redeemable shares is greater than the book value of those shares, the company should report the excess as a deficit (equity), even though the mandatorily redeemable shares are reported as a liability.

Common shares that are mandatorily redeemable are not included in the denominator when computing basic or diluted earnings per share. If any amounts, including contractual (accumulated) dividends, attributable to shares that are to be redeemed or repurchased have not been recognized as interest expense, those amounts are deducted in computing income available to common shareholders (the numerator of the calculation), consistent with the "two-class" method set forth in ASC 260. The redemption requirements for mandatorily redeemable shares for each of the next five years are required to be disclosed in the notes to the financial statements.

OBLIGATIONS TO ISSUE OR REPURCHASE SHARES

ASC 480 also requires that certain financial instruments that require an entity to purchase or issue its own equity shares be reported as liabilities. ASC 480 does not apply to financial instruments that are issued as contingent consideration in a business combination or obligations under stock-based compensation plans that are accounted for under ASC 718. It also does not apply to an embedded feature of a financial instrument unless that financial instrument is a derivative in its entirety.

Obligations to Issue Shares

If an entity enters into a contract that requires it or permits it at its discretion to issue a variable number of shares upon settlement, that contract is recognized as a liability if at inception the monetary value of the obligation is based solely or predominantly on one of these criteria:

1. A fixed monetary amount known at inception (e.g., a $100,000 payable can be settled by issuing shares worth $100,000 at the then-current market value)
2. An amount that varies based on something other than the fair value of the issuer's equity shares (e.g., a financial instrument indexed to the Dow that can be settled by issuing shares worth the index-adjusted amount at the then-current market value)
3. Variations inversely related to changes in the fair value of the entity's equity shares (i.e., a written put option that could be net share settled).

Contracts that meet one of the preceding criteria are recognized at fair value at the date of issuance and at every measurement date afterward. The changes in the fair value are recognized in earnings unless the contract falls within the scope of ASC 718 and that statement requires the changes to be recognized elsewhere.

Example of a contract with a fixed monetary amount known at inception

Smaga Corp. purchases equipment worth $100,000 and agrees to pay $110,000 at the end of one year or, at its option, to issue shares worth $112,000. The contract is recognized as a liability at issuance of $100,000. Subsequent to issuance the liability is remeasured at the fair value of the contract, which would be the accreted value of the cash payment amount ($110,000).

Obligations to Repurchase Shares

If an entity (the issuer) enters into a contract that obligates it to transfer assets to either repurchase its own equity shares or to pay an amount that is indexed to the price of its own shares, the contract is to be reported as a liability (or in certain cases, as an asset, if the fair value of the contract is favorable to the issuer). Examples of that type of financial instrument are written put options on the option writer's (issuer's) equity shares and forward contracts to repurchase an issuer's own equity shares if those instruments require physical or net cash settlement. (If the repurchase obligation is a redemption feature of common or preferred shares issued, see "Mandatorily Redeemable Shares and Similar Instruments" in this chapter.)

Written put options are measured initially and subsequently at fair value. Forward contracts are measured initially at the fair value of the shares to be repurchased (adjusted by any consideration or unstated rights or privileges) if the contract requires physical settlement for cash. The offset to the liability entry is a debit to equity. Subsequent to issuance, forward contracts are remeasured in one of two ways:

1. If both the amount to be paid and the settlement date are fixed, the contract is measured at the present value of the amount to be paid, computed using the rate implicit in the contract at inception.
2. If either the amount to be paid or the settlement date varies based on specified conditions, the contract is measured at the amount of cash that would be paid under the conditions specified in the contract if settlement occurred at the reporting date.

Under either measure, the amount of the change from the previous reporting date is recognized as interest cost.

Example of a written put option on a fixed number of shares

Millsap Corp. writes a put allowing the purchaser to sell 100 shares of Millsap common stock at $20 per share in six months. The purchaser pays Millsap $300 for the right to put the 100 shares. Millsap's common stock is currently trading at $23. Millsap reports a liability of $300. The liability is subsequently remeasured at the fair value of the put option.

Example of a forward contract with a variable settlement date

Kristi Corp. enters into a contract to purchase 200 shares of its subsidiary at $25 in two years. However, if the holder of the shares dies before the settlement date, Kristi agrees to purchase the shares at the present value of $25 at the settlement date computed using the then-current prime rate. The shares are currently trading at $22. The liability to repurchase shares is initially reported at $4,400. At each subsequent measurement date, Kristi would adjust the liability to the present value of $25 at the settlement date using the discount rate implicit in the contract, unless the holder of the shares had died. If the holder of the shares had died, Kristi would adjust the liability to the present value of $25 at the settlement date using the then-current prime rate. For example, if one year from issuance date the holder is still alive, the liability would be adjusted to $4,690 using the 6.6% rate implicit in the agreement. The adjustment amount of $290 would be charged to interest expense. If instead the holder had died and the prime rate was 5%, the liability would be adjusted to $4,762 ($5,000/1.05) and the adjustment of $362 would be charged to interest expense.

An entity that has entered into a forward contract that requires physical settlement by repurchase of a fixed number of its equity shares of common stock in exchange for cash does not include those shares in the denominator when computing basic or diluted earnings per share. If any amounts, including contractual (accumulated) dividends, attributable to shares that are to be redeemed or repurchased have not been recognized as interest expense, those amounts are deducted in computing income available to common shareholders (the numerator of the calculation), consistently with the "two-class" method set forth in ASC 260.

MEASURING LIABILITIES AT FAIR VALUE

Under GAAP, long-term debt, until extinguished, is measured at the amount recorded at the date of issuance, reduced by payments made and adjusted for any amortization since issuance. This historical cost-based approach is not, however, universally viewed as contributing to the most meaningful financial reporting. In recent years, the Financial Accounting Standards Board (FASB) has indicated its belief that more appropriate financial reporting would result if all financial liabilities (and assets) were reported at their respective fair values rather than at amounts based on historical cost. Fair value of a liability is an estimated market exit price, that is, an estimate of the amount that would have been paid if the entity had settled the liability on the date of the statement of financial position.

Many preparers and users of financial statements question the relevance of information about the fair value of a financial liability, given that management does not intend, and may not even be able, to settle the obligation before the stated maturity. In effect, the fair value amounts are purely hypothetical and do not alter the real obligation represented by the cost-based carrying amount of the liability at issue.

However, under the current reporting model, it is entirely possible that an entity will report gains from debt extinguishment as a result of the early retirement of a debt obligation carrying a below-market interest rate, even if that extinguishment is funded by the immediate issuance of debt bearing the current market rate. Notwithstanding that the entity's real economic position has not been improved (and may have been diminished), a gain has been reported, which many would agree is misleading. The next example illustrates this problem.

Example

Company A and Company B are competitors, they both are publicly held, and both have bonds outstanding. On December 31, 2009, Company A owes $2,000,000 due in 6 years that carries a fixed interest rate of 10%. Company B also owes $2,000,000 due in 6 years, but Company B issued its bonds in a less favorable interest rate environment. Its debt carries an interest rate of 14%. The two companies have equivalent credit ratings. The prevailing market interest rate for both companies changes to 12% on December 31, 2010. Under historical cost-based GAAP, each company will report $2,000,000 of outstanding debt in its statement of financial position dated December 31, 2010. The fair value of Company A's debt at that date is $1,835,500, while the fair value of Company B's debt is $2,164,500—both fair values computed at the present value of the interest and principal payments at the prevailing market rate of 12%.

If Company A paid off its bonds, it would recognize a gain of $164,500 ($2,000,000 – $1,835,500). But for Company A to recognize its gain, it would have had to repay debt that carried a favorable interest rate. Company A would lose its economically advantageous position of being a company with below-market financing. In addition, if Company A had not used $1,835,500 to repay the debt, it could have invested that amount in its own operations and perhaps earned a higher return. Moreover, if Company A continues to need financing, it will have to refinance at the higher current interest rate. Repurchasing its bonds might not have been the best way for Company A to invest its resources, and might have been motivated, in part, by the desire to manage reported earnings in 2010.

If Company B retired its bonds, it would recognize a loss of $164,500 ($2,000,000 – $2,164,500). As an alternative, Company B could leave its bonds outstanding and realize its loss by paying above-market rates during the remaining 6 years of their term. Depending on the available alternative uses of its money, repaying the bonds and relieving future operations of the burden of above-market interest payments may be the best use of its resources, but Company B would suffer a loss as a result—a loss that can be avoided simply by choosing to not repay its debt.

Company A's gain and Company B's loss would be caused by changes in interest rates—not by a decision to repay debt. The existing measurement model for liabilities sometimes provides an incentive for unwise actions. If Company A wanted to report a gain, it could pay off its debt, even though that might not have been the best use of its resources. If Company B wanted to avoid a loss, it could allow its bonds to remain outstanding, even though the best economic decision would have been to retire them.

Liabilities often are issued with credit enhancements obtained from a third party. Given the ever-increasing inclination to mandate fair value reporting for financial assets and liabilities, questions have arisen regarding whether an issuer would consider the effect of these third-party credit enhancements when measuring the liability at fair value. A new standard (ASC 820-10-05-3) was issued recently requiring the issuer of a liability with an inseparable third-party credit enhancement to not include the effect of the credit enhancement when calculating the fair value measurement of the liability.

Nonetheless, the project to replace historical data about financial liabilities with fair value data continues to be very controversial. Among opponents are financial institutions that would have to reprice virtually the entire statement of financial position at each reporting date and that might see a significant increase in periodic earnings volatility (albeit reflecting economic reality). It is not clear whether FASB will be successful in changing this long-standing tradition of reporting essentially all financial liabilities at historical cost.

MULTIPLE-CHOICE QUESTIONS

1. Which of the following is **not** a characteristic of a note?
    (a) It is a promise to pay a sum of money at a designated maturity date.
    (b) It contains a written agreement stating the amount of principal and interest and when they are to be paid.
    (c) It is primarily used to borrow funds from the general public.
    (d) It is a common form of exchange in business transactions for cash, property, goods and services.

2. When the market rate of a bond exceeds the stated rate, the bond will be issued at a
    (a) Discount.
    (b) Premium.

3. When a note is issued consideration such as property, the stated rate is presumed to be fair unless
    (a) No interest rate is stated.
    (b) The stated rate is unreasonable.
    (c) The face value of the debt is materially different from the consideration involved.
    (d) All of the above.

4. When a note is exchanged for property and the fair market value of the consideration is not determinable
    (a) The present value of the note must be determined using the effective rate of interest.
    (b) The present value of the note must be determined using the imputed interest rate.
    (c) The present value of the note must be determined using the market interest rate.
    (d) The present value of the note must be determined using the current interest rate.

5. Which of the following is an example of a mandatorily redeemable preferred share?
    (a) Callable preferred shares.
    (b) Convertible preferred shares.
    (c) Preferred stock with an unconditional obligation to redeem the shares at a specified date.
    (d) Preferred stock with a conditional obligation to redeem the shares at a specified date.

Chapter 19

LEASES (ASC 840)

BACKGROUND AND INTRODUCTION

This Standard prescribes the accounting treatment for leases in the financial statements of lessees and lessors.

DEFINITIONS OF KEY TERMS
(in accordance with ASC 840)

Bargain purchase option. A provision allowing the lessee the option of purchasing the leased property for an amount, exclusive of lease payments, which is sufficiently lower than the expected fair value of the property at the date the option becomes exercisable. Exercise of the option must appear reasonably assured at the inception of the lease.

Implicit interest rate. The discount rate that, when applied to the minimum lease payments, excluding that portion of the payments representing executory costs to be paid by the lessor, together with any profit thereon, and the unguaranteed residual value accruing to the benefit of the lessor, causes the aggregate present value at the beginning of the lease term to be equal to the fair value of the leased property to the lessor at the inception of the lease, minus any investment tax credit retained and expected to be realized by the lessor (and plus initial direct costs in the case of direct financing leases).

Incremental borrowing rate. The rate that, at the inception of the lease, the lessee would have incurred to borrow over a similar term (i.e., a loan term equal to the lease term) the funds necessary to purchase the leased asset.

Lease. An agreement conveying the right to use property, plant, or equipment (land or depreciable assets or both) usually for a stated period of time.

CLASSIFICATION OF LEASES

Lessee Classification

For accounting and reporting purposes, the lessee has two possible classifications for a lease: capital or operating. The classification is based on the extent to which risks and rewards of ownership of the leased asset are transferred to the lessee or remain with the lessor.

261

A lease is classified as a capital lease if it transfers substantially all the risks and rewards of ownership to the lessee. Substantially all of the risks and risks or benefits of ownership are deemed to have been transferred if any one of these criteria is met:

- Transfer of ownership to the lessee by the end of the lease term.
- The lease contains a bargain purchase option.
- The lease term is equal to 75% or more of the estimated economic life of the leased property, and the beginning of the lease term does not fall within the last 25% of the total economic life of the leased property.
- The present value (PV) of the minimum lease payments at the beginning of the lease term is 90% or more of the fair value to the lessor less any investment tax credit retained by the lessor. This requirement cannot be used if the lease's inception is in the last 25% of the useful economic life of the leased asset. The interest rate, used to compute the PV, is the incremental borrowing rate of the lessee unless the implicit rate is available and lower.

If a lease agreement does not meet any of the criteria set forth in the preceding sections, it is classified as an operating lease.

Lessor Classification

Four possible classifications apply to a lease from the standpoint of the lessor:

1. Operating
2. Sales type
3. Direct financing
4. Leveraged

The conditions surrounding the origination of the lease determine its classification by the lessor. If the lease meets any one of the four criteria for lessees and both of the qualifications set forth next, the lease is classified as a sales-type lease, a direct financing lease, or a leveraged lease depending on the conditions present at the inception of the lease.

- Collectibility of the minimum lease payments is reasonably predictable.
- No important uncertainties surround the amount of unreimbursable costs yet to be incurred by the lessor under the lease.

If a lease transaction does not meet the criteria for classification as a sales-type lease, a direct financing lease, or a leveraged lease as specified earlier, it is classified by the lessor as an operating lease. The classification testing is performed prior to considering the proper accounting treatment.

Sales-Type Lease

A lease is classified as a sales-type lease when the criteria set forth earlier have been met and the lease transaction is structured in such a way that the lessor (generally a manufacturer or dealer) recognizes a profit or loss on the transaction in addition to interest income. In order for this to occur, the fair value of the property (FV) must be different from the cost (carrying value). The essential substance of this transaction is that of a sale, thus its name.

Direct Financing Lease

A direct financing lease differs from a sales-type lease in that the lessor does not realize a profit or loss on the transaction other than interest income. In a direct financing lease, the fair value of the property at the inception of the lease is equal to the cost (carrying value). This type of lease transaction most often involves lessor entities engaged in financing operations. The lessor (a bank or other financial institution) purchases the asset and then leases the asset to the lessee. This transaction merely replaces the conventional lending transaction where the borrower uses the borrowed funds to purchase the asset.

Leveraged Lease

A leveraged lease meets all the definitional criteria of a direct financing lease but differs because it involves at least three parties: a lessee, a long-term creditor, and a lessor (commonly referred to as the equity participant). Two characteristics of a leveraged lease are

1. The financing provided by the long-term creditor must be without recourse to the general credit of the lessor, although the creditor may hold recourse with respect to the leased property. The amount of the financing must provide the lessor with substantial "leverage" in the transaction.
2. The lessor's net investment declines during the early years and rises during the later years of the lease term before its elimination.

LESSEE ACCOUNTING

Operating Leases

For an operating lease, the rental payments are charged to expense as the payments are made or become payable. This assumes that the lease payments are being made on a straight-line basis (i.e., an equal payment per period over the lease term).

If the lease agreement calls for either an alternative payment schedule or a scheduled rent increase over the lease term, the lease expense is recognized on a straight-line basis over the lease term unless another systematic and rational basis is a better representation of the actual physical usage of the leased property. In addition, the lessor may grant various incentives to the lessee during the lease term, such as a rent holiday or allowances to fund leasehold improvements. Incentives paid to or incurred on behalf of the lessee by the lessor are an inseparable part of the lease agreement. These amounts are recognized as reductions to rental expense on a straight-line basis over the term of a lease.

In the case of an operating lease, there is no recognition on the statement of financial position because the substance of the lease is merely that of a rental. There is no reason to expect that the lessee will derive any future economic benefit from the leased asset beyond the lease term.

Capital Leases

The lessee records a capital lease as an asset and an obligation (liability) at an amount equal to the present value of the minimum lease payments at the beginning of the lease term. For the purposes of the 90% test, the present value is computed using the incremental borrowing rate of the lessee unless it is practicable for the lessee to determine the implicit rate used by the lessor and the implicit rate is less than the incremental borrowing rate.

The asset is recorded at the lower of the present value of the minimum lease payments or the fair value of the asset. When the fair value of the leased asset is less than the present value of the minimum lease payments, the interest rate used to amortize the lease obligation will differ from the interest rate used in the 90% test. The interest rate used in the amortization will be the same as that used in the 90% test when the fair value is greater than or equal to the present value of the minimum lease payments.

The minimum lease payments generally include the minimum rental payments, any guarantee of the residual value made by the lessee, and the penalty for failure to renew the lease if applicable. If the lease includes a bargain purchase option (BPO), the amount required to be paid under the BPO is also included in the minimum lease payments.

The lease term used in this present value computation is the fixed, noncancelable term of the lease plus

- All periods covered by bargain renewal options.
- All periods for which failure to renew the lease imposes a penalty on the lessee.
- All periods covered by ordinary renewal options during which the lessee guarantees the lessor's debt on the leased property.
- All periods covered by ordinary renewals or extensions up to the date a BPO is exercisable.
- All periods representing renewals or extensions of the lease at the option.

- Collectibility of the minimum lease payments is reasonably predictable.
- No important uncertainties surround the amount of unreimbursable costs yet to be incurred by the lessor under the lease.

The amortization of the leased asset will depend on how the lease qualifies as a capital lease. If the lease transaction meets the criteria of either transferring ownership or containing a bargain purchase option, then the asset arising from the transaction is amortized over the estimated useful life of the leased property. If the transaction qualifies as a capital lease because it meets either the 75% of useful life or 90% of FV criteria, the asset is amortized over the lease term.

In some instances when the property is to revert back to the lessor, there may be a guaranteed residual value. This is an amount that the lessee guarantees to the lessor. If the FV of the asset at the end of the lease term is greater than or equal to the guaranteed residual value, then the lessee must make up the difference, usually with a cash payment. The guaranteed residual value often is used as a tool to reduce the periodic payments by substituting the lump-sum amount at the end of the term that results from the guarantee. In any event the amortization still must take place based on the estimated residual value. This results in a rational and systematic allocation of the expense to the periods of usage and avoids a large loss (or expense) in the last period as a result of the guarantee.

The annual (periodic) rent payments made during the lease term are allocated between a reduction in the obligation and interest expense in a manner such that the interest expense represents the application of a constant periodic rate of interest to the remaining balance of the lease obligation. This commonly is referred to as the effective interest method.

Case Study 1

Capital lease

Facts

An entity enters into a lease agreement on January 1, 2010, for equipment with an expected useful life of three years. The equipment reverts back to the lessor upon expiration of the lease agreement. The fair value of the equipment at lease inception is $135,000. Three payments are due to the lessor in the amount of $50,000 per year beginning 12/31/2010, and an additional sum of $1,000 is to be paid annually by the lessee for insurance. The lessee guarantees a $10,000 residual value on 12/31/2012 to the lessor; however, irrespective of the $10,000 residual value guarantee, the leased asset is expected to have only $1,000 salvage value on 12/31/2012. The lessee's incremental borrowing rate is 10%. (The lessor's implicit rate is unknown.)

Required

1. Calculate the present value of the lease obligation.
2. Make the entry necessary to record the lease.
3. Determine the proper allocation between interest and reduction of the lease obligation for each lease payment.
4. Make the necessary entry to record the amortization of the lease.

Solution

1. PV of guaranteed residual value = $10,000 × .7513*   =   7,513
   PV of annual payments = $50,000 × 2.4869**   = 124,345
                                                         $ 131,858

   * *The present value of an amount of $1 due in three periods at 10% is .7513.*
   ** *The present value of an ordinary annuity of $1 for three periods at 10% is 2.4869.*

2. The entry necessary to record the lease on 1/1/10 is

Leased equipment	131,858	
Lease obligation		131,858

   Note that the lease is recorded at the present value of the minimum lease payments that, in this case, is less than the FV. If the present value of the minimum lease payments had exceeded the FV, the lease would have been recorded at FV.

	Year	Cash Payment	Interest expense	Reduction in lease obligation	Balance of lease obligation
3.	Inception of lease				$131,858
	2010	$50,000	$13,186	$36,814	95,044
	2011	50,000	9.504	40,496	54,548
	2012	50,000	5,452	44,548	10,000

The effective interest method is used. The interest is calculated at 10% (the incremental borrowing rate) of the balance of the lease obligation for each period, and the remainder of each $50,000 payment is allocated as a reduction in the lease obligation. The lessee is also required to pay $1,000 for insurance on an annual basis.

4. The following entry will be made at the end of each year

Amortization expense	43,619	
Accumulated amortization		43,619 [($131,858 – 1,000)/3]

LESSOR ACCOUNTING

Operating Leases

The payments received by the lessor are recorded as rent revenues in the period in which the payment is received or becomes receivable. As with the lessee, if either the rentals vary from a straight-line basis, the lease agreement contains a scheduled rent increase over the lease term, or the lessor grants incentives to the lessee such as a rent holiday or leasehold improvement allowance, the revenue is recorded on a straight-line basis unless an alternative basis of systematic and rational allocation is more representative of the time pattern of physical usage of the leased property. If the scheduled increase(s) is due to the lessee leasing additional property under a master lease agreement, the increase is allocated proportionally to the additional leased property and recognized on a straight-line basis over the years that the lessee has control over the additional leased property. In this case, the total revised rent should be allocated between the previously leased property and the additional leased property based on their relative fair values.

The lessor presents the leased property on the statement of financial position under the caption "Investment in leased property." This caption is shown with or near the fixed assets of the lessor and depreciated in the same manner as the lessor's other fixed assets.

Any incentives made by the lessor to the lessee are treated as reductions of rent and recognized on a straight-line basis over the term of the lease.

Sales-Type Leases

In accounting for a sales-type lease, it is necessary for the lessor to determine these amounts:

- Gross investment
- Fair value of the leased asset
- Cost

The gross investment (lease receivable) of the lessor is equal to the sum of the minimum lease payments (excluding executor costs) plus the unguaranteed residual value. The difference between the gross investment and the present value of the two components of gross investment (minimum lease payment and unguaranteed residual value) is recorded as the unearned interest revenue.

The present value is computed using the lease term and implicit interest rate. The lease term used in this computation includes any renewal options exercisable at the discretion of the lessor. The resulting unearned interest revenue is to be amortized into income using the effective interest method. This will result in a constant periodic rate of return on the net investment. (The net investment is the gross investment less the unearned income.)

The fair value of the leased property is equal to the normal selling price of the asset adjusted by any residual amount retained. The adjusted selling price used for a sales-type lease is equal to the present value of the minimum lease payments. Thus, we can say that the normal selling price less the residual amount retained is equal to the present value of the minimum lease payments.

The cost of goods sold to be charged against income in the period of the sale is computed as the historic cost or carrying value of the asset (most likely inventory) plus any initial direct costs, less the present value of the unguaranteed residual value. The difference between the adjusted selling price and the amount computed as the cost of goods sold is the gross profit recognized by the lessor at the inception of the lease (sale). Thus, a sales-type lease generates two types of revenue for the lessor:

1. The gross profit on the sale
2. The interest earned on the lease receivable

Direct Financing Leases

Once a lease has been classified as a direct financing lease, these three numbers must be obtained:

1. Gross investment
2. Cost
3. Residual value

A direct financing lease generally involves a leasing company or other financial institution and results in only interest income being earned by the lessor. This is because the FV (selling price) and the cost are equal. Therefore, no profit is recognized on the actual lease transaction.

The gross investment still is defined as the minimum amount of lease payments exclusive of any executor costs plus the unguaranteed residual value. The difference between the gross investment as determined above and the cost (carrying value) of the asset is to be recorded as the unearned interest income because there is no manufacturer's/dealer's profit earned on the transaction.

The net investment in the lease is defined as the gross investment less the unearned interest income plus the unamortized initial direct cost related to the lease. Initial direct costs are defined in the same way that they were for purposes of the sales-type lease; however, the accounting treatment is different. For a direct financing lease, the unearned lease (interest) income and the initial direct costs are amortized to income over the lease term to yield a constant effective rate of interest on the net investment. Thus, the effect of the initial direct costs is to reduce the implicit interest rate, or yield, to the lessor over the life of the lease.

Case Study 2

Direct financing lease

Facts

Edwards, Inc. needs new equipment to expand its manufacturing operation; however, it does not have sufficient capital to purchase the asset at this time. Because of this, Edwards has employed Samuels Leasing to purchase the asset. In turn, Edwards (the lessee) will lease the asset from Samuels (the lessor). The following information applies to the terms of the lease:

Lease information

1. A three-year lease is initiated on 1/1/10 for equipment costing $131,858 with an expected useful life of five years. FV at 1/1/10 of the equipment is $131,858.
2. Three annual payments are due to the lessor beginning 12/31/10. The property reverts back to the lessor upon termination of the lease.
3. The unguaranteed residual value at the end of year three is estimated to be $10,000.
4. The annual payments are calculated to give the lessor a 10% return (implicit rate).
5. The lease payments and unguaranteed residual value have a PV equal to $131,858 (FMV of asset) at the stipulated discount rate.
6. The annual payment to the lessor is computed as

PV of residual value = $10,000 × .7513* = $7,513
PV of lease payments = Selling price – PV of residual value
= $131,858 – 7,513 = $124,345

Annual payment = $\dfrac{\$124,345}{PV_{3,\ 10\%}}$ = $\dfrac{\$124,345}{2.4869^{**}}$ = $50,000

* .7513 is the PV of an amount due in three periods at 10%.
** 2.4869 is the PV of an annuity of $1 for three periods at a 10% interest rate.

7. Initial direct costs of $7,500 are incurred by Samuels in the lease transaction.

Required

1. Determine the classification of the lease.
2. Determine the unearned interest and the net investment in the lease.
3. Make the entry to initially record the lease.
4. Record the entry for the payment of the initial direct costs.
5. Record the entry when the asset is returned to the lessor.

Solution

1. As with any lease transaction, the first step must be to determine the proper classification of the lease. In this case, the PV of the lease payments ($124,345) exceeds 90% of the FV (90% × $131,858 = $118,672). Assume that the lease payments are reasonably assured and that there are no uncertainties surrounding the costs yet to be incurred by the lessor. As such, it is a capital lease.
2. Next, determine the unearned interest and the net investment in the lease.

Gross investment in lease [(3 × $50,000) + $10,000]	$160,000
Cost of leased property	131,858
Unearned interest	$ 28,142

The unamortized initial direct costs are to be added to the gross investment in the lease and the unearned interest income is to be deducted to arrive at the net investment in the lease. The net investment in the lease for this example is determined as

Gross investment in lease	$160,000
Add: Unamortized initial direct costs	7,500
	$167,500
Less: Unearned interest income	28,142
Net investment in lease	$139,358

The net investment in the lease (Gross investment – Unearned revenue) has been increased by the amount of initial direct costs. Therefore, the implicit rate is no longer 10%. We must recompute the implicit rate. The implicit rate is really the result of an internal rate of return calculation. We know that the lease payments are to be $50,000 per annum and that a residual value of $10,000 is expected at the end of the lease term. In return for these payments (inflows), we are giving up equipment (outflow) and incurring initial direct costs (outflows) with a net investment of $139,358 ($131,858 + $7,500). The only way to obtain the new implicit manually rate is through a trial-and-error calculation as set up next.

$$\frac{50,000}{(1+i)^1} + \frac{50,000}{(1+i)^2} + \frac{50,000}{(1+i)^3} + \frac{10,000}{(1+i)^2} = \$139,358$$

Where i = implicit rate of interest

This computation is most efficiently performed using either spreadsheet or present value software. In doing so, the $139,358 is entered as the present value, the contractual payment stream and residual value are entered, and the software iteratively solves for the unknown implicit interest rate.

In this case, the implicit rate is equal to 7.008%. Thus, the amortization table would be set up in this way:

	(a)	*(b)* Reduction in unearned interest	*(c)* PV × implicit rate (7.008%)	*(d)* Reduction in initial direct costs (b–c)	*(e)* Reduction in PVI net invest. (a–b + d)	*(f)* PVI net invest. in lease $(f)_{(n+1)} = (f)_n - (e)$
	Lease payments					$139,358
1	$ 50,000	$13,186 *(1)*	$ 9,766	$3,420	$ 40,234	99,124
2	50,000	9,504 *(2)*	6,947	2,557	43,053	56,071
3	50,000	5,455 *(3)*	3,929	1,526	46,071	10,000
	$150,000	$28,145*	$20,642	$7,503	$129,358	

*   *Rounded*

(b.1) $131,858 × 10% = $13,186
(b.2) [$131,858 – ($50,000 – 13,186)] × 10% = $9,504
(b.3) {$131,858 – [($50,000 – 9,504) + ($50,000 – 13,186)]} × 10% = $5,455

Here the interest is computed as 7.008% of the net investment. Note again that the net investment at the end of the lease term is equal to the estimated residual value.

3. The entry made to initially record the lease is

> Lease receivable* [($50,000 × 3) + 10,000]   160,000
>   Asset acquired for leasing   131,858
>   Unearned interest   28,142

> *   *Also the "gross investment in lease."*

4. When the payment of (or obligation to pay) the initial direct costs occurs, this entry must be made:

> Initial direct costs   7,500
>   Cash (or accounts payable)   7,500

Using the previous schedule, these entries would be made during each of the indicated years:

	2010		2011		2012	
Cash	50,000		50,000		50,000	
Lease receivable*		50,000		50,000		50,000
Unearned interest	13,186		9,504		5,455	
Initial direct costs		3,420		2,557		1,526
Interest revenue		9,766		6,947		3,929

> *   *Also the "gross investment in lease."*

5. Finally, when the asset is returned to the lessor at the end of the lease term, it must be recorded by the following entry:

> Used asset   10,000
>   Lease receivable*   10,000

> *   *Also the "gross investment in lease."*

Leveraged Leases

In order to qualify as a leveraged lease, a lease agreement must meet these requirements, and the lessor must account for the investment tax credit (when in effect) in the manner described next.

- The lease must meet the definition of a direct financing lease (the 90% criterion does not apply as a direct financing lease must have its cost or carrying value equal to the fair value of the asset at the lease's inception).
- The lease must involve at least three parties.

  1. An owner-lessor (equity participant)
  2. A lessee
  3. A long-term creditor (debt participant)

- The financing provided by the creditor is nonrecourse as to the general credit of the lessor and is sufficient to provide the lessor with substantial leverage.

- The lessor's net investment (defined below) decreases in the early years and increases in the later years until it is eliminated.

SALE-AND-LEASEBACK TRANSACTIONS AND OTHER TRANSACTIONS INVOLVING THE LEGAL FORM OF A LEASE

Very often entities enter into complex financing arrangements involving lease-like arrangements. Careful analysis of such arrangements needs to be undertaken to ensure that the substance of the transaction is properly reflected, not just the legal form.

A sale-leaseback describes a transaction where the owner of property (seller-lessee) sells the property and then immediately leases all or part of it back from the new owner (buyer-lessor). If substantially all the rights to use the property are retained by the seller-lessee, and the agreement meets at least one of the criteria for capital lease treatment, the seller-lessee accounts for the lease-back as a capital lease and any profit on the sale is deferred and amortized in proportion to amortization of the leased asset. If the leaseback is classified as an operating lease, it is accounted for as such, and any profit on the sale is deferred and amortized over the lease term in proportion to gross rental charges. Any loss on the sale would also be deferred unless the loss were perceived to be a real economic loss, in which case the loss would be immediately recognized and not deferred.

Other more complex transactions need to be analyzed for their substance and often involve a series of transactions involving leases. On occasion, just tax benefits arise; sometimes there is no real transaction when the series of transactions is viewed in its entirety. In such cases, the substance needs to be clearly reflected in the financial statements.

EXTRACTS FROM PUBLISHED FINANCIAL STATEMENTS

Exxon Mobil Corporation

Notes to the Consolidated Annual Financial Statements

For the Year Ended December 31, 2008

10. Leased Facilities

At December 31, 2008, the Corporation and its consolidated subsidiaries held noncancelable operating charters and leases covering drilling equipment, tankers, service stations, and other properties with minimum undiscounted lease commitments totaling $11,188 million as indicated in the table. Estimated related rental income from noncancelable subleases is $155 million.

(millions of dollars)	*Lease payments under minimum commitments*	*Related sublease rental income*
2009	$ 2,278	$ 25
2010	1,939	22
2011	1,894	20
2012	1,385	16
2013	908	13
2014 and beyond	2,784	59
Total	$11,188	$155

Net rental expenses under both cancelable and noncancelable operating leases incurred during 2008, 2007, and 2006 were

(millions of dollars)	*2008*	*2007*	*2006*
Rental expense	$4,115	$3,367	$3,576
Less sublease rental income	123	168	172
Net rental expense	$3,992	$3,199	$3,404

MULTIPLE-CHOICE QUESTIONS

1. The classification of a lease as either an operating or finance lease is based on
  - (a) The length of the lease.
  - (b) The transfer of the risks and rewards of ownership.
  - (c) The minimum lease payments being at least 50% of the fair value.
  - (d) The economic life of the asset.

2. The accounting concept that is principally used to classify leases into operating and finance is
  - (a) Substance over form.
  - (b) Whether the lease meets certain criteria.
  - (c) Neutrality.
  - (d) Completeness.

3. Which of the following situations would prima facie lead to a lease being classified as an operating lease?
  - (a) Transfer of ownership to the lessee at the end of the lease term.
  - (b) Option to purchase at a value below the fair value of the asset.
  - (c) The lease term is for a major part of the asset's life.
  - (d) The present value of the minimum lease payments is 50% of the fair value of the asset.

4. The classification of a lease is normally carried out
  - (a) At the end of the lease term.
  - (b) After a cooling-off period of one year.
  - (c) At the inception of the lease.
  - (d) When the entity deems it to be necessary.

5. Which is the correct accounting treatment for an operating lease payment in the accounts of the lessee?
  - (a) Dr Cash
    - Cr Operating lease rentals/income statement
  - (b) Dr Operating lease rentals/income statement
    - Cr Cash
  - (c) Dr Asset account
    - Cr Cash
  - (d) Dr Cash
    - Cr Asset account

6. Which is the correct accounting treatment for a finance lease in the accounts of a lessor?
  - (a) Treat as a noncurrent asset equal to net investment in lease. Recognize all finance payments in income statements.
  - (b) Treat as a receivable equal to gross amount receivable on lease. Recognize finance payments in cash and by reducing debtor.
  - (c) Treat as a receivable equal to net investment in the lease. Recognize finance payment by reducing debtor and taking interest to income statement.
  - (d) Treat as a receivable equal to net investment in the lease. Recognize finance payments in cash and by reduction of debtor.

7. The profit on a finance lease transaction for lessors who are manufacturers or dealers should
  - (a) Not be recognized separately from finance income.
  - (b) Be recognized in the normal way on the transaction.
  - (c) Be recognized only at the end of the lease term.
  - (d) Be allocated on a straight-line basis over the life of the lease.

Chapter 20

SEGMENT REPORTING (ASC 280)

BACKGROUND AND INTRODUCTION

Segment information highlights the entity's risks and returns by showing the financial position and performance by each segment. Segment reporting is an important tool in analyzing companies that are diversified in terms of the types of businesses in which they engage or the geographic locations in which they operate.

SCOPE

This Standard applies to public companies. The Standard does not mandatorily apply to not-for-profit organizations or to nonpublic companies—which are, nevertheless, encouraged to voluntarily provide the segment disclosures prescribed by ASC 280.

DEFINITIONS OF KEY TERMS

Chief operating decision maker (CODM). The person(s) at the reporting entity level whose general function (not specific title) is to allocate resources to, and assess the performance of, the segments. Within a reporting entity, this authority does not necessarily need to be vested in a single individual; rather, the responsibilities can be fulfilled by a group of individuals.

Reportable segment. Segments considered to be significant to the operations of the reporting entity; a segment that has passed any one of the three defined 10% tests (assets, revenues, or profit and loss) or has been identified as being reportable through other criteria (e.g., aggregation).

OPERATING SEGMENTS

An operating segment is defined as a component of a reporting entity

- That engages in business activities that may generate revenues and incur expenses from transactions with external parties and/or with other components of the same reporting entity (intersegment transactions);
- About which discrete financial information is available; and

271

- Whose operating results are reviewed regularly by the reporting entity's chief operating decision maker (CODM) in order to assess the segment's performance and make resource allocation decisions.

Operating segments frequently have a segment manager function that communicates on an ongoing basis with the reporting entity's CODM. The segment manager is not necessarily a single individual; rather, the segment management responsibility can vest functionally in a committee or group of designated individuals. Additionally, an operating segment is not necessarily revenue generating from its inception, as it may be in the start-up phase.

Not all activities that occur within the reporting entity are allocable to its operating segments. Activities that are nonrevenue producing or that are incidental to the reporting entity, such as corporate headquarters or certain functional departments, are not considered to be operating segments. ASC 280 specifies that the reporting entity's pension and other postretirement benefit plans are not considered to be operating segments. This rather general definition means that management's judgment will be relied on to determine operating segment classifications.

REPORTABLE SEGMENTS

A segment is considered to be a reportable segment if it is significant to the entity as a whole because it satisfies one of the three quantitative 10% tests described next.

Revenue Test

Segment revenue (unaffiliated and intersegment) is at least 10% of the combined revenue (unaffiliated and intersegment) of all operating segments.

Profit and Loss Test

The absolute amount of segment profit or loss is at least 10% of the greater, in the absolute amount, of combined

- Profits of all operating segments reporting a profit.
- Losses of all operating segments reporting a loss.

If the CODM uses different measures of profit and loss to evaluate the performance of different segments (e.g., net income versus operating income), the reporting entity is to use a single, consistent measure for the purposes of this profit and loss test. This does not, however, affect the requirement that the reporting entity disclose the measure of profit or loss used by the CODM for the purpose of decision making regarding the segment's performance and resources to be allocated to the segment.

Assets Test

Segment assets are at least 10% of the combined assets of all operating segments. Segment assets include those assets used exclusively by the segment and the allocated portion of assets shared by two or more segments. Assets held for general corporate purposes are not assigned to segments.

Interperiod comparability must be considered in conjunction with the results of the 10% tests. If a segment fails to meet the tests in the current reporting period but has satisfied the tests in the past and is expected to in the future, it is considered as being reportable in the current year for the sake of comparability. Similarly, if a segment that rarely passes the tests does so in the current year as the result of an unusual event, that segment may be excluded to preserve comparability.

After the 10% tests are complete, a 75% test must be performed. The combined unaffiliated revenue of all reportable segments must be at least 75% of the combined unaffiliated revenue of all operating segments. If the 75% test is not satisfied, additional segments must be designated as reportable until the test is satisfied. The purpose of this test is to ensure that reportable segments account for a substantial portion of the entity's operations.

Case Study 1

Highlands Inc., a public limited company, has this information regarding operating segments:

Operating segment	Unaffiliated revenue	Intersegment revenue	Total revenue	Segment profit	Segment (loss)	Assets
A	$ 90	$ 12	$ 102	$11	$ —	$ 70
B	120	—	120	10	—	50
C	110	20	130	—	(40)	90
D	200	—	200	—	—	140
E	140	300	440	—	(100)	230
F	380	—	380	60	—	260
G	144	—	144	8	—	30
Total	$1,184	$332	$1,516	$89	$(140)	$870

Required

Determine which of the operating segments should be considered reportable segments and if the 75% test has been passed.

Solution

Operating segment	Total revenues (10% of $1,516=$152)	Segment profit/loss (10% of $140=$14)	Assets (10% of $870 = $87)	75% of unaffiliated revenues test
A				
B				
C		X	X	$110
D	X		X	200
E	X	X	X	140
F	X	X	X	380
G				
				830
			75% of $1,184	888
			Revenue shortfall	$(58)

Note that the aggregate revenues of the reportable segments that passed the 10% tests are $58 short of providing the required coverage of 75% of unaffiliated revenues. Consequently, an additional operating segment (A, B, or G) will need to be added to the reportable segments in order to obtain sufficient coverage.

Certain other factors must be considered when identifying reportable segments. Management may consider aggregating two or more operating segments if

- They have similar economic characteristics.
- Aggregation is consistent with the objective and basic principles of ASC 280.
- The segments are similar in all of these areas:

  - The nature of the products and services
  - The nature of the production processes
  - The type of customer for their products and services
  - The methods used to distribute their products or provide their services
  - The nature of the regulatory environment

The number of reportable segments should not be so great as to decrease the usefulness of segment reporting. As a rule of thumb, Financial Accounting Standards Board (FASB) suggests that if the number of reportable segments exceeds 10, segment information may become too detailed. In this situation, the most closely related operating segments should be combined into broader reportable segments, again, however, subject to the objectives inherent in ASC 280's requirements.

SEGMENT DISCLOSURES

General Information

An explanation of how management identified the reporting entity's reportable segments, including whether operating segments have been aggregated, is to be presented. Additionally, a description of the types of products and services from which each reportable segment derives its revenues is to be provided.

Certain Information about Reported Segment Profit and Loss, Segment Assets, and the Basis of Measurement

This information will include certain revenue and expense items included in segment profit and loss as well as certain amounts related to the determination of segment assets. Also, the basis of measurement for these items must be disclosed.

Reconciliations

Management must reconcile the segment amounts disclosed to the corresponding consolidated reporting entity amounts.

Interim-Period Information

Although the interim disclosures are not as extensive as in the annual financial report, certain segment disclosures are required in interim financial statements.

ENTITY-WIDE DISCLOSURES

Products and Services

Revenue from external customers for each product and service or each group of similar products and services is to be reported by the reporting entity unless impracticable. If deemed to be impracticable, that fact is to be disclosed. If the company's reportable segments have been organized around products and services, then this disclosure generally will not be required.

Geographic Areas

A reporting entity separately discloses revenues from external customers and long-lived assets attributable to its domestic operations and foreign operations. If the reportable segments have been organized around geographic areas, then these disclosures generally will not be required because they would be duplicative.

Domestic operations are those operations located in the reporting entity's home country that generate either unaffiliated or intersegment revenues. Foreign operations are similar operations located outside of the home country of the reporting entity. For the purposes of these disclosures, U.S. reporting entities' operations in Puerto Rico are not considered to be foreign operations, although management is not precluded from voluntary disclosure regarding Puerto Rican operations.

If the reporting entity functions in two or more foreign geographic areas, to the extent revenues or assets of an individual foreign geographic area are material, then these amounts are disclosed separately. In addition, disclosure is required of the basis for attributing revenue to different geographic areas. A geographic area is defined as an individual country. If providing this information is impracticable, that fact is to be disclosed.

Major Customers

If the reporting entity earns 10% or more of its revenues on sales to a single external customer, that fact and the amount of revenue from each such customer must be disclosed. Also, the segment making these sales must be disclosed.

For the purpose of this disclosure, a group of customers under common control, such as subsidiaries of a common parent, is regarded as a single customer. Similarly the various agencies of a government are considered to be a single customer. An insuring entity (such as Blue Cross) is not considered to be the customer unless that entity (rather than the patient) controls the decision as to the doctor, type of service, and so on.

RESTATEMENT OF PREVIOUSLY REPORTED SEGMENT INFORMATION

Segment reporting is required on a comparative basis when the associated financial statements are comparative. Therefore, the information must be restated to preserve comparability whenever the reporting entity has changed the structure of its internal organization in a manner that causes a change to its reportable segments. Management must explicitly disclose that it has restated the segment information of earlier periods.

EXTRACTS FROM PUBLISHED FINANCIAL STATEMENTS

Costco Wholesale Corporation, Annual Report 2009

Note 12. Segment Reporting

The Company and its subsidiaries are principally engaged in the operation of membership warehouses in the United States, Canada, Japan, Australia, the United Kingdom, and through majority-owned subsidiaries in Taiwan and Korea and through a 50%-owned joint venture in Mexico. The Company's reportable segments are based on management's organization of the operating segments for making operational decisions and assessments of financial performance, which considers geographic locations. The investment in the Mexico joint venture is only included in total assets under United States Operations in the table below, as it is accounted for under the equity method and its operations are not consolidated in the Company's financial statements.

Year Ended August 30, 2009	United States operations	Canadian operations	Other int'l operations	Total
Total revenue	$56,548	$ 9,737	$5,137	$71,422
Operating income	1,273	354	150	1,777
Depreciation and amortization	589	90	49	728
Capital expenditures, net	904	135	211	1,250
Property and equipment, net	8,415	1,394	1,091	10,900
Total assets	17,228	2,641	2,110	21,979
Net assets	7,458	1,470	1,090	10,018
Year Ended August 31, 2008				
Total revenue	$56,903	$10,528	$5,052	$72,483
Operating income	1,393	420	156	1,969
Depreciation and amortization	511	92	50	653
Capital expenditures, net	1,190	246	163	1,599
Property and equipment, net	8,016	1,371	968	10,355
Total assets	16,345	2,477	1,860	20,682
Net assets	6,882	1,292	1,018	9,192

The material accounting policies of the segments are the same as those described in Note 1. All intersegment net sales and expenses are immaterial and have been eliminated in computing total revenue and operating income.

MULTIPLE-CHOICE QUESTIONS

Segments	Sales	Profit	Segment assets
Suits	40%	45%	50%
Shirts	30%	35%	33%
Bed linen	15%	10%	7%
Blinds	8%	6%	5%
Cloth	7%	4%	5%
	100%	100%	100%

1. In order for an operating segment to be considered a reportable segment, it must

    (a) Pass a 10% revenue, profit and loss, and assets test.

    (b) Pass a 75% test.

    (c) Pass only one of the 10% tests related to revenue, profit and loss and assets.

    (d) Pass a 10% revenue, profit and loss, assets, and 75% test.

2. An entity is in the entertainment industry and organizes outdoor concerts in four different areas of the world: Europe, North America, Australia, and Japan. The entity reports to the board of directors on the basis of each of the four regions. The management accounts show the profitability for each of the four regions, with allocations for that expenditure that are difficult to directly charge to a region. The concerts are of two types: popular music and classical music. What is the appropriate basis for segment reporting in this entity?

    (a) The segments should be reported by class of business, that is, popular and classical music.

    (b) The segments should be reported by region, so Australia and Japan would be combined.

    (c) The segment information should be reported as North America and the rest of the world.

    (d) Segment information should be reported for each of the four different regions.

3. An entity has split its business segments on the basis of the law governing its different types of business. Two business segments that the entity has identified are insurance and banking. Within the banking group, several different services are provided: retail banking, merchant banking, and small business advisory service. The insurance entities sell travel insurance, health insurance, and property insurance. The entity operates throughout the world in several countries and continents. What basis should the entity report its segmental information?

    (a) On the basis of its business divisions.

    (b) By geographical location.

    (c) On the basis of the services it offers within those divisions.

    (d) The entity should just show one segment, entitled banking and insurance.

4. An entity manufactures suits, clothing, bed linen, and various cotton and man-made fiber products. It has several segments, which are reported internally as

The table represents the percentages of sales, profit, and segment assets that are attributable to the different segments. The entity wants to present bed linen and cloth as a single segment but is wondering whether the information can be aggregated. How will the segmental information be presented in the financial statements?

    (a) Bed linen and cloth, suits, and shirts, will all be shown as separate segments with blinds in the other category.

    (b) All of the segments should be presented separately.

    (c) Suits, shirts, and bed linen will be separate segments with blinds and cloth shown as a single segment.

    (d) Suits and cloth will be one segment with shirts, bed linen, and blinds shown as other separate segments.

Chapter 21

INTERIM REPORTING (ASC 270)

OBJECTIVE

The purpose of ASC 270, *Interim Reporting*, is to provide guidance on accounting and disclosure requirements for interim financial reports of publicly traded companies.

U.S. generally accepted accounting principles (GAAP) itself does not mandate interim financial reporting; however, the Securities and Exchange Commission (SEC) requires public companies to file quarterly financial information on Form 10-Q, which is due no later than 45 days after period-end (with shorter filing deadlines for larger entities).

DEFINITIONS OF KEY TERMS

Interim period. A financial reporting period shorter than a full financial year.

Interim financial report. A financial report that contains either a complete or condensed set of financial statements for an interim period.

Liquidation of LIFO inventories. A last-in, first-out (LIFO) liquidation occurs in an interim period when units sold during that period exceed the number of units purchased during that same period. This results in costs associated with one or more previous years' LIFO layers being released into cost of goods sold.

Seasonality. The normal, expected occurrence of a major portion of revenues or costs in the same one or two interim periods (on a consistent basis from year to year).

FORM AND CONTENT OF INTERIM REPORTS

ASC 270 defines the minimum content of an interim financial report as including condensed financial statements and selected explanatory notes. An entity should establish the level of detail provided to ensure that the condensed financial statements can be compared with the most recent previous annual financial statements. The interim financial report should provide an update on the latest financial statements.

If the entity publishes interim financial statements that are condensed, they should include only major captions, with the exception of inventories. For example, if a statement of financial position caption is less than 10% of total assets, and the amount in the caption has not increased or decreased by more than 25% since the end of the preceding fiscal year, the caption may be combined with others. Additional line items or notes should be included if omitting them would make the interim financial statements misleading.

DISCLOSURE OF INTERIM INFORMATION

It is presumed that users of interim financial statements have read or have access to the annual financial statements for the preceding fiscal year and that the adequacy of additional disclosure needed for fair presentation may be determined in that context, except in regard to material contingencies arising since the prior year-end. As the information presented in interim financial statements is significantly less detailed than in the annual financial statements, guidelines as to minimum disclosures are necessary. If information is reported at interim dates, this information should be disclosed, at a minimum:

- Sales or gross revenues, provision for income taxes, extraordinary items, net income, and comprehensive income
- Basic and diluted earnings per share data for each period presented
- Seasonal revenue, costs, or expenses
- Significant changes in estimates or provisions for income taxes
- Disposal of a component of an entity and extraordinary, unusual or infrequently occurring items
- Contingent items
- Changes in accounting principles or estimates
- Significant changes in financial position
- The information about the use of fair value to measure assets and liabilities recognized in the statement of financial position

Although these interim financial statements are informational tools used by investors, creditors, and analysts, they are not presented in sufficient detail to constitute a fair presentation of the reporting entity's financial position and results of operations in accordance with GAAP.

PERIODS TO BE PRESENTED BY INTERIM FINANCIAL STATEMENTS

ASC 270 requires this information to be presented:

- Statement of financial position as of the end of the current interim period and a comparative statement of financial position as of the end of the preceding fiscal year.
- Income statements for the current interim period, for the period between the end of the preceding fiscal year and the end of the most recent interim period, and for the corresponding periods of the preceding fiscal year.
- Cash flow statement for the current fiscal year to date, with a comparative statement for the comparable year to date period of the preceding fiscal year.

The operations of many businesses are subject to recurring material seasonal variations. Such businesses are required to disclose information about the seasonality of their activities to avoid the possibility of misleading interim reports. It is also recommended, but not required, that such businesses supplement their disclosures with information for 12-month periods ending at the interim date of the current and preceding year, the purpose of which is to eliminate seasonality concerns by reporting on one full annual cycle of activities.

MEASUREMENT

Revenues are recognized as earned during an interim period using the same principles followed in annual reports. With respect to contingent rental income of lessors, contingent rental income is not to be recognized during interim periods until the target that causes the contingent rental income to be earned is reached.

Product costs (and costs directly associated with service revenues) are treated in interim reports in the same manner as in annual reports. Entities generally should use the same inventory pricing methods and write-down provisions at interim dates that are used at annual inventory dates, except in these circumstances:

- The gross profit method may be used to estimate cost of goods sold and ending inventory for interim periods (which eliminates the need for a physical inventory count at the interim date).
- When a liquidation of LIFO inventories occurs at an interim date, and it is expected that this inventory will be replaced by year-end, the anticipated cost of replacing the liquidated inventory is included in cost of sales of the interim period. If a liquidation occurs that is not expected to be reinstated by year-end, the effect of the liquidation is recognized in the period in which it occurs to the extent that it can be reasonably determined.
- An inventory market decline reasonably expected to reverse by year-end (i.e., a decline deemed to be temporary in nature) need not be recognized in the interim period, as no loss is expected to be incurred in the fiscal year. If an inventory loss from a market decline that is recognized in one period is followed by a market price recovery, the reversal is recognized as a gain in the subsequent interim period, limited to the amount of loss previously recognized.
- Reporting entities using standard cost accounting systems ordinarily report purchase price, wage rate, and usage or efficiency variances in the same manner as at year-end. Planned purchase price and volume variances are deferred if expected to be absorbed by year-end.

Most other cost and expenses are recognized in interim periods as incurred. However, a cost that clearly benefits more than one interim period (e.g., annual repairs or property taxes) is allocated among the periods benefited. Allocation procedures are to be consistent with those used at year-end reporting dates. However, if a cost incurred during an interim period cannot be associated readily with other interim periods, it is not arbitrarily assigned to those periods. These parameters are used to account for certain types of interim expenses:

- Costs expensed at year-end dates that benefit two or more interim periods are assigned to interim periods through the use of deferrals or accruals.
- Quantity discounts given to customers based on annual sales volume are allocated to interim periods on the basis of sales to customers during the interim period relative to estimated annual sales.
- Property taxes (and like costs) are deferred or accrued at year-end date to reflect a full year's charge to operations. Charges to interim periods follow similar procedures.
- Advertising costs are permitted to be deferred to subsequent interim periods within the same fiscal year if the costs clearly benefit the later interim periods. Advertising costs may be accrued and allocated to interim periods on the basis of sales prior to actually receiving the service if the sales arrangement implicitly includes the advertising program.
- Lessees are to recognize contingent rental expense in the period before the end of the fiscal year when the achievement of the target that triggers the contingent rental expense becomes *probable*. If the assessment of probable target achievement changes during the year, previously recognized rental expense is reversed.

Costs and expenses subject to year-end determination, such as discretionary bonuses and profit-sharing contributions, are assigned to interim periods in a reasonable and consistent manner to the extent they can be reasonably estimated.

At each interim date, the reporting entity is required to make its best estimate of the effective income tax rate expected to apply to the full fiscal year. This estimate reflects the expected federal, state, local, and foreign income tax rates, income tax credits, and effects of applying income tax planning techniques. However, changes in income tax legislation are reflected in interim periods only after the enactment date of the legislation.

Extraordinary items and the effects of the disposal of a component of the entity are reported separately in the interim period in which they occur. The same treatment is given to other unusual or infrequently occurring events.

ACCOUNTING CHANGES

Any changes in accounting principle made from the prior fiscal year, the comparable interim period of the prior fiscal year, or the preceding interim periods of the current fiscal year are required to be disclosed in interim financial statements. The information included in these disclosures is the same as is required to be included in annual financial statements and should be provided in the interim periods in which the change occurs, subsequent interim periods of that same fiscal year, and the annual financial statements that include the interim period of change.

ASC 250 requires that changes in accounting estimate are accounted for currently and prospectively. Retroactive restatement and presentation of pro forma amounts are not permitted. This accounting is the same whether the change occurs at the end of the year or during an interim reporting period.

When an accounting change results in the financial statements presenting a different reporting entity than was presented in the past, the change is retrospectively applied to all prior periods presented in the new financial statements, including all previously issued interim financial information.

When a restatement is made due to correction of an error, the financial statements of each individual prior period presented (whether interim or annual) are to be adjusted to reflect the correction of the effects of the error that relate to that period. Full disclosure of the restatement is to be provided in the financial statements of the

- Interim period in which the restatement was first made.
- Subsequent interim periods during the same fiscal year that includes the interim period in which the restatement was first made.
- Annual period that includes the interim period in which the restatement was first made.

CONTINGENCIES

Contingencies and uncertainties that exist at an interim date are accrued or disclosed in the same manner as required for annual reports. For example, contingent losses that are probable and subject to reasonable estimation are to be accrued. Disclosures regarding material contingencies and uncertainties are to be repeated in all interim and annual reports until they have been removed or resolved, or become immaterial.

Case Study

Facts

Mendoza Inc. manufactures and sells high-end watches. There was a market decline in the value of its inventory that was not expected to be temporary in nature for $400,000 in the first quarter. In the third quarter, there was a price recovery of $600,000.

Required

Explain how market decline and subsequent price recovery should be treated in the interim financial statements.

Solution

As the price decline was not expected to be temporary in nature, a loss of $400,000 should be recorded in the first-quarter interim financial statements. In the third quarter, a gain of only $400,000 should be recognized as the gain is limited to the amount of loss previously recognized.

MULTIPLE-CHOICE QUESTIONS

1. Interim financial reports of a publicly traded company should be published
   (a) Once a year at any time in that year.
   (b) On a quarterly basis within 60 days after period-end.
   (c) On a quarterly basis within 45 days after period-end.
   (d) Whenever the entity wishes.

2. Interim reporting for publicly traded companies is mandated by
   (a) GAAP.
   (b) The SEC.
   (c) The AICPA.
   (d) The PCAOB.

3. Interim financial reports should include at a minimum a
   (a) Complete set of financial statements in compliance with GAAP.
   (b) Condensed set of financial statements and selected notes.
   (c) Statement of financial position and income statement only.
   (d) Condensed statement of financial position, income statement, and cash flow statement only.

4. ASC 270 states a presumption that anyone reading interim financial reports will
   (a) Understand all generally accepted accounting principles.
   (b) Have access to the records of the entity.
   (c) Have access to the most recent annual report.
   (d) Not make decisions based on the report.

5. A change in accounting principle that occurs in an interim period should be
   (a) Included in the interim period in which the change occurs.
   (b) Retrospectively applied to all prior periods presented.
   (c) Accounted for currently and prospectively.
   (d) Accounted for in the next set of annual financial statements.

6. An entity operates in the travel industry and incurs costs unevenly throughout the fiscal year. Advertising costs of $4 million were incurred on March 1, 2010, and staff bonuses are paid at year-end based on sales. Bonuses are expected to be around $20 million for the year, of which $6 million would relate to the period ending March 31, 2010. What costs should be included in the entity's quarterly financial report as of March 31, 2010?
   (a) Advertising costs $4 million; staff bonuses $5 million.
   (b) Advertising costs $1 million; staff bonuses $5 million.
   (c) Advertising costs $4 million; staff bonuses $6 million.
   (d) Advertising costs $1 million; staff bonuses $6 million.

Chapter 22

FOREIGN CURRENCY (ASC 830)

OBJECTIVES AND SCOPE

To facilitate the proper analysis of foreign operations by financial statement users, transactions and financial statements denominated in foreign currencies must be expressed in a common currency (i.e., U.S. dollars). The generally accepted accounting principles (GAAP) governing the translation of foreign currency financial statements and the accounting for foreign currency transactions are found primarily in ASC 830. Additional guidance in this area is provided by ASC 830-30-40.

These principles apply to the translation of

1. Foreign currency transactions (e.g., exports, imports, and loans) that are denominated in other than a company's functional currency.
2. Foreign currency financial statements of branches, divisions, subsidiaries, and other investees that are incorporated into the financial statements of a company reporting under U.S. GAAP by combination, consolidation, or application of the equity method.

DEFINITIONS OF KEY TERMS
(in accordance with ASC 830)

Closing rate. The spot exchange rate at the date of the statement of financial position.

Exchange difference. The difference resulting from translating a given number of units of one currency into another currency at different exchange rates.

Foreign operation. A subsidiary, associate, joint venture, or branch whose activities are based or conducted in a country or currency other than those of the reporting entity.

Functional currency. The currency of the primary economic environment in which the entity operates; normally, the currency of the environment in which the entity primarily generates and expends cash.

Spot rate. The exchange rate for immediate delivery of currencies exchanged.

Presentation currency. The currency that is used to present the financial statements.

FUNCTIONAL CURRENCY

The Financial Accounting Standards Board (FASB) defines functional currency but does not list definitive criteria that, if satisfied, would with certainty result in the identification of an entity's functional currency. Rather, realizing that such criteria would be difficult to develop, FASB listed various factors that were intended to give management guidance in making the functional currency decision. These factors include

1. *Cash flows.* Do the foreign entity's cash flows directly affect the parent's cash flows and are they immediately available for remittance to the parent?
2. *Sales prices.* Are the foreign entity's sales prices responsive to exchange rate changes and to international competition?
3. *Sales markets.* Is the foreign entity's sales market the parent's country, or are sales denominated in the parent's currency?
4. *Expenses.* Are the foreign entity's expenses incurred primarily in the parent's country?
5. *Financing.* Is the foreign entity's financing primarily from the parent, or is it denominated in the parent's currency?
6. *Intercompany transactions.* Is there a high volume of intercompany transactions between the parent and the foreign entity?

If the answers to these questions are predominantly yes, the functional currency is the reporting currency of the parent entity (i.e., the U.S. dollar). If the answers are predominantly no, the functional currency would most likely be the local currency of the foreign entity, although it is possible for a foreign currency other than the local currency to be the functional currency.

The entity's functional currency reflects the transactions, events, and conditions under which the entity conducts its business. Once chosen, the functional currency cannot be changed unless economic facts and circumstances have clearly changed. Additionally, previously issued financial statements are not restated for any changes in the functional currency.

TRANSLATION METHODS

To deal with discrete circumstances, FASB chose two different methods to translate an entity's foreign financial statements into U.S. dollars: the *current rate* method and the *remeasurement* method. These are not alternatives but rather are employed as circumstances dictate. The primary distinction between the methods is the classification of assets and liabilities (and their corresponding income statement amounts) that are translated at either the current or historical exchange rates.

The first method, known as the current rate method, is the approach mandated by ASC 830 when the functional currency is the foreign currency (e.g., the domestic currency of the foreign subsidiary or operation). All assets and liabilities are translated at the current rates while stockholders' equity accounts are translated at the appropriate historical rate or rates. Revenues and expenses are translated at rates in effect when the transactions occur, but those that occur evenly over the year may be translated at the weighted-average rate for the year.

NOTE: The weighted-average method, if used, must take into account the actual pace and pattern of changes in exchange rates over the course of the year, which often will not be varying at a constant rate throughout the period nor, in many instances, monotonically increasing or decreasing over the period. When these conditions do not hold, it is incumbent upon the reporting entity to develop a weighted-average exchange rate that is meaningful under the circumstances. When coupled with transactions (sales, purchases, etc.) that also have not occurred evenly throughout the year, this determination can become a fairly complex undertaking, requiring careful attention.

The second method, the remeasurement method, is also referred to as the monetary/nonmonetary method. This approach is required by ASC 830 when the foreign entity's accounting records are *not* maintained in the functional currency (e.g., when the U.S. dollar is designated as the functional currency for a Brazilian subsidiary).

This method translates monetary assets (cash and other assets and liabilities that will be settled in cash) at the current rate. Nonmonetary assets, liabilities, and stockholders' equity are translated at the appropriate historical rates.

The appropriate historical rate would be the exchange rate at the date the transaction involving the nonmonetary account originated. Also, the income statement amounts related to nonmonetary assets and liabilities, such as cost of goods sold (inventory), depreciation (property, plant, and equipment), and intangibles amortization (patents, copyrights), are translated at the same rate as used for the related statement of financial position translation.

Other revenues and expenses occurring evenly over the year may be translated at the weighted-average exchange rate in effect during the period, subject to the considerations just discussed.

Case Study 1

Example of the current rate method

Facts

Assume that a U.S. entity has a 100%-owned subsidiary in Italy that commenced operations in early 2010. The subsidiary's operations consist of leasing space in an office building. This building, which cost €1 million, was financed primarily by Italian banks. All revenues and cash expenses are received and paid in euros. The subsidiary also maintains its accounting records in euros. As a result, management of the U.S. entity has decided that the euro is the functional currency of the subsidiary.

The subsidiary's statement of financial position at December 31, 2010, and its combined statement of income and retained earnings for the year ended December 31, 2010, are presented next in euros.

Italian Company
STATEMENT OF FINANCIAL POSITION
at December 31, 2010
(€000 omitted)

Assets		*Liabilities and Stockholders' Equity*	
Cash	€ 100	Accounts payable	€ 60
Accounts receivable	40	Unearned rent	20
Land	200	Mortgage payable	800
Building	1,000	Common stock	80
Accumulated depreciation	(20)	Additional paid-in capital	320
		Retained earnings	40
		Total liabilities and	
Total assets	€1,320	stockholders' equity	€1,320

Italian Company
STATEMENT OF INCOME AND RETAINED EARNINGS
for the Year Ended December 31, 2010
(€000 omitted)

Revenues	€400
Expenses (including depreciation of €20)	340
Net income	60
Retained earnings, January 1, 2010	–
Less dividends declared	(20)
Retained earnings, December 31, 2010	€ 40

Various exchange rates for 2010 are

€1 = $1.50 at the beginning of 2010 (when the common stock was issued and the land and building were financed through the mortgage).

€1 = $1.55 weighted-average for 2010.

€1 = $1.58 at the date the dividends were declared and paid and the unearned rent was received.

€1 = $1.62 at the end of 2010.

Since the euro is the functional currency, the Italian Company's financial statements must be translated into U.S. dollars by the current rate method.

Required

Translate the Italian Company's financial statements into U.S. dollars using the current rate method.

Solution

Italian Company
STATEMENT OF FINANCIAL POSITION TRANSLATION
(Euro is the functional currency)
at December 31, 2010
(€/$000 omitted)

Assets	Euros	Exchange rate	U.S. dollars
Cash	€ 100	1.62	$ 162.00
Accounts receivable, net	40	1.62	64.80
Land	200	1.62	320.00
Building, net	980	1.62	1,587.60
Total assets	€1,320		$2,138.40
Liabilities and Stockholders' Equity			
Accounts payable	€ 60	1.62	$ 97.20
Unearned rent	20	1.62	32.40
Mortgage payable	800	1.62	1,296.00
Common stock	80	1.50	120.00
Additional paid-in capital	320	1.50	480.00
Retained earnings	40	See income statement	61.40
Translation adjustments	—	See computation below	51.40
Total liabilities and stockholders' equity	€1,320		$2,138.40

Italian Company
STATEMENT OF INCOME AND RETAINED EARNINGS
Statement Translation
(Euro is the functional currency)
for the Year Ended December 31, 2010
(€/$000 omitted)

	Euros	Exchange rate	U.S. dollars
Revenues	€ 400	1.55	$620.00
Expenses (including depreciation of €20 [$31.00])	340	1.55	527.00
Net income	60	1.55	93.00
Retained earnings, January 1	—	—	—
Less dividends declared	(20)	1.58	(31.60)
Retained earnings, December 31	€ 40		$ 61.40

Italian Company
STATEMENT OF CASH FLOWS
Statement Translation
(Euro is the functional currency)
for the Year Ended December 31, 2010
(€/$000 omitted)

	Euros	Exchange rate	U.S. dollars
Operating activities			
Net income	€ 60	1.55	$ 93.00
Adjustments to reconcile net income to net cash provided by operating activities			
Depreciation	20	1.55	31.00
Increase in accounts receivable	(40)	1.55	(62.00)
Increase in accounts payable	60	1.55	93.00
Increase in unearned rent	20	1.58	31.60
Net cash provided by operating activities	120		186.60
Investing activities			
Purchase of land	(200)	1.50	(300.00)
Purchase of building	(1,000)	1.50	(1,500.00)
Net cash used by investing activities	(1,200)		(1,800.00)

Financing activities			
Proceeds from issuance of common	400	1.50	600.00
Proceeds from mortgage payable	800	1.50	1,200.00
Dividends paid	(20)	1.58	(31.60)
Net cash provided by financing activities	1,180		1,768.40
Effect of exchange rate changes on cash	N/A		7.00
Increase in cash and equivalents	100		162.00
Cash at beginning of year	0		0
Cash at end of year	€ 100	1.62	$ 162.00

Note these points concerning the current rate method:

1. All assets and liabilities are translated using the current exchange rate at the date of the statement of financial position (€1 = $1.62). All revenues and expenses are translated at the rates in effect when these items are recognized during the period. Due to practical considerations, however, weighted-average rates can be used to translate revenues and expenses (€1 = $1.55).

2. Stockholders' equity accounts are translated by using historical exchange rates. Common stock was issued at the beginning of 2010 when the exchange rate was €1 = $1.50. The translated balance of retained earnings is the result of the weighted-average rate applied to revenues and expenses and the specific rate in effect when the dividends were declared (€1 = $1.58).

3. Translation adjustments result from translating all assets and liabilities at the current rate while stockholders' equity is translated by using historical and weighted-average rates. The adjustments have no direct effect on cash flows. Also, the translation adjustment is due to the net investment rather than the subsidiary's operations. For these reasons, the cumulative translation adjustments balance is reported as a component of accumulated other comprehensive income (AOCI) in the stockholders' equity section of the U.S. parent entity's consolidated statement of financial position. This balance essentially equates the total debits of the subsidiary (now expressed in U.S. dollars) with the total credits (also in dollars). It also may be determined directly, as shown next, to verify the translation process.

4. The translation adjustments credit of $30.70 is calculated as follows for the differences between the exchange rate of $1.62 at the end of the year and the applicable exchange rates used to translate changes in net assets:

Net assets at inception (land and building of $1,200,000 – Portion financed by mortgage of $800,000)	400 × ($1.62 – $1.50)	=	$48.00	credit
Net income	60 × ($1.62 – $1.55)	=	4.20	credit
Dividends declared	20 × ($1.62 – $1.58)	=	0.80	debit
Translation adjustment			$51.40	credit

5. The translation adjustments balance that appears as a component of AOCI in the stockholders' equity section is cumulative in nature. Consequently, the change in this balance during the year is disclosed as a component of other comprehensive income (OCI) for the period. In the illustration, this balance went from zero to $51.40 at the end of 2010. In addition, assume the following occurred during the following year, 2011:

Italian Company
STATEMENT OF FINANCIAL POSITION
at December 31
(€000 omitted)

Assets	*2011*	*2010*	*Increase/(Decrease)*
Cash	€ 200	€ 100	€100
Accounts receivable, net	—	40	(40)
Land	300	200	100
Building, net	960	980	(20)
Total assets	€1,460	€1,320	€140
Liabilities and Stockholders' Equity			
Accounts payable	€ 100	€ 60	€ 40
Unearned rent	0	20	(20)
Mortgage payable	900	800	100
Common stock	80	80	0
Additional paid-in capital	320	320	0
Retained earnings	60	40	20
Total liabilities and stockholders' equity	€1,460	€1,320	€140

Italian Company
STATEMENT OF INCOME AND RETAINED EARNINGS
for the Year Ended December 31, 2011
(€000 omitted)

Revenues	€440
Operating expenses (including depreciation of €20)	340
Net income	100
Retained earnings, Jan. 1, 2011	40
Less dividends declared	(80)
Retained earnings, Dec. 31, 2011	€ 60

Exchange rates were

€1 = $1.62 at the beginning of 2011

€1 = $1.65 weighted-average for 2011

€1 = $1.71 at the end of 2011

€1 = $1.68 when dividends were declared in 2011 and additional land bought by incurring mortgage.

The translation process for 2011 is illustrated next.

Italian Company
STATEMENT OF FINANCIAL POSITION TRANSLATION
(Euro is the functional currency)
at December 31, 2011
(€/$000 omitted)

Assets	*Euros*	*Exchange rate*	*U.S. dollars*
Cash	€ 200	1.71	$ 342.00
Land	300	1.71	513.00
Building, net	960	1.71	1,641.60
Total assets	€ 1,460		$2,496.60
Liabilities and Stockholders' Equity			
Accounts payable	€ 100	1.71	$ 171.00
Mortgage payable	900	1.71	1,539.00
Common stock	80	1.50	120.00
Additional paid-in capital	320	1. 50	480.00
Retained earnings	60	See income statement	92.00
Translation adjustments	—	See computation below	94.60
Total liabilities and stockholders' equity	€ 1,460		$2,496.60

Italian Company
STATEMENT OF INCOME AND RETAINED EARNINGS
STATEMENT TRANSLATION
(Euro is the functional currency)
for the Year Ended December 31, 2011
(€/$000 omitted)

	Euros	*Exchange rate*	*U.S. dollars*
Revenues	€ 440	1.65	$ 726.00
Expenses (including depreciation of €10 [$12.50])	340	1.65	561.00
Net income	100	1.65	165.00
Retained earnings, January 1, 2011	40	—	61.40
Less dividends declared	(80)	1.68	(134.40)
Retained earnings, December 31, 2011	€ 60		$ 92.00

Italian Company
STATEMENT OF CASH FLOWS
STATEMENT TRANSLATION
(Euro is the functional currency)
for the Year Ended December 31, 2011
(€/$000 omitted)

	Euros	Exchange rate	U.S. dollars
Operating activities			
Net income	€ 100	1.65	$165.00
Adjustments to reconcile net income to net cash provided by operating activities			
Depreciation	20	1.65	33.00
Decrease in accounts receivable	40	1.65	66.00
Increase in accounts payable	40	1.65	66.00
Decrease in unearned rent	(20)	1.65	(33.00)
Net cash provided by operating activities	180		297.00
Investing activities			
Purchase of land	(100)	1.68	(168.00)
Net cash used by investing activities	(100)		(168.00)
Financing activities			
Mortgage payable	100	1.68	168.00
Dividends	(80)	1.68	(134.40)
Net cash provided by financing activities	20		33.60
Effect of exchange rate changes on cash	N/A		17.40
Increase in cash and equivalents	100		180.00
Cash at beginning of year	100		162.00
Cash at end of year	€ 200	1.71	$342.00

Using the analysis presented before, the change in the translation adjustment attributable to 2011 is computed as

Net assets at January 1, 2011	€ 440	($1.71 – $1.62)	=	$39.60	credit
Net income for 2011	€ 100	($1.71 – $1.65)	=	6.00	credit
Dividends for 2011	€ 80	($1.71 – $1.68)	=	2.40	debit
Total				$43.20	credit

The balance in the cumulative translation adjustment component of AOCI at the end of 2011 is $94.60. ($51.40 from 2010 and $43.20 from 2011.)

6. The use of the equity method by the U.S. parent entity in accounting for the subsidiary would result in these journal entries (in $000s), based on the information just presented

Original investment

	2010		2011	
Investment in Italian subsidiary	600*		–	
Cash		600		–

   * €80 of common stock + €320 of additional paid-in capital = €400 translated at €1. 50 = $600.

Earnings pickup

	2010		2011	
Investment in Italian subsidiary	93.00		165.00	
Equity in subsidiary income		93.00		165.00

Dividends received

	2010		2011	
Cash	31.60		134.40	
Investment in Italian subsidiary		31.60		134.40

Translation adjustments

	2010		2011	
Investment in Italian subsidiary	51.40		43.20	
OCI—Translation adjustments		51.40		43.20

Note that in applying the equity method to record this activity in the U.S. parent entity's accounting records, the parent's stockholders' equity should be the same whether the Italian subsidiary is consolidated or not. Since the subsidiary does not report the translation adjustments on its financial statements, care should be exercised so that it is not forgotten in the application of the equity method.

7. If the U.S. entity disposes of its investment in the Italian subsidiary, the cumulative translation adjustments balance becomes part of the gain or loss that results from the transaction and is eliminated. For example, assume that on January 2, 2012, the U.S. entity sells its entire investment for €465,000. The exchange rate at this date is €1 = $1.71. The balance in the investment account at December 31, 2011, is $786,600 as a result of the entries made previously.

	Investment in Italian Subsidiary	
1/1/10	600.00	
	93.00	31.60
	51.40	
1/1/11 balance	712.80	
	165.00	
	43.20	134.40
12/31/11 balance	786.60	

These entries would be made by the U.S. parent entity to reflect the sale of the investment:

Cash (€465 × $1.71 conversion rate)	795.15	
Investment in Italian subsidiary		786.60
Gain from sale of subsidiary		8.55
AOCI—Translation adjustments	94.60	
Gain from sale of subsidiary		94.60

If the U.S. entity had sold only a portion of its investment in the Italian subsidiary, only a pro rata portion of the accumulated translation adjustments balance would have become part of the gain or loss from the transaction. To illustrate, if 80% of the Italian subsidiary was sold for €372 on January 2, 2012, these journal entries would be made:

Cash (€372 × $1.71 exchange rate)	636.12	
Investment in Italian subsidiary (80% × $786.60)		629.28
Gain from sale of subsidiary		6.84
AOCI—Translation adjustments (80% × $94.60)	75.68	
Gain from sale of subsidiary		75.68

An exchange rate might not be available if there is a temporary suspension of foreign exchange trading. This occurred, for example, when Israel announced on December 30, 1988, that it would devalue its currency, the shekel, on January 2, 1989, at which time it would resume settling unexecuted foreign currency transactions. ASC 830-30-55 provides that, if exchangeability between two currencies is temporarily lacking at a transaction date or the date of the statement of financial position, the first subsequent rate at which exchanges could be made is to be used to implement ASC 830. While this circumstance has been rare, it could happen again.

Case Study 2

Example of the remeasurement method

Facts

In the previous situation, the euro was the functional currency because the Italian subsidiary's cash flows were primarily in euros. Assume, however, that the financing of the land and building was denominated in U.S. dollars instead of euros and that the mortgage payable is denominated in U.S. dollars (i.e., it must be repaid in U.S. dollars). Although the rents collected and the majority of the cash flows for expenses are in euros, management has decided that, due to the manner of financing, the U.S. dollar is the functional currency. The accounting records, however, are maintained in euros.

Required

Translate the Italian Company's financial statements into U.S. dollars using the remeasurement method.

Solution

Italian Company
STATEMENT OF FINANCIAL POSITION (REMEASUREMENT)
(U.S. dollar is the functional currency)
at December 31, 2010
(€/$000 omitted)

Assets	Euros	Exchange rate	U.S. dollars
Cash	€ 100	1.62	$ 162.00
Accounts receivable, net	40	1.62	64.80
Land	200	1.50	300.00
Building, net	980	1.50	1,470.00
Total assets	€1,320		$1,996.80
Liabilities and Stockholders' Equity			
Accounts payable	€ 60	1.62	$ 97.20
Unearned rent	20	1.58	31.60
Mortgage payable	800	1.62	1,296.00
Common stock	80	1.50	120.00
Additional paid-in capital	320	1.50	480.00
Retained earnings	40	(See income statement)	(28.00)
Total liabilities and stockholders' equity	€1,320		$1,996.80

Italian Company
STATEMENT OF INCOME AND RETAINED EARNINGS (REMEASUREMENT)
(U.S. dollar is the functional currency)
for the Year Ended December 31, 2010
(€/$000 omitted)

	Euros	Exchange rate	U.S. dollars
Revenues	€ 400	1.55	$620.00
Expenses (not including depreciation)	(320)	1.55	496.00
Depreciation expense	(20)	1.50	(30.00)
Remeasurement loss	—	See analysis below	(90.40)
Net income (loss)	60	—	(3.60)
Retained earnings, January 1	—	—	—
Less dividends declared	(20)	1.58	(31.60)
Retained earnings, December 31	€ 40		$(28.00)

Italian Company
REMEASUREMENT LOSS
(U.S. dollar is the functional currency)
for the Year Ended December 31, 2010
(€/$000 omitted)

	Euros		Exchange rate	U.S. dollars	
	Debit	Credit		Debit	Credit
Cash	€ 100		1.62	$ 162.00	
Accounts receivable, net	40		1.62	64.80	
Land	200		1.50	300.00	
Building, net	980		1.50	1,470.00	
Accounts payable		€ 60	1.62		$ 97.20
Unearned rent		20	1.58		31.60
Mortgage payable		800	1.62		1,296.00
Common stock		80	1.50		120.00
Additional paid-in capital		320	1.50		480.00
Retained earnings		—	—	—	—
Dividends declared	20		1.58	31.60	
Revenues		400	1.55		620.00
Operating expenses	320		1.55	496.00	
Depreciation expenses	20		1.50	30.00	
Totals	€1,680	€1,680		$2,554.40	$ 2,644.80
Remeasurement loss				90.40	
Totals				$2,644.80	$ 2,644.80

Italian Company
STATEMENT OF CASH FLOWS (REMEASUREMENT)
(U.S. dollar is the functional currency)
for the Year Ended December 31, 2010
(€/$000 omitted)

	Euros	Exchange rate	U.S. dollars
Operating activities		See income	
Net income (loss)	€ 60	statement	$ 3.60
Adjustments to reconcile net income to			
net cash provided by operating activities			
		See income	
Remeasurement loss	—	statement	90.40
Depreciation	20	1.50	30.00
Increase in accounts receivable	(40)	1.55	(62.00)
Increase in accounts payable	60	1.55	93.00
Increase in unearned rent	20	1.58	31.60
Net cash provided by operating activities	120		186.60
Investing activities			
Purchase of land	(200)	1.50	(300.00)
Purchase of building	(1,000)	1.50	(1,500.00)
Net cash used by investing activities	(1,200)		(1,800.00)
Financing activities			
Proceeds from issuance of common	400	1.50	600.00
Proceeds from mortgage payable	800	1.50	1,200.00
Dividends paid	(20)	1.58	(31.60)
Net cash provided by financing activities	1,180		1,768.40
Effect of exchange rate changes on cash	N/A		7.00
Increase in cash and equivalents	100		162.00
Cash at beginning of year	0		0
Cash at end of year	€ 100	1.62	$ 162.00

Note these points concerning the remeasurement method:

1. Assets and liabilities that have historical cost balances (nonmonetary assets and liabilities) are remeasured by using historical exchange rates (i.e., the rates in effect when the transactions giving rise to the balance first occurred). Monetary assets and monetary liabilities, cash, and those items that will be settled in cash are remeasured by using the current exchange rate at the date of the statement of financial position. In 2011, the unearned rent from year-end 2010 of €10 would be remeasured at the rate of €1 = $1.58. The unearned rent at the end of 2010 is not considered a monetary liability. Therefore, the $1.58 historical exchange rate is used for all applicable future years. See the appendix at the end of this chapter for a listing of accounts that are remeasured using historical exchange rates.

2. Revenues and expenses that occur frequently during a period are remeasured, for practical purposes, by using the weighted-average exchange rate for the period. Revenues and expenses that represent allocations of historical balances (e.g., depreciation, cost of goods sold, and amortization of intangibles) are remeasured using historical exchange rates. Note that this is a different treatment as compared to the current rate method.

3. If the functional currency is the U.S. dollar rather than the local foreign currency, the amounts of specific line items presented in the reconciliation of net income to net cash flow from operating activities will be different for nonmonetary items (e.g., depreciation).

4. The calculation of the remeasurement gain (loss), in a purely mechanical sense, is the amount needed to make the dollar debits equal the dollar credits in the Italian entity's trial balance.

5. The remeasurement loss of $90.40 is reported on the U.S. parent entity's consolidated income statement because the U.S. dollar is the functional currency. When the reporting currency is the functional currency, as it is in this example, it is assumed that all of the foreign entity's transactions occurred in U.S. dollars (even if this was not the case). Accordingly, remeasurement gains and losses are taken immediately to the income statement in the year in which they occur as they can be expected to have direct cash flow effects on the parent entity. They are not deferred as a translation adjustments component of AOCI as they were when the functional currency was the euro (applying the current rate method).

6. The use of the equity method of accounting for the subsidiary would result in these entries by the U.S. parent entity during 2010:

Original investment

| Investment in Italian subsidiary | 600.00 | |
| Cash | | 600.00 |

Earnings (loss) pickup

| Investment in Italian subsidiary | 3.60 | |
| Equity in subsidiary income | | 3.60 |

Dividends received

| Cash | 31.60 | |
| Investment in Italian subsidiary | | 31.60 |

Note that remeasurement gains and losses are included in the subsidiary's net income (net loss) as determined in U.S. dollars before the earnings (loss) pickup is made by the U.S. entity.

7. In economies in which—per ASC 830-10-45—cumulative inflation is greater than 100% over a three-year period, FASB requires that the functional currency be the reporting currency, that is, the U.S. dollar. Projections of future inflation cannot be used to satisfy this threshold condition. The remeasurement method must be used in this situation even though the factors indicate the local currency is the functional currency. FASB made this decision in order to prevent the evaporation of the foreign entity's fixed assets, a result that would occur if the local currency was the functional currency.

RECOGNITION OF EXCHANGE DIFFERENCES

Exchange differences arising on monetary items are reported in profit or loss in the period, with one exception.

The exception is that exchange differences arising on monetary items that form part of the reporting entity's net investment in a foreign operation are recognized in the consolidated financial statements within a separate component of equity. They are recognized in profit or loss on disposal of the net investment.

The exchange difference arising on monetary items that form part of the reporting entity's net investment in a foreign operation is recognized in profit or loss in the entity financial statements.

TRANSLATION OF A FOREIGN OPERATION

When preparing consolidated financials, it is normal to deal with entities that utilize different currencies. The financial statements should be translated into the presentation currency.

Any goodwill and fair value adjustments are treated as assets and liabilities of the foreign entity and therefore are retranslated at each date of the statement of financial position at the closing spot rate.

Dividends paid in a foreign currency by a subsidiary to its parent company may lead to exchange differences in the parent's financial statements and will not be eliminated on consolidation but recognized in profit or loss.

Case Study 3

Facts

An entity has a foreign subsidiary whose functional currency is the euro. The functional currency of the entity is the dollar. On January 1, 2009, when the exchange rate was $1= €1.5, the entity loans the subsidiary $3 million. At December 31, 2009, the loan has not been repaid and is regarded as part of the net investment in the foreign subsidiary, as settlement of the loan is not planned or likely to occur in the foreseeable future. The exchange rate at December 31, 2009, is $1 = €2, and the average rate for the year was $1 = €1.75.

Required

Explain how this loan would be treated in the entity's and consolidated financial statements.

Solution

There is no exchange difference in the entity's financial statements, as the loan has been made in dollars. In the foreign subsidiary's financial statements, the loan is translated into its own functional currency (euro) at the rate of $1= €1.5, or €4.5 million as of January 1, 2010. At year-end, the closing rate will be used to translate this loan. This will result in the loan being restated at €6 million (= $3 million × 2), giving an exchange loss of €1.5 million, which will be shown in the subsidiary's income statement.

In the consolidated financial statements, this exchange loss will be translated at the average rate, as it is in the subsidiary's income statement, giving a loss of (= $1.5/1.75 million), or $857,000. This will be recognized in equity.

There will be a further exchange difference (gain) arising between the amount included in the subsidiary's income statement at the average rate and at the closing rate; that is, $857,000 minus $750,000 (= 1.5 million euros/2), or $107,000.

Thus the overall exchange difference is $750,000. This will be recognized in equity.

An alternative way of calculating this exchange loss follows. The loan at January 1, 2009, is €4.5 million. On retranslation, this becomes $2.25 million at December 31, 2009 (= €4.5/2).The original loan was $3 million, so there is an exchange loss of (= $3 − 2.25) million, or $0.75 million.

DISCLOSURE

An entity should disclose

- The aggregate transaction gain or loss included in determining net income for the period.
- A rate change that occurs after the date of the reporting entity's financial statements and its effects on unsettled balances pertaining to foreign currency transactions, if significant. If disclosed, the disclosure shall include consideration of changes in unsettled transactions from the date of the financial statements to the date the rate changed. In some cases, it may not be practicable to determine these changes; if so, that fact shall be stated.
- Management is encouraged to provide an analysis and discussion of the effects of rate changes on the reported results of operations. This type of disclosure might include the mathematical effects of translating revenue and expenses at rates that are different from those used in a preceding period as well as the economic effects of rate changes, such as the effects on selling prices, sales volume, and cost structures. The purpose is to assist financial report users in understanding the broader economic implications of rate changes and to compare recent results with those of prior periods.

EXTRACTS FROM PUBLISHED FINANCIAL STATEMENTS

Bingo.com, Ltd. for the fiscal year ended December 31, 2008

Notes to Consolidated Financial Statements

2. Summary of significant accounting policies

d) Foreign currency

The consolidated financial statements are presented in United States dollars, the functional currency of the Company. The Company accounts for foreign currency transactions and translation of foreign currency financial statements under Statement of Financial Accounting Standards (SFAS) No. 52, *Foreign Currency Translation* (SFAS 52). Transaction amounts denominated in foreign currencies are translated at exchange rates prevailing at the transaction dates. Carrying values of monetary assets and liabilities are adjusted at each balance sheet date to reflect the exchange rate at that date. Nonmonetary assets and liabilities are translated at the exchange rate on the original transaction date.

Gains and losses from restatement of foreign currency monetary and nonmonetary assets and liabilities are included in income. Revenues and expenses are translated at the rates of exchange prevailing on the dates such items are recognized in earnings.

Ico Inc., for the fiscal year ended September 30, 2009

Notes to Consolidated Financial Statements

1. Summary of significant accounting policies

Currency Translation

Amounts in foreign currencies are translated into U.S. dollars. When local functional currency is translated to U.S. dollars, the effects are recorded as a separate component of Other Comprehensive Income (Loss). Exchange gains and losses resulting from foreign currency transactions are recognized in earnings. Net foreign currency transaction gains (losses) were not significant in fiscal years 2009, 2008 and 2007.

The fluctuations of the U.S dollar against the euro, British pound sterling, New Zealand dollar, Brazilian real, Malaysian ringgit, and Australian dollar have impacted the translation of revenues and expenses of the Company's international operations. The table below summarizes the impact of changing exchange rates for the above currencies for fiscal years 2009, 2008 and 2007.

	Years ended September 30		
	2009	*2008*	*2007*
Revenues	$(33.7) million	$29.1 million	$20.4 million
Operating income	0.7 million	1.6 million	1.2 million
Pretax income (loss)	0.9 million	1.3 million	1.0 million
Net income (loss)	0.8 million	1.0 million	0.9 million

MULTIPLE-CHOICE QUESTIONS

1. Which of these considerations would **not** be relevant in determining the entity's functional currency?
   (a) The currency that influences the costs of the entity.
   (b) The currency in which finance is generated.
   (c) The currency in which receipts from operating activities are retained.
   (d) The currency that is the most internationally acceptable for trading.

2. Foreign operations that are an integral part of the operations of the entity would have the same functional currency as the entity. Where a foreign operation functions independently from the parent, the functional currency will be
   (a) That of the parent.
   (b) Determined using the guidance for determining an entity's functional currency.
   (c) That of the country of incorporation.
   (d) The same as the presentation currency.

3. An entity started trading in country A, whose currency was the dollar. After several years, the entity expanded and exported its product to country B, whose currency was the euro. The functional currency of the entity was deemed to be the dollar but, by the end of 2010, 80% of the business was conducted in country B using the euro. At the end of 2009, 30% of the business was conducted in the euro.

The functional currency should
   (a) Remain the dollar.
   (b) Change to the euro at the beginning of 2010.
   (c) Change to the euro at the end of 2010.
   (d) Change to the euro at the end of 2010 if it is considered that the underlying transactions, events, and conditions of business have changed.

4. An entity started trading in country A, whose currency was the dollar. After several years, the entity expanded and exported its product to country B, whose currency was the euro. The business was conducted through a subsidiary in country B. The subsidiary is essentially an extension of the entity's own business, and the directors of the two entities are common. The functional currency of the subsidiary is
   (a) The dollar.
   (b) The euro.
   (c) The dollar or the euro.
   (d) Difficult to determine.

5. An entity whose functional currency is the foreign currency should translate the entity's foreign financial statements using the
   (a) Weighted-average method.
   (b) Current rate method.
   (c) Remeasurement method.

6. An entity acquired all the share capital of a foreign entity at a consideration of €9 million on June 30, 2009. The fair value of the net assets of the foreign entity at that date was €6 million. The functional currency of the entity is the dollar. The financial year-end of the entity is December 31, 2009. The exchange rates at June 30, 2009, and December 31, 2009, were €1.5 = $1 and €2 = $1 respectively.

What figure for goodwill should be included in the financial statements for the year ended December 31, 2009?
   (a) $2 million
   (b) €3 million
   (c) $1.5 million
   (d) $3 million

7. An entity has a subsidiary that operates in a country where the exchange rate fluctuates wildly and there are seasonal variations in the income and expenditure patterns. Which of the following rates of exchange probably would be used to translate the foreign subsidiary's income statement?
   (a) Year-end spot rate.
   (b) Average for the year.
   (c) Average of the quarter-end rates.
   (d) Average rates for each individual month of the year.

9. An entity has a subsidiary that operates in a foreign country. The subsidiary issued a legal notice of a dividend to the parent of €2.4 million, and this was recorded in the parent entity's financial statements. The exchange rate at that date was €2 = $1. The functional currency of the entity is the dollar. At the date of receipt of the dividend, the exchange rate had moved to €3 = $1. The exchange difference arising on the dividend would be treated in which way in the financial statements?
   (a) No exchange difference will arise as it will be eliminated on consolidation.
   (b) An exchange difference of $400,000 will be taken to equity.
   (c) An exchange difference of $400,000 will be taken to the parent entity's income statement and the consolidated income statement.
   (d) An exchange difference of $400,000 will be taken to the parent entity's income statement only.

Chapter 23

EARNINGS PER SHARE (ASC 260)

BACKGROUND AND INTRODUCTION

Earnings per share (EPS) is an indicator widely used by both actual and prospective investors to gauge the profitability of a corporation. Its purpose is to indicate how effective an entity has been in using the resources provided by its common stockholders. In its simplest form, EPS is net income (loss) divided by the number of shares of outstanding common stock.

Any inconsistency of accounting policies between entities will result in a lack of comparability of the earnings per share figure. ASC 260 enhances financial reporting by ensuring that there is at least consistency in the calculation of the denominator in the earnings per share statistic.

ASC 260 applies to

- Entities whose common stock or potential common stock is publicly traded or that are in the process of issuing stock in the public markets.
- Entities that voluntarily choose to disclose.

DEFINITIONS OF KEY TERMS
(in accordance with IAS 33)

Antidilution. An increase in earnings per share or reduction in net loss per share resulting from the conversion, exercise, or contingent issuance of certain securities.

Basic earnings per share. The portion of net income available to each share of common stock outstanding during the reporting period.

Common stock. Stock that is subordinate to all other stock of the issuer.

Dilution. A reduction in earnings per share or an increase in net loss per share resulting from assuming that convertible securities have been converted or that options and warrants have been exercised or other shares have been issued upon the fulfillment of certain conditions.

Potential common stock. A security or other contract that may entitle its holder to obtain common stock during the reporting period or after the end of the reporting period.

COMMON STOCK

Common stock participates in profit for the period only after other types of stock, such as preferred stock, have participated.

An entity may have more than one class of common stock. For example, Entity A has two classes of "common" stock, Class X and Class Y. If Class X is entitled to a fixed dividend of $10 per share plus a dividend of 5%, and Class Y is entitled to a dividend of 5% only, then Class X stock is not common stock, as the fixed dividend per share ($10) creates a preference over Class Y shares, and hence Class Y shares are subordinate to Class X shares.

PRESENTATION OF EARNINGS PER SHARE

Entities with simple capital structures, those with only common stock outstanding, should present basic per-share amounts for income from continuing operations and for net income on the face of the income statement. All other entities should present on the face of the income statement both basic and diluted earnings per share for profit or loss from continuing operations and net income.

Basic and diluted earnings per share must be presented with equal prominence for all periods presented, even if the amounts are negative. If a discontinued operation is reported, then basic and diluted amounts per share for the discontinued operation must be disclosed on the face of the income statement or in the notes.

BASIC EARNINGS PER SHARE

Basic earnings per share =

$$\frac{\text{Net profit or loss attributable to common stockholders}}{\text{Weighted-average number of common shares outstanding during the period}}$$

Earnings are calculated

- As amounts attributable to the common stockholders in respect of profit or loss from continuing operations and net profit or loss.
- After all expenses including taxes and noncontrolling interests.
- After cumulative preferred dividend *for the period* whether earned or not.
- After noncumulative preferred dividend declared *for the period.*
- After other adjustments relating to preferred shares.

(Cumulative preferred dividends for the prior periods are ignored for purposes of the calculation but, however, must be disclosed in the notes to the financial statements.)

> **Basic Earnings per Share**
>
> The number of common shares is the weighted-average number of common shares outstanding during the period.

- The number of common shares at the beginning of the period are added to the number of shares issued during the period less the number of shares bought back in the period.
- Shares issued and bought back are multiplied by a time-weighting factor dependent on when the event took place.
- Shares are included from the date the consideration is receivable.
- Partly paid shares are included as fractional shares to the extent that they are entitled to participate in dividends during the period relative to a fully paid common share. To the extent that partly paid shares are not entitled to participate in dividends during the period, they are treated as the equivalent of warrants or options.
- Contingently issuable shares are included when the conditions have been satisfied.
- Common shares issued as part of a business combination are included from the acquisition date.

An entity may increase or reduce its common stock without a change in its resources. Examples of this are bonus issues, stock dividends, stock splits (i.e., where shares are issued for no consideration), and reverse stock splits (consolidation of shares). In these cases, the weighted-average number of shares is adjusted in line with the transaction as if the event had occurred at the beginning of the period. All periods presented should be adjusted for such events.

If the bonus issue, stock dividend, and other similar events occurred after the date of the statement of financial position but before the financial statements are authorized, then the earnings per share calculations should reflect these changes. This rule applies also to prior periods and to diluted earnings per share.

Case Study 1

Facts

Entity A has a profit after tax of $30 million for the year ended December 31, 2010. These appropriations of profit have not been included in this amount:

		$m
(1)	Arrears of cumulative preferred dividend for 2 years ended December 31, 2010	8
(2)	Common stock dividends	10
(3)	Preferred share premium payable on redemption—appropriation of profit	2
(4)	Exceptional profit (net of tax)	8

These share transactions occurred during the year ended December 31, 2010. The entity had 6 million common shares of $2 outstanding at January 1, 2010:

Date	Common shares issued/purchased	
January 1	500,000	Issued at $5 per share – $1 paid to date: entitled to participate in dividends to the extent paid up
April 1	1,200,000	Full market price $3 per share issue
July 1	(800,000)	Purchase of own shares at $3.5 per share

Required

Calculate basic earnings per share.

Solution

	$m
Profit after tax	30
Plus: Exceptional profit	8
Less: Preferred dividend (current year)	(4)
Preferred share appropriation	(2)
Profit available for common stockholders	32

Date	Number of shares ('000)	Weighting (months)	Weighted-average ('000)
1/1/10	6,000	1	6,000
1/1/10	(500 × 1/5)	1	100
4/1/10	1,200	9/12	900
7/1/10	(800)	6/12	(400)
			3,300
	('000)		
Basic earnings per share	32,000/6,600	=	$4.85

Case Study 2

Facts

A had a two-for-one share split on December 31, 2010, in which two shares were awarded for every share held, and in 2009 there was a reported basic earnings per share of $6.60.

Required

Show the effect on the basic earnings per share calculated in Case Study 1 and the previous year's basic earnings per share. State the effect on your answer if the share split had occurred on February 1, 2011, before the approval of the financial statements for the year ended December 31 2010.

Solution

2009:	Basic earnings per share	$6.60 \times 1/3$	=	$2.20
2010:	Basic earnings per share	$\dfrac{32,000}{(6,600 + 6,600 \times 2)}$	=	$1.62

If the share split had occurred on February 1, 2011, then this would still have been taken into account in the calculation, as such events after the date of the statement of financial position should be adjusted retrospectively.

RIGHTS ISSUES

An offer to existing stockholders to purchase additional shares of common stock in accordance with an agreement for a specified amount (which is generally substantially less than the fair value of the shares) for a given period.

A rights issue whose exercise price at issuance is below the fair value of the stock contains a bonus element. If a rights issue contains a bonus element (somewhat similar to a stock dividend) and is offered to all existing stockholders, basic and diluted EPS are adjusted retroactively for the bonus element for all periods presented.

If the ability to exercise the rights issue is contingent on some event other than the passage of time, this retroactive adjustment does not apply until the contingency is resolved.

DILUTED EARNINGS PER SHARE

Diluted earnings per share (DEPS) represents the earnings attributable to each share of common stock after giving effect to all potentially dilutive securities that were outstanding during the period. The computation of DEPS requires that two steps be performed:

1. Identify all potentially dilutive securities.
2. Compute dilution, the effects that the other dilutive securities have on net income and common shares outstanding.

Identification of Potentially Dilutive Securities

Dilutive securities are those that have the potential of being exercised and reducing the EPS figure. Some examples of dilutive securities identified by ASC 260 are convertible debt, convertible preferred stock, options, warrants, participating securities, two-class common stocks, and contingent shares.

Computation of DEPS

The second step in the process is the actual computation of DEPS. Basically two methods are used to incorporate the effects of other dilutive securities on EPS:

1. The treasury stock method
2. The if-converted method

Treasury Stock Method

The treasury stock method, which is used for the exercise of most warrants or options, requires that DEPS be computed as if the options or warrants were exercised at the beginning of the period (or actual date of issuance, if later) and that the funds obtained from the exercise were used to purchase (reacquire) the company's common stock at the average market price for the period. The incremental shares (the difference between the number of shares issued and the number of shares assumed purchased) are included in the denominator of the DEPS calculation.

If-Converted Method

The if-converted method is used for those securities that are currently sharing in the earnings of the company through the receipt of interest or dividends as preferred securities but that have the potential for sharing in the earnings as common stock (e.g., convertible bonds or convertible preferred stock). The if-converted method logically recognizes that the convertible security can share in the earnings of the company only as one or the other, not both. Thus, the dividends or interest less income tax effects applicable to the convertible security as a preferred security are not recognized in income available to common stockholders used to compute DEPS, and the weighted-average number of shares is adjusted to reflect the assumed conversion as of the beginning of the year (or actual date of issuance, if later).

Case Study 3

Facts

Net profit for year 2010	$3 million
Common shares outstanding during 2010	$10 million
Average fair value of one common share: year 2010	$8
Shares under option during 2010, convertible at $6 per share	2 million

Required

Calculate basic and diluted earnings per share using the treasury stock method.

Solution

Basic earnings per share

$$\frac{\$3 \text{ million}}{10 \text{ million}} = \$0.30$$

Diluted earnings per share

Shares under option	2 million
Number of shares that would have been issued at fair value if converted (2 million × $6 = $12 million): $12 million/$8 =	(1.5 million)
Therefore shares for "no consideration" (2 million – 1.5 million)	(0.5 million)

Diluted earnings per share

$$\frac{\$3 \text{ million}}{10.5 \text{ million}} = \$0.2857$$

Case Study 4

Facts

An entity issues 4 million convertible bonds at January 1, 2010. The bonds mature in three years and are issued at their face value of $10. The bonds attract interest arrears. Each bond can be converted into two common shares. The company can settle the principal amount of the bonds in common shares or in cash.

When the bonds are issued, the interest rate for a similar debt without the conversion rights is 10%. At the issue date the market price of a common share is $4. Ignore taxation. The company is likely to settle the contract by issuing shares.

Profit attributable to common shareholders to December 31, 2010	$33 million
Common shares outstanding	10 million

Allocation of proceeds of bond

Liability	$30 million
Equity	$10 million
Total	$40 million

Required

Calculate basic and diluted earnings per share for the year to December 31, 2010, using the if-converted method.

Solution

$$\text{Basic EPS} \qquad \frac{\$33 \text{ million}}{10 \text{ million}} = \$3.30 \text{ per share}$$

$$\text{Diluted EPS} \qquad \frac{(\$33 \text{ million} + \text{interest } 10\% \text{ of } \$30 \text{ million})}{10 \text{ million} + 8 \text{ million}} = \frac{\$36 \text{ million}}{18 \text{ million}} = \$2$$

PRESENTATION

An entity with a complex capital structure, whose securities are traded on a securities exchange or that is in process of public issuance, must present on the face of the income statement, basic and diluted earnings per share for both

- Profit or loss from continuing operations attributable to the common stockholders of the parent entity.
- Profit or loss attributable to the common stockholders of the parent entity for the period for each class of common shares that has a different right to share in profit for the period.

Basic and diluted EPS must be presented with equal prominence for all periods presented.

Basic and diluted EPS must be presented even if the amounts are negative (i.e., a loss per share).

If an entity reports a discontinued operation, basic and diluted amounts per share must be disclosed for the discontinued operation either on the face of the income statement or in the notes to the financial statements.

DISCLOSURES

- Basic and diluted EPS should be presented on the face of the income statement for each class of common stock.
- Basic and diluted EPS are presented with equal prominence.
- If an entity reports a discontinued operation, it should report the basic and diluted amounts per share for the discontinued operation.
- An entity should report basic and diluted EPS even if it is a loss per share.
- The amounts used as the numerators in calculating basic and diluted EPS, and reconciliation of those amounts to profit or loss attributable to the parent for the period.
- The effect that has been given to preferred dividends in arriving at income available to common stockholders in computing basic EPS.
- Instruments (including contingently issuable shares) that could potentially dilute BEPS in the future but were not included in the calculation of DEPS because they are antidilutive for the period(s) presented.
- A description of those common stock transactions or potential common stock transactions that occur after the date of the statement of financial position and that would have changed significantly the number of common stock or potential common stock outstanding at the end of the period if those transactions had occurred before the end of the reporting period. Examples include issues and redemptions of common stock, warrants, and options.

EXTRACTS FROM PUBLISHED FINANCIAL STATEMENTS

Whole Foods Market, Inc., for the fiscal year ended September 27, 2009

15. Earnings per Share

The computation of basic earnings per share is based on the number of weighted-average common shares outstanding during the period.

The computation of diluted earnings per share for fiscal year 2009 does not include options to purchase approximately 16.5 million shares of common stock or the conversion of Series A Preferred Stock to approximately 24.1 million shares of common stock due to their antidilutive effect. The computation of diluted earnings per share does not include approximately 70,000 shares of common stock related to the zero-coupon convertible subordinated debentures at the end of fiscal year 2008 and options to purchase approximately 13.4 million and 10.6 million shares of common stock at the end of fiscal years 2008 and 2007, respectively, due to their antidilutive effect.

A reconciliation of the numerators and denominators of the basic and diluted earnings per share calculations follows (in thousands, except per share amounts):

	2009	*2008*	*2007*
Income available to common shareholders (numerator for basic earnings per share)	$118,754	$114,524	$182,740
Interest on 5% zero-coupon convertible subordinated debentures, net of income taxes	—	—	98
Adjusted income available to common shareholders (numerator for diluted earnings per share)	$118,754	$114,524	$182,838
Weighted-average common shares outstanding (denominator for basic earnings per share)	140,414	139,886	140,088
Potential common shares outstanding:			
Assumed conversion of 5% zero-coupon convertible subordinated debentures	—	—	116
Incremental shares from assumed exercise of stock options	—	125	1,632
Weighted-average common shares outstanding and potential additional common shares outstanding (denominator for diluted earnings per share)	140,414	140,011	141,836
Basic earnings per share	$ 0.85	$ 0.82	$ 1.30
Diluted earnings per share	$ 0.85	$ 0.82	$ 1.29

MULTIPLE-CHOICE QUESTIONS

1. Entity A has a common "A" class, nonvoting share, which is entitled to a fixed dividend of 6% per annum. The "A" class common share will
   (a) Be included in the "per share" calculation after adjustment for the fixed dividend.
   (b) Be included in the "per share" calculation for EPS without adjustment for the fixed dividend.
   (c) Not be included in the "per share" calculation for EPS.
   (d) Be included in the calculation of diluted EPS.

2. Earnings per share is calculated before accounting for which of the following items?
   (a) Preferred dividend for the period.
   (b) Common stock dividend.
   (c) Taxation.
   (d) Noncontrolling interest.

3. Common stock issued as part of a business combination is included in the EPS calculation in the case of the "purchase" method from the
   (a) Beginning of the accounting period.
   (b) Date of acquisition.
   (c) End of the accounting period.
   (d) Midpoint of the accounting year.

4. When an entity makes a bonus issue/stock split/stock dividend or a rights issue, then
   (a) The previous year's EPS is not adjusted for the issue.
   (b) The previous year's EPS is adjusted for the issue.
   (c) Only a note of the effect on the previous year's EPS is made.
   (d) Only the diluted EPS for the previous year is adjusted.

5. If a stock option is converted on March 31, 20X1, then
   (a) The potential common stock (stock option) is included in diluted EPS up to March 31, 20X1, and in basic EPS from the date converted to the year-end (both weighted accordingly).
   (b) The common stock is not included in the diluted EPS calculation but is included in basic EPS.
   (c) The common stock is not included in the basic EPS but is included in diluted EPS.
   (d) The effects of the stock option are included only in previous year's EPS calculation.

6. In calculating whether potential common stock is dilutive, the profit figure used as the "control number" is
   (a) Net profit after taxation (including discontinued operations).
   (b) Net profit from continuing operations.
   (c) Net profit before tax (including discontinued operations).
   (d) Retained profit for the year after dividends.

7. An entity needs to disclose diluted EPS only if it differs from basic EPS by a material amount.
   (a) True.
   (b) False.

8. If a bonus issue occurs between the year-end and the date that the financial statements are authorized, then
   (a) EPS for both the current and the previous year is adjusted.
   (b) EPS for the current year only is adjusted.
   (c) No adjustment is made to EPS.
   (d) Diluted EPS only is adjusted.

9. The weighted-average number of shares outstanding during the period for all periods (other than the conversion of potential common shares) shall be adjusted for any
   (a) Change in the number of common shares without a change in resources.
   (b) Prior-year adjustment.
   (c) New issue of shares for cash.
   (d) Convertible instruments settled in cash.

Chapter 24

EMPLOYEE BENEFITS (ASC 715)

SCOPE

This Standard sets out the accounting and disclosure by employers for employee benefits.
The Standard identifies four main categories of employee benefits:

1. Short-term employee benefits, such as wages, salaries, vocational holiday benefit, sick pay, profit sharing or bonus plans paid within 12 months of the end of the period, and nonmonetary benefits, such as medical care and so on, for current employees
2. Postemployment benefits, such as pensions, postemployment medical benefits, and postemployment life insurance
3, Termination benefits, such as severance pay
4. Other long-term employee benefits, including long-service or sabbatical leave

Postemployment benefits are categorized as either defined contribution plans or defined benefit plans.

DEFINITIONS OF KEY TERMS
(in accordance with ASC 715)

Asset gains and losses. Differences between the actual return on plan assets during a period and the expected return on plan assets for that period. Asset gains and losses include both changes reflected in the market-related value of plan assets and changes not yet reflected in the market-related value (i.e., the difference between the fair value of assets and the market-related value).

Current service cost. The increase in the present value of the defined benefit obligation that occurs as a result of employee service in the current period.

Interest cost. The increase in the period in the present value of the defined benefit obligation that arises because the benefits payable are one year closer to the settlement of the plan.

Multiemployer plan. A pension plan or other postretirement benefit plan to which two or more unrelated employers contribute, usually pursuant to one or more collective bargaining agreements.

Past service cost. The increased present value of a defined benefit obligation for employee service in previous periods that has arisen because of the introduction of changes to the benefits payable to employees. Past service costs may be positive or negative depending on whether the benefits are improved or reduced.

Plan assets. Those assets held by the employee benefit fund, including any qualifying insurance policies.

Present value of a defined benefit obligation. The present value before deducting any plan assets or any expected payments required to settle the obligation that has occurred as a result of the service of employees in the current and previous periods.

Projected unfunded benefit obligation. The excess of the projected benefit obligation over the plan assets.

Return on plan assets. The interest, dividends, and any other income that is derived from the plan assets together with any realized or unrealized gains or losses on those assets less the cost of administering the plan and any tax payable by the plan.

DEFINED CONTRIBUTION PLANS AND DEFINED BENEFIT PLANS— CLASSIFICATION

In defined contribution plans, an entity pays a fixed contribution into a separate entity (fund), and that entity will have no legal or constructive obligation to pay further contributions if the fund does not have sufficient assets to pay employee benefits relating to employee service in the current and prior periods. An entity should recognize contributions to a defined contribution plan where an employee has rendered service in exchange for those contributions.

All other postemployment benefit plans are classified as defined benefit plans. Defined benefit plans can be unfunded, partly funded, or wholly funded.

DEFINED BENEFIT PLANS

ASC 715 requires an entity to account not only for its legal obligation to defined benefit plans but also for any constructive obligation that arises.

In accounting for defined benefit plans, an entity should determine the present value of any defined benefit obligation and the fair value of any plan assets with such regularity that the amount shown in the financial statements does not differ materially from the amounts that would be determined at the date of the statement of financial position.

Defined benefit plans should use the projected unit credit method to measure their obligations and costs.

DEFINED CONTRIBUTION PLANS

Under a defined contribution plan, payments or benefits provided to employees may be simply distributions of total fund assets, or a third party—for example, an insurance entity—may assume the obligation to provide the agreed level of payments or benefits to the employees. The employer is not required to make up any shortfall in the fund's assets.

CONTRASTING DEFINED BENEFIT AND DEFINED CONTRIBUTION

Under the defined benefits plan, the benefits payable to the employees are not based solely on the amount of the contributions, as in a defined contribution plan; rather, they are determined by the terms of the defined benefit plan.

This means that the risks remain with the employer, and the employer's obligation is to provide the agreed amount of benefits to current and former employees. The benefits normally are based on such factors as age, length of service, and compensation.

The employer retains the investment and actual risks of the plan. Consequently, the accounting for defined benefit plans is more complex than that for defined contributions plans.

Case Study 1

Facts

According to the pension plan of an entity, the employees and entity contribute 5% of the employee's salary to the plan, and the employee is guaranteed a return of the contributions plus 3% a year by the employer.

Required

What classification would be given to the above pension plan?

Solution

It is a defined benefit plan, as the employer has guaranteed a fixed rate of return and therefore carries the risk.

ACCOUNTING FOR DEFINED CONTRIBUTION PLANS

The accounting for a defined contribution plan is fairly simple because the employer's obligation for each period is determined by the amount that had to be contributed to the plan for that period.

Contributions can be based on a formula that uses employee compensation as the basis for its calculation.

There are no actuarial assumptions required to measure the obligation or expense, and there are no actuarial gains or losses to be experienced by the employer.

The employer recognizes the contribution payable at the end of each period based on employee service during that period. This amount is reduced by any payments made to employees in the period.

If the employer has made payments in excess of the required amount, this excess is treated as a prepayment to the extent that the excess will lead to reduction in future contributions or refund of cash.

ACCOUNTING FOR DEFINED BENEFIT PLANS

The obligation of an employer under a defined benefit plan is to provide an agreed amount of benefits to current and former employees in the future. Benefits may be in the form of cash payments or could be in-kind in terms of medical or other benefits.

Normally benefits will be based on age, length of service, and wage and salary levels. Pensions and other long-term benefits plans basically are measured in the same way. Actuarial gains and losses of long-term benefits plans other than pensions are reported immediately in net income.

The defined benefit plan can be unfunded, partially funded, or wholly funded by the employer. The employer's contributions, if any, are to a separate entity or fund that is legally separate from the reporting entity.

This fund then pays the benefits. The payment of benefits depends, to an extent, on the fund's financial position and the performance of its investments.

However, the payment of benefits also will depend on the employer's ability to pay and to make good any shortfall in the fund. The employer is essentially guaranteeing the fund's investment and actuarial risk. Absent a declaration of insolvency by the employer, it will be legally bound to pay the promised benefits, regardless of the condition of the separate retirement fund.

Accounting for defined benefit plans is more complex because actuarial assumptions are needed to determine the amount of the obligation as of any reporting date and the expenses to be recognized by the sponsor for the fiscal period then ended. Often the actual results differ from those determined under the actuarial valuation method. The difference between these results creates actuarial gains and losses.

Discounting is used because the obligations often will be settled several years after the employee gives the service. Usually actuaries are employed to calculate the defined benefit obligation and also the current and past service costs.

KEY INFORMATION: DEFINED BENEFIT PLANS

The entity must determine certain key information for each material employee benefit plan. The information required is listed next.

- A reliable estimate is required of the amount of the benefit that employees have earned in the current and prior period for services rendered.
- That benefit must be discounted using the projected unit credit method in order to determine the present value of the defined benefit obligation and the current service cost.
- The fair value of any plan assets should be determined.
- The total amount of actuarial gains and losses and the amount of those actuarial gains and losses that are to be recognized must be calculated.
- The past service costs should be determined in cases in which a plan has been introduced or an existing plan has been changed.
- The resulting gain or loss should be calculated in cases in which a plan has been curtailed, changed, or settled.

The entity must account not only for its legal obligation but also for any constructive obligation that arises from any informal practices. For example, the situation could arise wherein the entity has no realistic alternative but to pay employee benefits even though the formal terms of a defined benefit plan may permit an entity to terminate its obligation under the plan.

Case Study 2

Facts

A director of an entity receives a retirement benefit of 10% of his final salary per annum for his contractual period of three years. The director does not contribute to the plan. His anticipated salary over the three years is Year 1 $100,000, Year 2 $120,000, and Year 3 $144,000. Assume a discount rate of 5%.

Required

Calculate the current service cost, the pension liability, and the interest cost for the three years.

Solution

Year	$ Salary	$ Current service cost	$ Discounted current service cost	$ Interest cost (5% × liability)	$ Liability brought forward	$ Liability at year-end
1	100,000	14,400	13,061	–	–	13,061
2	120,000	14,400	13,714	653	13,061	27,428
3	144,000	14,400	14,400	1,372	27,428	43,200
Total		43,200	41,175	2,025		

STATEMENT OF FINANCIAL POSITION

The amount recognized in the statement of financial position could be either an asset or a liability calculated at the date of the statement of financial position.

The amount recognized will be

1. The present value of the defined benefit obligation, plus
2. Any actuarial gains less losses not yet recognized because the gains and losses fall outside the limits of the corridor, minus
3. Any past service cost not yet recognized, minus
4. The fair value of the plan assets at the date of the statement of financial position.

If the result of the preceding calculation is a positive amount, then a liability is incurred, and the unfunded projected benefit obligation is recorded in the statement of financial position. If the result is a negative amount, a pension asset is recorded.

Case Study 3

Facts

An entity has these balances relating to its defined benefit plan:

- Present value of the obligation: $33 million
- Fair value of plan assets: $37 million
- Actuarial losses: $3 million unrecognized
- Past service cost: $2 million unrecognized
- Present value of available future refunds and reduction in future contributions: $1 million

Required

Calculate the value that will be given to the net plan asset under ASC 715.

Solution

The negative amount (asset) determined under the Standard will be $33 million minus $37 million, minus $3 million, minus $2 million, which equals $9 million. An asset of $9 million will be recognized in the statement of financial position.

INCOME STATEMENT

The amount of the expense or income for a particular period is determined by a number of factors. The pension expense is the net of these items:

- Current service cost
- Interest cost
- The expected return on any plan assets and on any reimbursement rights
- Actuarial gains and losses to the extent recognized
- Past service cost to the extent that the Standard requires the entity to recognize it
- The effect of any curtailments or settlements

MEASURING THE DEFINED BENEFIT OBLIGATION

The entity should use the projected unit credit method to determine the present value of its defined benefit obligation, the related current service cost, and the past service cost.

This method looks at each period of service, which creates an additional increment of benefit entitlement. The method then measures each unit of benefit entitlement separately to build up the final obligation. The whole of the postemployment benefit obligation is discounted. The use of this method involves a number of actuarial assumptions. These assumptions are the entity's best estimate of the variables that will determine the final cost of the postemployment benefits provided. These variables include assumptions about mortality rates, change in retirement age, and financial assumptions, such as discount rates and benefit levels.

Any assumptions should be compatible, unbiased, and neither imprudent nor excessively conservative. The Standard provides guidance on certain key assumptions.

PLAN ASSETS

Plan assets are measured at fair value. Fair value is normally market value where available or an estimated value where it is not.

Fair value can be determined by discounting future expected cash flows using a discount rate that reflects risk and the maturity or expected disposal date of those assets. Plan assets specifically exclude

- Unpaid contributions due from the employer
- Nontransferable financial instruments issued by the entity and held by the fund
- Nonqualifying insurance policies

PENSION ASSETS AND LIABILITIES

Often an entity may have a number of employment benefit plans. Plan assets and plan liabilities from the different plans normally are presented separately in the statement of financial position.

The offsetting of assets and liabilities is permitted only where there is a legally enforceable right to use the surplus in one plan to settle the obligation in another. The employer also must intend to settle the obligations on a net basis or to realize the surplus in one plan and settle the obligation in another plan simultaneously.

Because of these requirements, it is unlikely that the offsetting of assets and liabilities will occur.

If an entity acquires another entity, then the purchaser recognizes the assets and liabilities arising from acquiree's postemployment benefits at the present value of the defined benefit obligation less the fair value of any plan assets. At the acquisition date, the present value of the obligation includes

- Actuarial gains and losses that arose before the acquisition date, whether inside or outside the 10% corridor.
- Past service costs that arise from benefit changes before the acquisition date.
- Amounts that had arisen under the transitional provisions that the acquiree had not recognized.

CURTAILMENTS AND SETTLEMENTS

A curtailment occurs when an entity either reduces the number of employees covered by the plan or amends the terms of a defined benefit plan. An amendment normally would be such that a material element of future service by current employees will no longer qualify for benefits or will qualify for a reduction in benefits.

Curtailments are likely to have a material impact on the entity's financial statements and often are linked to restructuring or reorganization. They should be recognized in the financial statements at the same time as the restructuring.

An entity settles its obligations when it enters into a transaction that eliminates a future legal and constructive obligation for part or all of the benefits provided under a defined benefit plan.

Settlements are usually lump-sum cash payments made to or on behalf of plan participants in exchange for the right to receive specified future benefits. A settlement occurs together with a curtailment if a plan is terminated such that the obligation is settled and the plan ceases to exist.

The plan does not cease to exist if the plan is replaced by a new plan that offers benefits that are in substance identical. If the entity acquires an insurance policy to fund some or all of the employee benefits, the acquisition of such a policy is not a settlement if the entity retains a legal or constructive obligation to pay further amounts if the insurance policy does not pay the employee benefits.

Where a curtailment relates to only some employees covered by the plan, the obligation is only partly settled, and any gain or loss calculated should include a proportionate share of the previously unrecognized past service cost and actuarial gains and losses.

The settlement gain and loss is based on

- Any resultant change in defined benefit obligation.
- Any resultant change in the fair value of the plan assets.

- Any related actuarial gains and losses and past service cost that have not been recognized previously.

Before determining the effect of a curtailment, the entity shall remeasure the obligation and plan assets using current actuarial assumptions.

Case Study 4

Facts

An entity closes down its subsidiary, and the employees of that subsidiary will earn no further pension benefits. The entity has a defined benefit obligation with a net present value of $20 million. The plan assets have a fair value of $16 million, and there are net cumulative and unrecognized actuarial gains of $8 million. The entity had adopted ASC 715 two years previously, and it has decided to recognize the increased liability of $10 million over a five-year period from that date. The curtailment reduces the net present value of the obligation by $2 million to $18 million.

Required

Calculate the curtailment gain and the net liability recognized in the balance sheet after the curtailment.

Solution

	Before curtailment $	Gain on curtailment $	After curtailment $
NPV of obligation	20	2	18
Fair value of plan assets	(16)	–	(16)
	4	(2)	2
Unrecognized actuarial gains	8	(0.8)	7.2
Unrecognized transitional amount (3/5 of 10)	(6)	0.6	(5.4)
Net liability in balance sheet	6	(2.2)	3.8

ASSET GAINS AND LOSSES—DEFINED BENEFIT PLANS

An entity should recognize a portion of its asset gains and losses as income or expense if the net cumulative unrecognized actuarial gains and losses at the end of the previous reporting period (i.e., at the beginning of the current financial year) exceeds the greater of

1. 10% of the present value of the defined benefit obligation at the beginning of the year; and
2. 10% of the fair value of the plan assets at the same date.

These limits should be calculated and applied separately for each defined plan. The excess determined by this method is then divided by the expected average remaining lives of the employees in the plan.

Case Study 5

Facts

An entity has a defined benefit pension plan. As of January 1, 20X4, these values relate to the pension plan:

- Fair value of plan assets: $50 million
- Present value of defined benefit obligation: $45 million
- Cumulative unrecognized actuarial gains: $8 million
- Average remaining working lives of employees: 20 years

At the end of the period at December 31, 20X4, the fair value of the plan assets has risen by $5 million. The present value of the defined benefit obligation has risen by $3 million. The actuarial gain is $10 million, and the average remaining working lives of the employees is 20 years. The entity wishes to know the difference between the corridor approach and the full recognition of actuarial gains and losses.

Required

How will the asset gain or loss for the period ending December 31, 20X4, be recognized in the financial statements?

Solution

Corridor Approach

The entity must recognize the portion of the net actuarial gain or loss in excess of 10% of the greater of defined benefit obligation or the fair value of the plan assets at the beginning of the year.

Unrecognized actuarial gain at the beginning of the year was $8 million. The limit of the corridor is 10% of $50 million, or $5 million. The difference is $3 million, which divided by 20 years is $0.15 million.

DISCLOSURE

The elements of the pension expense can be either segregated and presented as current service cost, interest cost, and return of plan assets or presented as a single amount within the income statement.

Sufficient disclosure is required to provide an understanding of the significance of the entity's employee benefit plans.

The pension disclosure requirements are extensive and quite detailed. Items that require disclosure are the accounting policy for recognizing actuarial gains and losses, description of the plan, components of the total expense in the income statement, principal actuarial assumptions used, reconciliation of the net liability for assets recognized in the statement of financial position from one year to the next, the funded status of the plan, the fair value of the plan assets for each category of the entity's own financial instruments, any property occupied or other assets used by the reporting entity, and disclosures about related-party transactions and contingencies.

Case Study 6

Facts

This information related to a defined benefit plan for the year ended December 31, 20X6:

(a) Current service cost of providing benefits for the year to December 31, 20X6: $30 million
(b) Average remaining working life of employees: 10 years
(c) Benefits paid to retired employees in the year: $31 million
(d) Contributions paid to the fund: $21 million
(e) Present value of obligation to provide benefits: $2,200 million at January 1, 20X6, and $2,500 million at December 31, 20X6
(f) Fair value of plan assets: $2,100 million at January 1, 20X6, and $2,400 million at December 31, 20X6
(g) Net cumulative unrecognized gains at January 1, 20X6: $252 million
(h) Past service cost: $115 million. All of these benefits have vested.
(i) Discount rates and expected rates of return on plan assets:

	January 1, 20X6	January 1, 20X7
Discount rate	5%	6%
Expected rate of return on plan assets	7%	8%

The entity wishes to use the corridor approach to recognizing actuarial gains and losses.

Required

Show the amounts that will be recognized in the statement of financial position and income statement for the year ended December 31, 20X6, and the movement in the net liability in the statement of financial position.

Solution

	At December 31, 20X6 $m
Amounts recognized in balance sheet:	
Present value of the obligation	2,500
Fair value of plan assets	(2,400)
	100
Unrecognized actuarial gains	336
Liability recognized in statement of financial position	436
Expense recognized in income statement for year ended December 31, 20X6:	
Current service cost	30
Interest cost	110
Expected return on assets	(147)
Past service cost	115
Asset gain recognized	(3)
Expense in income statement	105
Movement in net liability in balance sheet:	
Opening net liability (2,200 – 2,100 + 252)	352
Expense	105
Contributions	(21)
Closing liability	436
Changes in the present value of obligation and fair value of plan assets:	
Present value of obligation January 1, 20X6	2,200
Interest cost (5% of 2,200)	110
Current service cost	30
Past service cost	115
Benefits paid	(31)
Actuarial loss on obligation (balance)	76
Present value of obligation December 31, 20X6	2,500
Fair value of plan assets January 1, 20X6	2,100
Expected return on plan assets (7% of 2100)	147
Contributions	21
Benefits paid	(31)
Actuarial gain on plan assets (balance)	163
Fair value of plan assets December 31, 20X6	2,400

EXTRACTS FROM PUBLISHED FINANCIAL STATEMENTS

General Electric Company Annual Report, 2008

Note 6. Postretirement Benefit Plans

Retiree Health and Life Benefits

We sponsor a number of retiree health and life insurance benefit plans (retiree benefit plans). Principal retiree benefit plans are discussed below; other such plans are not significant individually or in the aggregate. We use a December 31 measurement date for our plans.

Principal Retiree Benefit Plans provide health and life insurance benefits to certain employees who retire under the GE Pension Plan with 10 or more years of service. Eligible retirees share in the cost of health-care benefits. These plans cover approximately 225,000 retirees and dependents.

Cost of Principal Retiree Benefit Plans

(In millions)	2008	2007	2006
Expected return on plan assets	$(131)	$(125)	$(127)
Service cost for benefits earned	326	286	229
Interest cost on benefit obligation	750	577	455
Prior service cost amortization	673	603	363
Net actuarial loss (gain) amortization	(49)	(17)	64
Retiree benefit plans cost	$1,569	$1,324	$984

Actuarial assumptions are described below. The discount rates at December 31 measured the year-end benefit obligations and the earnings effects for the subsequent year.

December 31	2008	2007	2006	2005
Discount rate	6.15%	6.31%[a]	5.75%	5.25%
Compensation increases	4.20	5.00	5.00	5.00
Expected return on assets	8.50	8.50	8.50	8.50
Initial healthcare trend rate[c]	7.00[b]	9.10	9.20	10.00

[a] *Weighted-average discount rate of 6.34% was used for determination of costs in 2008.*

[b] *Includes benefits from new healthcare supplier contracts.*

[c] *For 2008, ultimately declining to 6% for 2025 and thereafter.*

To determine the expected long-term rate of return on retiree life plan assets, we consider current and expected asset allocations, as well as historical and expected returns on various categories of plan assets. We apply our expected rate of return to a market-related value of assets, which stabilizes variability in the amounts to which we apply that expected return.

We amortize experience gains and losses as well as the effects of changes in actuarial assumptions and plan provisions over a period no longer than the average future service of employees.

Funding Policy. We fund retiree health benefits on a pay-as-you-go basis. We expect to contribute approximately $665 million in 2009 to fund such benefits. We fund retiree life insurance benefits at our discretion.

Changes in the accumulated postretirement benefit obligation for retiree benefit plans follow.

Accumulated Postretirement Benefit Obligation (APBO)

(In millions)	2008	2007
Balance at January 1	$12,983	$8,262
Service cost for benefits earned	326	286
Interest cost on benefit obligation	750	577
Participant contributions	51	47
Plan amendments[a]	–	4,257
Actuarial loss (gain)[b]	(1,351)	320
Benefits paid[c]	(811)	(796)
Other	1	30
Balance at December 31[d]	$11,949	$12,983

[a] *For 2007, related to labor agreements negotiated with U.S. unions.*

[b] *For 2008, primarily related to benefits from new healthcare supplier contracts.*

[c] *Net of Medicare Part D subsidy of $83 million and $73 million in 2008 and 2007, respectively.*

[d] *The APBO for the retiree health plans was $9,749 million and $10,847 million at year-end 2008 and 2007, respectively.*

A one percentage point change in the assumed healthcare cost trend rate would have the following effects.

(In millions)	1% increase	1% decrease
APBO at December 31, 2008	$990	$(848)
Service and interest cost in 2008	95	(80)

Fair Value of Plan Assets

(In millions)	2008	2007
Balance at January 1	$1,804	$1,710
Actual gain (loss) on plan assets	(486)	221
Employer contributions	617	622
Participant contributions	51	47
Benefits paid[a]	(811)	(796)
Balance at December 31	$1,175	$1,804

[a] *Net of Medicare Part D subsidy.*

Plan Asset Allocation

	2008		2007
December 31	*Target allocation*	*Actual allocation*	*Actual allocation*
U.S. equity securities	19-39%	25%	33%
Non-U.S. equity securities	18-38	15	20
Debt securities (including cash equivalents)	11-41	39	31
Real estate	2-12	7	6
Private equities	3-13	8	5
Other	0-10	6	5

Plan fiduciaries set investment policies and strategies for the trust and oversee its investment allocation, which includes selecting investment managers and setting long-term strategic targets. Long-term strategic investment objectives include preserving the funded status of the plan and balancing risk and return. Target allocation ranges are guidelines, not limitations, and occasionally plan fiduciaries will approve allocations above or below a target range.

Trust assets invested in short-term securities must generally be invested in securities rated A1/P1 or better, except for 15% of such securities that may be rated A2/P2. According to statute, the aggregate holdings of all qualifying employer securities (e.g., GE common stock) and qualifying employer real property may not exceed 10% of the fair value of trust assets at the time of purchase. GE securities represented 3.6% and 5.9% of trust assets at year-end 2008 and 2007, respectively.

Retiree Benefit Asset (Liability)

December 31 (In millions)	2008	2007
Funded status[a]	$(10,774)	$(11,179)
Liability recorded in the Statement of Financial Position		
Retiree health plans		
Due within one year	$ (644)	$ (675)
Due after one year	(9,105)	(10,172)
Retiree life plans	(1,025)	(332)
Net liability recognized	$(10,774)	$(11,179)
Amounts recorded in shareowners' equity (unamortized)		
Prior service cost	$ 5,027	$ 5,700
Net actuarial loss (gain)	(475)	210
Total	$ 4,552	$ 5,910

[a] *Fair value of assets less APBO, as shown in the preceding tables.*

In 2009, we estimate that we will amortize $675 million of prior service cost and $105 million of net actuarial gain from shareowners' equity into retiree benefit plans cost. Comparable amortized amounts in 2008 were $673 million of prior service cost and $49 million of net actuarial gains.

Estimated Future Benefit Payments

(In millions)	2009	2010	2011	2012	2013	2014-2018
Gross	$910	$930	$965	$980	$1,000	$5,200
Expected Medicare Part D subsidy	75	80	85	90	95	550
Net	$835	$850	$880	$890	$ 905	$4,650

Pension Benefits

We sponsor a number of pension plans. Principal pension plans, together with affiliate and certain other pension plans (other pension plans) detailed in this note, represent about 99% of our total pension assets. We use a December 31 measurement date for our plans.

Principal Pension Plans are the GE Pension Plan and the GE Supplementary Pension Plan.

The GE Pension Plan provides benefits to certain U.S. employees based on the greater of a formula recognizing career earnings or a formula recognizing length of service and final average earnings. Certain benefit provisions are subject to collective bargaining.

The GE Supplementary Pension Plan is an unfunded plan providing supplementary retirement benefits primarily to higher-level, longer-service U.S. employees.

Other Pension Plans in 2008 included 31 U.S. and non-U.S. pension plans with pension assets or obligations greater than $50 million. These defined benefit plans provide benefits to employees based on formulas recognizing length of service and earnings.

Pension Plan Participants

December 31, 2008	*Total*	*Principal pension plans*	*Other pension plans*
Active employees	**188,000**	**140,000**	**48,000**
Vested former employees	**231,000**	**190,000**	**41,000**
Retirees and beneficiaries	**246,000**	**220,000**	**26,000**
Total	**665,000**	**550,000**	**115,000**

Cost of Pension Plans

		Total		*Principal pension plans*			*Other pension plans*		
(In millions)	*2008*	*2007*	*2006*	*2008*	*2007*	*2006*	*2008*	*2007*	*2006*
Expected return on plan assets	**$(4,850)**	$(4,459)	$(4,211)	**$(4,298)**	$(3,950)	$(3,811)	**$(552)**	$(509)	$(400)
Service cost for benefits earned	**1,663**	1,727	1,719	**1,331**	1,355	1,402	**332**	372	317
Interest cost on benefit obligation	**3,152**	2,885	2,685	**2,653**	2,416	2,304	**499**	469	381
Prior service cost amortization	**332**	247	258	**321**	241	253	**11**	6	5
Net actuarial loss amortization	**316**	856	893	**237**	693	729	**79**	163	164
Pension plans cost	**$ 613**	$1,256	$1,344	**$244**	$755	$877	**$369**	$501	$467

Actuarial assumptions are described below. The discount rates at December 31 measured the year-end benefit obligations and the earnings effects for the subsequent year.

	Principal pension plans				*Other pension plans (weighted average)*			
December 31	*2008*	*2007*	*2006*	*2005*	*2008*	*2007*	*2006*	*2005*
Discount rate	**6.11%**	6.34%	5.75%	5.50%	**6.03%**	5.65%	4.97%	4.74%
Compensation increases	**4.20**	5.00	5.00	5.00	**4.47**	4.50	4.26	4.20
Expected return on assets	**8.50**	8.50	8.50	8.50	**7.41**	7.51	7.44	7.47

To determine the expected long-term rate of return on pension plan assets, we consider current and expected asset allocations, as well as historical and expected returns on various categories of plan assets. For the principal pension plans, we apply our expected rate of return to a market-related value of assets, which stabilizes variability in the amounts to which we apply that expected return.

We amortize experience gains and losses as well as the effects of changes in actuarial assumptions and plan provisions over a period no longer than the average future service of employees.

Funding policy for the GE Pension Plan is to contribute amounts sufficient to meet minimum funding requirements as set forth in employee benefit and tax laws plus such additional amounts as we may determine to be appropriate. We have not made contributions to the GE Pension Plan since 1987 and will not make any such contributions in 2009. In 2009, we expect to pay approximately $170 million for benefit payments under our GE Supplementary Pension Plan and administrative expenses of our principal pension plans and expect to contribute approximately $690 million to other pension plans. In 2008, comparative amounts were $153 million and $627 million, respectively.

Benefit obligations are described in the following tables. Accumulated and projected benefit obligations (ABO and PBO) represent the obligations of a pension plan for past service as of the measurement date. ABO is the present value of benefits earned to date with benefits computed based on current compensation levels. PBO is ABO increased to reflect expected future compensation.

Projected Benefit Obligation

(In millions)	Principal pension plans 2008	Principal pension plans 2007	Other pension plans 2008	Other pension plans 2007
Balance at January 1	$42,947	$43,293	$9,014	$9,034
Service cost for benefits earned	1,331	1,355	332	372
Interest cost on benefit obligations	2,653	2,416	499	469
Participant contributions	169	173	40	43
Plan amendments	–	1,470	16	26
Actuarial loss (gain)[a]	791	(3,205)	(923)	(665)
Benefits paid	(2,723)	(2,555)	(383)	(370)
Acquisitions (dispositions)—net	–	–	545	(311)
Exchange rate adjustments	–	–	(1,392)	416
Balance at December 31[b]	$45,168	$42,947	$7,748	$9,014

[a] *Principally associated with discount rate changes.*

[b] *The PBO for the GE Supplementary Pension Plan, which is an unfunded plan, was $3,505 million and $3,437 million at year-end 2008 and 2007, respectively.*

Accumulated Benefit Obligation

December 31 (In millions)	2008	2007
GE Pension Plan	$40,313	$38,155
GE Supplementary Pension Plan	2,582	2,292
Other pension plans	7,075	8,175

Plans with Assets Less than ABO

December 31 (In millions)	2008	2007
Funded plans with assets less than ABO		
Plan assets	$4,914	$3,639
Accumulated benefit obligations	5,888	3,974
Projected benefit obligations	6,468	4,595
Unfunded plans[a]		
Accumulated benefit obligations	3,352	3,111
Projected benefit obligations	4,303	4,283

[a] *Primarily related to the GE Supplementary Pension Plan.*

Fair Value of Plan Assets

(In millions)	Principal pension plans 2008	Principal pension plans 2007	Other pension plans 2008	Other pension plans 2007
Balance at January 1	$59,700	$54,758	$7,411	$6,435
Actual gain (loss) on plan assets	(16,569)	7,188	(1,743)	614
Employer contributions	153	136	627	730
Participant contributions	169	173	40	43
Benefits paid	(2,723)	(2,555)	(383)	(370)
Acquisitions (dispositions)—net	–	–	565	(372)
Exchange rate adjustments	–	–	(1,143)	331
Balance at December 31	$40,730	$59,700	$5,374	$7,411

Plan Asset Allocation

	Principal pension plans 2008 Target allocation	Principal pension plans 2008 Actual allocation	Principal pension plans 2007 Actual allocation
December 31			
U.S. equity securities	17–37%	25%	32%
Non-U.S. equity securities	17–37	14	20
Debt securities (including cash equivalents)	10–40	31	24
Real estate	4–14	12	9
Private equities	5–15	12	9
Other	1–14	6	6

Plan fiduciaries of the GE Pension Plan set investment policies and strategies for the GE Pension Trust and oversee its investment allocation, which includes selecting investment managers, commissioning periodic asset-liability studies, and setting long-term strategic targets. Long-term strategic investment objectives include preserving the funded status of the plan and balancing risk and return. Target allocation ranges are guidelines, not limitations, and occasionally plan fiduciaries will approve allocations above or below a target range.

GE Pension Trust assets are invested subject to the following additional guidelines:

- Short-term securities must generally be rated A1/P1 or better, except for 15% of such securities that may be rated A2/P2.
- Real estate investments may not exceed 25% of total assets.

Investments in restricted securities that are not freely tradable may not exceed 30% of total assets (actual was 16% of trust assets at December 31, 2008).

According to statute, the aggregate holdings of all qualifying employer securities (e.g., GE common stock) and qualifying employer real property may not exceed 10% of the fair value of trust assets at the time of purchase. GE securities represented 3.5% and 5.6% of trust assets at year-end 2008 and 2007, respectively.

	Other pension plans (weighted average)		
	2008		2007
December 31	*Target allocation*	*Actual allocation*	*Actual allocation*
Equity securities	**60%**	**57%**	67%
Debt securities	**30**	**32**	25
Real estate	**4**	**4**	4
Other	**6**	**7**	4

Pension Asset (Liability)

	Principal pension plans		Other pension plans	
December 31 (In millions)	**2008**	2007	**2008**	2007
Funded status[a]	**$(4,438)**	$16,753	**$(2,374)**	$(1,603)
Pension asset (liability) recorded in the Statement of Financial Position				
Pension asset	**$ –**	$20,190	**$ 9**	$ 258
Pension liabilities				
Due within one year[b]	**(117)**	(111)	**(51)**	(54)
Due after one year[b]	**(4,321)**	(3,326)	**(2,332)**	(1,807)
Net amount recognized	**$(4,438)**	$16,753	**$(2,374)**	$(1,603)
Amounts recorded in shareowners' equity (unamortized)				
Prior service cost	**$ 1,739**	$ 2,060	**$ 62**	$ 65
Net actuarial loss (gain)	**16,447**	(4,974)	**1,753**	654
Total	**$18,186**	$(2,914)	**$1,815**	$ 719

[a] *Fair value of assets less PBO, as shown in the preceding tables.*

[b] *For principal pension plans, primarily represents the Genentech Supplementary Pension Plan liability.*

In 2009, we estimate that we will amortize $323 million of prior service cost and $377 million of net actuarial loss for the principal pension plans from shareowners' equity into pension cost. For other pension plans, the estimated prior service cost and net actuarial loss to be amortized over the next fiscal year are $10 million and $125 million, respectively. Comparable amortized amounts in 2008, respectively, were $321 million and $237 million for principal pension plans and $11 million and $79 million for other pension plans.

Estimated Future Benefit Payments

(In millions)	2009	2010	2011	2012	2013	2014 – 2018
Principal pension plans	$2,725	$2,800	$2,850	$2,925	$2,950	$16,050
Other pension plans	345	350	360	370	375	2,105

Postretirement Benefit Plans

2008 Cost of Postretirement Benefit Plans and Changes in Equity other than Transactions with Shareowners

(In millions)	*Total post-retirement benefit plans*	*Retiree benefit plans*	*Principal pension plans*	*Other pension plans*
Cost of postretirement benefit plans	**$ 2,182**	**$1,569**	**$ 244**	**$ 369**
Changes in equity other than transactions with shareowners				
Net actuarial loss (gain)—current year	**$22,094**	**$ (734)**	**$ 21,658**	**$1,170**
Prior service cost—current year	**16**	**–**	**–**	**16**
Prior service cost amortization	**(1,005)**	**(673)**	**(321)**	**(11)**
Net actuarial gain (loss) amortization	**(267)**	**49**	**(237)**	**(79)**
Total changes in equity other than transactions with shareowners	**20,838**	**(1,358)**	**21,100**	**1,096**
Cost of postretirement benefit plans and changes in equity other than transactions with shareowners	**$23,020**	**$ 211**	**$ 21,344**	**$1,465**

MULTIPLE-CHOICE QUESTIONS

1. An entity contributes to an industrial pension plan that provides a pension arrangement for its employees. A large number of other employers also contribute to the pension plan, and the entity makes contributions in respect of each employee. These contributions are kept separate from corporate assets and are used together with any investment income to purchase annuities for retired employees. The only obligation of the entity is to pay the annual contributions. This pension plan is a
   (a) Multiemployer plan and a defined contribution plan.
   (b) Multiemployer plan and a defined benefit plan.
   (c) Defined contribution plan only.
   (d) Defined benefit plan only.

2. Which of these events will cause a change in a defined benefit obligation?
   (a) Changes in mortality rates or the proportion of employees taking early retirement.
   (b) Changes in the estimated salaries or benefits that will occur in the future.
   (c) Changes in the estimated employee turnover.
   (d) Changes in the discount rate used to calculate defined benefit liabilities and the value of assets.
   (e) All of the above.

3. An entity has decided to improve its defined benefit pension plan. The benefit payable will be determined by reference to 30 years' service rather than 40 years' service. As a result, the defined benefit pension liability will increase by $10 million. The average remaining service lives of the employees is 10 years. How should the increase in the pension liability by $10 million be treated in the financial statements?
   (a) The past service cost should be charged against retained profit.
   (b) The past service cost should be charged against profit or loss for the year.
   (c) The past service cost should be spread over the remaining working lives of the employees.
   (d) The past service cost should not be recognized.

4. Which of these elements are taken into account when determining the discount rate to be used?
   (a) Market yields at the date of the statement of financial position on high-quality corporate bonds.
   (b) Investment or actuarial risk.
   (c) Specific risk associated with the entity's business.
   (d) Risk that future experiences may differ from actuarial assumptions.

5. An entity operates a defined benefit plan that pays employees an annual benefit based on their number of years of service. The annual payment does allow the employer to vary the final benefit. Over the last five years, the entity has used this flexibility to increase employees' pensions by the current growth in earnings per share. How will employees' benefit be calculated if they retire in the current period?
   (a) It will be based on the existing plan rules with no additional award.
   (b) It will be based on the existing plan rules plus the current rate of growth of earnings per share.
   (c) It will be based on the plan rules plus the current rate of inflation.
   (d) It will be based on the plan rules plus the increase in earnings per share anticipated over the remaining working lives of the employees.

6. Which of these assets should be included within the valuation of plan assets?
   (a) Unpaid contributions.
   (b) Unlisted corporate bonds that are redeemable but not transferable without the entity's permission.
   (c) A loan to the entity that cannot be assigned to a third party.
   (d) Investments in listed companies.

7. An entity has decided to protect its pension obligation with an insurance policy. The insurance policy permits the entity to cash in the insurance policy. Is this insurance policy a qualifying insurance policy that will be included in plan assets?
   (a) Yes.
   (b) No.

8. An entity operates a defined benefit pension plan and changes it on January 1, 20X4, to a defined contribution plan. The defined benefit plan still relates to past service but not to future service. The net pension liability after the plan amendment is $70 million, and the net pension liability before the amendment was $100 million. How should the entity account for this change?
   (a) The entity recognizes a gain of $30 million.
   (b) The entity does not recognize a gain.
   (c) The entity recognizes a gain of $30 million over the remaining service lives of the employees.
   (d) The entity recognizes the gain but applies the 10% corridor approach to it.

9. An entity on December 31, 20X5, changes its defined benefit pension plan to a defined contribution plan. The entity agrees with the employees to pay them $9 million in total on the introduction of a defined contribution plan. The employees forfeit any pension entitlement for the defined benefit plan. The pension liability recognized in the balance sheet at December 31, 20X4, was $10 million. How should this curtailment be accounted for in the balance sheet at December 31, 20X5?

   (a) A settlement gain of $1 million should be shown.

   (b) The pension liability should be credited to reserves, and a cash payment of $9 million should be shown in expense in the income statement.

   (c) The cash payment should go to reserves, and the pension liability should be shown as a credit to the income statement.

   (d) A credit to reserves should be made of $1 million.

Chapter 25

ACCOUNTING AND REPORTING BY RETIREMENT BENEFIT PLANS (ASC 960 AND 962)

INTRODUCTION

ASC 960 and 962 deal with defined benefit pension plans and defined contribution pension plans, respectively. The Standards set out the form and content of the general-purpose financial reports of retirement benefit plans. The Standards apply to

- *Defined contribution plans.* Where benefits are determined by contributions to the plan together with investment earnings thereon.
- *Defined benefit plans.* Where benefits are determined by a formula based on employees' earnings and/or years of service.

ASC 960 and 962 are sometimes confused with ASC 715, because both Standards address employee benefits. But there is a difference: While ASC 960 and 962 address the financial reporting considerations for the benefit plan itself, as the reporting entity, ASC 715 deals with employers' accounting for the cost of such benefits as they are earned by the employees. These Standards are thus somewhat related, but there will not be any direct interrelationship between amounts reported in benefit plan financial statements and amounts reported under ASC 715 by employers.

DEFINITIONS OF KEY TERMS

Actuarial present value. Value, as of a specified date, of an amount or series of amounts payable or receivable thereafter, with each amount adjusted to reflect (1) the time value of money (through discounts for interest) and (2) the probability of payment (by means of decrements for events such as death, disability, withdrawal, or retirement) between the specified date and the expected date of payment.

Defined benefit plans. Pension plan that defines an amount of pension benefit to be provided, usually as a function of one or more factors, such as age, years of service, or compensation. Any pension plan that is not a defined contribution pension plan is, as described in ASC 715-30, a defined benefit pension plan.

Defined contribution plans. Plan that provides pension benefits in return for services rendered, provides an individual account for each participant, and specifies how contributions to the individual's account are to be determined instead of specifying the amount of benefits the individual is to receive. Under a defined contribution pension plan, the benefits a participant will receive depend solely on the amount contributed to the participant's account, the returns earned on investments of those contributions, and forfeitures of other participants' benefits that may be allocated to such participant's account.

Funding policy. Program regarding the amounts and timing of contributions by the employer(s), participants, and any other sources (e.g., state subsidies or federal grants) to provide the benefits a pension plan specifies.

Net assets available for benefits. The assets of a retirement benefit plan less its liabilities other than the actuarial present value of promised retirement benefits.

Participants. The members of a retirement benefit plan and others who are entitled to benefits under the plan.

Vested benefits. Entitlements, the rights to which, under the terms of a retirement benefit plan, are not conditional on continued employment.

DEFINED CONTRIBUTION PLANS

Retirement benefit plans either can be defined contribution plans or defined benefit plans. When the amount of the future benefits payable to the participants of the retirement benefit plan is determined by the contributions made by the participants' employer, the participants, or both, together with investment earnings thereon, such plans are defined contribution plans. Defined benefit plans guarantee certain defined benefits, often determined by a formula that takes into consideration factors such as number of years of service of employees and their salary level at the time of retirement, irrespective of whether the plan has sufficient assets; thus the ultimate responsibility for payment (which may be guaranteed by an insurance company, the government, or some other entity, depending on local law and custom) remains with the employer.

According to ASC 962, the report of a defined contribution plan should contain a "Statement of the Net Assets Available for Benefits" and a "Statement of Changes in Net Assets Available for Benefits." In preparing the statement of the net assets available for benefits, the plan investments should be carried at "fair value," which in the case of marketable securities would be their "market value." If an estimate of fair value is not possible, the entity must disclose why "fair value" has not been used.

PRACTICAL INSIGHT

In practice, in many cases "plan assets" will have determinable market values, because in discharge of their fiduciary responsibilities, plan trustees generally will mandate that the retirement plans hold only marketable investments.

Example

An example of a statement of net assets available for plan benefits, for a defined contribution plan, is presented next.

Benevolent Corp. Defined Contribution Plan
STATEMENT OF NET ASSETS AVAILABLE FOR BENEFITS
December 31, 2010
(in thousands of U.S. $)

Assets	
Investments at fair value:	
U.S. government securities	$10,000
U.S. municipal bonds	13,000
U.S. equity securities	13,000
EU equity securities	13,000
U.S. debt securities	12,000
EU corporate bonds	12,000
Others	11,000
Total investments	84,000
Receivables:	
Amounts due from stockbrokers on sale of securities	25,000
Accrued interest	15,000
Dividends receivable	12,000
Total receivables	52,000
Cash	15,000
Total assets	151,000
Liabilities	
Accounts payable:	
Amounts due to stockbrokers on purchase of securities	20,000
Benefits payable to participants—due and unpaid	21,000
Total accounts payable	41,000
Accrued expenses	21,000
Total liabilities	62,000
Net assets available for benefits	89,000

DEFINED BENEFIT PLANS

Defined benefit plans are those plans where the benefits are guaranteed amounts and amounts to be paid as retirement benefits are determined by reference to a formula, usually based on employees' earnings and/or number of years of service. The critical factors are thus the retirement benefits that are fixed or determinable, without regard to the adequacy of assets that may have been set aside for payment of the benefits. This clearly is different from the way defined contribution plans work; they provide the employees, upon retirement, amounts that have been set aside, plus or minus investment earnings or losses that have been accumulated thereon, however great or small that amount may be.

ASC 960 requires that the report of a defined benefit plan should contain a statement that shows

1. The net assets available for benefits.
2. The changes during the year in net assets available for benefits.
3. The actuarial present value of accumulated plan benefits as of either the beginning or end of the plan year.
4. Information regarding the effects, if significant, of certain factors affecting the year-to-date change in actuarial present value of accumulated plan benefits.

As in the case of defined contribution plans, investments of a defined benefit plan should be carried at fair value, which for marketable securities would be "market values."

Example

Examples of the alternative types of reports prescribed for a defined benefit plan follow.

Excellent Inc. Defined Benefit Plan
**STATEMENT OF NET ASSETS AVAILABLE FOR BENEFITS, ACTUARIAL
PRESENT VALUE OF ACCUMULATED RETIREMENT
BENEFITS AND PLAN EXCESS OR DEFICIT**
December 31, 2009
(in thousands of U.S. $)

1. Statement of net assets available for benefits

   Assets
   Investments at fair value:

U.S. government securities	155,000
U.S. municipal bonds	35,000
U.S. equity securities	35,000
EU equity securities	35,000
U.S. debt securities	25,000
EU corporate bonds	25,000
Others	15,000
Total investments	325,000

   Receivables:

Amounts due from stockbrokers on sale of securities	155,000
Accrued interest	55,000
Dividends receivable	25,000
Total receivables	235,000
Cash	55,000
Total assets	615,000

   Liabilities
   Accounts payable:

Amounts due to stockbrokers on purchase of securities	150,000
Benefits payable to participants–due and unpaid	150,000
Total accounts payable	300,000
Accrued expenses	120,000
Total liabilities	420,000
Net assets available for benefits	195,000

2. Actuarial present value of accumulated plan benefits

Vested benefits	120,000
Nonvested benefits	30,000
Total	150,000

3. Excess of net assets available for benefits over actuarial present value of accumulated plan benefits

	45,000

Excellent Inc. Defined Benefit Plan
STATEMENT OF CHANGES IN NET ASSETS AVAILABLE FOR BENEFITS
December 31, 2009
(in thousands of U.S. $)

Investment income:

Interest income	45,000
Dividend income	15,000
Net appreciation (unrealized gain) in fair value of investments	15,000
Total investment income	75,000

Plan contributions:

Employer contributions	55,000
Employee contributions	50,000
Total plan contributions	105,000
Total additions to net asset value	180,000

Plan benefit payments:

Pensions (annual)	25,000
Lump-sum payments on retirement	35,000
Severance pay	10,000
Commutation of superannuation benefits	15,000
Total plan benefit payments	85,000

Total deductions from net asset value	85,000
Net increase in asset value	95,000
Net assets available for benefits	
Beginning of year	100,000
End of year	195,000

ADDITIONAL DISCLOSURES REQUIRED BY THE STANDARDS

In both defined benefit plans and defined contribution plans, ASC 960 and 962 require that the reports of a retirement benefit plan should also contain this information:

- A statement of changes in net assets available for benefits
- A summary of significant accounting policies
- A description of the plan and the effect of any changes in the plan during the period

Reports provided by retirement benefit plans may include, if applicable,

1. A statement of net assets available for benefits disclosing:

   a. Assets at the end of the period suitably classified.
   b. The basis of valuation of assets.
   c. Details of any single investment exceeding either 5% of the net assets available for benefits or 5% of any class or type of security.
   d. Details of any investment in the employer.
   e. Liabilities other than the actuarial present value of promised retirement benefits.

2. A statement of changes in net assets available for benefits showing

   a. Employer contributions.
   b. Employee contributions.
   c. Investment income such as interest and dividends.
   d. Other income.
   e. Benefits paid or payable (analyzed, e.g., as retirement, death, and disability benefits, and lump-sum payments).
   f. Administrative expenses.
   g. Other expenses.
   h. Taxes on income.
   i. Profits and losses on disposal of investments and changes in value of investments.
   j. Transfers from and to other plans.

3. A description of the funding policy.
4. A description of significant plan amendments adopted during the year ending on the latest benefit information date.
5. A brief, general description of the priority order of participants' claims to the assets of the plan upon plan termination and benefits guaranteed by the Pension Benefit Guaranty Corporation, including a discussion of the application of its guaranty to any recent plan amendment.
6. The policy regarding the purchase of contracts with insurance entities that are excluded from plan assets.
7. The federal income tax status of the plan, if a favorable letter of determination has not been obtained or maintained. Disclosure of the plan's tax status is not prescribed in other circumstances.
8. Significant real estate or other transactions in which the plan and any of the following parties are jointly involved:

   a. The sponsor.
   b. The employer(s).
   c. The employee organization(s).

9. Unusual or infrequent events or transactions occurring after the latest benefit information date but before the financial statements are issued or are available to be issued that might significantly affect the usefulness of the financial statements in an assessment of the plan's present and future ability to pay benefits.
10. For defined benefit plans, the total actuarial value of accumulated benefits as of the benefit information date shall be segmented into at least the following three categories:

   a. Vested benefits of participants currently receiving payments, including benefits due and payable as of the benefit information date.
   b. Other vested benefits.
   c. Nonvested benefits.

Since the report of a retirement benefit plan contains a description of the plan, either as part of the financial information or in a separate report, it may contain

1. The names of the employers and the employee groups covered.
2. The number of participants receiving benefits and the number of other participants, classified as appropriate.
3. The type of plan—defined contribution or defined benefit.
4. A note as to whether participants contribute to the plan.
5. A description of the retirement benefits promised to participants.
6. A description of any plan termination terms.
7. Changes in items 1 through 6 during the period covered by the report.

Furthermore, it is not uncommon to refer to other documents that are readily available to users in which the plan is described and to include in the report only information on subsequent changes.

MULTIPLE-CHOICE QUESTIONS

1. In rare circumstances, when a retirement benefit plan has attributes of both defined contribution and defined benefit plans, according to ASC 715 it is deemed to be
- (a) A defined benefit plan.
- (b) A defined contribution plan.
- (c) Neither a defined benefit nor a defined contribution plan.
- (d) For aspects of the hybrid plan that are similar to a defined benefit plan, provisions of IAS 26 applicable to such plans are to be applied; for aspects of the hybrid plan that are similar to a defined contribution plan, provisions of IAS 26 that apply to such plans are to be applied.

2. Which of the following is **not** a criteria for determining benefits as part of a defined benefit plan?
- (a) Years of service.
- (b) Compensation.
- (c) How much the employee has contributed to the plan.
- (d) Age.

Chapter 26

STOCKHOLDERS' EQUITY (ASC 505)

BACKGROUND AND INTRODUCTION

ASC 505 defines stockholders' equity as the residual interest in the assets of an entity after deducting its liabilities. Stockholders' equity is comprised of all capital contributed to the entity plus its accumulated earnings less any distributions that have been made.

ASC 505 applies to all public and nonpublic entities, unless more specific guidance for those entities is provided in other ASC topics.

DEFINITIONS OF KEY TERMS
(in accordance with ASC 505)

Additional paid-in capital. Amounts received at issuance in excess of the par or stated value of capital stock and amounts received from other transactions involving the entity's stock and/or stockholders. It is classified by source.

Outstanding stock. Stock issued by a corporation and held by shareholders (i.e., issued shares that are not held in the treasury).

Par value method. A method of accounting for treasury shares that charges the treasury stock account for the aggregate par or stated value of the shares acquired and charges the excess of the purchase cost over the par value to paid-in capital and/or retained earnings. A deficiency of purchase cost is credited to paid-in capital.

Restricted share. A share for which sale is contractually or governmentally prohibited for a specified period of time. Most grants of shares to employees are better termed nonvested shares because the limitation on sale stems solely from the forfeitability of the shares before employees have satisfied the necessary service or performance condition(s) to earn the rights to the shares. Restricted shares issued for consideration other than employee services, however, are fully paid immediately. For those shares, there is no period analogous to a requisite service period during which the issuer is unilaterally obligated to issue shares when the purchaser pays for those shares, but the purchaser is not obligated to buy the shares. ASC 718 uses the term "restricted shares" to refer only to fully vested and outstanding shares whose sale is contractually or governmentally prohibited for a specified period of time.

Retained earnings. The undistributed earnings of a firm.

Stock-based compensation. Compensation arrangements under which employees receive shares of stock, stock options, or other equity instruments, or under which the employer incurs obligations to the employees based on the price of the company's shares.

Stock rights. Enables present shareholders to purchase additional shares of stock of the corporation. They are used commonly if a preemptive right is granted to common shareholders by some state corporation laws.

Treasury stock. Shares of a corporation that have been repurchased by the corporation. This stock has no voting rights and receives no cash dividends. Some states do not recognize treasury stock. In such cases, reacquired shares are treated as having been retired.

LEGAL CAPITAL AND CAPITAL STOCK

Legal capital typically refers to that portion of the stockholders' investment in a corporation that is permanent in nature and represents the interests in assets that will continue to be available for the satisfaction of creditor's claims.

Traditionally, legal capital was comprised of the aggregate par or stated value of common and preferred shares issued. In recent decades, however, many states have eliminated the requirement that corporate shares have a designated par or stated value. States that have adopted provisions of the Model Business Corporation Act have eliminated the distinction between par value and the amount contributed in excess of par.

The specific requirements regarding the preservation of legal capital are a function of the business corporation laws in the state in which a particular entity is incorporated. Accordingly, any action by the corporation that could affect the amount of legal capital (e.g., the payment of dividends in excess of retained earnings) must be considered in the context of the relevant laws of the state where the company is incorporated.

Ownership interest in a corporation is made up of common and, optionally, preferred shares. The common shares represent the residual risk-taking ownership of the corporation after the satisfaction of all claims of creditors and senior classes of equity.

Preferred Stock

Preferred shareholders are owners who have certain rights superior to those of common shareholders. Preferences as to earnings exist when the preferred shareholders have a stipulated dividend rate (expressed either as a dollar amount or as a percentage of the preferred stock's par or stated value). Preferences as to assets exist when the preferred shares have a stipulated liquidation value. If a corporation were to liquidate, these preferred holders would be paid a specific amount before the common shareholders would have a right to participate in any of the proceeds.

In practice, preferred shares are more likely to have preferences as to earnings than as to assets. Although unusual, preferred shares may have both preferential rights. Preferred shares may also have these optional features:

- Participation in earnings beyond the stipulated dividend rate
- The cumulative feature, ensuring that dividends in arrears, if any, will be fully satisfied before the common shareholders participate in any earnings distribution
- Convertibility or callability by the corporation

Preferences must be disclosed adequately in the financial statements, either on the face of the statement of financial position or in the notes thereto.

In exchange for the preferences, the preferred shareholders' other rights or privileges often are limited. For instance, the right to vote may be restricted to common shareholders. The most important right denied to the preferred shareholders, however, is the right to participate without limitation in the earnings of the corporation. Thus, if the corporation has exceedingly large earnings for a particular period, most of these earnings would accrue to the benefit of the common shareholders. This statement is true even if the preferred stock is participating (a fairly uncommon feature) because participating preferred stock usually has some upper limitation placed on the extent of participation.

Occasionally, several classes of stock will be categorized as common (e.g., Class A common, Class B common, etc.). Since there can be only one class of shares that represents the true residual risk-taking ownership in a corporation, it is clear that the other classes, even though described as common shareholders, must in fact have some preferential status. Typically, these preferences relate to voting rights.

Issuance of Shares

The accounting for the sale of shares by a corporation depends on whether the stock has a par or stated value. If there is a par or stated value, the amount of the proceeds representing the aggregate par or stated value is credited to the common or preferred stock account. The aggregate par or stated value generally is defined as legal capital not subject to distribution to shareholders. Proceeds in excess of par or stated value are credited to an additional paid-in capital account. The additional paid-in capital represents the amount in excess of the legal capital that may, under certain defined conditions, be distributed to shareholders.

A corporation selling stock below par value credits the capital stock account for the par value and debits an offsetting discount account for the difference between par value and the amount actually received. If the discount is on original issue capital stock, it serves to notify the actual and potential creditors of the contingent liability of those investors. As a practical matter, corporations avoided this problem by reducing par values to an arbitrarily low amount. This reduction in par eliminated the chance that shares would be sold for amounts below par.

Where the Model Business Corporation Act has been adopted or where corporation laws have been conformed to the guidelines of that Act, there is often no distinction made between par value and amounts in excess of par. In those jurisdictions, the entire proceeds from the sale of stock may be credited to the common stock account without distinction between the stock and the additional paid-in capital accounts.

Case Study 1

Facts

1. A corporation sells 100,000 shares of $5 par common stock for $8 per share cash.
2. A corporation sells 100,000 shares of no-par common stock for $8 per share cash.

Required

Prepare the necessary journal entries for each transaction.

Solution

A)	Cash	800,000		
	Common stock		500,000	
	Additional paid-in capital		300,000	
B)	Cash	800,000		
	Common stock		800,000	

Preferred stock often will be assigned a par value because in many cases, the preferential dividend rate is defined as a percentage of par value (e.g., 10%, $25 par value preferred stock will have a required annual dividend of $2.50).

If the shares in a corporation are issued in exchange for services or property rather than for cash, the transaction should be reflected at the fair value of the property or services received. If this information is not readily available, then the transaction should be recorded at the fair value of the shares that were issued.

Where necessary, appraisals should be obtained in order to properly reflect the transaction. As a final resort, a valuation of the stock issued can be made by the board of directors.

Stock issued to employees as compensation for services rendered should be accounted for at the fair value of the services performed, if determinable, or the value of the shares issued. If shares are given by a major shareholder directly to an employee for services performed for the entity, this exchange should be accounted for as a capital contribution to the company by the major shareholder and as compensation expense incurred by the company. Only when accounted for in this manner will there be conformity with the general principle that all costs incurred by an entity, including compensation, should be reflected in its financial statements.

In certain instances, common and preferred shares may be issued to investors as a unit (e.g., one share of preferred and two shares of common sold as a package). Where both of the classes of stock are publicly traded, the proceeds from a unit offering should be allocated in proportion to the relative market values of the securities.

If only one of the securities is publicly traded, the proceeds should be allocated to the one that is publicly traded based on its known market value. Any excess is allocated to the other. Where the market value of neither security is known, appraisal information may be used. The imputed fair value of one class of security, particularly the preferred shares, can be based on the stipulated dividend rate. In this case, the amount of proceeds remaining after the imputing of a value of the preferred shares would be allocated to the common stock.

Equity offerings generally involve the incurrence of various costs, such as legal and accounting fees and underwriting commissions. These are offset against the proceeds of the offering, generally reducing paid-in capital, which is thus reported net of costs. If a unit offering involves debt and equity, the offering costs should be allocated proportionally against equity and debt, possibly creating a discount on the debt issuance that will be amortized as additional interest expense in the usual manner.

STOCK SUBSCRIPTIONS

Occasionally, particularly in the case of a newly organized corporation, a contract is entered into between the corporation and prospective investors, whereby the latter agree to purchase specified numbers of shares to be paid for over some installment period. These stock subscriptions are not the same as actual stock issuances, and the accounting differs.

The amount of stock subscriptions receivable by a corporation occasionally is accounted for as an asset on the statement of financial position and is categorized as current or noncurrent in accordance with the terms of payment. However, in accordance with Securities and Exchange Commission requirements, most subscriptions receivable are shown as a reduction of stockholders' equity in the same manner as treasury stock. Since subscribed shares do not have the rights and responsibilities of actual outstanding stock, the credit is made to a stock subscribed account instead of to the capital stock accounts.

ASC 310-10-45-14 states that a contribution to a company's equity made in the form of a note receivable generally should not be reported as an asset unless circumstances indicate both the ability and intent to pay in a short period of time. EITF noted that the most widespread practice is to report these notes as a reduction of equity. However, if the cash is received prior to the issuance of the financial statements, the note may be reported as an asset.

If the common stock has par or stated value, the common stock subscribed account is credited for the aggregate par or stated value of the shares subscribed. The excess over this amount is credited to additional paid-in capital. No distinction is made between additional paid-in capital relating to shares already issued and shares subscribed for. This treatment follows from the distinction between legal capital and additional paid-in capital. Where there is no par or stated value, the entire amount of the common stock subscribed is credited to the stock subscribed account.

As the amount due from the prospective shareholders is collected, the stock subscriptions' receivable account is credited and the proceeds are debited to the cash account. Actual issuance of the shares, however, must await the complete payment of the stock subscription. Accordingly, the debit to common stock subscribed is not made until the subscribed shares are fully paid for and the stock is issued.

When a subscriber defaults on an obligation under a stock subscription agreement, the accounting will follow the provisions of the state in which the corporation is chartered. In some jurisdictions, the subscriber is entitled to a proportionate number of shares based on the amount already paid on the subscriptions, sometimes reduced by the cost incurred by the corporation in selling the remaining defaulted shares to other stockholders. In other jurisdictions, the subscriber forfeits the entire investment upon default. In this case, the amount already received is credited to an additional paid-in capital account that describes its source.

Case Study 2

Facts

1. 10,000 shares of $50 par preferred are subscribed at a price of $65 each; a 10% down payment is received.
2. 2,000 shares of no-par common shares are subscribed at a price of $85 each, with one-half received in cash.
3. All preferred subscriptions are paid and subscribed preferred shares are issued, and one-half of the remaining common subscriptions are collected in full.
4. The remaining common subscriptions are collected in full.

Required

Prepare the necessary journal entries.

Solution

1. 10,000 shares of $50 par preferred are subscribed at a price of $65 each; a 10% down payment is received.

Cash	65,000	
Stock subscriptions receivable	585,000	
Preferred stock subscribed		500,000
Additional paid-in capital		150,000

2. 2,000 shares of no-par common shares are subscribed at a price of $85 each, with one-half received in cash.

Cash	85,000	
Stock subscriptions receivable	85,000	
Common stock subscribed		170,000

3. All preferred subscriptions are paid and subscribed preferred shares are issued, and one-half of the remaining common subscriptions are collected in full.

Cash [$585,000 + ($85,000 × .50)]	627,500	
Stock subscriptions receivable		627,500
Preferred stock subscribed	500,000	
Preferred stock		500,000

4. The remaining common subscriptions are collected in full.

Cash ($85,000 × .50)	42,500	
Stock subscriptions receivable		42,500
Common stock subscribed	170,000	
Common stock		170,000

ADDITIONAL PAID-IN CAPITAL

Additional paid-in capital represents all capital contributed to a corporation other than that defined as par, stated value, no-par stock, or donated capital. Additional paid-in capital can arise from proceeds received from the sale of common and preferred shares in excess of their par or stated values. It also can arise from transactions related to

1. Sale of shares previously issued and subsequently reacquired by the corporation (treasury stock).
2. Retirement of previously outstanding shares.
3. Payment of stock dividends in a manner that justifies the dividend being recorded at the market value of the shares distributed.
4. Lapse of stock purchase warrants or the forfeiture of stock subscriptions, if these result in the retaining by the corporation of any partial proceeds received prior to forfeiture.

5. Warrants that are detachable from bonds.
6. Conversion of convertible bonds.
7. Other "gains" on the entity's own stock, such as that which results from certain stock option plans.

When the amounts are material, the sources of additional paid-in capital should be described in the financial statements.

Examples of additional paid-in capital transactions

ABC Company issues 2,000 shares of common stock having a par value of $1, of a total price of $8,000. This entry records the transaction:

Cash	8,000	
Common stock		2,000
Additional paid-in capital		6,000

ABC Company buys back 2,000 shares of its own common stock for $10,000 and then sells these shares to investors for $15,000. These entries record the buyback and sale transactions, respectively, assuming the use of the cost method of accounting for treasury stock:

Treasury stock	10,000	
Cash		10,000
Cash	15,000	
Treasury stock		10,000
Additional paid-in capital		5,000

ABC Company buys back 2,000 shares of its own $1 par value common stock (which it had originally sold for $8,000) for $9,000 and retires the stock, which it records with the next entry:

Common stock	2,000	
Additional paid-in capital	6,000	
Retained earnings	1,000	
Cash		9,000

ABC Company issues a small stock dividend of 5,000 common shares at the market price of $8 per share. Each share has a par value of $1. This entry records the transaction:

Retained earnings	40,000	
Common stock		5,000
Additional paid-in capital		35,000

ABC Company previously has recorded $1,000 of stock options outstanding as part of a compensation agreement. The options expire a year later, resulting in this entry:

Stock options outstanding	1,000	
Additional paid-in capital		1,000

ABC Company sells 2,000 of par $1,000 bonds as well as 2,000 attached warrants having a market value of $15 each. Pro rata apportionment of the $2,000,000 cash received between the bonds and warrants results in this entry:

Cash	2,000,000	
Discount on bonds payable	29,557	
Bonds payable		2,000,000
Additional paid-in capital—		
warrants		29,557

ABC's bondholders convert a $1,000 bond with an unamortized premium of $40 and a market value of $1,016 into 127 shares of $1 par common stock whose market value is $8 per share. This results in the next entry:

Bonds payable	1,000	
Premium on bonds payable	40	
Common stock		913
Additional paid-in capital		127

When the amounts are material, the sources of additional paid-in capital should be described in the financial statements.

Donated Capital

Donated capital can result from an outright gift to the corporation (e.g., a major shareholder donates land or other assets to the company in a nonreciprocal transfer) or may result when services are provided to the corporation. Under ASC 958-605-25-2, such nonreciprocal transactions are recognized as revenue in the period the contribution is received. Donated capital should be adequately disclosed in the financial statements.

It is now required that donations be reflected in the income statement, which means that, after the fiscal period has ended and the books have been closed, the effect of donations will be incorporated in the reporting entity's retained earnings.

In the case of donations, historical cost is not adequate to properly reflect the substance of the transaction, since the historical cost to the corporation would be zero. Accordingly, these events should be reflected at fair market value (ASC 845-10-30-1). If long-lived assets are donated to the corporation, they should be recorded at their fair value at the date of donation, and the amount so recorded should be depreciated over the normal useful economic life of such assets. If donations are conditional in nature, they should not be reflected formally in the accounts until the appropriate conditions have been satisfied. However, disclosure still might be required in the financial statements of both the assets donated and the conditions required to be met.

Example of donated capital

A board member of the for-profit Adirondack Boys' Club (ABC) donates land to the organization that has a fair market value of $1 million. ABC records the donation with the next entry:

Land	1,000,000	
Revenue—donations		1,000,000

The same board member donates one year of accounting labor to ABC. The fair value of services rendered is $75,000. ABC records the donation with the next entry:

Salaries—accounting department	75,000	
Revenue—donations		75,000

The board member also donates one year of free rent of a local building to ABC. The annual rent in similar facilities is $45,000. ABC records the donation with the next entry:

Rent expense	45,000	
Revenue—donations		45,000

Finally, the board member pays off a $100,000 debt owed by ABC. ABC records the donation with the next entry:

Notes payable	100,000	
Revenue—donations		100,000

Following the closing of the fiscal period, the effect of all the foregoing donations will be reflected in Adirondack's retained earnings account.

RETAINED EARNINGS

Legal capital, additional paid-in capital, and donated capital collectively represent the contributed capital of the corporation. The other major source of capital is retained earnings, which represents the accumulated amount of earnings of the corporation from the date of inception (or from the date of reorganization) less the cumulative amount of distributions made to shareholders and other charges to retained earnings (e.g., from treasury stock transactions). The distributions to shareholders generally take the form of dividend payments but may take other forms as well, such as the reacquisition of shares for amounts in excess of the original issuance proceeds. The key events impacting retained earnings are

- Dividends.
- Certain treasury stock resales at amounts below acquisition cost.
- Certain stock retirements at amounts in excess of book value.

- Prior period adjustments.
- Recapitalizations and reorganizations.

Examples of retained earnings transactions

Merrimack Corporation declares a dividend of $84,000, which it records with this entry:

Retained earnings	84,000	
Dividends payable		84,000

Merrimack acquires 3,000 shares of its own $1 par value common stock for $15,000 and then resells it for $12,000. The next entries record the buyback and sale transactions respectively, assuming the use of the cost method of accounting for treasury stock:

Treasury stock	15,000	
Cash		15,000
Cash	12,000	
Retained earnings	3,000	
Treasury stock		15,000

Merrimack buys back 12,000 shares of its own $1 par value common stock (which it had originally sold for $60,000) for $70,000 and retires the stock, which it records with this entry:

Common stock	12,000	
Additional paid-in capital	48,000	
Retained earnings	10,000	
Cash		70,000

Merrimack's accountant makes a mathematical mistake in calculating depreciation, requiring a prior period reduction of $30,000 to the accumulated depreciation account and corresponding increases in its income tax payable and retained earnings accounts. Merrimack's income tax rate is 35%. It records this transaction with the next entry:

Accumulated depreciation	30,000	
Income taxes payable		10,500
Retained earnings		19,500

Retained earnings also are affected by action taken by the corporation's board of directors. Appropriation serves disclosure purposes and restricts dividend payments but does nothing to provide any resources for the satisfaction of the contingent loss or other underlying purpose for which the appropriation has been made. Any appropriation made from retained earnings eventually must be returned to the retained earnings account. It is not permissible to charge losses against the appropriation account; nor is it permissible to credit any realized gain to that account. The use of appropriated retained earnings has diminished significantly over the years.

It is axiomatic that transactions in a corporation's own stock can result in a reduction of retained earnings (i.e., a deficiency on such transactions can be charged to retained earnings) but cannot result in an increase in retained earnings (any excesses on such transactions are credited to paid-in capital, never to retained earnings).

If a series of operating losses have been incurred or distributions to shareholders in excess of accumulated earnings have been made, and if there is a debit balance in retained earnings, the account generally is referred to as accumulated deficit.

Dividends

Dividends are the pro rata distribution of earnings to the owners of the corporation. The amount and the allocation between the preferred and common shareholders is a function of the stipulated preferential dividend rate; the presence or absence of (1) a participation feature, (2) a cumulative feature, and (3) arrearages on the preferred stock; and the wishes of the board of directors. Dividends, even preferred stock dividends, where a cumulative feature exists, do not accrue. Dividends become a liability of the corporation only when declared by the board of directors.

Traditionally, corporations were not allowed to declare dividends in excess of the amount of retained earnings. Alternatively, a corporation could pay dividends out of retained earnings and additional paid-in capital but could not exceed the total of these categories (i.e., it could not impair legal capital by the payment of dividends). States that have adopted the Model Business Corporation Act grant more latitude to the directors. Corporations can now, in certain jurisdictions, declare and pay dividends in excess of the book amount of retained earnings if the directors conclude that, after the payment of such dividends, the fair value of the corporation's net assets will still be a positive amount. Thus, directors can declare dividends out of unrealized appreciation that, in certain industries, can be a significant source of dividends beyond the realized and recognized accumulated earnings of the corporation. This action, however, represents a major departure from traditional practice and demands both careful consideration and adequate disclosure.

Three important dividend dates are

1. The declaration date.
2. The record date.
3. The payment date.

The declaration date governs the incurrence of a legal liability by the corporation. The record date refers to that point in time when a determination is made as to which specific registered stockholders will receive dividends and in what amounts. Finally, the payment date relates to the date when the distribution of the dividend takes place.

Case Study 3

Facts

On May 1, 2010, the directors of River Corp. declared a $.75 per share quarterly dividend on River Corp.'s 650,000 outstanding common shares. The dividend is payable May 25 to holders of record May 15.

Required

Record the necessary journal entries on the appropriate dates

Solution

May 1	Retained earnings (or dividends)	487,500	
	Dividends payable		487,500
May 15	No entry		
May 25	Dividends payable	487,500	
	Cash		487,500

If a dividends account is used, it is closed to retained earnings at year-end.

Dividends may be made in the form of cash, property, or scrip. Cash dividends are either a given dollar amount per share or a percentage of par or stated value. Property dividends consist of the distribution of any assets other than cash (e.g., inventory or equipment). Finally, scrip dividends are promissory notes due at some time in the future, sometimes bearing interest until final payment is made.

Occasionally, what appear to be disproportionate dividend distributions are paid to some, but not all, of the owners of closely held corporations. Such transactions need to be analyzed carefully. In some cases, these actually may represent compensation paid to the recipients. In other instances, these may be a true dividend paid to all shareholders on a pro rata basis, to which certain shareholders have waived their rights. If the former, the distribution should not be accounted for as a dividend but rather as compensation or some other expense category and included on the income statement. If the latter, the dividend should be grossed up to reflect payment on a proportional basis to all the shareholders, with an offsetting capital contribution to the company recognized as having been effectively made by those to whom payments were not made.

Property dividends. If property dividends are declared, the paying corporation may incur a gain or loss. Since the dividend should be reflected at the fair value of the assets distributed, the difference between fair value and book value is recorded at the time the dividend is declared and charged or credited to a loss or gain account.

Scrip dividends. If a corporation declares a dividend payable in scrip that is interest bearing, the interest is accrued over time as a periodic expense. The interest is not a part of the dividend itself.

Liquidating dividends. Liquidating dividends are not distributions of earnings but rather a return of capital to the investing shareholders. A liquidating dividend normally is recorded by the declarer through charging additional paid-in capital rather than retained earnings. The exact accounting for a liquidating dividend is affected by the laws where the business is incorporated, and these laws vary from state to state.

Stock dividends. Stock dividends represent neither an actual distribution of the assets of the corporation nor a promise to distribute those assets. For this reason, a stock dividend is not considered a legal liability or a taxable transaction.

Despite the recognition that a stock dividend is not a distribution of earnings, the accounting treatment of relatively insignificant stock dividends (defined as being less than 20% to 25% of the outstanding shares prior to declaration) is consistent with it being a real dividend. Accordingly, retained earnings are debited for the fair market value of the shares to be paid as a dividend, and the capital stock and additional paid-in capital accounts are credited for the appropriate amounts based on the par or stated value of the shares, if any. A stock dividend declared but not yet paid is classified as such in the stockholders' equity section of the statement of financial position. Since such a dividend never reduces assets, it cannot be a liability.

The selection of 20% to 25% as the threshold for recognizing a stock dividend as an earnings distribution is arbitrary, but it is based somewhat on the empirical evidence that small stock dividends tend not to result in a reduced market price per share for outstanding shares. The aggregate value of the outstanding shares should not change, but the greater number of shares outstanding after the stock dividend should necessitate a lower per-share price. As noted, however, the declaration of small stock dividends tends not to have this impact, and this phenomenon supports the accounting treatment.

When stock dividends are larger in magnitude, however, it is observed that per share market value declines after the declaration of the dividend. In such situations, it would not be valid to treat the stock dividend as an earnings distribution. Rather, logic suggests that it should be accounted for as a split. The precise treatment depends on the legal requirements of the state of incorporation and on whether the existing par value or stated value is reduced concurrent with the stock split.

If the par value is not reduced for a large stock dividend and if state law requires that earnings be capitalized in an amount equal to the aggregate of the par value of the stock dividend declared, the event should be described as a stock split effected in the form of a dividend, with a charge to retained earnings and a credit to the common stock account for the aggregate par or stated value. When the par or stated value is reduced in recognition of the split and state laws do not require treatment as a dividend, there is no formal entry to record the split but merely a notation that the number of shares outstanding has increased and the pershare par or stated value has decreased accordingly. It should be noted that many companies account for stock splits as if they were a large stock dividend. By doing this, par value per share remains unchanged. The concepts of small versus large stock dividends are illustrated in the next examples.

Assume that stockholders' equity for the Wasatch Corp. on November 1, 2010, is

Common stock, $1 par, 100,000 shares outstanding	$ 100,000
Paid-in capital in excess of par	1,100,000
Retained earnings	750,000

Small Stock Dividend: On November 10, 2010, the directors of Wasatch Corp. declared a 15% stock dividend, or a dividend of 1.5 shares of common stock for every 10 shares held. Before the stock dividend, the stock is selling for $23 per share. After the 15% stock dividend, each original share worth $23 will become 1.15 shares, each with a value of $20 ($23/1.15). The stock dividend is to be recorded at the market value of the new shares issued, or $300,000 (15,000 new shares at the post-dividend price of $20). The entries to record the declaration of the dividend and the issuance of stock (on November 30) by Wasatch Corp. are

Nov. 10	Retained earnings	300,000	
	Stock dividends distributable		15,000
	Paid-in capital in excess of par		285,000
Nov. 30	Stock dividends distributable	15,000	
	Common stock, $1 par		15,000

Large Stock Dividend: Because the focus of the Committee on Accounting Procedure was on small stock dividends, the accounting requirements for governing large stock dividends are less specific than those for small stock dividends. In practice, ASC 505-20-30-3 results in the par or stated value of the newly issued shares being transferred to the capital stock account from either retained earnings or paid-in capital in excess of par. To illustrate, assume that on November 10, 2010, Wasatch Corp. declares a 50% large stock dividend, a dividend of one share for every two held. Legal requirements call for the transfer to capital stock of an amount equal to the par value of the shares issued. Entries for the declaration on November 10 and the issuance of 50,000 new shares (100,000 × .50) on November 30 are

Nov. 10	Retained earnings	50,000	
	Stock dividends distributable		50,000
	or		
	Paid-in capital in excess of par	50,000	
	Stock dividends distributable		50,000
Nov. 30	Stock dividends distributable	50,000	
	Common stock, $1 par		50,000

Treasury Stock

Treasury stock consists of a corporation's own stock that has been issued, subsequently reacquired by the firm, and not yet reissued or cancelled. Treasury stock does not reduce the number of shares issued but does reduce the number of shares outstanding as well as total stockholders' equity. These shares are not eligible to receive cash dividends.

Three approaches exist for the treatment of treasury stock: the cost, par value, and constructive retirement methods.

Cost method. Under the cost method, the gross cost of the shares reacquired is charged to a contra equity account (treasury stock). The equity accounts that were credited for the original share issuance (common stock, paid-in capital in excess of par, etc.) remain intact. When the treasury shares are reissued, proceeds in excess of cost are credited to a paid-in capital account. Any deficiency is charged to retained earnings (unless paid-in capital from previous treasury share transactions exists, in which case the deficiency is charged to that account, with any excess charged to retained earnings). If many treasury stock purchases are made, a cost flow assumption (e.g., first-in, last-out or specific identification) should be adopted to compute excesses and deficiencies upon subsequent share reissuances. The advantage of the cost method is that it avoids identifying and accounting for amounts related to the original issuance of the shares and is, therefore, the simpler, more frequently used method.

Par value method. Under the par value method, the treasury stock account is charged only for the aggregate par (or stated) value of the shares reacquired. Other paid-in capital accounts (excess over par value, etc.) are relieved in proportion to the amounts recognized upon the original issuance of the shares. The treasury share acquisition is treated almost as a retirement. However, the common (or preferred) stock account continues at the original amount, thereby preserving the distinction between an actual retirement and a treasury share transaction.

When the treasury shares accounted for by the par value method are subsequently resold, the excess of the sale price over par value is credited to paid-in capital. A reissuance for a price below par value does not create a contingent liability for the purchaser. It is only the original purchaser who risks this obligation to the entity's creditors.

Constructive retirement method. The constructive retirement method is similar to the par value method, except that the aggregate par (or stated) value of the reacquired shares is charged to the stock account rather than to the treasury stock account. This method is superior when (1) it is management's intention not to reissue the shares within a reasonable time period or (2) the state of incorporation defines reacquired shares as having been retired. In the latter case, the constructive retirement method is probably the only method of accounting for treasury shares that is not inconsistent with the state Business Corporation Act, although the state law does not necessarily dictate such accounting. Certain states require that treasury stock be accounted for by this method.

Treasury shares originally accounted for by the cost method subsequently can be restated to conform to the constructive retirement method. If shares were acquired with the intention that they would be reissued and it is later determined that such reissuance is unlikely (due, e.g., to the expiration of stock options without their exercise), then it is proper to restate the transaction.

Case Study 4

Example of accounting for treasury stock

Facts

1. 100 shares ($50 par value) that were originally sold for $60 per share are later reacquired for $70 each.
2. All 100 shares are subsequently resold for a total of $7,500.

Required

Make the necessary entries to record the acquisition and resale of the treasury stock under the cost method, par value method, and constructive retirement method.

Solution

To record the acquisition, the entry is

Cost method			Par value method			Constructive retirement method		
Treasury stock	7,000		Treasury stock	5,000		Common stock	5,000	
Cash		7,000	Additional paid-in capital—common stock	1,000		Additional paid-in capital—common stock	1,000	
			Retained earnings	1,000		Retained earnings	1,000	
			Cash		7,000	Cash		7,000

To record the resale, the entry is

Cost method			Par value method			Constructive retirement method		
Cash	7,500		Cash	7,500		Cash	7,500	
Treasury stock		7,000	Treasury stock		5,000	Common stock		5,000
Additional paid-in capital—treasury stock		500	Additional paid-in capital—common stock		2,500	Additional paid-in capital—common stock		2,500

If the shares had been resold for $6,500, the entry is

Cost method			Par value method			Constructive retirement method		
Cash	6,500		Cash	6,500		Cash	6,500	
Retained earnings*	500		Treasury stock		5,000	Common stock		5,000
Treasury stock		7,000	Additional paid-in capital—common stock		1,500	Additional paid-in capital—common stock		1,500

*"Additional paid-in capital—treasury stock" or "Additional paid-in capital—retired stock" of that issue would be debited first to the extent it exists.

APPENDIX A

FINANCIAL STATEMENT PRESENTATION

This appendix provides an illustration of the various financial statements that may be required to be presented and are related to the stockholders' equity section of the statement of financial position.

Stockholders' Equity Section of a Statement of Financial Position

Capital stock:		
Preferred stock, $100 par, 7% cumulative, 30,000 shares authorized, issued, and outstanding		$ 3,000,000
Common stock, no par, stated value $10 per share, 500,000 shares authorized, 415,000 shares issued		4,150,000
Total capital stock		$ 7,150,000
Additional paid-in capital:		
Issued price in excess of par value—preferred	$ 150,000	
Issued price in excess of stated value—common	845,000	995,000
Total paid-in capital		$ 8,145,000
Donated capital		100,000
Retained earnings:		
Appropriated for plant expansion	$2,100,000	
Unappropriated	2,110,000	4,210,000
Accumulated other comprehensive income		165,000
Total capital, retained earnings, and accumulated other comprehensive income		$12,620,000
Less 10,000 common shares held in treasury, at cost		(120,000)
Total stockholders' equity		$12,500,000

Retained Earnings Statement

Balance at beginning of year, as reported	$ 3,800,000
Prior period adjustment—correction of an error in method of depreciation (less tax effect of $77,000)	115,000
Balance at beginning of year, restated	$ 3,915,000
Net income for the year	583,000
Cash dividends declared during the year	
Preferred stock	(210,000)
Common stock	(78,000)
Balance at end of year	$ 4,210,000

MULTIPLE-CHOICE QUESTIONS

1. Which of the following is **not** true regarding preferred shares?

   (a) Preferred shareholders have superiority over common shareholders.

   (b) Preferred shareholders may have preferences to assets when preferred shares have a stipulated liquidation value.

   (c) Preferred shareholders are guaranteed a dividend payment.

   (d) Common shareholders cannot be paid a dividend payment until preferred dividends have been paid.

2. Which of the following is **not** likely to result in additional paid-in capital?

   (a) Retirement of previously outstanding shares.

   (b) Proceeds received from the sale of common shares that are less than the stated value of the stock.

   (c) Payment of stock dividends in a manner that justifies the dividend being recorded at the market value of the shares distributed.

   (d) Treasury stock transactions.

3. On January 15, 2010, the directors of Pervan Corp. declared a $1 per share quarterly dividend on Pervan Corp.'s 200,000 outstanding common shares. The dividend is payable February 15 to holders of record February 1. Which of the following is true?

   (a) On February 15, a dividend payable should be recorded.

   (b) On January 15, a debit to dividends payable and a credit to cash should be made for $200,000.

   (c) On February 1, a debit to retained earnings and a credit to dividends payable should be made for $200,000.

   (d) On January 15, a debit to retained earnings and a credit to dividends payable should be made for $200,000.

4. 200 shares ($25 par value) that were originally sold for $30 per share are later reacquired for $35 each. What is the entry to record the acquisition of shares using the par value method?

   (a) Treasury stock 5,000
      Additional paid-in capital 1,000
      Retained earnings 1,000
      Cash 7,000

   (b) Treasury stock 7,000
      Cash 7,000

   (c) Common stock 5,000
      Additional paid-in capital 1,000
      Retained earnings 1,000
      Cash 7,000

Chapter 27

PERSONAL FINANCIAL STATEMENTS (ASC 274)

INTRODUCTION

ASC 274 addresses the preparation and presentation of personal financial statements or, more specifically, financial statements of individuals or groups of related individuals (i.e., families). Personal financial statements generally are prepared to organize and plan an individual's financial affairs on a more formal basis. Specific purposes that might require the preparation of personal financial statements include the obtaining of credit, income tax planning, retirement planning, gift and estate planning, or public disclosure of financial affairs. Third-party recipients of personal financial statements use them in deciding whether to grant credit, in evaluating the financial condition of individuals, in assessing the financial affairs of public officials and candidates for public office, and for other purposes.

SCOPE

ASC 274 applies to all individuals and all groups of related individuals (families).

DEFINITIONS OF KEY TERMS

Estimated current amount of liabilities. Payables and other liabilities are to be presented at the discounted amounts of future cash to be paid. The interest rate used to discount the debt is the rate implicit in the transaction in which the debt was incurred. If, however, the debtor is able to repay the debt currently at a lower amount, the debt is to be presented at that reduced figure.

Estimated current value of an asset. The amount for which an item could be exchanged between a buyer and a seller, each of whom is well informed and willing, and neither of whom is compelled to buy or sell.

Net worth. The difference between total assets and total liabilities, after deducting estimated income taxes on the differences between the estimated current values of assets and the estimated current amounts of liabilities and their income tax bases.

PURPOSE AND COMPONENTS OF FINANCIAL STATEMENTS

Personal financial statements can be prepared for an individual, jointly for a husband and wife, or collectively for a family.

Personal financial statements consist of

1. *Statement of financial condition.* The only required financial statement, the statement of financial condition presents the estimated current values of assets and the estimated current amounts of liabilities. A liability is recognized for estimated income taxes on the difference between the asset and liability amounts set forth in the statement of financial condition and their respective income tax bases. Naturally, the residual amount after deducting the liabilities (including the estimated income tax liability) from the assets is presented as net worth at that date.

2. *Statement of changes in net worth.* This optional that presents the primary sources of increases and decreases in net worth over a period of time.

3. *Comparative financial statements.* The inclusion of a comparison of the current period's financial statements with one or more previous period's financial statements is optional.

MEASUREMENT

The accrual basis, rather than the cash basis of accounting, is used in preparing personal financial statements. The presentation of personal financial statements does not require the classification of assets and liabilities as current and noncurrent. Instead, assets and liabilities are presented in order of liquidity and maturity.

In personal financial statements, assets are presented at their estimated current values. This is defined as the amount at which the item could be exchanged between a buyer and a seller, assuming both parties are well informed, and neither party is compelled to buy or sell. Disposal costs, if material, are deducted to arrive at current values.

A specialist may need to be consulted in the determination of the current value of certain types of assets (e.g., works of art, jewelry, restricted securities, investments in closely held businesses, and real estate). If property is held in joint tenancy, as community property, or through a similar joint ownership arrangement, the financial statement preparer may require the advice of an attorney to determine, under applicable state law, the portion of the property interest that should be included in the individual's assets.

Liabilities are presented at the lesser of the discounted amount of cash to be paid or the current cash settlement amount. The discount rate should be the rate implicit in the transaction that gave rise to the liability. As a practical matter, the preparer may decide to use the individual's incremental borrowing rate at the inception of the transaction to discount the remaining cash flows.

The use of information about recent transactions involving similar types of assets and liabilities, in similar circumstances, constitutes a satisfactory means of determining the estimated current value of an asset and the estimated current amount of a liability. If recent transactional information cannot be obtained, it is permissible to use other methods (e.g., capitalization of past or prospective earnings, liquidation values, adjustment of historical cost based on changes in a specific price index, appraisals, and discounted amounts of projected cash receipts and payments). The methods used should be followed consistently from period to period unless the facts and circumstances dictate a change to different methods.

Income taxes payable are to include unpaid income taxes for completed tax years and the estimated amount for the elapsed portion of the current tax year. Additionally, personal financial statements are required to include estimated income tax on the difference between the current value (amount) of assets (liabilities) and their respective income tax bases as if they had been realized or liquidated.

Business interests that comprise a large portion of a person's total assets should be presented separately from other investments. An investment in a separate entity that is marketable as a going concern (e.g., a closely held corporation) should be presented as one amount. If the investment is a limited business activity, not conducted in a separate legal entity, separate asset and liability amounts should be shown (e.g., investment in real estate and related mortgage; only the person's beneficial interest in the investment is included in his/her personal financial statements).

The preparer must decide whether to value the net investment him-/herself or to engage a qualified specialist. The possible valuation methods available are discounted cash flow, appraised value, liquidation value, multiple of earnings, reproduction value, adjustment of book value (e.g., equity method), or cost. In some cases it is appropriate to use a combination of approaches to reasonably estimate the current value.

The next table summarizes the methods of determining "estimated current values" for assets and "estimated current amounts" for liabilities.

Assets and liabilities	*Discounted cash flow*	*Quoted market price*	*Appraised value*	*Other*
Receivables	x			
Marketable debt and equity securities		x		If traded on valuation day: closing price. If not traded: valuation must fall in range (between bid and ask price); adjustments may be required for factors such as the holding of a large block of equity securities in an enterprise (blockage factor) or for restrictions on transfer of the securities
Options—securities		x		If a quoted market price for the option is not available, compute based on the value of the asset subject to option considering factors such as the exercise price and length of option period
Options—other assets*				Difference between the exercise price and the current value of the contracted asset, discounted at the interest rate that would be available to the individual to borrow with the asset under option as collateral
Investment in life insurance				Cash surrender value less outstanding loans
Investment in closely held business	x		x	Liquidation value, multiple of earnings, reproduction value, adjustment of book value or cost
Real estate (including leaseholds)	x		x	By reference to sales of comparable property, appraisals used for the purpose of borrowing, by reference to assessed values used for property tax purposes, and to the relationship of assessed value to current value of properties in the geographic area
Intangible assets	x			Net proceeds from current sale or discounted cash flows from asset; otherwise, may use cost of purchasing a similar asset, if available
Future interests (nonforfeitable rights)**	x			
Payables and other liabilities	x			Discharge amount if lower than discounted amount
Noncancelable commitments***	x			
Income taxes payable				Unpaid income tax for completed tax years and estimated income tax for elapsed portion of current tax year to date of financial statements
Estimated income tax on difference between current values of assets and current amounts of liabilities and their respective tax bases				Computed as if current value of assets and liabilities had been respectively realized or liquidated considering applicable tax laws and regulations, recapture provisions and carryovers
Uncertain obligations*				Not covered by SOP 82-1; follow recognition, measurement, and disclosure guidance in ASC 450

   * *Adapted from: Michael D. Kinsman and Bruce Samuelson, "Personal Financial Statements: Valuation Challenges and Solutions," Journal of Accountancy (September 1987): 138–148.*

  ** *Rights have all of these attributes: (1) are for fixed or determinable amounts; (2) are not contingent on holder's life expectancy or occurrence of a particular event (e.g., disability/death), and (3) do not require future performance of service by holder.*

 *** *Commitments have all of these attributes: (1) are for fixed or determinable amounts; (2) are not contingent on others' life expectancies or occurrence of a particular event (e.g., disability/death); and (3) do not require future performance of service by others.*

DISCLOSURES

The next disclosures typically are made in either the body of the financial statements or in the accompanying notes. (This list is not all inclusive.)

1. A clear identification of the individuals covered by the financial statements
2. That assets are presented at their estimated current values and liabilities are presented at their estimated current amounts
3. The methods used in determining the estimated current values of major assets and the estimated current amounts of major liabilities or major categories of assets and liabilities, and changes in methods from one period to the next
4. If assets held jointly by the person and by others included in the statements, the nature of the joint ownership
5. If the person's investment portfolio is material in relation to his or her other assets and is concentrated in one or a few companies or industries, the names of the companies or industries and the estimated current values of the securities
6. If the person has a material investment in a closely held business,

   a. The name of the company
   b. The person's percentage of ownership
   c. The nature of the business
   d. Summarized financial information about assets, liabilities, and results of operations for the most recent year based on the business's own financial statements as well as the basis of presentation (e.g., generally accepted accounting principles, cash basis, income tax basis, etc.), and any significant loss contingencies

7. Description of intangible assets and their estimated useful lives
8. The face amount of life insurance the individual owns
9. Certain nonforfeitable rights, such as pensions based on life expectancy
10. The methods and assumptions used to calculate estimated income taxes on the differences between the estimated current values of assets and the estimated current amounts of liabilities and their tax bases as well as a statement that the provision probably will differ from the amounts eventually paid because the timing and method of disposal as well as changes in the tax laws and regulations will affect the actual taxes to be paid
11. Unused operating loss and capital loss carryforwards and any other unused deductions or credits and, if applicable, the tax year in which they expire (Under the current income tax code, there frequently will be unused alternative minimum tax credit carryforwards.)
12. The differences between the estimated current values of major assets and the estimated current amounts of major liabilities or categories of assets and liabilities and their tax bases
13. Maturities, interest rates, collateral, and other pertinent details relating to receivables and debt
14. Certain noncancelable commitments such as operating leases

HYPOTHETICAL SET OF PERSONAL FINANCIAL STATEMENTS

Marcus and Alyssa Victoria Stafford
STATEMENTS OF FINANCIAL CONDITION
December 31, 2010 and 2009

	2010	*2009*
Assets		
Cash	$ 381,437	$ 207,621
Certificate of deposit	20,000	10.000
Securities		
Marketable (Note 2)	128,787	260,485
Tax-exempt bonds (Note 3)	1,890,222	986,278
Loans receivable (Note 4)	262,877	362,877
Partnership and joint venture interests (Note 5)	935,000	938,000
Real estate interests (Note 6)	890,000	2,500,000
David Corporation (Note 7)	2,750,687	2,600,277

	2010	2009
Cash surrender value of life insurance (Note 8)	388,000	265,000
Personal residences (Note 9)	2,387,229	2,380,229
Deferred losses from partnerships	68,570	60,830
Vested interest in David Corporation benefit plan	545,960	530,960
Personal jewelry and furnishings (Note 10)	513,000	6,700
Total assets	$11,161,769	$11,109,257

Liabilities

Mortgage payable (Note 11)	$ 254,000	$ 267,000
Security deposits—rentals	—	5,700
Income taxes payable—current year balance	9,800	10,680
Total liabilities	263,800	283,380
Estimated income taxes on difference between estimated current values of assets and estimated current amounts of liabilities and their tax bases (Note 12)	555,400	731,000

Net Worth

	10,342,569	10,094,877
Total liabilities and net worth	$11,161,769	$11,109,257

Marcus and Alyssa Victoria Stafford
STATEMENT OF CHANGES IN NET WORTH
for the Years Ended December 31, 2010 and 2009

	2010	2009
Realized increases in net worth		
Salary and bonus	$ 200,000	$ 175,000
Dividends and interest income	184,260	85,000
Distribution from limited partnerships	280,000	260,000
Gain on sales of marketable securities	58,240	142,800
	722,500	662,800
Realized decreases in net worth		
Income taxes	180,000	140,000
Interest expense	25,000	26,000
Real estate taxes	21,000	18,000
Personal expenditures	242,536	400,000
	468,536	584,000
Net realized increase in net worth	253,964	78,800
Unrealized increases in net worth		
Marketable securities (net of realized gains on securities sold)	37,460	30,270
Benefit plan—David Corporation	15,000	14,000
Personal jewelry and furnishings	20,000	18,000
	72,460	62,270
Unrealized decreases in net worth		
Estimated income taxes on the difference between the estimated current values of assets and the estimated current amounts of liabilities and their tax bases	78,732	64,118
Net unrealized decrease in net worth	(6,272)	(1,848)
Net increase in net worth	247,692	76,952
Net worth at the beginning of year	10,094,877	10,017,925
Net worth at the end of year	$10,342,569	$10,094,877

Marcus and Alyssa Victoria Stafford
NOTES TO FINANCIAL STATEMENTS

Note 1: The accompanying financial statements include the assets and liabilities of Marcus and Alyssa Victoria Stafford. Assets are stated at their estimated current values, and liabilities at their estimated current amounts.

Note 2: The estimated current values of marketable securities are either (1) their quoted closing prices or (2) for securities not traded on the financial statement date, amounts that fall within the range of quoted bid and asked prices.

Marketable securities consist of:

| | December 31, 2010 | | December 31, 2009 | |
| | Number of | Estimated current | Number of | Estimated current |
Stocks	shares	values	shares	values
Susan Schultz, Inc.			1,000	$122,000
Ripley Robotics Corp.	500	$ 51,927	1,000	120,485
L.A.W. Corporation	300	20,700	100	5,000
Jay & Kelly Corp.	300	20,700	200	5,000
J.A.Z. Corporation	200	35,460	200	8,000
		$128,787		$260,485

Note 3: The interest income from state and municipal bonds is generally not subject to federal income taxes but is, except in certain cases, subject to state income tax and federal alternative minimum tax.

Note 4: The loan receivable from Carol Parker, Inc. matures January 2017 and bears interest at the prime rate.

Note 5: Partnership and joint venture interests consist of

	Percent owned	Cost	Estimated current value 12/31/2010	Estimated current value 12/31/2009
East Third Partnership	50.0%	$ 50,000	100,000	100,000
631 Lucinda Joint Venture	20.0	10,000	35,000	38,000
27 Wright Partnership	22.5	10,000	40,000	50,000
Eannarino Partnership	10.0	40,000	60,000	50,000
Sweeney Joint Venture	30.0	100,000	600,000	600,000
Kelly Parker Group	20.0	20,000	100,000	100,000
707 Lucinda Joint Venture	50.0	(11,000)	—	—
			$935,000	$938,000

Note 6: Mr. and Mrs. Stafford own a one-half interest in an apartment building in DeKalb, Illinois. The estimated current value was determined by Mr. and Mrs. Stafford. Their income tax basis in the apartment building was $1,000,000 for both 2010 and 2009.

Note 7: Alyssa Stafford owns 75% of the common stock of the David Corporation. A condensed statement of assets, liabilities, and stockholders' equity (income tax basis) of David Corporation as of December 31, 2010 and 2009 is summarized next.

	2010	2009
Current assets	$2,975,000	$3,147,000
Investments	200,000	200,000
Property and equipment (net)	145,000	165,000
Loans receivable	110,000	120,000
Total assets	$3,430,000	$3,632,000
Current liabilities	$2,030,000	$2,157,000
Other liabilities	450,000	400,000
Total liabilities	2,480,000	2,557,000
Stockholders' equity	950,000	1,075,000
Total liabilities and stockholders' equity	$3,430,000	$3,632,000

Note 8: At December 31, 2010 and 2009, Marcus Stafford owned a $1,000,000 whole life insurance policy. Mrs. Stafford is the sole beneficiary under the policy.

Note 9: The estimated current values of the personal residences are their purchase prices plus their cost of improvements. Both residences were purchased in 2008.

Note 10: The estimated current values of personal effects and jewelry are the appraised values of those assets, determined by an independent appraiser for insurance purposes.

Note 11: The mortgage (collateralized by the residence) is payable in monthly installments of $2,479, including interest at an annual rate of 6% through 2022.

Note 12: The estimated current amounts of liabilities at December 31, 2010, and December 31, 2009, equaled their income tax bases. Estimated income taxes have been provided on the excess of the estimated current values of assets over their tax bases as if the estimated current values of the assets had been realized on the dates of the statements of financial condition, using applicable income tax laws and regulations. The provision probably will differ from the amounts of income taxes that eventually will be paid because those amounts are determined by the timing and the method of disposal or realization and the income tax laws and regulations in effect at the time of disposal or realization.

The excess of estimated current values of major assets over their income tax bases are

	December 31	
	2010	*2009*
Investment in David Corporation	$1,400,000	$1,350,000
Vested interest in benefit plan	350,000	300,000
Investment in marketable securities	100,000	120,300
	$1,850,000	$1,770,300

MULTIPLE-CHOICE QUESTIONS

1. Which of the following financial statements is required?
    (a) Statement of changes in net worth.
    (b) Statement of cash flows.
    (c) Statement of financial condition.
    (d) Comparative financial statements.

2. In personal financial statements, assets should be presented at
    (a) Their estimated current values.
    (b) Historical cost.
    (c) The current cash settlement amount.
    (d) Their discounted cash flow amount.

3. For an investment in real estate
    (a) The market value of the entire property should be presented.
    (b) Only the person's beneficial interest in the investment is presented.
    (c) The historical cost of the entire property should be presented.

4. Which one of the following is **not** true in regard to personal financial statements?
    (a) The accrual basis of accounting is used.
    (b) The statement of financial condition is the only required financial statement.
    (c) Personal financial statements can be prepared for an individual or collectively for a family.
    (d) Assets and liabilities should be presented as current and noncurrent.

ANSWERS FOR MULTIPLE-CHOICE QUESTIONS

Chapter 2

1. c   2. d   3. a   4. a   5. b

Chapter 3

1. c   2. b   3. c

Chapter 4

1. b   2. a   3. d   4. b   5. c

Chapter 5

1. c   2. a   3. c   4. c

Chapter 6

1. c   2. b   3. e   4. a   5. c

Chapter 7

1. b   2. d   3. e   4. a

Chapter 8

1. b   2. c   3. c   4. a

Chapter 9

1. d   2. c   3. d   4. b   5. a
6. d   7. d

Chapter 10

1. a   2. b   3. b

Chapter 11

1. c   2. c   3. b   4. d   5. d
6. c   7. a   8. d   9. c   10. a
11. c   12. c   13. b   14. a   15. d
16. d   17. a   18. c

Chapter 12

1. d   2. a   3. c   4. c   5. d
6. b

Chapter 13

1. d   2. d   3. b   4. d   5. a

Chapter 14

1. d   2. b   3. c   4. a   5. d
6. d   7. b

Chapter 15

1. c   2. d   3. a   4. d   5. a
6. a   7. d   8. c   9. b   10. a
11. d   12. c*   13. b   14. d**

*At January 1, 2008: cost $10 million – 30% of
$20 million=

At January 1, 2009: cost $15 million – 40% of
$25 million =

	Goodwill
At January 1, 2008: cost $10 million – 30% of $20 million=	4
At January 1, 2009: cost $15 million – 40% of $25 million =	5
	9

(Entity A has not accounted for the initial purchase as an associate.)

** Cost of acquisition (Mask's shareholders own 60% of equity of Man)

In order for 40% of Mask's shares to be owned by shareholders of Man, Mask needs to issue 4 million shares. Therefore, cost of acquisition is

4 million × $6 each	$24 million
Fair value of assets of Man	($18 million)
Goodwill	$6 million

Chapter 16

1. a   2. c*   3. b   4. a

* ($4m – $3m) × 30%

Chapter 17

1. a   2. c   3. b   4. c   5. d

Chapter 18

1. c   2. a   3. d   4. b   5. c

Chapter 19

1. b   2. b   3. d   4. c   5. b
6. c   7. b

Chapter 20

1. c   2. d   3. c   4. a

Chapter 21

1. c   2. b   3. b   4. c   5. a
6. c

Chapter 22

1. d   2. b   3. d   4. a   5. b
6. c   7. d   8. c

Chapter 23

1. c   2. b   3. b   4. b   5. a
6. b   7. b   8. a   9. a

Chapter 24

1. a   2. e   3. b   4. a   5. b
6. d   7. b   8. a   9. a

Chapter 25

1. a   2. b

Chapter 26

1. c   2. b   3. d   4. a

Chapter 27

1. c   2. a   3. b   4. d

INDEX